# TELEVISION
# AND
# SOCIAL BEHAVIOR

## REPORTS AND PAPERS, VOLUME III:
## TELEVISION AND ADOLESCENT AGGRESSIVENESS

### A TECHNICAL REPORT TO THE
### SURGEON GENERAL'S SCIENTIFIC ADVISORY COMMITTEE
### ON TELEVISION AND SOCIAL BEHAVIOR

Edited By
**George A. Comstock and Eli A. Rubinstein**
Editorial Coordination: Susan Lloyd-Jones

U.S. DEPARTMENT OF HEALTH, EDUCATION, AND WELFARE
Health Services and Mental Health Administration

National Institute of Mental Health
5600 Fishers Lane
Rockville, Maryland

# Staff Members

| | |
|---|---|
| Eli A. Rubinstein | Vice Chairman, Surgeon General's Scientific Advisory Committee |
| George A. Comstock | Senior Research Coordinator |
| John P. Murray | Research Coordinator |
| Michael Adler | Staff Assistant |
| Eileen Marchak | Research Assistant |
| Susan S. Lloyd-Jones | Editor |
| Joseph D. Reckley | Administrative Officer |
| Margaret D. Salladay | Secretary |
| Laura A. De Lisi | Secretary |

# Former Staff Members

| | |
|---|---|
| Douglas A. Fuchs | Senior Research Coordinator (through 6/70) |
| John P. Robinson | Research Coordinator (through 9/70) |
| Harold Leigh | Administrative Officer (through 10/70) |
| Thomas Brubeck | Information Officer (through 5/71) |
| Deborah Cutler | Research Assistant (through 8/70) |
| Jan W. Lipkin | Secretary (through 4/70) |

# Advisory Committee Members

| | |
|---|---|
| Ira H. Cisin | Charles A. Pinderhughes |
| Thomas E. Coffin | Ithiel de Sola Pool |
| Irving L. Janis | Alberta E. Siegel |
| Joseph T. Klapper | Anthony F. C. Wallace |
| Harold Mendelsohn | Andrew S. Watson |
| Eveline Omwake | Gerhart D. Wiebe |

# Preface

This document is one of five volumes of technical reports resulting from a broad scientific inquiry about television and its impact on the viewer. In the spring of 1969, by Congressional request, the DHEW initiated a special program under the general auspices of a Surgeon General's Scientific Advisory Committee on Television and Social Behavior. The major emphasis was to be on an examination of the relationship between televised violence and the attitudes and behavior of children. During the ensuing two years, more than fifty scientists participated directly in this program of research and produced over forty scientific reports.

The reports which are included in these five volumes are the independent work of the participating researchers. These results have all been made available to the Scientific Advisory Committee as evidence which the Committee could then evaluate and draw its own conclusions in the preparation of its own report. However, this work is of significance in its own right and is being published independently as source material for other researchers and for such interest as the general public may have in these technical reports.

In any broad scientific undertaking of this nature, where many individuals are involved, a careful balance between collaboration and independence of responsibility must be established. During the two and half years that this program of research was active, a constant effort was made to protect the scientific independence of the individual investigators and, at the same time: 1) to foster both cooperation and exchange among the researchers, 2) to develop as much of a total program structure as possible, and 3) to permit maximum communication and feedback among the researchers, the full-time staff responsible for planning and implementing the total research program, and the Scientific Advisory Committee responsible for the final assessment and evaluation of the research.

This is not the place to describe in detail how that balance of collaboration and independence was established and maintained. I believe, however, that these five volumes of technical reports provide an accurate and meaningful indication of our success in achieving the goal. The reports themselves are the products of the respective authors. They have been edited only to insure some comparability of format and to delete any excessive redundancies in review of the literature or introductory material. In some instances, where a report seemed initially too long the author was requested to reduce the report without deleting any critical material. All editing done by staff was submitted for the author's approval. We believe the result has made each of these five volumes a more readable and integrated totality than would otherwise be expected from a collection of research reports produced under the time constraints of this program.

In each instance, the integration of the five volumes was further established by the inclusion of an overview paper which attempts to summarize and relate the papers in that volume. These overview papers are also the independent work of the respective authors.

It would be difficult to convey to the reader the extraordinary efforts required by all participants in this research program to bring the endeavor to its published conclusion within the time allotted. Despite that time pressure, these volumes demonstrate an unusually high level of both productivity and quality for an area of research which has had more than its share of complexity and controversy.

In addition to the work of all persons directly engaged in this program, a very large number of individuals at one time or another provided advice and guidance to the researchers, to the staff, and to the Scientific Advisory Committee. It would be impossible to provide a complete list of these additional consultants. The total count is in the hundreds. While their names are not visible in these products, their counsel was often a very significant factor in the course of an individual piece of research or in a decision on the direction of the research program. To all those individuals, this program owes a special debt of gratitude for the collective wisdom made available to us.

And finally, on behalf both of the members of the Scientific Advisory Committee and of the staff who served the program, I wish especially to express much appreciation to the participating researchers who did the work and wrote the reports that contributed the new knowledge contained in these volumes.

Eli A. Rubinstein
Vice-Chairman, Surgeon General's
Scientific Advisory Committee on Television
and Social Behavior

# Contents

vi

# Television and Adolescent Aggressiveness (Overview)

Steven H. Chaffee

This paper is an introduction to reports of eight field studies of adolescents, focusing on their exposure to violent television programs and on their aggressive social behaviors and feelings. The concepts, samples, measures, and modes of analysis of these studies differ greatly. The purpose of this paper, then, is to attempt to set the studies in a comparative context so they can be interpreted in relation to one another and to other research. This is neither a substitute for, nor a critique of, the studies themselves, and cannot itself be interpreted without direct reference to the original research reports (which can be found elsewhere in this volume).

To avoid pointless redundancy, the eight present studies will be consistently referred to by number throughout the text, as follows:

(*1*) Steven H. Chaffee and Jack M. McLeod. Adolescent television use in the family context.

(*2*) Herbert L. Friedman and Raymond L. Johnson. Mass media use and aggression: a pilot study.

(*3*) Monroe M. Lefkowitz, Leonard D. Eron, Leopold O. Walder, and L. Rowell Huesmann. Television violence and child aggression: a followup study.

(*4*) Jennie J. McIntyre and James J. Teevan, Jr. Television and deviant behavior.

(*5*) Jack M. McLeod, Charles K. Atkin, and Steven H. Chaffee. Adolescents, parents, and television use. This report was issued in two parts, which will be referred to where necessary as follows:

(*5a*) Adolescent self-report measures from Maryland and Wisconsin samples.

(*5b*) Self-report and other-report measures from the Wisconsin sample.

(*6*) Joseph R. Dominick and Bradley S. Greenberg. Attitudes toward violence: the interaction of television exposure, family attitudes and social class.

(*7*) John P. Robinson and Jerald G. Bachman. Television viewing habits and aggression.

(*8*) Raymond L. Johnson, Herbert L. Friedman, and Herbert S. Gross. Four masculine styles in television programming: a study of the viewing preferences of adolescent males.

The central research question guiding all these studies is whether aggressive or violent social behavior by adolescents can be attributed in some degree to violent television programming. This paper will build systematically toward evidence on that hypothesis, according to the following outline:

I.    Samples and settings for the nine studies

II.    Measures of adolescent television use and their correlates
    A.  Time spent viewing
    B.  Program preferences
    C.  Frequency of viewing
    D.  Perceptions of television

III.    Measures of adolescent aggressiveness and their correlates
    A.  Reports by others
    B.  Self-reported aggressive behavior
    C.  Feelings of aggressiveness

IV.    Correlations between viewing and aggressiveness measures
    A.  Correlations with violent program preferences
    B.  Correlations with viewing of violent programs
    C.  Possible causal inferences

# SAMPLES AND SETTINGS

The procedures for data-gathering are described in detail in each of the studies. Only a few elementary comparisons will be made here, to introduce the studies in a common context.

Two of the studies use small (N=80) samples of boys from racially mixed junior high schools in Baltimore, Md. (2; 8). Neither of the samples is random; instead, both are purposefully stratified on the basis of high or low "aggressiveness" as determined by school officials.

Three studies used data from ongoing surveys that had begun before initiation of the Television and Social Behavior project. In two of these, a new wave of data-gathering was added to the previous measures (3; 7). Secondary analyses from the third of these (1) provided the "pretest" basis for a new study with a different sample (5).

The major longitudinal study (3) was conducted in a rural county of upstate New York, and spans a ten-year period in the lives of the panel members. They were originally measured in school in the third grade, when their modal age was 8. A five-year followup study was attempted but provided quite incomplete data. A ten-year followup, called the "thirteenth" grade wave, was completed in 1969 as part of the Television and Social Behavior project. There are 436 respondents for whom both third- and thirteenth-grade data are available.

The other ongoing study is longitudinal to the limited extent that some measures were repeated one year apart in 1969 and 1970 (7). It is an all-male sample, consisting of some 2,200 post-high school students (age 19) "scattered throughout the United States."

The secondary analysis report is based on data from some 1,300 junior and senior high students and their parents, gathered in five eastern Wiscon cities in 1968 (1). In the later study by the same research group, two samples were interviewed (5). The first consists of separate measures from adolescents and their mothers in a south-central Wisconsin suburb. There were two waves, in fall 1969 and fall 1970. The first wave of child measures occurred at school (sixth and ninth grades), and all other measures took place at home. This sample included 225 mother-child pairs in the first wave; attrition reduced it to 151 in the second wave. The other sample consisted of 473 seventh and tenth graders, who filled out questionnaries at school in Prince Georges County, Md., in spring 1970.

Prince Georges County was also the site of the most comprehensive sample among the present studies (4). In this survey 2,260 students, evenly distributed across grades 7 through 12, completed questionnaires at school in spring 1970. The sample includes large numbers of both black and white adolescents, a variable that was also coded in three other studies (2; 7; 8).

The remaining study (6) barely reaches the borderline of what is usually considered "adolescence," since the samples consist of fourth, fifth, and sixth graders in six Michigan schools in spring 1970. Data were analyzed separately for the 434 males and the 404 females. The studies are included in this group despite the age discrepancy, primarily because the measures are similar to those in several of the other surveys here.

## ADOLESCENT TELEVISION USE

These studies use three types of measures of adolescent viewing behavior: time spent viewing, program preferences, and frequency of viewing recurrent programs. Although these measures obviously have something in common, they do not produce consistently similar results. Separate examination of each can tell us something about the uses adolescents make of television, and about the specific role of violent programming in these patterns of use.

## Time spent viewing

Most of the present studies use variants of the Roper (1969) method of asking the respondent to estimate his viewing on "an average day" (3; 4; 7); others ask about the prior day (Lyle and Hoffman, 1971) or combine the "average day" and "yesterday" items into a single best-estimate (1; 5). Two studies note that estimates tend to be higher for "average day" than for "yesterday" (2; LoSciuto, 1971). The wisdom of ascertaining separate estimates for weekend vs. daily viewing (as in 3) is indicated by the detailed measures gathered by Lyle and Hoffman (1971). They presented local program logs for each day and asked their respondents to check the ones they had watched the previous day. Total viewing time on Sunday was about double the figures for weekdays. Schramm et al. (1961) had found a less dramatic but similar difference ten years earlier.

The "average" amount of time spent viewing by the "average" adolescent is a decidedly elusive quantity, one that varies greatly according to details of sampling, question phrasing, and the method of averaging. (But it appears a reasonable guess that on a given day, approximately one-half of American adolescents spend some three hours or more with an operating television set.) A substantial number watch twice that much, and of course a good many do not watch television at all. But overall there is a general impression of "many youngsters spending hours in front of a television set" (4).

More interesting than the synthetic notion of an "average" are the relationships between viewing time and other variables. The most consistent finding is that (viewing time decreases throughout adolescence)

Schramm et al. (1961) estimated that children's viewing is (heaviest at about the sixth grade) which is also roughly the beginning of adolescence. Their finding of a steady decline after the sixth grade is replicated, with rare exceptions, in each of the present studies that make age-group or grade-level comparisons (*1; 4; 5a;* Lyle and Hoffman, 1971). Further, a study of junior high boys comments that they "watch a good deal of television," some two to six hours daily, often simply to "kill time" (*2*); by contrast, a study of boys one year beyond high school remarks on how little they watch television, in comparison with general population norms (*7*).

The evidence on sex differences is mixed. Schramm et al. (1961) found no significant male-female difference, nor does LoSciuto (1971). Two of the present studies report that (adolescent males view more than females)(*1; 5a*), but two others show slight trends in the opposite direction (*4;* Lyle and Hoffman, 1971). These same data indicate a greater adolescent developmental trend away from heavy viewing among girls in three studies (*1; 4; 5*) but not in the fourth (Lyle and Hoffman, 1971).

Mental ability presents a more consistent picture. Almost all the studies agree that brighter adolescents watch less television. Schramm et al. (1961) found a negative correlation between IQ and viewing time among adolescents, and one of the present studies replicates this (*3*). Another study shows a negative correlation with academic performance in school (*5a*). If we assume that continued education beyond high school indicates higher mental ability, there is pertinent evidence in two samples of post-high-school boys. One finds the expected negative correlation between viewing time and years of education (*3*), but the other reports no more than a "trivial difference" between those who are in college and those who are not (*7*). Viewing time is also negatively related to indices of social skills such as leadership and achievement (*3*), popularity (*3*), and integration with peers (*5b*).

Socioeconomic status tends to be negatively related to adolescent viewing time. That is, those whose parents' occupations and education levels place them in the lower SES strata spend more time with television (*3; 4; 5a*). In several studies the authors control SES statistically, to examine residual relationships between viewing time and other variables (*1; 4; 5; 7*).

The possibility of parental influences on adolescent viewing has been examined in several ways. There is a significant correlation between viewing time measures for adolescents and their parents, particularly their mothers (*1; 5b*). Although Schramm et al. (1961) concluded that "parental example" exercises "a very potent kind of influence" over adolescent viewing, a review of more extensive data does not support so strong an inference (*1;* see also Chaffee et al., 1971). It seems that adolescents are at least as likely to influence their parents' viewing as vice-versa, and a good portion of the parent-adolescent viewing similarity can probably be explained by the fact that two persons living in the same household will tend to be exposed to the same television programs without influencing one another socially. Their mutual opportunity to view the same programs is simply greater, regardless of "example."

As will be seen shortly (below), a considerable portion of adolescent viewing time is spent with programs that often depict violence. It is not surprising, then, that part-whole correlations between viewing time and violence-viewing measures are reported in several studies (1; 3; 5a). There is also evidence that those who watch more television tend slightly toward a stronger preference for violent programs (4).

Many factors could account for the dwindling of "the TV habit" during adolescence. The developing youngster increasingly finds competing activities that might occupy his time. The developmental trend away from television is particularly marked among those who are most likely to find other things to do: the brighter and more socially skilled, and those in higher socioeconomic strata. It is against this background of developmental and "life-space" factors that we turn to specific measures of preference for and viewing of violent programs.

## Program preferences

Four studies employ measures of the violent content in the youngsters "favorite" programs (2; 3; 4; 7). One of these (7) uses a list of three or four favo'·tes, and the mean violence rating across this list based on the Greenberg and Gordon (1971) ratings. Another (4) ascertains both the single favorite program and the four favorites, and applies the Greenberg-Gordon ratings to each; the one-favorite-program measure is used in most analyses. In the longitudinal study, different measures were used in different waves of interviews. At the third-grade stage, the child's parents were asked what the youngster's three favorite programs were; in the five- and ten-year followup measurements, the adolescent's own list of his four favorites was used. The third grade parent report is probably more a measure of observed "frequent viewing" by the child than of "program preferences," since the child's viewing behavior is the most likely indicator a parent has of his preferences; therefore this measure is classed with the "frequency of viewing" measures (below). This assumption, that the parent-reports of child's favorites differ from the child's self-reports, is supported by the fact that they do not correlate significantly over time, for either sex (3). These differences in the viewing measure seriously affect attempts at longitudinal causal inference, as discussed later here. In both waves, staff coders rated the programs, and their ratings (3) correlate highly with those of Greenberg and Gordon. The fourth study (2) used both a checklist and an open-ended "favorite program" question, again applying the Greenberg-Gordon ratings; the two forms of the question yielded similar results.

Even more than in the case of viewing time, it is bootless to attempt to ascertain the "average" level of violence in adolescent program preferences. Lyle and Hoffman (1971) constructed a list of the 20 most popular programs, based on the youngsters' four favorite shows. Only two from their sixth-grade list, and three from their tenth-grade list, are also among the 20 most-violent shows (Greenberg and Gordon, 1971). However, Lyle and Hoffman elicited a decidedly more violent flavor when they asked which programs the youngsters actually watched (see discussion below).

( Preference for violent programs predominates in the favorite shows of a group of junior high boys that was partly sampled for high aggressiveness (2)) Of their nine most-preferred programs, five are also among the six most-violent according to ratings by critics and by the public (Greenberg and Gordon, 1971). Rather few of these boys complained of too much violence on television (2), whereas this was the second most frequent complaint about television in a national sample of adolescents and adults (LoSciuto, 1971). Lyle and Hoffman (1971) also report that few adolescents complain about television violence, especially at the tenth-grade level. Adolescent boys also have a strong interest in football telecasts, most of which are of the maximally violent professional game (2; 7).

Unlike total viewing time, age appears not to be much of a factor in preferences for violent programs. If anything, there is a slightly greater tendency for older adolescents to name a violent program as their favorite (4; Lyle and Hoffman, 1971).

The longitudinal study shows rather strong correlations between eighth- and thirteenth-grade preferences for violent programs (3). Neither of these measures is significantly related to the earlier third-grade violence-viewing measure, which could be due to developmental shifts or to the fact that the third-grade measure was derived from parent reports (3). At any rate, a youngster's preference for (or against) violent programs appears to be well defined early in adolescence, and to persist despite the general drift away from heavy viewing during that period in life.

Sex and SES are both related to violence-preference. Males and high-SES youngsters are more likely to have no "favorite" program than are girls and low-SES respondents. When a favorite is named, it is again the males, but also the low-SES youngsters, who are most likely to mention a violent one (4). A seemingly related finding is that boys with high mobility aspirations are more likely to prefer violent programs than are those whose aspirations are lower (3).

In all, the present studies add rather little to our knowledge of the psychological origins of preferences for television violence, other than the degree to which they can be attributed to the youngster's general level of aggressiveness. That question is considered in detail later in this paper.

# Frequency of viewing

The most common method of ascertaining violence viewing in these studies was to present the respondent with a checklist of recurrent programs, and ask him how often he watched each (5; 6; 8). A more laborious but also more precise technique was to show him the previous day's local television log and ask him to check the programs he had watched; this procedure was repeated daily for an entire school week by Lyle and Hoffman (1971). A decidedly imprecise method was to list program categories ("westerns" and "spy and adventure shows"), and ask for an estimate of the frequency of viewing each (1).

These raw frequency measures were converted into violence-viewing indices by a variety of methods. In one study 28 programs were listed, including the 20 that had been judged "most violent" in the Greenberg and Gordon (1971) study; the number of shows from this 20 that the respondent viewed each week was his or her violence-viewing score (6). A more elaborate procedure was to develop a composite violence rating based on the two Greenberg and Gordon samples plus a Minnesota study (Murray et al., 1970); then to multiply this by a five-level viewing-frequency measure for each of 65 programs; and finally to sum the 65 products of frequency-by-violence measures (5a).

As mentioned above, the third-grade measure of viewing consisted of asking the parent to list the child's three favorite programs; these programs were then coded according to their frequency of violence (3). While it is difficult to determine exactly what behavior of the child's is being measured by these reports, it seems reasonable to assume that parents would be better able to name programs the child *frequently* watches than to assess the child's *liking* of programs. The latter would have required information about affective responses to programs that we have no reason to expect parents would possess.

Lyle and Hoffman (1971) made no attempt to build a violence-viewing index from their data, but their list of most-viewed programs indicates a developmental trend toward more violent (and quite probably more adult) shows. Of the 22 most-viewed prime time programs, the number that are also among the 20 most-violent (Greenberg and Gordon, 1971) jumps from four at the sixth grade to nine in the tenth-grade norms (Lyle and Hoffman, 1971). As mentioned earlier, this measure of actual viewing contrasts markedly with program-preference measures in the same study, in which the youngsters listed only two or three violent shows among their favorites. There seems to be a tendency for adolescents to watch violent programs more than to admit that they like them.

In terms of real viewing, exposure to television violence probably does not increase during adolescence, because total viewing time decreases (see above). For example, *Mod Squad* is the second-most-watched program among tenth graders and ranks only fifth on the sixth-grade list (Lyle and Hoffman, 1971), but the difference between grade levels in the percentage who watched it is small. Similarly, *Ironside* ranks eighteenth at both grade levels but was seen by slightly more sixth graders.

Another study shows a decrease in violence viewing from junior to senior high samples that holds for both sexes and for all four family-communication-patterns types (*1*). This finding was replicated for both sexes in each of two other samples (*5a*). Consistently higher violence viewing by males than females is found at both grade levels (*1; 5a*).

The brighter youngsters, and those from higher socioeconomic levels, are less likely to watch violent programs. Significant negative correlations with SES and measures of IQ or school performance are reported for three samples (*1; 5a*). A mild negative relationship between violence viewing and SES can also be discerned from the cell Ns in the study of younger children (*6*). The negative SES relationship holds for samples of both sexes at two grade levels (*5b*).

It appears, however, that this raw correlation can be better explained by more functional variables than by the demographic construct of SES. When other measures of television use and parent-child relations are controlled, the SES-violence viewing correlation falls to zero (*1*). Looking at it another way, controls for SES fail to alter appreciably the correlations between violence viewing and a number of aggressiveness indices (*5a*).

By contrast, the negative relationship between IQ and violence viewing survives extensive partialing (*1*), and school performance proves an important control variable in the aggressiveness-viewing analyses (*5a*). The tendency for brighter adolescents to watch less television (see above) is echoed by a corresponding tendency to watch less violent programs; this specific pattern holds regardless of the youngster's total television use or various parental factors (*1*). In one small-sample analysis (*5b*), it appears that SES is negatively related to violence viewing only among boys, and to school performance only among girls.

Parental behaviors bear some relationships to the adolescent's frequency of viewing violent programs. Perhaps the strongest, at least at the junior high level, is the parent's own level of violence viewing; this correlates significantly with the child's viewing, even when television time is controlled for both parent and child (*1*). These parent-child correlations hold for specific programs and for all major categories of programs (*5b*). Regardless of the child's sex, the correlation with the mother's viewing is stronger than with the father's (*1*). This lack of a sex-role link, plus other data, lead the authors to conclude that the correlations are due to reciprocal causation at most and may be spurious (*1*).

Three other parent-child interaction variables are positively associated with adolescent violence viewing in several samples. These include restriction as a method of punishing the child (*1; 5a; and 5b*); socio-oriented family communication (*1; 5b*); and parental interpretation of television violence (*5a* and *5b*). These correlations are readily understood for two of the three measures. A restricted youngster has unanticipated "time at home" on his hands, and television is an easily available activity to fill it. Parental interpretation of television violence is obviously more likely to be offered to youngsters who watch more violent programs. The correlation with family socio-oriented communication suggests somewhat more subtle sociopsychological processes at work; it has survived considerable partialing, at least at the junior high level (*1; 5b*).

## Perceptions of television

As has already been mentioned, adolescents do not complain often about the level of violence on television. Their most frequent complaints are that there are too many commercials and news programs (*2;* Lyle and Hoffman, 1971). It is rare to complain about potential material that is missing; instead, objections are raised against what is presented, which suggests that adolescents have an essentially passive consumer orientation toward television.

It is clear from the Lyle and Hoffman (1971) data that television is primarily associated with entertainment and relaxation in the typical adolescent mind. When a youngster is angry or has had his feelings hurt, he is more likely to want to converse, go off alone, listen to music, or engage in sports than to turn on the television set. A sample of adolescent boys cited "enjoyment" and "time-killing" as their most usual reasons for viewing and said that about three of every ten programs they watched "just came on" (*2*).

Violent programs are seen as highly realistic by adolescents, even more so than news and documentary programs (*4*). Involvement with television violence is reported more frequently for crime shows than for westerns (*5b*). Girls report more feelings of involvement with violent programs, but boys identify more with violent characters (*5a*). Younger adolescents are more likely to say they have learned aggressive behaviors from television (*5a*). These specific reactions to television violence are only mildly correlated with the amount of violence viewing; they are somewhat more strongly correlated with aggressive behavior, indicating that they may be key intervening variables in any process of learning of social aggression *via* television (*5a*).

One study (*4*) measured the adolescent's perception of the role played by aggression in his favorite program; since these variables are related only to indices of aggressive behavior, discussion of them will be deferred until later in this paper.

A provocative attempt to discern the latent dimensions of role perceptions in adolescent viewing was made in one study (*8*). Beginning with a four-fold sample (blacks *vs.* whites, aggressives *vs.* normals) of 80 eighth-grade boys, the authors focus on those programs that have a peculiar appeal to only one of the four groups. They conclude that the chief characters in these programs can be characterized by status (low *vs.* high) and reactions to problem situations (active *vs.* passive) that are analogous to those of the boys who watch them. The authors assume that selective television viewing is a form of information seeking, in which "the adolescent is highly motivated to search for prototypes of adult masculine behavior" on television, which provides "a readily accessible source of high-definition portraits of the masculine styles common in our mass culture." This implies a more purposeful approach to the television set than other studies would suggest for most adolescents, who appear to be quite casual in their viewing (see above). But this assumption is supported to an extent by the finding that one-fifth of a general adolescent sample felt that aggressive behavior by the main characters in their favorite programs "shows the way people ought to act" (4). Also, boys in early adolescence are the most likely to say they have learned aggressive modes of behavior from television (5a). The hypothesis of role-modeling *via* television need not extend to all kinds of adolescents to be socially significant.

## ADOLESCENT AGGRESSIVENESS

An enormous variety of conceptions of "aggressiveness" are found in the present studies. The measures can be conveniently broken down into four categories: reports of aggression by others, self-reports of aggression and delinquent behavior, self-reports of aggressive feelings and attitudes, and self-reports of cognitive and effective reactions to aggression. As with the various indices of television use (above), these different measures yield somewhat different results. In this section they will be compared with one another, and their correlates will be reviewed. The following section deals with their relationships to television violence.

# Reports by others

Three kinds of "experts" on an adolescents's aggressive social behavior have been used in the present studies: school officials, peers, and parents. (A fourth potential source, siblings, was not used, probably because data would not have been comparable from one youngster to another due to varying ages and numbers of brothers and sisters.)

Two studies rely on school administrators and counselors, to pick samples of students with "records" or "histories" of aggressive behavior (2; 8). In the first of these there was a validity check based on self-reports, which showed a substantially higher incidence of fighting and use of weapons by the "aggressives" than by other students (2). The aggressives were also more likely to come from low-SES homes and to get low grades in school. It is difficult to determine whether the school officials were influenced by these factors in their nomination of aggressives; aggressiveness measures based on self-report do not consistently correlate with SES, but tend to be related to poorer school performance (see below).

A single-item teacher report was used in one junior high sample, and it did not discriminate very strongly between the sexes (5b). This measure correlated only modestly with peer ratings, and even less with self- and mother-ratings.

In this same study, a ten-item peer report of "assault aggression" appears to have been much more satisfactory. It discriminates by sex and age, in that boys and younger adolescents are rated more aggressive by their peers. This was also the only study to use parent reports, a four-item index based on interviews with the mother. Like the teacher report, this measure did not distinguish between sexes or grade levels, and it correlated quite weakly with other measures of aggressiveness. It was, nevertheless, combined with peer and teacher reports into a single "other-report" index of aggressiveness. Although such a multiple-operation measure would seem to offer maximum validity, this index does not correlate as strongly with self-reported aggression as does the peer report alone.

Peer reports also provide the most important aggressiveness measures in the longitudinal study; they were repeated, with modifications, in the third, eighth, and "thirteenth" grade waves (3). In the third grade, a ten-item "guess who" list of aggressive acts was given to each child; he was instructed to name the other child in the class who was most likely to have committed the act. In the eighth grade, one of the ten items was dropped, and there were some changes in wording; more importantly, only a small portion of the original sample could be re-interviewed. So the eighth-grade measure is unsatisfactory for longitudinal analysis, and the authors make little use of it except as a validity check. Respondents in the larger thirteenth-grade wave were given the nine eighth-grade items, all of which had been changed to retrospective measures by converting the wording to past tense. For example, "Who starts a fight over nothing?" from the first two waves became "Who started a fight over nothing?" Instead of nominating a single "most likely" classmate from their own third-grade rooms, the respondents were invited to check the names of "all those people who fit that question." For this purpose, each respondent was given a roster of students with whom he had gone to school. Arithmetical corrections were made to neutralize differences in opportunity for nomination.

Correlations among these three waves of peer-rated aggression are highest for pairs of measures nearer in time among the boys, but for girls the third:eighth grade correlation is quite the weakest. Measures of "psychopathology" in the thirteenth grade correlate most strongly with thirteenth-grade peer-rated aggression, and successively less strongly with each earlier measure. The thirteenth-grade aggressiveness indices were positively related to social status and negatively with IQ for both sexes (3).

Overall, the peer-based aggressiveness measures appear to be the most valid of the various other-ratings in the present studies. This should be expected, since they are based on more items and larger pools of "experts" and since peers are more usual victims of adolescent aggression, compared with the various types of adult raters.

## Self-reported aggressive behavior

It could easily be argued that the most competent "expert" on an adolescent's aggressive acts would be that person himself. There is, however, a danger that the youngster would be reluctant to admit many transgressions and would distort his answers to achieve a modicum of social approval from the researcher. In most of the present studies, the researchers were willing to take that kind of risk, although most of them opted for various forms of multiple operationism in an effort to "surround" the key variable of aggressiveness.

In the study where the main measure of aggressiveness was selection by school officials, the nominated "aggressives" more often admitted fighting, hitting a teacher, and using a gun or knife to "get something" from someone (2). Thus self-report provided a validity check on the main measure.

Repeated measures one year apart on an eight-item index were gathered in the large-sample study of post-high-school boys (7). The most frequent aggressive acts were fighting, participating in a gang fight, hurting someone so that he needed medical attention, and getting something by threatening another person. These same items were used to create an index of "aggressive or violent acts" in another study with a more comprehensive sample (4).

Much less frequently reported by the post-high-school males were hitting a parent or other adult and using a weapon to get something. The eight-item index, including these and the more frequent delinquent acts, was negatively related to indicators of SES (7). When it was substituted for the aggressiveness reports of school officials (see above), the results of the study were quite different.

In addition to the five-item measure of "aggressive or violent acts" (see above), there were four other indices of delinquent behavior in the Maryland study (4). At least one of them consists of fairly serious behavior, as indicated by "involvement with legal officials." In lieu of direct behavioral questions that might have incriminated the respondents, they were asked how often they had been stopped by police, taken to the police station, arrested, brought to juvenile court, and spent time in a juvenile facility. The other three indices were "petty delinquent acts" (trespassing, intentionally damaging school property), "defiance of parents" (staying out late, running away from home, arguing or fighting with parents, drinking without permission), and "political action" (joining a sit-in, asking a school official to change a policy or course). These latter three measures are dropped from portions of the reported analyses, and are clearly less "aggressive" in nature.

The authors do not report intercorrelations among these five measures, but they do assess each of them in terms of several demographic indicators (4). On both of the measures of serious deviance, boys report a higher incidence of aggressive acts than girls. SES is negatively related to legal involvement, and accounts for racial differences on that measure. On the measure of aggressive acts, SES is also negatively correlated among white respondents, but positively correlated among blacks.

Two batteries of self-report items were adapted from previous research to supplement teacher-mother-peer measures in one study (5a). One is a six-item measure called "manifest physical aggression," in which four of the items consist of admitting hitting someone. The other two items indicate a readiness to fight when provoked. A response scale based on the degree to which the item is "like me" is used. The second scale, "aggressive behavioral delinquency," consists of three items on the frequency of fighting.

These two scales correlated fairly well with one another and with a number of other self-report aggression measures in two samples (5a). Both show the expected boy-girl difference, and clearly decline with age in adolescence. They are unrelated to SES, but in one sample are negatively correlated with school performance. The authors combine them with several other measures to construct major indices for their later analyses (see below).

The final (thirteenth-grade) wave of the longitudinal study (3) included a number of self-reported aggression and delinquency items. These included two three-item indices of "aggressive habit" and a measure of "antisocial behavior" consisting of 26 delinquent acts. The respondents were also asked how often they had been arrested. These measures all correlated positively with earlier peer-rated aggressiveness indices and with "psychopathology." But the authors prefer the "external" peer-ratings for their main analyses and rely very little on these self-reported acts in drawing their inferences.

## Feelings of aggressiveness

Whereas reports by other persons may be more objective than self-reports where overt behavior is concerned, only the respondent himself can explain how he "feels"—including the extent to which he feels like behaving aggressively, or his internal reactions to aggression. Four sets of authors included such mentalistic measures in their studies.

Two studies used the generalized aggressiveness inventory devised by Zaks and Walters (1959). This measure includes several items that appear only obliquely related to aggression on their face, but its authors report satisfactory validity checks (Walters and Zaks, 1959). Their full 12-item battery was administered in both the third and thirteenth grades in the longitudinal study (3). The other study adapted seven of the 12 items to a modified response scale (5a). The 12-item version correlated positively with "psychopathology" and negatively with "achievement" (3). The seven-item measure showed boys more aggressive than girls in only one of two samples and correlated rather weakly with other aggressiveness measures in both samples (5a). It is somewhat negatively correlated with SES and school performance (5a). Data from mothers on this measure show positive correlations with children of both sexes at two grade levels (5b). It is negatively related to the degree of concept-orientation in the family's communication structure (5b). In all, this measure appears to be somewhat different in nature from more direct assessments of aggression, and is best employed as a supplementary index of adolescent aggressiveness; in both studies, the authors use it in that fashion.

Hypothetical situations were posed as potential settings for aggressive behavior by the respondent in both these studies, and by the authors of another study (3; 5; 6). In the longitudinal study, 24 items assessed the degree to which the respondent said he would use punishment if he were the parent of an eight-year-old child (3). Hypothetical aggressive reactions to four possible conflict situations involving peers yielded an index that distinguished as well between sexes and grade levels as any direct report of aggressive behavior, and correlated well with the other measures (5a). This measure was independent of SES and displayed inconsistent patterns of correlation with school performance (5a). It was very slightly related to both dimensions of family communication structure (5a). The other study (6) used four open-ended "What would you do if . . . ?" items involving hypothetical conflict situations with peers, and coded the responses on a dichotomous scale. These measures were negatively related to SES for boys only, and positively correlated with perceived parental approval of aggression.

Various items and indices from the Buss and Durkee (1957; Buss, 1961) inventory were employed in several studies. In one, it was concluded that only a few of the items discriminated validly between aggressive boys and others (2). Many of the Buss-Durkee items represent a measurement borderline between feelings and actual behavior; they are included in this section because most of the authors did not ask their respondents for specific reports of their past behavior.

The study of preadolescents asked for agree-disagree responses on five Buss-Durkee items and combined these into an index of "willingness to use violence" (6). As was the case with the measure based on hypothetical conflict situations (see above), aggressive responses were negatively related to SES for boys only, and were associated with parental approval of aggression.

Buss-Durkee items were used in another study (5a) to construct a four-item index of "assault aggression" and a three-item index of "irritability." The assault aggression measure, which included three of the six items from the "manifest physical aggression" measure (see self-reported behavior, above), correlated well with all other aggressiveness indices. It also yielded the expected distinctions between sexes and grade levels (males and younger adolescents being more aggressive), whereas irritability correlated weakly with other aggressiveness indices and was somewhat higher for females. Neither measure correlates consistently with SES or school performance (5a). Mother-child correlations are mostly positive for assault aggression, but not for irritability (5b). Generally, then, the irritability measure seems to tap a dimension that is rather different from most of the indices under review here.

A four-item Buss-Durkee index of "verbal aggression" was employed as a supplementary measure in this study, and as expected it was higher among boys (5b). However, it did not correlate strongly with measures of aggressive overt behavior, being instead apparently a manifestation of aggressive inner feelings.

The longitudinal study (3) included a four-item measure called "aggressive drive" that was mostly verbal in the nature of aggressiveness represented. However, no relationships between this and other variables are reported, presumably because they were not significant. In general, verbal expressions of hostility appear to be orthogonal to physically aggressive behavior, perhaps providing a functionally equivalent "outlet" for aggressive feelings.

Approval of aggression or violence was measured in various ways by three sets of authors of the present studies. The simplest was the degree of agreement with two items that suggested conditions under which "it's all right to hit an enemy" (5a). Boys ranked higher than girls on this measure, and it correlated rather well with measures of aggressive behavior and feelings. It was negatively correlated with SES and school performance in two samples and showed positive mother-child correlations (5b).

An eight-item approval-of-violence index was used in the study of preadolescents (6). The form of the measure was agreement with statements such as, "It's all right if a man slaps his wife." Another index that is in the general vein of "approval" in this study is the "perceived effectiveness of violence," a five-item measure using such statements as, "A fight is the best way to settle an argument once and for all." Both these indices correlated negatively with SES for boys only and positively with parental approval of violence for both sexes.

The most extensive analysis of approval of violence broke it down into three aggressor roles: adult males, teenage males, and police officers (*4*). Five possible provoking situations were posed (*e.g.*, a stranger had broken into the man's house, or had knocked him down and was trying to rob him), and the respondent was asked if he approved of an adult male punching or shooting the stranger. The teenage measure was similar, involving punching or knifing another teenage male under various provoking circumstances. The policeman questions asked about striking or shooting an adult male in response to insults or criminal acts. The authors found no consistent relationships between these measures and either sex or race.

This study (*4*) included one additional index that is at least partly based on inner feelings and perceptions (although it has some basis in objective reality as well). This is the respondent's estimate of the frequency of various crimes of violence in his neighborhood, in an adjacent metropolitan center, and in "this part of the country." This measure was related to firsthand experience as a crime victim, but only for the local-neighborhood crime level. Interestingly, the authors report that adolescent belief in a high crime rate beyond the local neighborhood is "nearly unanimous." The crime-rate estimates are higher among older adolescents and whites, but are unrelated to SES or sex.

## CORRELATIONS BETWEEN VIEWING AND AGGRESSIVENESS

The foregoing review of the major variables in the present studies has established a number of similarities between measures of violence viewing and measures of aggressiveness. There is some evidence that both these kinds of behaviors are more common early in adolescence, among males, in the lower socioeconomic strata, and among those with lesser intellectual capabilities. But none of those relationships is especially strong or consistent across different samples and measures. In this final section of the paper, the focus turns to the direct issue that has been purposely avoided until this point: empirical relationships between violence viewing and aggressiveness.

Two opposing (although not mutually incompatible) research hypotheses bring us to this juncture. (Put very simply, it could be hypothesized that aggressiveness leads an adolescent to prefer violent programs, or that the experience of seeing violent programs develops aggressive tendencies in the youngster.) Schramm et al. (1961) accepted the first hypothesis and rejected the second, because they could find no differences in aggressiveness between youngsters in a town with television and a town that lacked it.

Absence of correlation between the two variables, or a negative correlation, would provide evidence against both hypotheses. Positive correlations can be interpreted either way, or as evidence consistent with other hypotheses in which some third factor "causes" both violence viewing and aggressiveness. Correlations that remain when other variables have been partialed out can be taken as evidence that those specific variables are not plausible "third factors" for alternative hypotheses of this latter type.

To attempt to make some further use of the present findings for causal interpretations, the present review is divided into two sections. The first examines correlations between aggressiveness and preferences for violent programs, on the premise that this is the most appropriate "dependent variable" to consider in testing the hypothesis that aggressiveness induces tendencies to watch violent programs. The second section reviews correlations between aggressiveness and actual viewing of violent programs, a measure that is much closer to the kind of "independent variable" that often leads to minor forms of aggression in laboratory experiments.

The distinction between these two types of measures is scarcely iron-clad, of course. We should assume that program preferences correlate rather well with actual viewing, although the study showing comparative data demonstrates marked discrepancies between the two measures (Lyle and Hoffman, 1971). And in the only other research that reports indices of both measures, the correlation between them is a modest .25 (Chaffee and McLeod, 1971). But the scientific purposes of this total body of studies will be best served if we can attempt to eliminate one hypothesis at a time. If some rival hypotheses can be eliminated by disconfirming evidence, the presumptive case for the other hypotheses that "survive" becomes somewhat stronger. At the same time, however, purely correlational evidence cannot "prove" or "confirm" a hypothesis in a positive sense. We are necessarily limited to the cumbersome and plodding procedure of attempting to falsify each alternative hypothesis. A final section of the paper will consider possible causal inferences more fully.

## Correlations with violent program preferences

Four of the present studies relate a violence index based on the youngster's "favorite" programs to one or more measures of aggressiveness (2; 3; 4; 7). Although all the authors infer that there is some kind of overall correlation, they note that their evidence is not particularly strong or consistent. In another study, the authors were so disappointed by the lack of correlation between violent program preference and many aggressiveness measures that they omitted the data from their report, and relied instead on measures of actual viewing (5). Subsequent analyses that include the viewing-preference measures from that study have since been reported (Chaffee and McLeod, 1971), and are incorporated into this paper.

Only one study reports findings for both kinds of viewing measure (2); the results for actual viewing are reviewed in the next section of this paper. The preference measure was a single item asking the youngster to list his four favorite programs. The sample was equally divided between 40 "aggressives" (as nominated by school officials) and 40 other students, all urban junior high males. The aggressive boys listed an average of 1.8 violent programs, while the corresponding figure for the nonaggressives was 1.6. Given the small Ns, this is not a particularly impressive difference; no significance test is reported. Larger differences were found on some related measures, such as a greater tendency for the nonaggressives to list "family comedy" shows and to complain that television offers too much violence and too little comedy.

A second measure of aggressiveness, based on a battery of self-report items about aggressive feelings, produced somewhat stronger results (2). When the sample was split on this index (the aggressives were found to have listed an average of 2.2 violent programs, compared to 1.5 for the less aggressives) Regardless of the aggressiveness measure used (the aggressives were found to spend more time watching television, to be more selective in their television use, to pay more attention to newspaper stories about robberies and civil disorders—and to prefer listening to music over watching television.)

There is a danger of overinterpreting such findings, since the sample is so small and specialized and was clearly not selected by anything approaching a random process. Moreover, another member of the same research group has suggested that it is not the violent content that specifically accounts for the varying program preferences that are reported (8). Using similar data and a circumplicial analysis, he suggests instead that it is the social role of the major male character in the show that draws a young adolescent boy's attention. Such a youngster is in need of a "model for manhood" that is appropriate to his ascribed social status and personality, it is argued (Aggressiveness is a manifestation of a generally "active" personality, which in turn is drawn to observe adult male protagonists who actively deal with the problems that confront them each week; their methods of coping frequently involve violence, but not necessarily) An analogous line of reasoning, to account for black-white differences in terms of the male lead's social standing in the program, is also suggested.

The study of post-high-school males (7) also found a positive correlation between an index of violence in the youngster's four favorite programs and an aggressiveness measure. In this case aggression was indexed by eight items self-reporting specific delinquent acts. The largest differences (between those with "a great deal" of violence in their favorite programs and those with "almost none") are found on items reporting fighting. (The difference was, strangely, strongest among those who spend very little time watching television.) But when the data were controlled for aggressiveness indicated in a similar measure the previous year, the differences disappeared except among those who had initially been very aggressive. As the authors point out, this does not necessarily render their findings less disturbing socially. If highly aggressive young men find "reinforcement" for aggressive behavior in the television programs they select, there is ample reason for concern about such programs. And as Klapper (1963) has stated, the usual effect of media violence is to reinforce behavioral tendencies regardless of whether they are "socially wholesome or socially unwholesome." The term "reinforce" generally means that "the probability that a response will recur" in a similar situation has been increased (English and English, 1963). The reinforcement of aggressive behavioral tendencies, whatever their origin, may indeed be considered socially unwholesome by many.

The longitudinal study (3) provides two kinds of viewing-aggressiveness correlations, synchronous and time-lagged. Surprisingly, the latter data are much stronger than the former. (The strongest data, the time-lagged correlations stemming from the third-grade viewing measure, will be taken up in the next section, since they are interpreted here as measures of actual viewing, not of viewing preference.)

At both points in adolescence, in fact, the synchronous correlations between aggressiveness and stated preferences for violent programs are slightly negative. The time-lagged correlation from eighth-grade viewing preference to thirteenth-grade aggressiveness is positive, however. The eighth-grade data, being drawn from an inadequate subsample of the study's total panel, are inconclusive. The more important longitudinal findings involve the third-grade parental report of the child's viewing (below). It should be noted here, however, that there is no correlation between third-grade aggressiveness and thirteenth-grade violence program preferences, which there presumably should have been if aggressiveness were a "cause" of viewing preference.

Rather weak overall relationships are shown in the other study using a "favorite program" measure (4). In this large-sample survey spanning most of the adolescent years, the incidence of "high deviance" on five different measures increases by only a few percentage points from "low violence, favorite program" to "high violence, favorite program." For the two measures that most clearly involve serious aggressive behavior, the differences are 2.5 percent and 1.1 percent. When the more reliable measure "average violence rating of four favorite shows" is used, however, the differences are much more convincing: 11.1 percent and 10.2 percent, respectively. This justifies the authors' conclusion that the relationship is positive, albeit weak. In their subsequent partialing analyses they show only the less-reliable single-program measure. These partialed tables fairly consistently demonstrate that the association between program preference and behavioral deviance is limited to one of their four major subgroups: male whites. The trend is in the opposite direction for female whites and male blacks, and varies between measures for female blacks. Differences on the two principal measures of deviant behavior tend to vanish when perceptions of the instrumental role of violence in the favorite program are controlled; only eight of 16 comparisons are in a positive direction, which is the number that would be expected by chance alone. Controls for demographic and aspirational variables do not appreciably alter the authors' conclusion that the preference-deviance correlation is a weak one.

Feelings about violence, as indexed by approval of adult, teen, and police violence, are all weakly but positively correlated with a preference for a violent "favorite" program (4). Breaking the sample down by race and gender, however, shows that these findings also hold only for white males. There is no relationship between estimated frequency of violent crime and preference for violent programs, a finding that holds up under a variety of controls for other variables.

A consistent thread runs through these diverse studies, in that evidence of any link between adolescent aggressiveness and preference for television violence is limited to white males. That is certainly the dominant conclusion to be reached from the only sample with large numbers of respondents of both sexes and races (4). There are no relationships in the longitudinal study (3), the synchronous correlations being slightly negative for both sexes. In the large-sample national survey of post-high-school boys, the relationship is monotonic (although weak) for whites, but not for blacks (2). And in the small-sample study of equal numbers of black and white males in junior high, the whites listed more violent shows among their favorites than the blacks; this was true of both aggressives and nonaggressives, as determined by two very different measures (2).

One rather simple explanation for this specific pattern has been suggested in the present studies. The overwhelming majority of violent acts on evening series television programs are committed by white males. So if program preferences are guided to any extent by the search for adult role models (see 8), it is the aggressive white male adolescent who would be most likely to be peculiarly drawn to shows that frequently depict violence. The general absence of more positive findings for other sectors of the population in these field studies may, then, be partly an artifact of the kinds of program content that are to be found on television. With more detailed research attention to specific sources of attraction to specific programs, including those that are favored by smaller portions of the total audience, it might be possible to establish closer relationships than the present studies suggest.

# Correlations with viewing of violent programs

Four studies present new data relating various measures of exposure to violent television content to several indicators of aggressiveness (2; 3; 5; 6).

In one small-sample study of junior high boys (2) the results are mixed, at most. Those boys designated as "aggressives" by school officials reported that they spent more time viewing than did the other youngsters, but they also indicated less viewing of individual programs from a list of evening shows. The lists of ten-most-watched shows for these two groups differ in that there is one more violent program on the aggressives' lists, plus considerably less viewing of family comedy shows. However, when a self-report aggressiveness measure was substituted for the school-report, these differences disappeared.

In the study of preadolescent boys and girls (6), the violence-viewing measure consists of the number of programs watched each week, from the list of 20-most-violent (Greenberg and Gordon, 1971). Since all the data tables are partialed on SES and parental attitudes toward violence, they provide in effect a total of eight replications of the viewing-aggressiveness relationship in different samples of youngsters. On the measure of willingness to use violence, there were significant positive relationships with violence viewing for both sexes; the means are in this direction for three of the four subsamples of boys and all four subsamples of girls. On the measure of suggested use of violence in hypothetical conflict situations, the results are significant for the girls only, and in the positive direction for all four subsamples. For boys the difference is nonsignificant, holds for only two of four subsamples, and is entangled in an uninterpreted three-way interaction with SES and parental approval of violence. There are strong main effects of violence viewing on the perceived effectiveness of violence, for both sexes and in seven of eight subsamples; violence viewing does not interact with other variables in either study. The fourth criterion measure, approval of aggression, is not related to violence viewing for either sex.

In the study that provides the greatest number of measures of aggressiveness, and of replications in different subsamples, the correlations with violence viewing are overwhelmingly positive (5a). The correlations with an overall index of self-reported aggression are significant in two widely separated communities. For the four subtests that make up this overall index, all eight correlations are positive and seven significantly so. The partialed data by sex and grade level provide a total of 38 correlation coefficients, of which 35 are positive, 12 significantly; none of the three negative correlations approaches significance. All told, this is a fairly impressive array of evidence, considering the smallness of Ns.

These self-report aggressiveness measures are also correlated to an extent with time spent viewing (5a). But when viewing time is controlled, the pattern of positive correlation between violence viewing and aggressiveness remains in 34 of the 38 subsample entries. The most strongly related aggressiveness index is the one based on hypothetical situations; it is perhaps noteworthy, though, that this does not hold for the younger males, a finding that corresponds to the study of preadolescent boys (6). Unlike the findings reviewed earlier on program preference, there is no appreciable sex difference. There is, however, an interaction between sex and grade level, in that the overall partial correlation is stronger (in both samples) for girls at the junior high level but for boys in senior high (5a). This interaction, and the overwhelmingly positive trend of the overall data, tend to hold up well when controls for SES and school performance are instituted.

Viewing of any type of program tends to be correlated with the overall self-report aggressiveness measure, which might be expected from the correlation with viewing time (5a). However, when viewing of other types of programs is controlled, only specific exposure to crime-detective, adventure-drama, and Saturday morning programs retains a partial correlation with aggressiveness. There are several variables that, added to violence viewing, increase the likelihood of high self-reported aggressiveness; these include the perceived learning of aggression from television and irritability. Controls for these two variables tend to reduce the power of violence viewing to predict aggressiveness, but it remains significant. Another variable that reduces the correlation is parental emphasis on nonaggressive behavior; even when this kind of constraint operates on the youngster, however, there remains a significant correlation between violence viewing and aggressiveness.

These factors should be allocated to different roles in an attempt to explain what accounts for the viewing:aggressiveness correlations. Irritability would seem to be a contingent condition, perhaps one that increases the likelihood that viewing violence would instigate aggression. Learning of aggressive behavior, by contrast, is part of the hypothetical process by which exposure to violence might be translated into aggression. And finally, parental emphasis on nonaggression is a form of social control that could be instituted to modify any undesirable influences of violence viewing. This last area is taken up more fully later.

When the measure of aggressiveness is based on reports by persons other than the youngster himself, the results are less strong, but they are still positive for all measures except mother-report and significantly positive for the overall index constructed from the various reports by others (5b). This low positive correlation with the overall other-report index holds for both sexes and grade levels, which can be thought of as separate replications of the finding. It also holds up when time spent viewing, SES, and school performance are controlled, although the relationship is limited to junior high girls and senior high boys. Only when irritability, perceived learning of aggression from television, and parental affection and punishment are simultaneously controlled does the partial correlation of violence viewing and other-report aggressiveness drop to zero for the junior high subsample and to a nonsignificant level for the overall sample (5b).

Perhaps the best single index of aggressiveness is the gra.. combination of self-reports and those by peers, mothers, and teachers. This measure is significantly correlated with overall violence viewing, even when irritability, perceived learning of aggression from television, and parental affection and punishment are simultaneously controlled (5b).

Although not based on adolescent viewing, the data from the longitudinal study provide some of the most impressive evidence of a link between violence viewing and aggressiveness. The third-grade parent-report viewing measure correlates significantly with third-grade aggressiveness and even *more strongly* with thirteenth-grade aggressiveness for boys (3). (In female sample, both relationships are null and even slightly negative.) This time-lagged evidence of time-order is even more impressive in light of the fact that third-grade aggressiveness does not predict thirteenth-grade aggressiveness much better than third-grade violence viewing does. The parent-report of boys' viewing also correlates positively with their self-reported antisocial behavior and "psychopathology" ten years later. The authors conclude that "exposure to a diet of violent television" as a child is "a probable cause of the expression of aggressive behavior" in late adolescence, for males. Problems of causal inference will be taken up more fully later in this paper.

There is other evidence that violence viewing at an earlier age is more closely associated with aggressiveness than is the adolescent's present level of violence viewing. Retrospective self-reported viewing correlates somewhat more strongly with the self-report aggressiveness measure (5b) and much more strongly with the combined self-other measure in a multiple regression analysis that also involves two other good predictors of aggressiveness.

Approval of aggression, a variable that was unrelated to violence viewing in the study of preadolescents (6), is mildly positively related in this study (5b). It is more strongly correlated with violence viewing at a younger age than at present.

To summarize the findings of this key section of the paper, the different subsamples from the present studies that relate violence viewing to aggressiveness are roughly compared in Table 1. Samples of boys have been separated from samples of girls, and each group has been arrayed in order of grade level. For the boys, there are positive relationships in five of six samples, plus the time-lagged positive relationship from the longitudinal study (3). For the girls, out of six samples only the data from the longitudinal study (3) are null. The pattern of stronger correlations for the younger girls and the older boys can also be seen in a general fashion in this table.

For comparison, Table 2 summarizes the analogous relationships found between aggressiveness and self-reported preferences for vio-

Table 1: Summary of correlations between violence viewing and aggressiveness

| Study | Locale | Grade | N | Self-report aggressive behavior | Other-report aggressive behavior |
|-------|--------|-------|---|--------------------------------|----------------------------------|
| | | | Samples of boys | | |
| (3) | New York | 3 | 211 | | ++ |
| (6) | Michigan | 4-5-6 | 434 | | ++ |
| (5) | Wisconsin | 6-7 | 38 | + | + |
| (5) | Maryland | 7 | 122 | + | 0 |
| (2) | Maryland | 8-9 | 80 | 0 | |
| (5) | Wisconsin | 9-10 | 43 | + | ++ |
| (5) | Maryland | 10 | 107 | ++ | ++ |
| | | | Samples of girls | | |
| (3) | New York | 3 | 216 | | 0 |
| (6) | Michigan | 4-5-6 | 404 | | +++ |
| (5) | Wisconsin | 6-7 | 30 | ++ | ++ |
| (5) | Maryland | 7 | 108 | ++ | ++ |
| (5) | Wisconsin | 9-10 | 40 | + | ++ |
| (5) | Maryland | 10 | 136 | + | + |

Note: Cell entries indicate presence of positive (+) or null (0) correlation between the amount of violence viewing reported by the adolescent, and an aggressiveness index based on the type of report listed in the column heading. Stronger or more consistent positive relationships are indicated by repeating the sign (++). These are very approximate estimates of the strength of the evidence that the correlation is non-zero.

lence viewing. Since rather few analyses had been reported, Table 2 also includes findings from a later report (Chaffee and McLeod, 1971) based on data from one of these studies (5). Among the samples of boys, null relationships are reported in four of the eight cases; the other four are positive but low (the highest correlation coefficient is +.13). No positive relationships are reported for any of the five samples of girls. While one hesitates to generalize when most of the samples are from one state (Maryland), the relationship appears to be peculiar to the younger white males. Overall, Table 2 contrasts markedly with Table 1, where the correlations were stronger and not specific to any sex or age group. (Race was not coded in the samples in Table 1.)

Obviously Table 1 oversimplifies a great deal of complex data and obscures a number of nice distinctions. Assuming that these matters have been dealt with sufficiently already in this paper, we can at this stage direct our attention to the central fact of Table 1. There is clearly a preponderance of evidence in these studies to support the conclusion that adolescent aggressiveness and the viewing of violent television programs are statistically associated. This relationship is considerably more impressive and pervasive than the weak and limited correlations between aggressiveness and expressed preference for violent programs, which are shown in Table 2. Where tested by partialing out additional

Table 2: Summary of correlations between aggressiveness and preference for violent programs

| Study | Locale (race) | Grade | N | Self-report aggressive behavior | Other-report aggressive behavior |
|---|---|---|---|---|---|
| | | | Samples of boys | | |
| (5)* | Maryland | 7 | 122 | + | |
| (2) | Maryland | 8-9 | 80 | + | 0+ |
| (4) | Maryland (white) | 7-12 | 857 | 0+ | |
| (4) | Maryland (black) | 7-12 | 125 | 0 | |
| (5)* | Maryland | 10 | 107 | 0 | |
| (7) | Nationwide (white) | 12 | 1351 | + | |
| (7) | Nationwide (black) | 12 | 167 | 0 | |
| (3) | New York | 13 | 211 | | 0 |
| | | | Samples of girls | | |
| (5)* | Maryland | 7 | 108 | 0 | |
| (4) | Maryland (white) | 7-12 | 963 | 0 | |
| (4) | Maryland (black) | 7-12 | 159 | 0 | |
| (5)* | Maryland | 10 | 136 | 0– | |
| (3) | New York | 13 | 216 | | 0 |

Note: Cell entries indicate positive (+), negative (–) or null (0) correlation between amount of violence in the child's self-reported "favorite" programs, and an aggressiveness index of the listed type. Asterisk (*) indicates later analyses that do not appear in the report here, but are shown in Chaffee and McLeod (1971).

variables, the positive relationships in Table 2 tended to vanish, whereas those in Table 1 did not. In all, then, there seems to be a strong association between aggressiveness and violence viewing that cannot be explained by an intervening preference for violent programs.

## Possible causal inferences

Only one of the present studies (3) ventures so far as to state an inference of positive, unidirectional causation, and even that is in terms of violence viewing as a "probable cause" of adolescent aggressiveness among boys only. Accordingly, let us examine the supporting data in that case first. Surprisingly, it is one of the few studies that find no synchronous correlations within adolescence, between a viewing measure and an aggressiveness measure. The positive evidence is entirely time-lagged, and there are no instances of an aggressiveness measure predicting a delayed effect on a viewing measure. The positive findings are either synchronous within childhood or time-lagged from childhood viewing to adolescent aggressiveness ten years later. It is this last finding, of course, that provides the single basis of the causal claim by the authors. The finding holds only for males. (It is the only sex-specific relationship between two such measures in the present studies.)

The authors take a decidedly statistical approach to interpretation, basing their inference on several variants of cross-lagged correlation. The time-lagged correlation of + .31 is the strongest of the four correlations relating a viewing preference measure to an aggression measure. As they point out, such data stand up under several statistical analyses. The simple cross-lagged comparison shows + .31 vs. − .01. When third-grade aggression levels are controlled, the partial correlation is still + .21. When the authors make reasonable estimates of reliability and apply the Rozelle and Campbell (1961) baseline, the + .31 figure is substantially above the baseline of + .06; the latter, in turn, is only slightly greater than the reverse-time correlation of − .01, which would suggest that it is unlikely that third grade aggressiveness diminishes the youngster's preference for violent television ten years later. Yet another procedure, which the authors did not attempt, would be to apply Bohrnstedt's (1969) formula that combines the cross-lagged and partial tests (see also Chaffee et al., 1970). That approach would yield time-lagged correlations of + .35 (p. <.001) for boys, and − .10 (n.s.) for girls. Those figures would seem to provide an even more conclusive case for longitudinal causal inference.

But models of statistical inference are no more valid than the assumptions underlying them. And in the case of all the time-lagged models reported in the previous paragraph, the assumptions are quite difficult to meet in one respect: the measures of the "same" variable at different times must be equivalent. On a narrow statistical basis this is dubious in this study. It is not unlikely that the two measures of viewing preference differ from one another in reliability, and perhaps in their approximations to a normal distribution. The third-grade measures are based on "three favorite programs," for instance, whereas "four favorite programs" provide the basis for the thirteenth-grade index; more items generally improve reliability, as was found in a similar situation in another study ( 4 ). For peer-rated aggressiveness, differential reliabilities are even more likely, since many more peers could nominate a given youngster in the thirteenth-grade measure than in the third-grade version. In the third grade, one's peers were limited to those in his classroom; in the thirteenth-grade measure, all other respondents in the entire sample could conceivably nominate a given boy as aggressive. An increase in the number of "expert" judges could increase reliability of the measure appreciably, which would account for its relating more strongly to a third variable (i.e., third-grade viewing) than did the third-grade aggressiveness measure. (In the absence of any reliability coefficients, one can only guess at this, of course.) It is also unlikely that the distribution of aggressive behavior at age eight is particularly similar to the distribution for the same boys ten years later. However, Kenny (1971) has concluded, on the basis of an ingenious test involving correlations with a third variable (IQ), that the third-grade aggressiveness measure is probably not less reliable than the thirteenth-grade measure. Pending more direct evidence, then, the issue appears unresolved.

Equivalence of these measures in terms of substantive meaning and validity is an even less tenable assumption, setting aside statistical niceties of reliability and distribution. The measures simply are not the same, even on their face. Parent-report program preferences cannot be assumed equivalent to self-reported preferences, and the two measures are uncorrelated longitudinally. Peer nominations of likely social aggression "now" (the third-grade measure) cannot be assumed equivalent to similar statements about some time in the past (the thirteenth-grade measure). Most importantly, perhaps, the social background and context of both variables are surely different in the two time periods. To begin with, television programs circa 1960 quite probably contained more violence than ten years later (Clark and Blankenburg, 1971). Eight-year-olds do not watch the same set of programs, nor even the same time slots, as they will in late adolescence. Television is a relatively new experience, of a few years' duration typically, in the life of a third-grader; it is a familiar artifact of daily living, and one that he is growing away from, for the usual "thirteenth" grader. The developmental differences regarding television demonstrated by Schramm et al. (1961), and replicated and amplified by Lyle and Hoffman (1971), suggest strongly that even seemingly identical questions will not have the same meaning to youngsters at ten-year intervals in their growth.

But it is the aggressiveness measures that are more critical, since the thirteenth-grade viewing preferences can be ignored in some modes of longitudinal analysis. Developmental change in the personal and social meaning of aggressive behavior must be massive, and constitutes the most serious single threat to the assumption of equivalent measurement. This point can perhaps be amply demonstrated by considering the different meanings, to children and to late adolescents, of some of the items that were used: saying "mean things," making "unfriendly gestures," pushing or shoving students, taking other students' things without asking, "always getting into trouble," starting fights "over nothing." The fact that the social meaning of these items in adolescence may be quite different from their meaning in childhood does not necessarily render the measures noncomparable. The third-and thirteenth-grade aggressiveness indices do, after all, correlate .38, so they surely have something in common. (One cannot say the same for the corresponding viewing measures.)

These developmental and metrical problems can scarcely be blamed on the researchers. Their attempts to gather equivalent measures over time could not be substantially improved upon. The "fault" instead seems to be inherent in longitudinal research that cuts across radically different phases in child development. At about the time that the third-grade data were being gathered, Schramm et al. (1961: pp.186-88) concluded their major volume on television and children with the suggestion that a ten-year longitudinal study much like the present one was "of first importance, if we are to push steadily ahead in understanding the uses children make of television." Now that a skilled research team has persevered long enough to complete such a study, it can be seen that this research model held out a false promise. The tools for causal inference from nonexperimental data require assumptions that will be met for few, if any, of the variables that interest us in developmental research. (Schramm et al. also suggested that many more variables should be included in the ten-year study, but that would not have alleviated the basic problem that is faced here.) A longitudinal study extending over two or three years within a homogeneous life-cycle period (either childhood or adolescence, but not from one to the other) would seem highly desirable. While not quite as ambitious in its total scope as the present study ( 3 ), it would provide a somewhat less ambiguous test of the causal hypothesis.

When all that is said, however, and the formal time-lagged tests are abandoned (which seems appropriate), an undeniable fact remains: one of the strongest correlation coefficients in all of the present studies is the +.31 between this third-grade parent-report viewing preference measure and retrospective peer-rated aggressiveness ten years later. The first index is, as indicated above, at least questionable; the latter is one of the very few aggressiveness measures that fails to correlate with an adolescent viewing measure in the present studies. With such fragile measures and yet such a healthy correlation, one must suspect that "something" has been going on in this panel of young men. Although a simple causal viewing:aggressiveness function cannot reasonably be considered proven, neither can it be easily rejected. Of the various possible explanations for the finding, it has parsimony on its side, and it is probably the most commonly held "folk hypothesis" about television violence. At this stage in research on television violence, the present longitudinal finding (in the context of a wide variety of supportive experimental and field studies) appears to stand as the strongest evidence on behalf of the main causal hypothesis.

Any challenge to that hypothesis must come from an alternative explanation that is at least equally consistent with the data. One possibility would be "simultaneous" causation by a third variable, whose effect on television preferences occurs in childhood but which does not manifest itself in social aggressiveness until well into adolescence. One such variable might be a hypothetical personality trait we could call "attraction to

adult forms of aggression." An eight-year-old boy cannot very effectively aggress in adult fashion, but if that sort of behavior fascinates him he
may well enjoy watching it on television. Some years later, as he ma-
tures physically and acquires various social and combative skills, he
should find more situations in which to act out his "predisposition" to
adult forms of aggression. Meanwhile, television is a progressively less
likely locus for the manifestation of this trait; he spends less time watching it, there are fewer violent scenes, and he has become more or less
habituated to the stock cliches of television aggression. Hence we could
expect a time-lagged correlation but little or no synchronous correlation
in adolescence.

All of that is wholly speculative, and a competent developmental psychologist could surely improve on it as an alternative explanation. It is
sketched out briefly here, simply to demonstrate that plausible explanations other than the direct causal hypothesis can account for the data
that have been reported. Future research could profitably explore this
area of the different sociopsychological meanings of both television and
aggressive behavior at different stages in childhood and adolescence.

To the time-honored call for "more research" it seems prudent to add
the proviso that future studies should be designed to eliminate alternative explanations that challenge the hypothesis that viewing violence
induces aggression. The present studies are of some further help in this
regard.

When two variables are statistically associated, either could be "causing" the other, without reference to third variables. As suggested earlier, any influence of aggressiveness as a "cause" of viewing should be
indicated most clearly in an adolescent's preferences for violent programs. The evidence from these studies is that any such link is limited to
white males, the particular demographic type that is most likely to be
seen behaving aggressively on television. When, on the other hand, we
examine correlations between aggressiveness and actual viewing of violence, there is no sex difference. The positive findings here are, then,
consistent in a rough fashion with those of experimental studies where
exposure to media violence has been manipulated. But that inference is
based on a "face-validity" distinction between the two media violence
measures, preference and exposure. It would be much preferable to
examine each of these with the other held constant, before more than
tentative conclusions are drawn.

If one were limited to a choice between the two possible two-variable
causal hypotheses, there is decidedly more support here for the viewing-
induces-aggressiveness interpretation than for the reverse. The data
supporting that conclusion have survived a number of statistical controls for likely "third variables," but of course there is a potentially infinite list of such additional factors that might account for the correlations
that have been found.

# Potential approaches to social control

The authors of these papers have tended to concern themselves primarily with detailed presentation of original data, and secondarily with testing the hypothesis that exposure to television violence increases the likelihood of aggressive social behavior among adolescents. They have generally not addressed the question of what might be done about this hypothetical influence, if indeed it does exist. As indicated in the previous section, we have in these studies considerably stronger evidence for the hypothesis than had been the case before. So without declaring flatly that the hypothesis of aggressive effects of television violence is "true" in a scientific sense, we might well assume it to be true as a tentative proposition and direct some attention to potential forms of social control over this relationship.

In one of these studies, families were divided according to the degree to which the parents emphasized nonaggressive behavior by their youngsters. This parental constraint on aggression, without direct reference to television, appears to reduce the viewing-aggressiveness correlations consistently for eight subsamples of varying grades, sexes, and locales (5a).

In subsequent analyses reported elsewhere (Chaffee and McLeod, 1971) these authors found more mixed results from parental controls directed at television itself. Limitations by the parent on the programs the child could view also diminish the viewing-aggressiveness correlation, but rather few parents appear to control adolescent viewing in this fashion. Parental discussion of television violence, as an attempt to "interpret" its meaning in relation to real life, does not appear to affect the adolescent viewing-aggressiveness relationship at all; this latter type of parental behavior is probably rare. It is possible that either control might be effective if attempted more often.

There also appears to be some danger that attempts to control adolescent aggression by minimizing violence viewing might "boomerang." That inference could be drawn from the widely discussed field experiment by Feshbach and Singer (1971). They manipulated the viewing of groups of junior high boys into "high violence" and "low violence" television conditions. Earlier here it was noted that violent programs are among those most-watched by junior high boys, and another study found a positive correlation between aggressiveness (self-reported) and parental control over the youngster's viewing ( 5b ). So we might expect the counternormative "low violence viewing" condition to be associated with more negative affective reactions to the programs and with more aggression rather than less; one might posit a frustration-aggression hypothesis in making such a prediction. The "low violence" manipulation did produce both significantly more disliking of programs viewed (Feshbach and Singer, 1971) and more reported aggressive behavior.

The authors adopt a "catharsis" explanation, assuming that the "high violence" manipulation provided more covert outlets for aggressive impulses than the "low violence" manipulation. In the absence of any direct indicators of the hypothetical construct of "catharsis," this interpretation remains conceivable but operationally moot. The catharsis hypothesis is inconsistent with the great bulk of evidence from the present studies, which instead suggest that the usual outcome of exposure to television violence is more aggressive behavior, not less.

In all, the question of effective social controls that might modify socially undesirable aggression that could result from television violence remains practically untouched by research. It seems, then, an obvious direction for future study.

## SUMMARY

What, in the light of these new studies, can be said of the scientific standing of the proposition that viewing of violent television programs induces tendencies toward aggressive behavior in adolescents? In several ways, that rather hazy hypothesis has been enhanced, in comparison with competing theories about the relationship between these variables.

A significant positive correlation has been found much more often than not, and there is no negative correlational evidence. That correlation stands up consistently in varying samples of different sexes, age levels, and locales, and with a variety of measures of aggressiveness. It persists in the face of attempts to partial out many other variables that might have explained it away. And its most obvious theoretical rival, the reverse causal hypothesis, has not fared nearly so well here. Measures of viewing preference, as opposed to actual viewing, relate to aggressiveness only for white males, and generally quite weakly. Longitudinal data on this point are null, whereas longitudinal data on the viewing-induces-aggressiveness hypothesis are about as strong as any of the synchronous correlational findings in any of these studies.

All of this is unsurprising, perhaps, since one can hardly expect that media experiences would have absolutely *no* influence on the social behavior of *any* developing child. A minor effect on rather few youngsters can produce positive correlations, and none of the present studies suggests that viewing television violence could account for more than about ten percent of the total variance in the measures of adolescent aggressiveness. Whether more precise and reliable measurement would increase that figure appreciably remains a question for future research.

Meanwhile, the present studies have also demonstrated that adolescent aggressiveness is associated with a number of other factors that have nothing to do with television. Their "effects" tend to remain when violence viewing is controlled statistically, and several of them are more strongly correlated with aggressiveness. These studies rather conclusively eliminate the hypothesis that television violence is the sole, or principal, cause of aggressive behavior by adolescents. In all, it appears to make a relatively minor contribution. And the findings here cannot conclusively eliminate the possibility that this apparent contribution is an artifact of other causal processes that have yet to be discovered.

# REFERENCES

Bohrnstedt, G.W. Observations on the measurement of change. In Borgatta, E.F. (Ed.) *Sociological methodology 1969*. San Francisco: Jossey-Bass, 1969.

Buss, A.H. Aggression and hostility inventories. In *The psychology of aggression*. New York: John Wiley, 1961.

Buss, A.H., and Durkee, A. An inventory for assessing different kinds of hostility. *Journal of Consulting Psychology*, 1957, **21**, 343-49.

Chaffee, S.H., and McLeod, J.M. Adolescent television use in the family context. In *Television and social behavior*, Vol. 3 (this volume). Referred to in this paper as ( *1* ).

Chaffee, S.H., and McLeod, J.M. Adolescents, parents, and television violence. Paper presented at annual meeting of the American Psychological Association, Washington, D.C., September 1971.

Chaffee, S.H., McLeod, J.M., and Atkin, C.K. Parental influences on adolescent media use. *American Behavioral Scientist*, 1971, **14**, 323-40.

Chaffee, S.H., Ward, L.S., and Tipton, L.P. Mass communication and political socialization. *Journalism Quarterly*, 1970, **47**, 647-59.

Clark, D.G., and Blankenburg,W.B. Trends in violent content in selected mass media. In *Television and social behavior*, Vol. 1 (this series). Washington, D.C.: U.S. Government Printing Office, 1971.

Dominick, J.R., and Greenberg, B.S. Attitudes toward violence: the interaction of television exposure, family attitudes, and social class. In *Television and social behavior*, Vol. 3 (this volume). Referred to in this paper as ( *6* ).

English, H.B., and English, A.C. *A comprehensive dictionary of psychological and psychoanalytical terms*. New York: David McKay, 1958.

Feshbach, S., and Singer, R.D. *Television and aggression*. San Francisco: Jossey-Bass, 1971.

Friedman, H.L., and Johnson, R.L. Mass media use and aggression: a pilot study. In *Television and social behavior*, Vol. 3 (this volume). Referred to in this paper as ( *2* ).

Greenberg, B.S., and Gordon, T.F. Perceptions of violence in television programs: critics and the public. In *Television and social behavior*, Vol. 1 (this series). Washington, D.C.: U.S. Government Printing Office, 1971.

Johnson, R.L., Friedman, H.L., and Gross, H.S. Four masculine styles in television programming. In *Television and social behavior*, Vol. 3 (this volume). Referred to in this paper as ( *8* ).

Klapper, J.T. The social effect of mass communication. In Schramm, W. (Ed.) *The science of human communication*. New York: Basic Books, 1963.

Lefkowitz, M.M., Eron, L.D., Walder, L.C., and Huesmann, L.R. Television violence and child aggression: a followup study. In *Television and social behavior*, Vol. 3 (this volume). Referred to in this paper as ( *3* ).

LoSciuto, L.A. A national inventory of television viewing behavior. In *Television and social behavior*, Vol. 4 (this series). Washington, D.C.: U.S. Government Printing Office, 1971.

Lyle, J., and Hoffman, H.R. Children's use of television and other media. In *Television and social behavior*, Vol. 4 (this series). Washington, D.C.: U.S. Government Printing Office, 1971.

McIntyre, J.J., and Teevan, J.J. Television and deviant behavior. In *Television and social behavior*, Vol. 3 (this volume). Referred to in this paper as ( *4* ).

McLeod, J.M., Atkin, C.K., and Chaffee, S.H. Adolescents, parents, and television use: adolescent self-report measures from Maryland and Wisconsin samples. In *Television and social behavior*, Vol. 3 (this volume). Referred to in this paper as (*5a*).

McLeod, J.M., Atkin, C.K., and Chaffee, S.H. Adolescents, parents, and television use: self-report and other-report measures from the Wisconsin sample. In *Television and social behavior*, Vol. 3 (this volume). Referred to in this paper as (*5b*).

Murray, R.L., Cole, R.R., and Fedler, F. Teenagers and TV violence: how they rate and view it. *Journalism Quarterly*, 1970, **47**, 247-55.

Robinson, J.P., and Bachman, J.G. Television viewing habits and aggression. In *Television and social behavior*, Vol. 3 (this volume). Referred to in this paper as ( *7* ).

Rozelle, R.M., and Campbell, D.T. More plausible hypotheses in the cross-lagged panel correlation technique. *Psychological Bulletin*, 1969, **71**, 74-80.

Schramm, W., Lyle, J., and Parker, E.B. *Television in the lives of our children*. Stanford, Calif.: Stanford University Press, 1961.

Walters, R., and Zaks, M. Validation studies on an aggression scale. *Journal of Psychology*, 1959, **47**, 209-18.

Zaks, M., and Walters, R. First steps in the construction of a scale for the measurement of aggression. *Journal of Psychology*, 1959, **47**, 199-208.

# Television Violence and Child Aggression: A Followup Study

Monroe M. Lefkowitz, Leonard D. Eron, Leopold O.
Walder, and L. Rowell Huesmann

*New York State Department of Mental Hygiene*
*Albany, New York*

The current project[1] is a continuation of a project begun in 1955, entitled *Psychosocial Development of Aggressive Behavior.* The 1955 project was initiated by the research unit of the Rip Van Winkle Foundation in Columbia County, New York, and supported in part by USPHS Grant No. M1726. Because of the public health orientation of the host institution, the research had originally been conceived as epidemiological and preventive in nature. The charge to the research unit at that time was to study the prevalance of mental illness in a rural area, Columbia County in New York state. Applying epidemiological techniques to the area of mental health presented two related problems. One problem was arriving at an adequate or appropriate definition of mental health; the other

35

was obtaining a representative sample of the population in which to measure this condition. A first step in resolving the definition problem was selecting for study one behavior which most investigators would accept as an aspect of mental health. This behavior had to be amenable to reliable observation and objective measurement. Aggression was considered to be such a variable. (In the current study the idea that aggression is a facet of psychopathology is also examined.)

The original definition of aggression was that developed by Dollard, Doob, Miller, Mowrer, and Sears (1939): "an act whose goal response is injury to another object." As the research progressed, however, a more limited definition developed: "an act which injures or irritates another person." This definition is concerned specifically with extrapunitive aggression directed toward another person (Walder, Abelson, Eron, Banta, and Laulicht, 1961).

The sampling problem was resolved by the decision to study a 100 percent sample of a specific population. All the children in the third grade in Columbia County were selected for the study. The modal age of these children was eight years. It was felt that this was the earliest age at which children would cooperate with the group paper-and-pencil procedures used in a large-scale survey study. Moreover, stable patterns of behavior amenable to reliable observation have probably been established by this age (Goodenough and Tyler, 1959).

The basic research plan was to obtain data about each child from four independent sources: his classmates, his mother, his father, and himself. One purpose of studying this population was to determine the extent of aggressive behavior at school and at home and attempt to account for the variation in aggression by familial, social, geographic, economic, and cultural factors. A second goal was to gain an understanding of the learning conditions for aggression. The experimenters tried to relate the ways in which children act out their aggression to the kinds of training in its expression and control they receive from such socializing agents as parents and peers. A third aim was to study the consistency of aggressive behavior across time as a function of new learning situations by studying the same subjects in the eighth and twelfth grades. This aim is related to a body of theory which holds that behavior is characterized by stability (Goodenough and Tyler, 1959; Cattell, 1965), and that from such stable behavior the construct of personality is deduced.

The major dependent variable, then, was aggression as observed in the school situation; the major class of independent variables was defined by parents' socialization practices. These variables included contingent responses to the expression of aggressive behavior, instigation of aggression, the child's identification with his parents, and sociocultural factors (the family's socioeconomic status, their educational and occupational aspiration for the child, and the child's IQ).

The measure of aggression in the classroom was obtained by a peer rating instrument in which each child could be nominated by every other child in his class for ten "guess who" items describing aggressive behavior. These items were interspersed among a series of other peer nomination questions. Since these items with only slight modification constitute the major dependent variable in the five- and ten-year followup studies,[2] the three versions are presented in Table 1.

Table 1: Comparison of peer rating items for three time periods

| 3rd grade | 5-year follow up 8th grade | 10-year followup 13th grade |
|---|---|---|
| 1. Who does not obey the teacher? | Who does not obey the teacher? | Who did not listen to the teacher? |
| 2. Who often says, "Give me that!"? | OMITTED | OMITTED |
| 3. Who gives dirty looks or sticks out their tongue at other children? | Who gives dirty looks or unfriendly gestures to other students? | Who gave dirty looks or made unfriendly gestures to other students? |
| 4. Who makes up stories and lies to get other children into trouble? | Who makes up stories and lies to get other students into trouble? | Who made up stories and lies to get other students into trouble? |
| 5. Who does things that bother others? | Who does things that bother others? | Who did things that bothered others? |
| 6. Who starts a fight over nothing? | Who starts a fight over nothing? | Who started fights over nothing? |
| 7. Who pushes or shoves children? | Who pushes or shoves students? | Who pushed or shoved students? |
| 8. Who is always getting into trouble? | Who is always getting into trouble? | Who was always getting into trouble? |
| 9. Who says mean things? | Who says mean things? | Who used to say mean things? |
| 10. Who takes other children's things without asking? | Who takes other students' things without asking? | Who took other students' things without asking? |

The development of this peer rating technique, pilot studies concerning it, and data pertaining to reliability and validity are presented in Walder et al. (1961) and Eron, Walder, and Lefkowitz (1971).

Each child's aggression score was based on the number of judges choosing him as fitting a particular behavioral description. Thus, if ten of the 27 members of a class crossed out Johnny Jones's name as someone who said mean things, Johnny's raw score was ten for that item. If he was selected a total of 45 times for the nine other items, his total raw score on the complete set of aggression items would be 55; his mean raw score on the ten aggression items would be 5.5. These mean raw scores were converted into percentages (of the total number who were present and made nominations) in order to make scores of subjects who were in different sized classrooms more comparable. In addition to the aggression measure, other peer ratings were obtained from items designed to measure aggression anxiety, success in aggression, popularity, and activity level. Such measures as IQ, masculine-feminine identification, occupational aspirations, human figure drawings, and self-description of expressive behavior were also obtained from the children. These measures are described in greater detail in Eron, Walder, and Lefkowitz (1971).[3]

Measures of the independent variables were primarily obtained from an objective, precoded child rearing interview administered face-to-face with mothers and fathers independently. The interview contained 286 items comprising 41 variables, which were categorized largely into four types: reinforcers of aggression, instigators to aggression, identification of child with family, and sociocultural variables. A copy of the interview and a history of its development and psychometric properties are presented in Eron et al., 1971.

A number of individual questions were included in the interview because of popular notions about the antecedents of aggressive behavior. These questions concerned frequency of television watching in the home, types of programs watched, the child's reading of comic books, parents' PTA membership, and parents' familiarity with Dr. Spock and other child care publications. Because of their content, these questions also tended to serve as buffer items; the insouciance with which they were treated or viewed by the investigators at that time is shown by their grouping under the initials LHJ (for Ladies Home Journal).

In 1959-60 all the children in 38 third-grade classrooms in all public and parochial schools in Columbia County were tested in their classrooms. This population was 900 children, of whom 875 were third graders. During this period 713 of their mothers and 570 of their fathers were interviewed separately; data on 557 mother-father pairs were thereby obtained.[3]

Because of the increasing interest in the effect of television viewing on children's behavior, the investigators analyzed the relation between the violence ratings of the child's favorite television programs (as reported by parents) and the child's peer ratings of aggression in the classroom (Eron, 1963). Ratings of the violence contained in these programs were made independently by two raters, and each child's putative television diet was assigned a violence rating. This rating, as well as the number of hours the child was said to watch television, was compared in an analysis of variance design with his peer rating aggression score. A significant positive relationship was found among boys between television violence and peer ratings of aggression. In addition, but again only for boys, a significant inverse relationship was found between the number of hours subjects watched television and peer ratings of aggression.

Funding for the project was terminated in 1962 and the research team was dispersed. However, an attempt was made by the present researchers to carry out the second step in the longitudinal design. Five years later, in 1964-65, when the modal age of the subjects was 13 years and their modal grade was eight, the schools in Columbia County were approached and asked for their continuing cooperation. Because of adverse newspaper publicity and opposition to the program by some dissident groups during the third-grade study (Eron and Walder, 1961), several of the schools did not wish to participate. However, 382 children were tested in eighth-grade classrooms. Of this group, 252 were in the original third-grade population.

Slight modifications of the peer rating items were necessary to insure face validity for 13-year-old subjects (see Table 1). The nominating procedure was altered slightly, and the peer rating measure and other tests were administered in the classroom by teachers, school psychologists, and other school personnel. The subjects themselves, rather than their parents, were asked to report their favorite television programs and the amount of time they watched television. The measures used in Columbia County at this stage of the study had previously been modified and tested in pilot studies of eighth graders in the Duke Street School in Alexandria, Virginia.

The attenuation of the number of subjects tested in the eighth grade in Columbia County reflected the limited effort the research team was able to muster rather than attrition from the third to the eighth grades. Unable to obtain support for this phase of the study, the team confined itself to those schools most readily accessible and to a circumscribed number of subjects.

Lists of television programs were assembled and rated for violence by three Columbia County school personnel. Each rated the television programs independently, and each received $10 for this service.

A violence score could range from a low of 0 to a high of 5. Each child's television violence score was the average rating of the shows he named. For example, if the child named three programs with violence scores of 2, 3, and 3 respectively, his total violence score would be 2.67. If he named only two programs with ratings of 2 and 4, his average score would be 3. Separate ratings of these same programs were made by two NBC television censors.[4]

The relation between television violence and aggressive behavior among the eighth grade subjects in Alexandria, Virginia, was also analyzed. These subjects differed from the Columbia County population in that they lived in an urban area. Again, the ratings of television violence and aggressive behavior remained methodologically independent. A statistically significant relation in the same direction (r = .31, p <.01) as that found for the third graders in Columbia County was found for the 73 eighth-grade male and female subjects in Alexandria, Virginia: the greater the amount of television violence viewed, the higher the peer ratings of aggression.

The peer rating procedure was also administered to large groups of third graders in Cedar Rapids, Iowa, and scores were meaningfully related to available school data (Semler and Eron, 1967; Semler, Eron, Meyerson, and Williams, 1967) and to overt behavior in a controlled laboratory situation (Williams, Meyerson, Eron, and Semler, 1967).

In 1968 the third-grade study was replicated on a smaller scale in Amsterdam under the direction of Dr. Eron. The peer rating procedure and the parent interview were translated into Dutch. The classroom procedures were administered in six classrooms of eight-year-old children located in divergent socioeconomic areas of Amsterdam. An attempt was made to interview all the mothers and fathers of these children, but the effort met with considerably less success than it had in Columbia County. However, scorable interviews were obtained from 72 mothers; these data were analyzed in relation to the peer rating scores and other classroom measures of their children. The results were surprisingly similar to the Columbia County findings (Stroo, 1970). These cross-national data are presented in Eron et al. (1971). Because of limited access to television and rigorous control of programming by the Dutch government, data on television behavior were not collected in the Amsterdam study.

The present research is directly related to the foregoing third-grade and eighth-grade studies and to the cross-national study. The current project has three specific aims: (1) to complete (within the financial limitations of NIMH support) the longitudinal study of the psychosocial development of aggressive behavior for which data were collected in Columbia County in 1960 and 1965; (2) to investigate the longitudinal relationships between violence content in television and aggressive behavior on the part of viewers; and (3) to examine the consequences of childhood aggression during late adolescence and young adulthood. A relationship between violent content and viewer aggression could be determined if the present subjects selected the same level of violence in their television preferences that they had selected in the eighth grade and if these television preferences were still related to aggression. The third aim deals with the ramifications of aggressiveness (as assessed in childhood) on critical spheres of functioning during late adolescence. Specific questions about educational and occupational achievement and aspiration, psychopathology, prosocial and antisocial behavior in the community, and military status are scrutinized. A corollary of this objective was determining the relation between variables obtained in the third grade and aggressiveness as measured in the ten-year followup. Moreover, the relation between the early measures of aggression and later measures of psychopathology is important in determining if aggression was indeed well chosen as a component of mental health.

## Hypotheses

Three hypotheses were derived from the foregoing rationale:
1. When examined longitudinally, positive relationships obtain between violent television preferences and aggressive behavior.
2. Early aggressive behavior is positively related to later aggressive behavior.
3. Aggressive behavior is positively related to psychopathology.

To test these hypotheses, the investigators adduced data concerning the manner and extent to which viewing of violent television programs is related to aggressive behavior. The relation between violent television preferences and a host of other variables is also open to inspection through the test of the foregoing hypotheses.

## METHOD

The present research employed survey techniques. The overall goal was to obtain data from as many as possible—but at least half—of the original 875 third-grade subjects. Each subject was to give two hours of his time, the first hour in an individual face-to-face interview and the second taking written psychological tests. Two incentives were offered to encourage the subjects to participate. The importance of the research was explained to the subjects in a letter, and they were offered $20 for their time.

## Subjects

In order to estimate the number of subjects available for the ten-year followup study, a preliminary survey of the Columbia County high school graduates of June 1969 was undertaken. Information was obtained from New York State Department of Education records and from various newspaper files in Columbia County. It was determined that approximately 52 percent of the original subject pool was still in Columbia County as of June 1969. The investigators assumed that this was a conservative estimate of the number of subjects potentially available, since this tally did not account for those subjects who dropped out of school or who had not yet been graduated.

Letters were written to the seven district superintendents of the county's public and parochial schools (see Appendix A). They were reminded of the investigators' past efforts and of their own cooperation with those efforts. The superintendents were asked to supply addresses for these former third grade children and other information from their school records. Most of these officials were very cooperative and asked their principals and guidance counselors to furnish the requested information. Perhaps because of problems encountered with certain parents and community groups during the third grade survey in the Chatham and Hudson areas (Eron and Walder, 1961) and because of adverse publicity there in 1965, the district superintendents in these two localities thought it necessary to present our request to their school boards. In both cases, the school boards were concerned about the possible controversy which might again arise from the study and refused to cooperate in providing address lists or information from school records. Despite these refusals, more than 400 addresses for third-grade subjects were furnished by officials of the other school districts. A major effort was exerted to locate as many of the remaining subjects as possible, especially those in the non-cooperating school districts.

It was reasoned that sampling bias would be minimized by inviting for interview as many of the original subjects as could be traced. An intensive search was made for those subjects for whom the schools refused to give current addresses and for those subjects for whom cooperating schools could provide no addresses. We examined high school yearbooks, old and current telephone directories, voter lists, tax lists, and a county directory. In addition, each of the interviewees who did appear was questioned about the whereabouts of any of the missing subjects.

This effort, in conjunction with the addresses furnished by the schools, resulted in letters sent to 735 of the 875 subjects, or 84 percent of the original sample. If a subject did not respond within three to four weeks and the letter was not returned by the Post Office for insufficient address, a followup letter was sent. (Copies of these letters are presented in Appendix A.) Consequently, 236 second letters were sent, totaling 971 first and second letters. Of the 735 subjects to whom letters were sent (see Appendix A), 460 indicated willingness to be interviewed; the remaining 275 subjects were categorized as shown in Table 2.

Table 2:  Classification of 735 subjects to whom letters were sent

|                     | N   | %    |
|---------------------|-----|------|
| Acceptances         | 460 | 63   |
| Post office returns  | 45  | 6    |
| Definite refusals    | 81  | 11   |
| In military service  | 38  | 5    |
| Deceased            | 4   | .5   |
| In prison           | 2   | .2   |
| No replies          | 105 | 14   |
| TOTAL               | 735 | 99.7 |

Of the 460 subjects who responded positively to the interview request, 436 were interviewed. (The remaining 24 subjects either lived at too great a distance, did not appear after several appointments, or requested an appointment after the field operation was terminated.) Of the

436 subjects interviewed, 427 contributed data which could be compared across the ten-year span. The sample was composed of 211 boys and 216 girls. The modal age of this group was 19 years. The mean number of years of school completed was $12.57 \pm .82$. Based on 103 cases for whom current test scores were available, the mean IQ was $109.12 \pm 11.57$. Using father's occupation as reported by subject to determine socioeconomic status (Warner, Meeker and Eells, 1960), the sample may be described as predominantly middle class.

Sampling bias was evinced in the ten-year followup when an analysis of the number of subjects in the upper and lower quartiles of aggression in the third grade was performed. Of the 130 boys in the lower quartile of aggression at age eight, 74 (or 57 percent) consented to be interviewed in the ten year followup at age 19. However, of the 125 boys in the upper quartile of aggression at age eight, only 34 (or 27 percent) consented to be interviewed at age 19. Girls responded similarly: 63 percent of the low aggressive group consented to be interviewed in the ten-year followup, while only 33 percent of those in the upper quartile of aggression consented to be interviewed at age 19. That approximately twice as many high as compared to low aggressive subjects—of both sexes—were unavailable for interview stands as a datum by itself and is relevant to survey research. In part the effect of this sampling bias was controlled statistically where the data were analyzed by analysis of variance. In this technique, the independent variable was partitioned in a manner so that the upper and lower 10 percent and the middle 80 percent entered into the analysis. Thus both extremes were equally represented.

A field office was established in Hudson, N. Y., seat of Columbia County, from June 1 through September 30, 1970. The results of the preliminary survey had indicated that this time of year would be the most propitious for maximizing the number of subjects sampled. In addition to the authors of this report, additional temporary staff was employed.[5]

Shortly after the field office was established, staff training sessions were held. The confidentiality of the data being gathered and the necessity of maintaining locked files were stressed. The ethics of conducting research with human subjects was discussed. The trainees first familiarized themselves with the interview schedule, being themselves interviewed and interviewing one another. Finally they observed a senior staff member, who had participated in the third grade study, in a live interview session. The trainees were observed in a live interview session. Throughout, they received feedback on their performances from the staff members and from an interviewer manual which had been developed early in the data collection phase.

## Measures: peer ratings

The measure of aggressive behavior for these 19-year-old subjects included essentially the same items used in the eighth-grade study, which in turn had been slightly modified from the third-grade items (see Table 1). Tested in a brief pilot study in the Washington, D.C., area for wording, the measure was made final at the Hudson field office on the first few Columbia County subjects.

In addition to the nine aggression items, the questionnaire contained six items which yielded scores on aggression anxiety, popularity, activity level, and leadership. The fifteen items were administered to each subject individually with relevant instructions (see Appendix B).

"Ten years ago, when you were in the third grade, you answered a series of questions about yourself and about your classmates. I would like your cooperation in answering a similar series of questions.

"I have lists of people who might have gone to school with you. Put a check in the box next to the names of the people you know well enough to answer some questions about. Generally, these would be people who had been in class with you. You might remember the way they acted in school." (At this point the subject was given appropriate class lists to check [see below].) After the subject checked the names of those he knew he was given the following instructions:

"I shall ask you questions, one at a time. For each question, tell me the identification numbers of all those people who fit that question. Do not name yourself for any of these questions. You may name any number of people for each question. Notice that to these questions there are no answers that are right for everybody. Base your answers on what you last knew of each person from personal observation and contact.

"You may give any number of answers. You may check more names if you think of them as I ask the questions."

Since the subjects were no longer grouped together in classrooms as they had been in the third and eighth grades, the problem arose as to how nominations would be made and who was to make them. This problem was resolved by asking each subject for the schools he attended after the third grade. The subject was then presented with rosters of all the original third-grade subjects who might have attended the last Columbia County school the subject himself said he attended in addition to his own third-grade class. For example, if the subject said the last school he attended was Hudson High School, he was presented with rosters of the twelve grade school classes in Hudson and its environs which were the feeder elementary schools for Hudson High School. On these rosters were only those subjects who were in the original third-grade study. Thus, subjects in the larger schools might review several hundred names for each of the peer rating items. In the smaller schools, subjects might review as few as 60 names for each of the items.

As the interviewer read each peer rating item, the subject responded with the identification numbers of any of the individuals on the roster of subjects to which that item applied. The aggression score for any subject was then computed. For the nine aggression items the number of people giving a particular subject's name was counted. This sum was divided by nine (the number of items). This average was then divided by the number of people who said they knew the particular subject. For example, if a subject received 45 nominations for the nine items, 45 was divided by 9 to yield an average of five nominations per item. If ten people said they knew the subject, this quotient of 5 was divided by 10 to yield an aggression score of .50.

The same general technique for computing peer rating scores was used for aggression-anxiety, popularity, activity level, and leadership. Peer-rated aggression-anxiety and popularity are composite categories made up of two items each. Thus the numerator of each of these scores was the average number of nominations that the subject received on the two aggression-anxiety items (or the popularity items). The numerators of peer-rated activity level and leadership were each based on one item and therefore were simply the number of nominations that the subject received on each item.

In addition to these percentage scores for aggression-anxiety, popularity, activity level, and leadership, there were two other peer rating scores, which were simply the average number of nominations a subject received on the nine aggression items and the number of nominations he received in answers to the question, "Whom do you know well enough to rate?"

## The interview schedule

Interview items were derived from five sources: (1) The Rip Van Winkle Child Rearing Interview used with parents in the third-grade study (Eron et al., 1971); (2) an interview written by the staff of the Television and Social Behavior program of the National Institute of Mental Health;[6] (3) Project Talent (Flanagan, Davis, Dailey, Shaycoft, Orr, Goldberg, and Neyman, 1964); (4) Youth in Transition (Bachman, 1967); and (5) The Teen Age Interview (Lange, Baker, and Ball, 1969). In addition, interview questions were formulated by the research staff. Consisting of 180 items, the interview was almost entirely precoded and required about one hour for administration (see Appendix B).

A pilot study of the interview was conducted to determine the applicability, clarity of directions, and general meaningfulness for 19-year-old individuals. This study was done at the University of Illinois at Chicago Circle, and 15 introductory psychology students served as subjects. Final revisions were made on the basis of experience with the first few Columbia County subjects.

For the purpose of the present study, subsets of the 180 items were formed to build variables bearing on the hypotheses under study. Like the Rip Van Winkle Child Rearing Survey, the present interview was regarded as a test consisting of a number of subscales.

The following variables were derived from the interview schedule (see Appendix C for detailed derivations):

1. Respondents' aggression
   a. Respondent as object of aggression (VAG)
   b. Respondent as witness of aggression (WAG)
   c. Aggressive habit—A (AHA)
   d. Aggressive habit—B (AHB)
   e. Total aggressive habit (TAH)
   f. Antisocial behavior (ASB)
   g. Aggressive drive (AGD)
   h. Total aggressive environment (TAG)
   i. Personal opinion inventory (WAZ)
   j. Potential punishment for aggression (PUN-TOP)
2. Social status factors
   a. Social status of family (ISS)
      (1) Number of books (NOB)
      (2) Occupation of father (FOC)
      (3) Total number of rooms
      (4) Composite social status index (CIS)
   b. Respondent's occupational status (CSR)
      (1) Occupation (ROC)
      (2) Education (EDR)
   c. Mobility aspirations (ASP)
      (1) Total aspiration (TAS)
      (2) Mobility orientation (MOO)
   d. Church attendance (REL-RAT)
3. Psychopathology
   a. Minnesota Multiphasic Personality Inventory (MMPI)
   b. Z-Test
      (1) Hostility (Z-HOS-2)
      (2) Psychopathology (Z-SUM)
4. Television variables
   a. Hours of watching (TV-HW-A)
   b. TV violence—Hudson (TV-VIOL-H)
   c. TV violence—Greenberg (TV-VIOL-G)
   d. Sports programs (TV-SPT)
   e. Realism of TV (ROT)
5. Height
   a. Height of subject (SHT)
   b. Discrepancy between subject's height and average of mother's and father's height (DAH)
6. School records
   a. Achievement (ACH)
   b. IQ
   c. Times tardy (TARDY)

7. Number of arrests

Data for varying numbers of subjects were collected from six sources: (1) peer ratings (N = 427); (2) individual face-to-face interviews (N = 427); (3) height (N = 427); (4) psychological tests, objective and projective (N = 427); (5) IQ as measured in the twelfth grade and obtained from school records (N = 103), standardized achievement test scores obtained from twelfth grade school records (N = 120), tardiness obtained from twelfth grade school records (N = 49); (6) Number of arrests in New York State of boys in the upper and lower quartiles of aggression as measured in the third grade (N = 255).

## Data analyses

A basic data set comprised of 49 third-grade variables, five five-year followup variables, and 40 ten-year followup variables was stored on magnetic tape. A code manual listing the 94 variables is presented in Appendix E. The following types of analyses were performed for the above data set: descriptive statistics, histograms, correlations, partial correlations, multiple correlations, cross-lagged correlations, principal components factor analyses, regression analyses, analyses of variance, and contingency analyses. These analyses were applied where appropriate to the data and to the hypothesis in question. In the main, the data were analyzed for each sex group and for the total.

## RESULTS

## Television and aggression

Data bearing on the first hypothesis—that positive relations exist between preference for violent television programs and aggressive behavior—confirmed previous findings of a contemporaneous relation between the two variables (Eron, 1963). Table 3 presents these findings in a longitudinal context—the intercorrelations[7] among four variables: peer ratings of aggression at two stages (third grade (AGG3) and thirteenth grade (AGG13)[8], and violence ratings of preferred television programs at these same two stages (TVVL3 and TVVL13).

At the time of the third-grade study, each parent was asked what his child's three favorite television programs were. All programs mentioned were then categorized as violent or nonviolent by two independent raters who were familiar with television programs. There was 94 percent agreement in their ratings. Differences in the remaining six percent of the programs were resolved by discussion between the raters. Each subject received a score according to the number of violent programs he

Table 3: Correlations among violence ratings of preferred
TV programs and peer ratings of aggression
at two different periods

| | Boys | | | | Girls | | | |
|---|---|---|---|---|---|---|---|---|
| | TVVL3 | AGG3 | TVV13 | AGG13 | TVVL3 | AGG3 | TVV13 | AGG13 |
| TVVL3[b] | 1.00 | .21** | .05 | .31** | 1.00 | .02 | .08 | -.13 |
| AGG3 | | 1.00 | .01 | .38** | | 1.00 | -.08 | .47** |
| TVVL13 | | | 1.00 | -.05 | | | 1.00 | -.05 |
| AGG13[a] | | | | 1.00 | | | | 1.00 |
| M | 7.15 | 12.12 | 6.39 | 80.46 | 5.29 | 7.51 | 5.07 | 26.51 |
| S.D. | 5.05 | 12.73 | 6.09 | 96.98 | 4.72 | 9.87 | 4.71 | 37.68 |
| N | 184 | 211 | 211 | 211 | 175 | 216 | 216 | 216 |

[a]The AGG13 score, when being calculated, was multiplied by 10. Otherwise it was calculated in the same manner as was AGG3.

[b]The number 3, 8, or 13 following a variable indicates the period, 3rd, 8th, or 13th grades when the data were obtained.

**indicates significance of r at or beyond .01 level of confidence.

was reported to favor. Scores ranged from 1 (for no violent programs) to 4 (for three violent programs).

The same scoring procedure was used in the five-year followup study (eighth grade) except that the programs were rated for violence by two professional censors employed by NBC—with an equally high degree of agreement between them. These ratings were made approximately four years after the data were collected.[9]

In the ten-year followup study (thirteenth grade), each subject was himself asked to mention his four current favorite television programs. All programs were then categorized for presence or absence of violence by two independent raters of different sex and educational background who were only a few years older than the subjects themselves. Scores were assigned to each program on the basis of agreement between the raters. If they agreed a program was nonviolent, the program received a score of zero; if they agreed it was violent, the score was two; if they disagreed in categorization, the score was one. There was much agreement between the two raters. They agreed on 81 percent of 125 programs mentioned by the subjects. (The list of programs categorized according to violence rating is presented in Appendix D.)

Their designation of violent and nonviolent programs agreed very well with the assignment of programs by Feshbach and Singer (1971) to aggressive and nonaggressive diets in their field experiment. Furthermore, the judgments of these two raters were in close agreement with the results obtained by Greenberg and Gordon (1970). The latter research team did an intensive rating study, using as raters both established television critics (approximately 45) and 300 subjects randomly selected from the Detroit telephone book. Of the 20 programs which Greenberg and Gordon indicated had the highest violence ratings, 19 were selected as violent by our raters. For the 427 cases in the ten-year followup study, there was a correlation of .94 between the Greenberg-Gordon average ratings and our ratings. There can be little doubt that these programs were accurately rated for presence or absence of violence.

It is apparent, in Table 3, from the intercorrelations that a relation exists between the violence of the television programs preferred by boys when they are in the third grade and their aggressive behavior ten years later. The relation between third-grade television and later behavior is in fact stronger than that between third-grade television and aggressive behavior at that time. Furthermore, there is no relation between later television preference and earlier aggressive behavior. Such a finding supports the notion that preference for violent programs in the third grade is causally related to aggressive behavior ten years later.[10] This becomes clear when the pertinent correlations are viewed in a cross-lagged context as shown in Figure 1. The large and significant difference (Fisher's $Z$ = 3.07, $p$ = .002) between the cross-lagged correlations on the diagonals lends strong support to the hypothesis that watching violent television causes aggressive habits.[11] However, this hypothesis, which is diagrammed in Figure 2a, is not the only possible interpretation of the correlations, and several rival hypotheses deserve consideration.

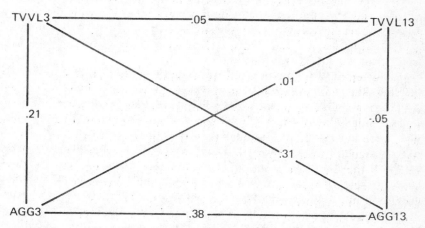

Figure 1:  The correlations between television violence and aggression for 211 boys over a ten-year lag

The first alternative is that television violence has only a synchronous effect on aggression at the third-grade level and that this effect, coupled with the temporal reliability of the aggression measure, explains the cross-lagged correlation from television violence to later aggression. The corresponding causal chain is diagrammed in Figure 2b. This interpretation can be rejected because, if it were true, the cross-lagged correlation would be less than the product of the synchronous correlation and

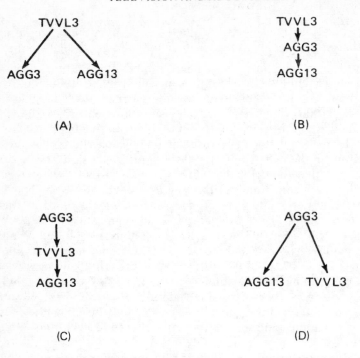

Figure 2: Four feasible causal hypotheses for the correlations presented in Figure 1

the reliability. For the same reason, the causal chain in Figure 2c can be eliminated as a contending hypothesis. However, one cannot reject so easily the hypothesis (diagrammed in Figure 2d) that early aggression causes both concomitant watching of violent television and later aggression. We can compare the partial correlation between AGG3 and AGG13 holding TVVL3 constant (r = .33) with the partial correlation between TVVL3 and AGG13 holding AGG3 constant (r = .21). Since both partials remain substantial, we can conclude that neither of these possibilities provides a complete causal explanation. The higher partial correlation between AGG3 and AGG13 is not surprising, since that correlation is partly a reliability measure. It is more interesting to compare the two relevant longitudinal correlations in Figure 1 (r = .38 and r = .31) with the synchronous correlation between AGG3 and TVVL3. Both relevant longitudinal correlations are larger than the synchronous correlation (r = .21). This is easily explainable for the correlation between AGG3 and AGG13 (r = .38) since (as indicated) that correlation contains a reliability component. However, it is difficult to explain why the cross-lagged correlation from TVVL3 to AGG13 should be greater than the synchronous correlation between TVVL3 and AGG3 except in terms of the causal model in Figure 2a. Hence, on the basis of the cross-lagged correlations, the most plausible single causal hypothesis would appear to be that watching violent television in the third grade leads to the building of aggressive habits.

Another point to be considered, as Rozelle and Campbell (1969) have indicated, is that a cross-lagged correlation may be viewed as a deviation from the initial synchronous correlation. Under this view the correlations in Figure 1 could be interpreted as indicating that early aggression causes a decrease in the watching of violent television because .01 is farther below the .21 synchronous correlation than .31 is above it. However, following the method of Rozelle and Campbell, the most appropriate baseline is not the early synchronous correlation, but the average of the two synchronous correlations attenuated for the reliability of the two variables. The higher the reliabilities, the less is the attenuation. With a conservative assumption of a very high temporal reliability of .70, the base line for Figure 1 would be $\{ [.21 + (-.05)] \sqrt{.7 \times .7} \} /2 = .06$. With this correction, the hypothesis that aggression causes diminished watching of violent television becomes untenable.

The relation between third-grade aggression of boys and eighth-grade television violence is not significantly different from zero (n = −.16); nor is the relation between eighth-grade television violence and eighth-grade aggression (r = −.10), although the relation between third- and eighth-grade aggression for boys is moderately positive (r = .48). For girls the relation between third- and eighth-grade aggression is also positive (r = .30), while the relations between aggression and television violence at the between the two age levels is not different from zero. It should be remembered, however, that in the pilot study done in Alexandria, Virginia, with eighth graders, the same findings were obtained as in the third grade in Columbia County.

As has been pointed out (Eron et al., 1971), the Pearson product moment correlations may very likely be masking more marked relations in these data due to the kurtosis of the distributions. That this is so can be seen in the table of means (Table 4) and the resultant analyses of variance. In Table 4 the independent variable is violence of preferred television programs in the third grade. There is a three-way partition of the sample of 184 boys into three groups—low, medium, and high television violence preferences. The breakdown into three parts was made by inspection of the frequency distribution at approximately the tenth and ninetieth percentiles. The relation of third-grade television habits to later behavior now appears even more impressive. Not only is violence of programs preferred in third grade related to peer-rated aggression in the third grade and ten years later, but it is also related positively to self-disclosure of antisocial behavior ten years later and to the sum of $T$ scores on scales 4 and 9 of the MMPI at that time. This pair of scales has been demonstrated to discriminate potential and actual delinquents from normal populations (Hathaway and Monachesi, 1963). Further data bearing on the sum of scales 4 and 9 are presented below.

Table 4: Mean aggression scores as a function of TV violence ratings
of programs preferred by boys in third grade

| | | AGG3 | | AGG13 | | ASB[a] | | MMPI-49S[b] | |
|---|---|---|---|---|---|---|---|---|---|
| TVVL3 | N | M | SD | M | SD | M | SD | M | SD |
| Lo | 31 | 9.06 | 9.91 | 51.39 | 50.54 | 25.58 | 12.12 | 121.97 | 20.50 |
| Med | 139 | 11.19 | 11.54 | 81.39 | 98.80 | 22.06 | 12.69 | 122.50 | 19.33 |
| Hi | 14 | 21.00 | 13.79 | 164.64 | 132.98 | 30.86 | 14.23 | 135.86 | 18.14 |
| Total | 184 | 11.58 | 11.75 | 82.67 | 98.58 | 23.33 | 12.90 | 123.424 | 19.67 |
| F | | 5.43 | | 6.82 | t=4.04[c] | 3.63 | | 3.105 | |
| P | | <.005 | | <.001 | <.01 | <.03 | | <.05 | |

[a] ASB = Self-rating of frequency of antisocial behavior
[b] MMPI-49S = Sum of T scores on scales 4 and 9 of MMPI
[c] Because of heterogeneity of variance a $t$ test, between the two most discrepant means for
AGG13, was performed. The $t$ was conservatively evaluated by using df equal to N for the
smallest group, i.e., 14. Means and variances are significantly different.

Although current television behavior, in terms both of violence score
of preferred programs and of total number of hours the subject watches
television per week, are not related to current aggressive behavior as
rated by peers, both aspects of television viewing are related to other
measures of current behavior, as seen in Table 5. Especially meaningful
are the relations between the number of hours the subject estimates he
watches television and his achievement test scores, educational attainment, social status as measured by father's occupation, and peer-rated
popularity and leadership. The more the subject watches television, the
lower are his measured abilities and his social and educational accomplishments. Realism of television (extent to which the subject states that
life as depicted on television westerns and crime stories is realistic) is

Table 5: Correlation between TV viewing habits at grade 13
and other contemporaneous variables

| Variable | Hours watched | | | | TV violence | | | |
|---|---|---|---|---|---|---|---|---|
| | N | Boys | N | Girls | N | Boys | N | Girls |
| Achievement 13 | 58 | −.39 | | | | | | |
| Judgment of TV realism 13 | 210 | .28 | 216 | .34 | 211 | .36 | 216 | .18 |
| Social status 13 | 208 | .24 | 210 | .22 | | | | |
| Subject's education 13 | 210 | −.26 | | | | | | |
| Subject's mobility aspirations 13 | | | | | 211 | .18 | | |
| Personal opinion inventory —Walters-Zak 13 | 210 | .19 | | | | | | |
| POP 13 | 210 | −.26 | | | | | | |
| Leadership 13 | 210 | −.19 | 216 | −.19 | | | | |
| TVVL 13 | 210 | .20 | 216 | .25 | | | | |
| TV-SPT 13 | 210 | .24 | | | | | | |

related moderately positively both to number of hours television is watched currently and to the violence score of preferred programs.

It is also interesting that the number of hours the subject watches television at this later period is negatively related to measures taken ten years earlier. These measures, presented in Table 6, included IQ at grade three, popularity, father's educational aspirations for the child at that time, mother's educational aspirations for the child, and father's and mother's achieved education.[12] There is no relation between number of hours the subject watched television in grade three as reported by mother and the number of hours he watches at grade thirteen as reported

Table 6:  Correlations[a] between amount of TV viewing at grade 13 and measures taken at grade 3 for boys

| Measure | Correlation | N |
| --- | --- | --- |
| IQ3 | −.33 | 204 |
| Father's educational aspiration for child 3 | −.21 | 143 |
| Mother's educational aspiration for child 3 | −.41 | 185 |
| Popularity 3 | −.22 | 210 |
| Father's education 3 | −.25 | 143 |
| Mother's education 3 | −.27 | 185 |

[a]Only those correlations significant at or beyond .01 level of confidence are presented.

by himself. As shown in Figure 3, the child's peer-rated popularity at grade three has the same order of relation to hours of television watched ten years later as does the later rating of popularity. Popularity at grade three is related to popularity ten years later (r = .38). Although IQ at grade three is not related to the number of hours television was watched

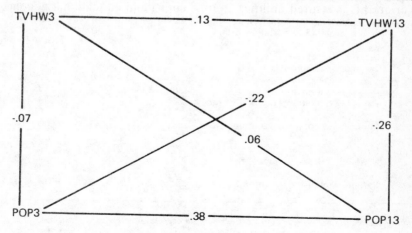

Figure 3:  The correlations between television hours and popularity for 211 boys over a ten-year lag

at that time, it is inversely related to number of hours television is currently watched. However, the relation between twelfth-grade IQ and number of hours television is watched in the thirteenth grade, although in a negative direction, does not reach significance at our accepted level ($r = -.20$, $N = 53$). This occurs despite the fact that the two IQ measures are moderately positively related ($r = .51$). Since different measures of IQ were used and the number of subjects in the later period included only a subsample of the original number of subjects it is surprising that the latter relation is as high as it is. The relation of judged realism of television to current IQ is negligible, although it is related to third-grade IQ ($r = -.21$). Again it should be pointed out that IQ measures at the later period were available for only a small subsample of subjects; the true relation between the two variables was probably not permitted to emerge.

These correlations apply only to boys. As previously indicated, aggression in girls does not enter into as many antecedent-consequent relations as does aggression in boys. The same is generally true for television violence and number of hours per week during which the subject watches television. This is apparent in Table 5.

Tables 7, 8, and 9 represent the multiple correlations of increasing sets of predictors to peer-rated aggression in the third, eighth, and thirteenth grades. (These correlations again refer to boys only.) The violence of the programs boys prefer at the third-grade level enters into the multiple

Table 7: Multiple correlation of third-grade predictor variables to third-grade peer-rated aggression for boys[a]

| $X$[b] | Predictor | $R^2$ | $R$ | Partialed r | r | N |
|---|---|---|---|---|---|---|
| 1 | IQ3 | .09 | .29 | - - - | −.29 | 205 |
| 2 | Social status 3 | .12 | .34 | −.19 | −.16 | 144 |
| 3 | Discrepancy in identification with Father 3 | .15 | .39 | .20 | .25 | 132 |
| 4 | Father's lack of nurturance 3 | .18 | .43 | −.18 | −.14 | 144 |
| 5 | TV hours watched 3 | .21 | .46 | −.17 | −.19 | 186 |
| 6 | TV violence 3 | .24 | .49 | .20 | .21 | 184 |
| 7 | Father's punishment 3 | .26 | .51 | .17 | .13 | 144 |
| 8 | Father's occupational aspirations for child 3 | .27 | .52 | −.13 | −.16 | 144 |
| 9 | Mother's occupational aspirations for child 3 | .28 | .53 | −.13 | −.03 | 186 |
| 10 | Father's generational level 3 | .30 | .55 | −.15 | −.13 | 144 |
| 11 | Mother's educational aspirations for child 3 | .31 | .56 | .13 | −.04 | 186 |
| 12 | Father's mobility orientation 3 | .32 | .57 | .12 | .14 | 144 |

[a]The number of variables entering into the multiple correlations in this and the two subsequent tables is contingent upon the requirement that any variable add at least 1% to the variance explained.

[b]Final standardized regression equation: $\text{AGG3} = -.232X_1 - .133X_2 + .223X_3 - .176X_4 - .190X_5 + .188X_6 + 134X_7 - .146X_8 - .116X_9 - .155X_{10} + .132X_{11} + .105X_{12}$

correlations of predictor variables to aggression at each grade level. However, the number of hours boys watch television is included among the multiple predictions only for aggression in the third grade.

Table 8: Multiple correlations of third-grade predictor variables to eighth-grade peer-rated aggression for boys

| $X^a$ | Predictor | $R^2$ | R | Partialed r | r | N |
|---|---|---|---|---|---|---|
| 1 | Discrepancy in identification with mother 3 | .22 | .46 | - - - | .47 | 56 |
| 2 | Father's occupational aspirations for child 3 | .30 | .54 | −.32 | −.35 | 53 |
| 3 | Father's punishment 3 | .36 | .60 | .31 | .30 | 53 |
| 4 | Father's lack of nurturance | .42 | .65 | −.29 | −.26 | 53 |
| 5 | Father's generational level | .46 | .68 | −.26 | −.29 | 53 |
| 6 | Mother's judgment of punishment harshness 3 | .50 | .71 | .29 | .24 | 64 |
| 7 | Discrepancy in identification with father 3 | .55 | .74 | .29 | .45 | 47 |
| 8 | Father's mobility aspirations for himself 3 | .60 | .78 | −.36 | −.20 | 53 |
| 9 | Mother's educational aspirations for child 3 | .67 | .82 | .40 | −.12 | 64 |
| 10 | Father's education 3 | .69 | .83 | −.28 | .15 | 53 |
| 11 | TV violence 3 | .72 | .85 | .29 | .16 | 64 |
| 12 | Residential mobility 3 | .74 | .86 | −.28 | −.03 | 53 |
| 13 | IQ 3 | .76 | .87 | −.25 | −.30 | 68 |
| 14 | Father's aggression on Walters-Zak scale 3 | .77 | .88 | .25 | .31 | 53 |
| 15 | Mother's education 3 | .78 | .88 | −.24 | .18 | 64 |
| 16 | Parental disharmony 3 | .79 | .89 | .20 | .04 | 64 |

$^a$Final standardized regression equation: $AGG8 = -.134X_1 - .229X_2 + .328X_3 - .272X_4 - .341X_5 + .423X_6 + .655X_7 - .326X_8 + .321X_9 - .151X_{10} + .162X_{11} - .201X_{12} - .181X_{13} + .156X_{14} - .168_{15} + .100X_{16}$

Table 9: Multiple correlations of third-grade predictors to 13th-grade peer-rated aggression for boys

| $X^a$ | Predictor | $R^2$ | R | Partialed r | r | N |
|---|---|---|---|---|---|---|
| 1 | TV violence 3 | .09 | .31 | - - - | .31 | 184 |
| 2 | Father's mobility 3 | .13 | .36 | .20 | .19 | 144 |
| 3 | Discrepancy in identification with mother 3 | .16 | .39 | .17 | .17 | 167 |
| 4 | Father's lack of nurturance 3 | .17 | .41 | −.12 | −.12 | 144 |
| 5 | Parental disharmony 3 | .18 | .42 | .12 | .14 | 186 |
| 6 | Father's punishment 3 | .19 | .44 | .12 | .14 | 144 |
| 7 | Mother's church attendance 3 | .20 | .45 | .09 | .02 | 186 |

$^a$Final standardized regression equation: $AGG13 = .276X_1 + .193X_2 + .130X_3 - .147X_4 + .132X_5 + .112X_6 + .087X_7$

These regressions were computed by a stepwise method that entered the variables into the equation in order of their utility in predicting the criterion aggression variable. Hence, the increment in $R^2$ when a variable is entered reveals the proportion of the variance it predicts when used in conjunction with the variables previously entered.

From this fact and from the data in Table 9, one can see that for predicting aggression in the thirteenth grade, the third-grade television violence variable was the single most useful predictor of all third-grade causal variables. It accounted for nine percent of the total variance and about 40 percent of the variance that could be explained by all 20 third-grade causal variables. In predicting third- and eighth-grade aggression, the third-grade television violence variable was the sixth and eleventh best predictor respectively, but accounted for three percent of the total variance in each case.

This regression demonstrates that a substantial component of aggression at all three grade levels and a particularly large component at the thirteenth grade can be predicted better by the amount of television violence the child watched in the third grade than by any other causal variable measured and reinforces the contention that there is a cause and effect relation between the violence content of television and overt aggressive behavior. However, as shown in Table 7, the best predictor of third-grade aggression is third-grade IQ.

As Darlington (1968) has pointed out, one can treat the standardized coefficients in a multiple regression equation as measures of the causal contributions of the predictor variables to the criterion variable. This approach, called "path analysis," assumes that all causal variables not in the regression equation are uncorrelated with those that are. While it is clear that this assumption is violated, it is still worthwhile to examine the coefficients as approximate measures of causal contributions.

Table 9 reveals that of all the third-grade causal variables, third-grade television violence is the major "cause" of thirteenth-grade aggression with a beta weight of .276. Similarly, as indicated in Table 7, not watching television and television violence watched are the fifth and sixth most important "causes" of concurrent third-grade aggression with standardized betas of $-.190$ and .188, respectively. On the other hand, third-grade television violence is not revealed to be a major "cause" of eighth-grade aggression as seen in Table 8.

## Relation of early to later aggression

The second hypothesis states that early aggression is a predictor of and a basis for later aggression. Table 10 contains the intercorrelations among the peer-rated aggression scores for boys obtained in the third grade (AGG3), the eighth grade (AGG8), and at the thirteenth (AGG13). Table 11 contains the same type of information about girls. The six correlations in Table 10 and 11 are all dependably nonzero (significant at the

Table 10: Intercorrelations for boys among peer nominations of aggression obtained in 3rd, 8th, and 13th grades

|  | AGG3 | AGG8[a] | AGG13 |
|---|---|---|---|
| AGG3 | 1.00 | .48 | .38 |
| AGG8 |  | 1.00 | .65 |
| AGG13 |  |  | 1.00 |
| Mean | 12.12 | 79.47 | 80.46 |
| S.D. | 12.73 | 89.05 | 96.98 |
| N | 211 | 71 | 211 |

[a]The AGG8 and AGG13 scores presented here and in the next table were multiplied by 10. Otherwise they were calculated in the same manner as was AGG3.

Table 11: Intercorrelations for girls among peer nominations of aggression obtained in 3rd, 8th and 13th grades

|  | AGG3 | AGG8 | AGG13 |
|---|---|---|---|
| AGG3 | 1.00 | .30 | .47 |
| AGG8 |  | 1.00 | .52 |
| AGG13 |  |  | 1.00 |
| Mean | 7.51 | 39.98 | 26.51 |
| S.D. | 9.87 | 49.85 | 37.68 |
| N | 216 | 79 | 216 |

.01 level). For each sex group the highest correlation was the one between the aggression scores at eighth and thirteenth grades. All the scores are obviously skewed to the high end. This *J* curve phenomenon has been discussed in Walder et al. (1961) and Eron et al. (1971).

Each of the correlations among these early and later aggression scores needs to be examined for its dependence upon some third variable such as IQ, social status, or aggressive milieu. Table 12 includes data relevant

Table 12: Correlations for boys between early and later aggression with selected controls

|  |  |  |  | Control variables for partialed $r$ s |  |  |
|---|---|---|---|---|---|---|
| Predictor | Outcome | r | IQ3 | Father's occupational status 3 | Father's aggression 3 | N |
| AGG3 | AGG8 | .48 | .43 | .51 | .50 | 71 |
|  | AGG13 | .38 | .34 | .39 | .38 | 211 |
| AGG8 | AGG13 | .65 | .64 | .65 | .65 | 71 |
|  | ASB13 | .39 | .37 | .38 | .38 | 70 |
|  | TAH13[a] | .48 | .46 | .47 | .47 | 71 |
|  | TAG13[b] | .48 | .47 | .47 | .47 | 71 |

[a]TAH = Admission by the subject that he has displayed aggressive and antisocial behaviors.
[b]TAG = Statements by the subject that he has expressed, witnessed, and experienced aggression.

to this type of concern. For the boys' data each of the three intercorrelations has been partialed with respect to the boys' IQs in the third grade, the occupational (social) status of the boys' fathers as measured by the 1960 Bureau of the Census index (low numbers here refer to high occupational status), and the fathers' aggression levels (the fathers' scores on Walters and Zak's Personal Opinion Inventory). These three third-grade measures were used as controls since the interest here was to predict from early aggression.

The first three rows of Table 12 contain the three correlations which were presented in Table 10. The remaining three rows contain other predictor-outcome correlations. These are the survivors from a selection procedure which first looked for dependably nonzero correlations between early aggression measures (AGG3 or AGG8) and any other measures that were obtained from or about the children at any later time in the five- or ten-year followup studies. This involved examining the relevance of early aggression to later peer rating measures, school and occupational variables, television scores, test results (e.g., MMPI and Z-Test scores), self-descriptions, and attitude responses. A number of these later measures could, in fact, be predicted from aggression scores which had been obtained five and ten years earlier. These substantial correlations over long periods of developmental time represent impressive *post hoc* evidence of reliability for these measures of aggression and of other behaviors. (See, e.g., Nunnally, 1967, p. 172 ff. for his discussion of reliability as a necessary but not sufficient condition for validity.)

The second aspect of this selection procedure required that each dependably nonzero predictive correlation be partialed with respect to one of the three control variables, as listed in Table 12. Predictor-outcome pairs whose correlations became markedly smaller when any one of these three variables was controlled were not retained for presentation here. Outcome variables such as peer-rated aggression-anxiety, school achievement test scores, later IQ scores, some school behaviors such as tardiness and attainment in school, and selected television behaviors did not survive this test in the data for boys. Thus Table 12 contains predictor-outcome correlations which demonstrate validities over five- and ten-year spans of time and which are not functions of any of the control variables examined. Table 13 presents variables which were selected on the same basis for girls.

A third selection procedure was employed to determine which predictor-outcome pairs should be presented here. Predictive correlations which were dependably nonzero and whose partial correlations were not lowered were subjected to this third requirement. Specifically, a one-way analysis of variance using unweighted means with the predictor as the independent variable and the outcome as the dependent variable yielded a significant $F$. Tables 14 and 15 present the six surviving predictor-outcome relations for the boys, and Table 16 and 17 present the five

Table 13: Correlations for girls between early and later aggression
with selected controls

| Predictor | Outcome | r | IQ3 | Control variables for partialed _r_ s | | N |
| | | | | Father's occupational status 3 | Father's aggression 3 | |
|-----------|---------|-----|-----|------------------------------|------------------|-----|
| AGG3 | AGG13 | .47 | .44 | .46 | .47 | 216 |
| | TV-SPT13 | .22 | .25 | .22 | .22 | 216 |
| AGG8 | AGG13 | .52 | .51 | .51 | .52 | 79 |
| | TAH13 | .37 | .38 | .40 | .37 | 79 |
| | TAG13 | .41 | .42 | .45 | .41 | 79 |

Table 14: Mean predicted scores as a function of earlier aggression in boys

| AGG3 | N | AGG8 | | AGG13 | |
| | | M | SD | M | SD |
|------|-----|------|------|--------|--------|
| Low | 44 | | | 24.61 | 35.14 |
| Med | 139 | not | | 83.10 | 92.77 |
| Hi | 28 | available | | 155.07 | 127.67 |
| Total | 211 | | | 80.46 | 96.98 |
| F | | | | 18.195 | t=6.50** |
| P | | | | < .0009 | |

surviving predictor-outcome relations for the girls. (An error in scoring has temporarily delayed the availability of the ANOVA for the AGG3 to AGG8 relation.)

The boys' data indicated that one can predict from aggression in the third grade to aggression in the eighth and thirteenth grades. Also one can predict from aggression in the eighth grade not only to peer-rated aggression in the thirteenth grade but also to various self-ratings of aggression obtained in that grade. These self-ratings were Antisocial Behavior, Total Aggressive Habit, and Total Aggressive Environment. Tables 14 and 15 show that heterogeneity of variance occurs for the AGG13 variables. In each case a $t$ test between means of the two groups differing most on variances was calculated. The $t$ was evaluated conservatively using as the number of degrees of freedom the N of the smaller group, 28 and 11, respectively. The prediction from third to thirteenth-grade aggression was unaffected but that from eighth to thirteenth (Table 15) was less certain, t = 2.63, p <.05. Similar $t$ tests were performed for certain of the girls' data, as illustrated in Tables 16 and 17 where the variance was heterogeneous. Only television sports failed to survive this test—$t$ was not statistically significant.

The girls' data indicated that one can predict from aggression in the third grade to aggression ten years later (AGG13). From aggression in the eighth grade (AGG8) predictions can be made not only to aggression in the thirteenth grade but to two self-descriptive aggression scores (TAH and TAG) which have already been described for the boys.

Table 15: Mean predicted scores as a function of earlier aggression in boys

| AGG8 | N | AGG13 | | ASB | | TAH | | TAG | |
|---|---|---|---|---|---|---|---|---|---|
| | | M | SD | M | SD | M | SD | M | SD |
| Lo | 13 | 9.39 | 12.39 | 9.83[a] | 7.55 | 14.46 | 8.47 | 30.23 | 14.85 |
| Med | 47 | 66.77 | 71.72 | 21.70 | 12.51 | 29.53 | 14.73 | 45.89 | 19.19 |
| Hi | 11 | 120.73 | 146.32 | 25.73 | 4.61 | 36.64 | 7.62 | 58.55 | 12.79 |
| TOTAL | 71 | 75.47 | 97.03 | 20.30 | 11.90 | 27.87 | 14.51 | 44.99 | 19.31 |
| F | | 15.512 | t=2.63 | 7.215 | | 9.860 | | 7.838 | |
| P | | <.0009 | <.05 | <.001 | | <.0009 | | <.001 | |

[a]This mean is based upon 12 cases; the mean of the total is therefore based upon 70 cases, df = 2 and 67.

Table 16: Mean predicted scores as a function of earlier aggression in girls

| AGG3 | N | AGG13 | | TV-SPT | |
|---|---|---|---|---|---|
| | | M | SD | M | SD |
| Lo | 29 | 9.21 | 13.94 | 5.41 | 0.91 |
| Med | 165 | 22.78 | 28.71 | 5.62 | 1.65 |
| Hi | 22 | 77.27 | 67.95 | 6.73 | 2.12 |
| Total | 216 | 26.51 | 37.68 | 5.71 | 1.66 |
| F | | 30.340 | t=5.36 | 4.990 | t=1.05 |
| P | | < .009 | < .01 | < .008 | ns |

Table 17: Mean predicted scores as a function of earlier aggression in girls

| AGG8 | N | AGG13 | | TAH | | TAG | |
|---|---|---|---|---|---|---|---|
| | | M | SD | M | SD | M | SD |
| Lo | 13 | 2.77 | 5.10 | 18.39 | 8.20 | 29.31 | 9.67 |
| Med | 53 | 19.94 | 27.96 | 19.51 | 10.17 | 30.42 | 11.89 |
| Hi | 13 | 56.15 | 65.38 | 28.23 | 9.44 | 42.62 | 12.21 |
| Total | 79 | 23.08 | 37.96 | 20.76 | 10.21 | 32.24 | 12.38 |
| F | | 8.280 | t=4.12 | 4.621 | | 6.250 | |
| P | | < .001 | < .01 | < .013 | | < .003 | |

To be assured that one can reasonably predict later scores from earlier aggression, the predictive relations with the greatest heterogeneity of variance (AGG3 to AGG13) are presented in Table 18 for boys and 19

Table 18: Predictability of AGG13 from AGG3 for boys

| | %-ile | | AGG13 | | | | % of row | Sum | % of Col. |
|---|---|---|---|---|---|---|---|---|---|
| | | | 28 | 50 | 75 | 99 | | | |
| | 28 | % of row | 40.9 | 29.5 | 15.9 | 13.6 | 99.9 | | |
| | | N | 18 | 13 | 7 | 6 | | 44 | 20.9 |
| | 50 | % of row | 2.5 | 35.0 | 35.0 | 27.5 | 100.0 | | |
| | | N | 1 | 14 | 14 | 11 | | 40 | 19.0 |
| A G G 3 | 75 | % of row | 20.0 | 16.4 | 23.6 | 40.0 | 100.0 | | |
| | | N | 11 | 9 | 13 | 22 | | 55 | 26.1 |
| | 99 | % of row | 2.8 | 9.7 | 30.6 | 56.9 | 100.0 | | |
| | | N | 2 | 7 | 22 | 41 | | 72 | 34.1 |
| | | SUM | 32 | 43 | 56 | 80 | | 211 | 100.1 |
| | | % of row | 15.2 | 20.4 | 26.5 | 39.7 | 100.0 | | |

Chi-square = 60.538***
df = 9, P < 0.0009

for girls. For best prediction, the highest row percentage indicated as the top number in each cell should be on the diagonal. The table should

Table 19: Predictability of AGG13 from AGG3 for girls

| %-ile | | AGG13 28 | 50 | 75 | 99 | % of row | Sum | % of Col. |
|---|---|---|---|---|---|---|---|---|
| 28 | % of row | 56.2 | 25.0 | 16.2 | 2.5 | 99.9 | | |
| | N | 45 | 20 | 13 | 2 | | 80 | 37.0 |
| 50 | % of row | 41.5 | 24.5 | 24.5 | 9.4 | 99.9 | | |
| | N | 22 | 13 | 13 | 5 | | 53 | 24.5 |
| A 75 | % of row | 34.1 | 29.5 | 25.0 | 11.4 | 100.0 | | |
| G G N | N | 15 | 13 | 11 | 5 | | 44 | 20.4 |
| 3 99 | % of row | 23.1 | 10.3 | 28.2 | 38.5 | 100.1 | | |
| | N | 9 | 4 | 11 | 15 | | 39 | 18.1 |
| | SUM | 91 | 50 | 48 | 27 | | 216 | 100.0 |
| | % of row | 42.1 | 23.1 | 22.2 | 12.5 | 99.9 | | |

Chi-square = 41.631**
df = 9, P < 0.0009

approximate a simplex with percentages high at the diagonal and decreasing in the cells farther from the diagonal. This monotonic relation is expressed by the correlations already provided for the AGG3 and AGG13 relation. By inspection one can see that for both sex groups the best prediction is from the extreme categories of third-grade aggression. It should be noted that the percentile score groupings were established for each aggression score by examining each distribution of pooled scores of both sexes. The obvious relation between sex and aggression shows up in the resulting skew to the high scores in the two middle rows of the girls' table (Table 19) and a smaller skew to the low scores in the two middle rows of the boys' table (Table 18). In spite of these shortcomings, inspection of these two tables gives assurance that one can predict fairly well that a person's relative position on AGG3 will generally be maintained ten years later in AGG13. This prediction is possible in spite of the considerable skewness of both distributions.

It seems fair to say that the second hypothesis is supported by our ability to predict from earlier aggression scores to aggression and other related scores obtained five and ten years later. These predictions are not a function of the child's IQ or the social status or aggression level of the father. Coupled with the support of the first hypothesis, we may say from hypothesis one that precursors including television behaviors are related to contemporary and later aggression. From hypothesis, two one can say that aggression is related to subsequent peer- and self-rated aggression. The examination of the data so far has revealed, once more, a difference between boys and girls in the distribution of aggression scores and in the relations of these scores to other variables.

# Aggression and psychopathology

Hypothesis three deals with the relation of aggression to psychopathology. This hypothesis was tested by examining the correlations between various measures of aggression and measures of maladjustment. These latter measures were composed of certain components of the MMPI, the psychopathology score of the Z-Test, school achievement, and arrest record.

Table 20 presents the Pearson product moment correlation coefficients for boys between various measures of aggression and the clinical scales of the MMPI. These measures were obtained from the subjects'

Table 20: Correlations for boys between various measures of aggression and psychopathology

| Aggression | N | MMPI Clinical scales (Psychopathology) | MMPI Scales 4+9 Partialed | MMPI Scales 4+9 |
|---|---|---|---|---|
| Frequency of home aggression—Father 3 | 144 | .14 | | .09 |
| Frequency of home aggression—mother 3 | 186 | .06 | | −.04 |
| Recency of home aggression—father 3 | 144 | .22** | .13 | .19 |
| Recency of home aggression—mother 3 | 186 | .16 | | .11 |
| AGG3 | 211 | .07 | −.07 | .21** |
| AGG8 | 71 | −.07 | | .20 |
| AGG13 | 211 | .23** | −.02 | .39** |
| Personal opinion inventory (Walters-Zak) 13 | 211 | .11 | | .17 |
| Antisocial behavior 13 | 209 | .28** | .00 | .50** |
| Total aggressive habit 13 | 211 | .27** | −.04 | .48** |
| Total aggressive environment 13 | 211 | .27** | −.03 | .48** |
| IQ3 | 205 | −.12 | | −.16 |
| Social status 13 | 209 | .15 | | .15 |

parents or from the subjects themselves in the third, eighth, and/or thirteenth grade. The criterion measures (e.g., MMPI, achievement, arrests) were obtained only at the period of the thirteenth grade.

Because MMPI scale 4 and scale 9 may be more a measure of delinquent behavior (Hathaway and Monachesi, 1963) or an active hostility index (Dahlstrom and Welsh, 1960) than a measure of psychopathology, the effects of these scales were removed by partial correlation technique. With this control, five if the variables in Table 20 entered into significant relations with the MMPI clinical scales—the criterion measure. As a result of the control for the 4 plus 9 scale, all of these correlations were reduced to zero order as seen in column 4. The correlations of aggression measures with the sum of scales 4 and 9 are presented in column 5. The peer nominations of aggression obtained in the third grade (AGG3) and those obtained in the ten-year followup (AGG13) related significantly to this later putative measure of delinquency. Moderate correlations also occur between scales 4 plus 9 and the following self-ratings of aggression: Antisocial Behavior (ASB), Total Aggressive Habit (TAH) and Total Aggressive Environment (TAG). These three latter measures were obtained concurrently with the MMPI. Neither IQ nor social status enters into a significant relation with the psychopathology measure or scales 4 plus 9. Since the Z-Test proved unrelated to any of the aggression measures, the results are not presented.

Table 21: Correlations for girls between various measures of aggression and psychopathology

| Aggression | N | MMPI Clinical scales (Psychopathology) | MMPI Scales 4+9 Partialed | MMPI Scales 4+9 |
|---|---|---|---|---|
| Frequency of home aggression— father 3 | 157 | .00 | | .00 |
| Frequency of home aggression— mother 3 | 184 | .07 | | .05 |
| Recency of home aggression— father 3 | 157 | −.07 | | .00 |
| Recency of home aggression— mother 3 | 184 | −.04 | | .00 |
| AGG3 | 216 | .03 | | .12 |
| AGG8 | 79 | .12 | | .27 |
| AGG13 | 216 | .10 | | .28** |
| Personal opinion inventory 13 | 216 | .15 | | .23** |
| Antisocial behavior 13 | 211 | .29** | −.00 | .45** |
| Total aggressive habit 13 | 216 | .27** | −.03 | .45** |
| Total aggressive environment 13 | 216 | .30** | .01 | .45** |
| IQ3 | 207 | −.15 | −.07 | −.14 |
| Social status 13 | 210 | .03 | | .07 |

Table 21 presents similar data for girls. The only significant relations between the measures of aggression and psychopathology occurred for those measures obtained concurrently: ASB, TAH, TAG. However, when the effect of scales 4 plus 9 was controlled by partial correlation, these relations were reduced to zero order as shown in column 4.

Table 22: Comparison of MMPI mean scores in grade 13
for boys rated high or low
on aggression in grade 3

| MMPI Scale | Low (74) | | High (34) | | |
|---|---|---|---|---|---|
| | M | SD | M | SD | t |
| L | 47.54 | 6.66 | 49.35 | 7.04 | 1.29 |
| F | 57.30 | 9.08 | 61.32 | 14.46 | 1.76 |
| K | 51.54 | 8.38 | 50.26 | 8.13 | .74 |
| 1 | 53.38 | 11.57 | 53.62 | 6.66 | .11 |
| 2 | 55.97 | 11.21 | 55.91 | 12.64 | .03 |
| 3 | 55.36 | 11.30 | 56.62 | 7.48 | .59 |
| 4 | 56.73 | 9.86 | 63.32 | 11.96 | 3.01** |
| 5 | 60.80 | 10.29 | 58.94 | 8.73 | .91 |
| 6 | 54.53 | 9.82 | 59.26 | 12.50 | 2.13 |
| 7 | 58.74 | 10.42 | 59.41 | 12.13 | .29 |
| 8 | 59.58 | 12.33 | 64.79 | 16.10 | 1.85 |
| 9 | 61.68 | 11.82 | 66.21 | 12.64 | 1.81 |
| 0 | 53.38 | 9.97 | 52.26 | 9.37 | .55 |
| IQ | 111.31 | 12.39 | 99.18 | 11.55 | 4.83** |
| Social status | 4.23 | 2.69 | 4.12 | 1.74 | .22 |

Inspection of column 5 shows that scales 4 plus 9 relate to these three measures of aggression positively as they did for boys: all increase considerably in magnitude. Consequently, the relation between the measures of aggression and the MMPI clinical scales was only apparent; the variance in this relation was accounted for by scales 4 plus 9. Again, neither IQ nor social status entered into significant relations with the MMPI measures of psychopathology and delinquency.

Because some of the relations between aggression and the MMPI may have been obscured by compressing the 11 clinical scales into one measure, a more extensive analysis of the MMPI was conducted. Presented

Table 23: Comparison of MMPI mean scores in grade 13 for
girls rated high or low on aggression in grade 3

| MMPI Scale | Low (80) | | High (39) | | |
|---|---|---|---|---|---|
| | M | SD | M | SD | t |
| L | 49.29 | 6.84 | 50.59 | 7.18 | .96 |
| F | 54.09 | 7.61 | 59.03 | 13.21 | 2.58 |
| K | 53.16 | 7.65 | 52.23 | 7.40 | .63 |
| 1 | 50.30 | 7.56 | 51.33 | 8.90 | .66 |
| 2 | 52.45 | 8.74 | 53.85 | 13.02 | .69 |
| 3 | 54.61 | 7.51 | 54.72 | 6.47 | .08 |
| 4 | 57.31 | 10.97 | 62.31 | 13.30 | 2.17 |
| 5 | 46.55 | 8.83 | 54.03 | 8.71 | 4.36** |
| 6 | 56.72 | 9.27 | 57.51 | 11.07 | .41 |
| 7 | 55.92 | 7.13 | 56.62 | 9.07 | .45 |
| 8 | 55.56 | 8.43 | 59.82 | 13.14 | 2.14 |
| 9 | 59.05 | 11.11 | 62.74 | 9.97 | 1.76 |
| 0 | 53.10 | 9.32 | 51.21 | 9.55 | 1.03 |
| IQ | 108.61 | 12.56 | 97.26 | 13.45 | 4.52** |
| Social status | 3.79 | 1.65 | 4.13 | 1.88 | 1.01 |

Table 24: Comparison of MMPI mean scores in grade 13 for
boys rated high or low in aggression in grade 8

| MMPI Scale | Low (18) | | High (19) | | |
|---|---|---|---|---|---|
| | M | SD | M | SD | t |
| L | 47.33 | 5.65 | 45.21 | 8.27 | .91 |
| F | 57.72 | 6.52 | 60.63 | 10.51 | 1.00 |
| K | 53.06 | 6.49 | 49.37 | 9.38 | 1.38 |
| 1 | 51.67 | 13.30 | 54.32 | 8.41 | .73 |
| 2 | 57.22 | 14.97 | 56.26 | 9.83 | .23 |
| 3 | 56.67 | 8.90 | 57.16 | 9.87 | .16 |
| 4 | 55.28 | 10.12 | 62.63 | 11.49 | 2.06 |
| 5 | 61.00 | 7.61 | 59.21 | 12.09 | .54 |
| 6 | 52.39 | 9.56 | 59.53 | 11.38 | 2.06 |
| 7 | 59.22 | 12.78 | 61.26 | 12.23 | .50 |
| 8 | 57.17 | 14.81 | 63.58 | 15.49 | 1.29 |
| 9 | 54.94 | 12.53 | 64.47 | 11.93 | 2.37 |
| 0 | 58.72 | 11.06 | 51.63 | 6.49 | 2.39 |
| IQ | 118.39 | 13.28 | 105.05 | 11.52 | 3.27** |
| Social status | 3.39 | 1.46 | 3.37 | 1.61 | .04 |

in Table 22 are the means and standard deivations of the 13 basic MMPI scales for boys in the upper and lower quartiles of aggression as determined by peer nominations in the third grade. Again, values for IQ and social status serve as control measures. Inspection of this table demonstrates that high aggressive boys have a significantly higher mean score on scale 4 as indicated by the *t* test between means. Furthermore the IQs differ significantly: the high aggressive group has a lower mean IQ. Also evident in Table 22 is the absence of a significant relation between aggression and social status.

The same analysis is presented for girls in Table 23. These data show that girls who received the highest peer nominations for aggression

Table 25: Comparison of MMPI mean scores in grade 13 for
girls rated high or low in aggression in grade 8

| MMPI Scale | Low (20) | | High (21) | | |
|---|---|---|---|---|---|
| | M | SD | M | SD | t |
| L | 50.85 | 7.95 | 46.71 | 4.92 | 2.01 |
| F | 50.85 | 5.75 | 55.33 | 9.60 | 1.80 |
| K | 58.10 | 5.99 | 52.52 | 7.78 | 2.56 |
| 1 | 49.40 | 3.50 | 49.24 | 6.50 | .10 |
| 2 | 51.35 | 9.66 | 50.24 | 7.13 | .42 |
| 3 | 54.05 | 5.83 | 55.76 | 6.22 | .91 |
| 4 | 53.50 | 9.25 | 59.86 | 13.61 | 1.74 |
| 5 | 46.65 | 10.46 | 48.38 | 9.07 | .57 |
| 6 | 56.10 | 9.30 | 55.81 | 8.32 | .11 |
| 7 | 56.80 | 10.31 | 56.43 | 7.79 | .13 |
| 8 | 57.20 | 10.07 | 56.52 | 7.87 | .24 |
| 9 | 57.55 | 9.71 | 61.43 | 10.31 | 1.24 |
| 0 | 53.45 | 8.77 | 50.29 | 8.28 | 1.19 |
| IQ | 108.50 | 14.70 | 108.14 | 10.37 | .09 |
| Social status | 3.35 | 2.01 | 3.38 | 1.56 | .06 |

when they were in the third grade have significantly higher scores on scale 5 ten years later than girls categorized in the low aggressive group. This scale is a measure of masculinity-femininity and a high score for girls is in the masculine direction. Again, IQ was negatively related to aggression whereas social status was unrelated to aggression.

The relations between ratings of aggression for boys in the eighth grade and the MMPI administered in the thirteenth grade are presented in Table 24. Although several of the clinical scales are elevated in the predicted direction, none of the *t*s reaches the stipulated level of significance. IQ was negatively related to aggression for this group, and social status was unrelated.

Table 26: Comparison of MMPI mean scores in grade 13 for boys rated high or low in aggression at the same period

| MMPI Scale | Low (58) | | High (53) | | | |
|---|---|---|---|---|---|---|
| | M | SD | M | SD | t | Welch's t |
| L | 49.26 | 7.45 | 47.79 | 6.71 | 1.09 | |
| F | 56.02 | 7.66 | 66.58 | 14.38 | 4.89** | 4.76** |
| K | 54.10 | 7.43 | 49.64 | 7.31 | 3.18** | |
| 1 | 53.09 | 10.33 | 54.96 | 9.45 | .99 | |
| 2 | 55.67 | 11.29 | 58.04 | 12.79 | 1.03 | |
| 3 | 55.53 | 10.40 | 56.60 | 10.13 | .55 | |
| 4 | 55.66 | 8.71 | 66.13 | 10.81 | 5.64** | |
| 5 | 60.00 | 10.05 | 58.53 | 9.73 | .78 | |
| 6 | 53.55 | 9.47 | 60.72 | 12.65 | 3.40** | |
| 7 | 59.45 | 11.18 | 62.68 | 13.05 | 1.40 | |
| 8 | 58.74 | 11.41 | 69.60 | 16.53 | 4.06** | |
| 9 | 59.33 | 12.03 | 69.40 | 10.71 | 4.64** | |
| 0 | 54.64 | 10.30 | 51.68 | 8.07 | 1.67 | |
| IQ | 111.48 | 13.14 | 105.30 | 12.94 | 2.49 | |
| Social status | 3.83 | 1.74 | 4.34 | 1.53 | 1.64 | |

Table 27: Comparison of MMPI mean scores in grade 13 for girls rated high or low in aggression at the same period

| MMPI Scale | Low (58) | | High (54) | | | |
|---|---|---|---|---|---|---|
| | M | SD | M | SD | t | Welch's t |
| L | 49.41 | 7.24 | 50.30 | 7.13 | .65 | |
| F | 50.86 | 5.17 | 59.17 | 11.91 | 4.84** | 4.73** |
| K | 53.91 | 7.11 | 52.44 | 7.77 | 1.04 | |
| 1 | 48.66 | 5.61 | 50.98 | 8.18 | 1.76 | |
| 2 | 51.66 | 8.58 | 52.85 | 9.65 | .69 | |
| 3 | 52.66 | 5.47 | 55.02 | 7.05 | 1.99 | |
| 4 | 54.50 | 9.65 | 64.72 | 12.37 | 4.90** | |
| 5 | 46.38 | 9.37 | 52.80 | 9.13 | 3.66** | |
| 6 | 54.67 | 8.71 | 58.07 | 10.85 | 1.84 | |
| 7 | 55.52 | 7.32 | 55.98 | 7.85 | .32 | |
| 8 | 54.60 | 8.54 | 58.98 | 11.25 | 2.33 | |
| 9 | 57.60 | 10.32 | 63.30 | 10.57 | 2.88** | |
| 0 | 54.14 | 8.49 | 50.76 | 8.29 | 2.13 | |
| IQ | 108.22 | 11.49 | 102.80 | 13.77 | 2.27 | |
| Social status | 3.91 | 1.78 | 4.02 | 1.49 | .34 | |

Table 28: Comparison of MMPI mean scores in grade 13
for boys rated high-high or low-low on
ratings of aggression in grades 3 and 13

| MMPI Scale | Low (31) | | High (17) | | |
|---|---|---|---|---|---|
| | M | SD | M | SD | t |
| L | 47.26 | 6.63 | 48.12 | 7.11 | .42 |
| F | 57.16 | 7.07 | 65.94 | 18.24 | 2.39 |
| K | 54.45 | 7.89 | 51.29 | 6.53 | 1.41 |
| 1 | 53.87 | 11.95 | 52.59 | 7.59 | .40 |
| 2 | 57.23 | 12.96 | 58.00 | 14.97 | .19 |
| 3 | 56.03 | 13.15 | 57.47 | 9.27 | .40 |
| 4 | 56.55 | 8.79 | 68.06 | 11.56 | 3.88** |
| 5 | 63.55 | 10.21 | 59.88 | 9.95 | 1.20 |
| 6 | 54.32 | 9.56 | 60.76 | 14.55 | 1.85 |
| 7 | 60.06 | 10.75 | 61.71 | 14.39 | .45 |
| 8 | 59.77 | 11.53 | 70.41 | 19.33 | 2.39 |
| 9 | 60.55 | 13.04 | 71.71 | 9.78 | 3.08** |
| 0 | 54.52 | 11.17 | 50.65 | 9.73 | 1.20 |
| IQ | 113.74 | 13.28 | 98.53 | 9.55 | 4.16** |
| Social status | 3.90 | 1.58 | 4.82 | 1.33 | 2.04 |

For girls the same analysis is illustrated in Table 25. No significant differences occurred between MMPI scales or the control measures of IQ and social status.

Table 26 presents the analysis of mean differences on MMPI scores for boys grouped into the lower and upper quartiles of aggression according to peer nominations received synchronously. The high aggressive boys have significantly higher mean scores on the F-scale and on scales 4, 6, 8, and 9. In addition, this group manifests significantly lower scores on the K-scale when compared with the low aggressive group. IQ

Table 29: Comparison of MMPI mean scores in grade 13 for
girls rated high-high or low-low on
ratings of aggression in grades 3 and 13

| MMPI Scale | Low (23) | | High (24) | | | |
|---|---|---|---|---|---|---|
| | M | SD | M | SD | t | Welch's t |
| L | 50.85 | 7.97 | 53.13 | 6.47 | 1.15 | |
| F | 50.73 | 4.95 | 60.46 | 14.22 | 3.65** | 3.16** |
| K | 54.30 | 6.56 | 53.50 | 7.71 | .42 | |
| 1 | 48.91 | 5.30 | 52.00 | 8.41 | 1.70 | |
| 2 | 51.39 | 8.40 | 54.17 | 11.14 | 1.07 | |
| 3 | 52.85 | 5.15 | 54.50 | 6.61 | 1.06 | |
| 4 | 54.03 | 9.31 | 65.13 | 13.71 | 3.64** | |
| 5 | 47.48 | 10.10 | 54.92 | 7.98 | 2.99** | |
| 6 | 54.58 | 9.09 | 58.92 | 11.97 | 1.56 | |
| 7 | 54.45 | 7.32 | 57.38 | 8.29 | 1.41 | |
| 8 | 53.24 | 8.90 | 59.75 | 13.61 | 2.18 | |
| 9 | 56.55 | 10.21 | 63.25 | 10.86 | 2.38 | |
| 0 | 54.48 | 8.34 | 50.25 | 7.74 | 1.95 | |
| IQ | 107.33 | 11.63 | 95.29 | 15.07 | 3.41** | |
| Social status | 4.12 | 1.83 | 4.00 | 1.62 | .26 | |

and social status were not significantly related to aggression. In the case of the F-scale, the variance between groups proved to be heterogeneous (F = 3.508 for 52 and 57 degrees of freedom). This scale was reanalyzed using Welch's *t* (Winer, 1962), and both the mean and variability on the F-scale were found to be significantly greater for the high aggressive group.

The same data are presented for girls in the thirteenth grade in Table 27. High aggressive girls evinced significantly higher mean scores on the F-scale and on scales 4, 5, and 9. IQ and social status were not signifi-

Table 30: Correlations for boys between various measures of aggression and intellectual functioning

| Aggression | N | Achievement | IQ partialed | Social status partialed |
|---|---|---|---|---|
| Frequency of home aggression — father 3 | 34 | .05 | | |
| Frequency of home aggression — mother 3 | 45 | −.08 | | |
| Recency of home aggression — father 3 | 34 | .16 | | |
| Recency of home aggression — mother 3 | 45 | .00 | | |
| AGG3 | 58 | −.32 | | |
| AGG8 | 23 | −.30 | | |
| AGG13 | 58 | −.36** | −.31 | −.32 |
| Personal opinion inventory 13 | 58 | −.59** | −.54** | −.57** |
| Antisocial behavior 13 | 57 | −.26 | | |
| Total aggressive habit 13 | 58 | −.29 | | |
| Total aggressive environment 13 | 58 | −.25 | | |
| MMPI 4+9 13 | 58 | −.25 | | |
| IQ3 | 57 | .53** | | .51** |
| Social status 13 | 57 | −.37** | −.33** | |

cantly related to aggression for this sample. Again group variances on the F-scale were heterogeneous: $F = 5.259$, p <.01 for df = 53 and 57. According to Welch's *t*, both the means and variances on the F-scale appear to be related to the classification by aggression.

Tables 28 and 29 present analyses for boys and girls who met the conditions of being consistently in either the upper or lower quartiles of aggression at *both* the third and thirteenth grades. Table 28 demonstrates that the high-high aggressive boys have significantly higher mean scores on scales 4 and 9. In addition IQ for this group is significantly lower compared with the low-low aggressives; social status is unrelated to aggression.

Table 31: Correlations for girls between various measures of
aggression and intellectual functioning

| Aggression | N | Achievement | IQ partialed | Social status partialed |
|---|---|---|---|---|
| Frequency of home aggression — father 3 | 43 | .23 | | |
| Frequency of home aggression — mother 3 | 50 | .17 | | |
| Recency of home aggression — father 3 | 43 | .29 | | |
| Recency of home aggression — mother 3 | 50 | .03 | | |
| AGG3 | 62 | −.30 | | |
| AGG8 | 37 | −.44** | −.47** | −.45** |
| AGG13 | 62 | −.39** | −.34** | −.39** |
| Personal opinion inventory 13 | 62 | −.19 | | |
| Antisocial behavior 13 | 60 | −.08 | | |
| Total aggressive habit 13 | 62 | −.08 | | |
| Total aggressive environment 13 | 62 | −.04 | | |
| MMPI 4+9 13 | 61 | −.20 | | |
| IQ3 | 59 | .60** | | |
| Social status 13 | 61 | −.26 | | |

Table 29 shows that the high-high aggressive girls have significantly elevated scores on the F-scale and on scales 4 and 5. The low-low aggressives have significantly higher mean IQs. A test of the variances of the F-scale yielded the following: $F = 8.416$, $df = 23$ and $72$, $p < .01$. According to Welch's $t$ for this scale, both the means and variances seem to have been directly affected by the aggression groupings. Again, IQ is significantly higher for the low-low aggressives.

Table 30 presents the correlations for boys between the various measures of aggression and intellectual functioning. The latter variable was measured by standardized achievement test scores obtained when the subjects were in the twelfth grade. Because IQ and social status are correlated with achievement ($r = .53$ and $-.37$, respectively) the effects of these variables on achievement were controlled by partial correlation. Inspection of Table 30 illustrates that none of the third-grade measures of home aggression obtained from the parents' interview predicted later school functioning. Among the peer nomination measures, aggression as measured in the thirteenth grade was apparently related to achievement but did not quite survive the control by partial correlation for the effects of IQ and social status. The only measure of aggression related to achievement irrespective of these controls was the Personal Opinion

Inventory administered in the thirteenth grade. The higher the aggression, the lower the achievement.

Similar data for girls is presented in Table 31. The peer nominations of aggression in the eighth (AGG8) and thirteenth grades (AGG13) were negatively related to achievement. These relations did withstand the controls for IQ and social status. Again, aggression was negatively related to achievement. Because of the nature of the measures, it is improbable that method variance is contributing to these relations.

The contingency relation between peer nominations of aggression in the third grade and arrest during adolescence is presented in Table 32.

Table 32: Chi-square analysis of arrests
by levels of aggression

| | Boys | | |
|---|---|---|---|
| AGG3 | Arrests | | |
| | Yes | No | Total |
| High | 7 | 118 | 125 |
| Low | 2 | 128 | 130 |
| | 9 | 246 | 255 |

Chi-square = 3.087
p = .075

The classification of aggression is by upper and lower quartile. Only those arrests which occurred in New York State were available and only in aggregate form. Arrest charges were as follows: burglary, grand larceny, larceny 3rd, attempted grand larceny, sexual misconduct, criminal mischief, petty larceny. Although more than three times as many boys were arrested in the high as compared to the low aggression group, the chi-square of 3.087 does not reach statistical significance.

# DISCUSSION

The above results would tend to indicate that television habits established by age eight influence aggressive and other behaviors at that time and at least through late adolescence. This is more true for boys than for girls, although many of the relations for girls are in the same direction as those for boys, though less strong. The more violent the programs preferred by boys in the third grade, the more aggressive is their behavior both at that time and ten years later. This positive relation between early television habits and later behavior prevails both for peer-rated aggression and for self-ratings of aggression. Actually these early television habits seem to be more influential than current viewing patterns, since the number of hours per week that the subject watches television in the thirteenth grade and the violence ratings of his preferred programs at that time are not at all related to current aggressive behavior; nor are early television habits related to later television habits. Similarly there is a stronger negative relation between IQ at grade three and number of hours television is watched at grade thirteen than between IQ at grade twelve and extent of television watching at grade thirteen. However, the attenuation in relation to the two later obtained measures may be a function of the smaller number of subjects for whom the investigators could obtain IQ scores at the later age (N = 53).

It should be noted that the lack of relation between later television habits and later aggression is not a result of inadequate measurement operations. The television ratings, as pointed out above, were reliably made and were closely correlated with ratings independently made in at least two other studies (Greenberg and Gordon, 1970; Feshbach and Singer, 1971). Furthermore, although unrelated to current aggressive behavior, these violence ratings are related significantly to other current and past behaviors, as noted above. It is unlikely that the findings presented are a result of unreliable and/or invalid ratings of either television violence or aggressive behavior. We can surmise that the absence of a concurrent relation between television violence and aggressive behavior in the thirteenth grade is due to the fact that this behavior has already been established and is no longer responsive to conditions which influence such behavior in the young.

The multiple R analyses provide further evidence that the violence of preferred television programs at the third grade level retains a strong predictive relation to aggression five and ten years later. Of 20 different variables which entered significantly into any of the three multiple R s, television violence is one of only three which made a significant contribution to all three levels. It can be assumed that children who prefer violent programs in the third grade will continue to watch such programs as they get older; since the relation with aggression is stronger in the thirteenth grade than it is in the third grade, we can hypothesize that the effect of television violence on aggressive behavior is cumulative. It has been demonstrated that the more hours a subject watches television and the more he prefers violent programs, the more likely he is to judge that the situations depicted in television westerns and crime stories are realistic representations of life. One might speculate that subjects continually exposed to television violence would not perceive their own aggressive behavior as deviant or unusual—this is the way life is and the way one goes about solving problems. Inhibitions against expressing overt aggression would thus be diminished.

These findings showing a direct positive relation between the viewing of television violence and aggressive behavior on the part of the viewer corroborate in a field study what has been demonstrated in the laboratory (Bandura, Ross, and Ross, 1961, 1963a, 1963b; Berkowitz, 1964; Berkowitz and Rawlings, 1963; Berkowitz, Corwin, and Heironimus, 1960). Because the foregoing are manipulative studies in which systematically varied treatments were administered to randomly selected subjects under controlled conditions, statements about cause and effect relations based on their findings can be made with more confidence perhaps than those based on findings of naturalistic studies. In such studies, many uncontrolled variables are unaccounted for, and observation and measurement cannot be as precise. The investigators feel that their recent finding relating television violence and behavior over a ten-year period strengthens the conviction that this is indeed a real relation. The direction indicated for the relation is that viewing violence regularly on television at age eight leads to more aggressive behavior on the part of the viewer at that time and also in subsequent years than does viewing nonviolent programs.

Feshbach and Singer (1971), in a bold attempt to compromise between laboratory manipulation and a field setting, provided findings which would indicate that the viewing of aggressive programs on television leads to a diminution of aggressive behavior on the part of the viewers, at least for some types of subjects. They regulated the amount of television aggression viewed by their subjects over a six-week period by prescribing an aggressive or nonaggressive diet of television programs to groups of subjects. (The authors believed they were able to do this successfully because the subjects were enrolled in residential private schools and homes for boys.) The researchers employed a number of behavioral, attitudinal, and fantasy measures, both self-ratings and ratings by peers and supervisors, before the experiment began and at various times throughout the study. It was found in general that the boys who were exposed to an aggressive television diet decreased in manifestations of aggression over this period while the control subjects increased in aggression.

Actually the research by Feshbach and Singer addressed itself to a different question than did the present research, which is more concerned with the long-range effects of viewing television violence and with more pervasive aggressive dispositions. In this regard it is of interest that Feshbach and Singer used the peer rating measure which we had developed for our studies (Walder et al., 1961) in order to assess preexperimental aggressive levels of their subjects and thereby separate them into high and low aggressive subsamples. They found: "Regardless of experimental group, boys who score high on the peer aggression nomination measure display about twice as much aggressive behavior towards peers as boys who score low on the peer nomination measure" (Feshbach and Singer, 1971, p. 91). Thus any manipulation that changes the peer nomination score would indeed have powerful effects.

It is this measure that is affected by television preference. The findings of Feshbach and Singer are smaller and perhaps more transient.

Feshbach and Singer criticize laboratory studies of aggression in that they do not ". . .replicate real life viewing and behavioral conditions sufficiently to permit extrapolation to the effects of the depiction of violence in the media on daily behavior" (p. 43). However, although these researchers have come a long way from the laboratory in setting up their research arena, they are still themselves far from approximating natural situations. The subjects watched television in groups of ten to 18 boys at precise times either in their classrooms or in their headmaster's or teacher's living rooms, for a minimum of six hours a week. In two of the schools, participation by the subjects was compulsory; in five it was voluntary. There was of course no voluntary choice of television programs since the boys were restricted to the television diet to which they were assigned according to the experimental design. There is some indication that at least at first this lack of preference was resented by boys assigned to the nonviolent diet, since it meant they could not watch their favorite programs. In a few cases the experimenters, in order to retain the cooperation of the subjects, permitted the boys in the nonaggressive diet to watch *Batman* even though it was one of the aggressive programs. Although all subjects were given the same cover story, that the researchers were interested in the relation between certain personality factors and evaluation of television programs, some (it is not stated how many and at which schools) guessed the real purpose. All of these conditions just described do not resemble those under which most youngsters in this culture watch television. Nor is their independent measure comparable to our predictor measure, preference for specific programs.

Furthermore, their subjects are not really representative of any given segment of the population. They ranged from elementary through high school level at seven different residential schools and institutions in California and New York. These included a military school, a coeducational boarding school, a school described as "very similar to a better New England prep school," and four boys' homes for "boys with inadequate home care facilities or with minor social adjustment problems." What kind of population to which their results are generalizable is unclear. The findings hold up significantly only in the homes for boys, not in the private schools. It is not unlikely that conditions in the private schools approximate more closely real-life viewing and behavioral conditions than those in the homes for boys. The one instance in which the Feshbach and Singer findings were reversed was at the junior high level in the private schools. The researchers preferred to ascribe this to chance occurrence, but it may indeed be a real effect, given those more natural conditions in the private school. In a recent review of the literature pertaining to aggression and filmed material, Bryan and Schwartz (1971) conclude that scant support can be marshaled for a catharsis principle from experimental studies. The preponderance of studies indicated that exposure to an aggressive model increases the viewer's aggressive behavior.

Another important difference between the Feshbach and Singer study and the present research is that in the former, the viewing and performance situations are the same—the boys watched television in the same setting in which their behavior was evaluated. In the current study television viewing took place in the home and the aggressive behavior was noted in the school setting. We submit that this is the more natural situation, allowing for displacement and wider generalization of expression of the aggression.

The investigators' criticism of the biased sampling represented by Feshbach and Singer's subject population behooves us to justify our own sampling representativeness. Our subjects represent a given population: 19-year-old boys and girls who had been in the third grade in Columbia County ten years previously. The demographic, socioeconomic, educational, intellectual and other social characteristics of this group have been delineated. As was pointed out in the method section above, a greater proportion of low than high aggressive subjects from the third grade volunteered for the ten-year followup study. This bias in composition of the subject pool was in part controlled statistically in the ANOVA (analysis of variance) procedure.

A graphic example of how sampling bias can influence the direction of findings, especially when contemporaneous relations are being considered without reference to longitudinal effects, is in the data presented

Table 33: Mean scores on selected variables as a function of
violence of preferred TV programs in grade 8

|  | TVVL3 | AGG3 | TVVL8 | AGG8 | TVVL13 | AGG13 | PID3[a] | N |
|---|---|---|---|---|---|---|---|---|
| LOW TVVL8 | 4.46 | 16.25 | 16.5 | 85.5 | 2.42 | 70.2 | 5.70 | 12 |
| MED TVVL8 | 7.45 | 11.11 | 98.0 | 87.2 | 5.62 | 82.5 | 5.94 | 42 |
| HIGH TVVL8 | 6.50 | 9.50 | 176.2 | 51.7 | 6.90 | 88.1 | 5.25 | 10 |

[a]PID3 was a 3rd grade measure concerned with discrepancy in identification with mother (see Eron et al., 1971 for explanation of this measure).

here. It appeared that in the eighth grade we had found a negative relation between peer-rated aggression of boys and violence score of preferred television programs. This correlation coefficient ($r = .245$, $p = .05$) missed the predetermined acceptable alpha level of .01. Table 33 shows the mean aggression and television violence scores of subjects separated according to their eighth-grade television violence scores. It appears that the negative correlation between concurrent television violence and aggression in the eighth grade is caused primarily by a small number of subjects with very high television violence scores and very low aggression scores. From Table 33 one can see that the preference of these children for violent television was not present in the third grade.

Hence, if the effect of violent television is primarily longitudinal, one would not expect these children to be highly aggressive in the eighth grade. Moreover, one would expect those subjects watching violent television to be more aggressive by the thirteenth grade. In fact this is the case, as Table 33 reveals. By the thirteenth grade, the ten high violence watchers have become highly aggressive. But why was there a negative correlation between television violence and aggression rather than a zero order correlation in the eighth grade? This phenomenon can be explained by sampling bias. Apparently the ten crucial subjects were exposed to a third-grade environment that made them low in aggression in the eighth grade. This hypothesis is supported by the data. As indicated in Table 33, these ten subjects identified very closely with their mothers and this variable turns out to be the best predictor of low aggression in the eighth grade (see Table 8). This finding illustrates the necessity for both longitudinal and multivariate study when attempting to specify cause and effect in a correlation design.

Thus far in this discussion the investigators have dealt primarily with the causal relation between television viewing and aggressive behavior. However, television variables also enter into other interesting relations both contemporaneous and longitudinal. The more hours the young adult watches television, the lower is his school achievement and peer-rated leadership. However, the direction of the antecedent-consequent relation cannot yet be stated, since the cross-lagged correlations that were available for the television-aggression relation are not at hand.

For the peer nomination of popularity, however, some of the ingredients for establishing such a relation exist. Figure 3 represents the correlations between peer-rated popularity and number of hours television is watched over a ten-year period. While there is no relation between the number of hours a child watches television in the third grade and his popularity at that time, a negative relationship does exist between his popularity in the third grade and the number of hours he watches television in the thirteenth grade. Furthermore, there is a negative relation between hours watched in the thirteenth grade and popularity at that time. Of course, a component of the relation between the measures of popularity is probably attributable to the temporal reliability of the measure. However, this would not explain the relations between popularity and television hours watched in the third or thirteenth grades. The child who is unpopular in the third grade tends to watch television more as he gets older and continues to be unpopular. Although it is undetermined at this time whether he is unpopular because he watches television or watches television because he is unpopular, there is no doubt that popularity at grade three is negatively related to television hours watched at grade thirteen and positively related to popularity at this grade.

In summary, therefore, it appears (for boys) that preference for a violent television diet in the third grade leads to aggressive behavior at that time and also in late adolescence. Furthermore, the third-grade child who is unpopular with his peers tends to spend more time watching television during adolescence. During late adolescence, the more unpopular he is the more time he devotes to television. However, the antecendent-consequent direction of this relation is undeterminate. Similarly unknown is the cause and effect direction in the negative relations between amount of time spent watching television and achievement variables.

## Aggression in childhood and adolescence

The relation of early aggression to aggression five and ten years later may appear to be a test reliability index rather than a stability of behavior index. The evidence available supports a stability of behavior interpretation of the correlations. The scores each time were based upon overlapping but different sets of raters, who were basing their ratings upon different observations. Some raters were rating the same classmates on two or three of the three rating occasions. Perhaps these raters were indeed influenced by their own memory of how they answered the questions on a single day five and/or ten years before, or perhaps their ratings stem from descriptive labels about each child which were learned by each classmate from his social group (teacher and peers). The latter notion, reminiscent of reputation, seems more substantial than the former. However, data from earlier studies of this peer rating measure (see Walder et al., 1961; Eron et al., 1971) suggest that, while reputation is a factor, the raters were responding to the rated child's behaviors in addition to any response to other people's descriptions of the rated child.

Writers about psychological measurement have been concerned with such issues as the role of method compared with content. Method refers to the form of the test or measuring device and the procedures for obtaining and calculating the score; content refers to the goal of the test maker—that, if measured, makes some call the test "valid." Feshbach (1970), for example, in his recent comprehensive review of aggression, states that peer nomination (or sociometric) techniques have adequate reliability and that initial reports concerning their validities as measures of overt aggressive tendencies have been encouraging. He then writes, "However, the predictive utility of sociometric, projective, and inventory measures is limited by the substantial method variance yielded by each procedure, and it is evident that the more dissimilar the test of aggression is to the aggression criterion, the weaker are the relationships obtained" (p. 181).

We have reported elsewhere (Eron et al., 1971) data which bear upon the above concern: (1) The application of Campbell and Fiske's multitrait, multimethod matrix to patterns of correlations demonstrated that the measuring devices of the authors yielded sufficient content variance. (2) The factor analytic studies of the investigators' peer rating, parent rating, and self rating questionnaire measures of aggressive and of other behaviors showed essentially the same results. (3) The relation of peer rating measures to performance on the *Iowa Aggression Machine* to such other independent events as clinical referral and the content of the clinical request, and to teacher ratings, revealed that the investigators had developed a psychometrically sound measure of important aggressive behaviors.

These data add support to claims we made in the past and make here once again that one can avoid undue method variance in comparison to content variance if the measures are built and/or selected with some care and sophistication. The present findings have demonstrated the relations between a variety of different types of measures representing different methods and different contents secured at different times. In this case the time spans are five and ten years during importan. development periods of childhood and adolescence. In point of fact, peer-rated aggression scores from the eighth grade related substantially to peer-rated aggression scores at the thirteenth grade; they also related just as substantially to self-ratings of aggression for both boys and girls. The pattern of relations does, of course, suggest that method variance accounts for part of the size of the correlations; the pattern also suggests that relations obtain across method and across content.

This finding in the thirteenth grade that self ratings relate to ratings by others was not found in the third grade (Walder et al., 1961). The study of third graders shows that self-ratings of several behaviors are positively intercorrelated in spite of different contents but are not related to scores on the same behaviors as rated by others. In the thirteenth grade at least, self-ratings of aggression relate to peer ratings of aggression. Perhaps the eight-year-old school child had not learned to describe himself as well as he had learned to describe others. Another possibility is that the testing conditions may have changed in that in the third grade the investigators were perhaps identified as being in league with the school; in the thirteenth grade this was obviously not so. A third possibility is that the youngster today, irrespective of his age or the testing conditions, is less inhibited in describing himself than even the same children were ten years ago. These possibilities require further tests.

## Aggression and psychopathology

Support for the hypothesis that aggression is a facet of psychopathology was partially afforded by the data. When a global measure of the MMPI—the number of clinical scales elevated above a T score of 70—was used as the criterion, aggression was unrelated. The partial correlation technique demonstrated that when aggression does appear to relate to the clinical scales it is really the component of scales 4 plus 9 which accounts for this relation. Since these scales are typically peaked or receive the highest codes in the profiles of delinquents (Dahlstrom and Welsh, 1960; Hathaway and Monachesi, 1961 and 1963), it seems that aggression as measured in its various aspects in the present study is a fair predictor of potential delinquency or socially maladaptive behavior. The synchronous correlations between measures of aggression and MMPI scales 4 plus 9 are fairly substantial. Although a small portion of the relation may be attributed to method variance between some of the measures, the nature of other measures makes this explanation less likely. For example, method variance would be less likely involved in the relation between peer nominations and scales 4 plus 9 or between scales 4 plus 9 and Total Aggressive Environment. The latter variable is one in which the subject reports on the extent of his experience with aggression.

Because of the pronounced sex differences in aggression which have been found in the present study as well as in other studies (Feshbach, 1970), the moderate correlations for girls between various concurrent measures of aggression and scales 4 plus 9 deserve further comment. Sex differences in aggression have been variously attributed to causes such as biological (Lorenz, 1966), biochemical-hormonal (Scott, 1963; Hamburg and Lunde, 1966; Harris and Levine, 1962), and child rearing-cultural (Sears, 1961; Montagu, 1968). These broad reasons are obviously not mutually exclusive, and the topic is highly polemical. The present findings strongly suggest that attitude also plays a role in the difference in aggression between males and females. The high as compared to the low aggressive girls have significantly higher scores on scale 5 of the MMPI, the measure of masculinity-feminity. A high score for girls suggests a masculine pattern of interests in work, sports, and hobbies (Pearson and Swenson, 1967). Significantly, peer nominations of aggression for girls also relate positively to the watching of contact sports—football, boxing, wrestling, hockey—on television. Thus, aggressive girls seem to have acquired masculine attitudes and interests. It seems pertinent, in this regard, to note that when scale 5 is high for males (i.e., in the feminine direction), the inhibition of manifest delinquent behavior is indicated (Dahlstrom and Welsh, 1960). Femininity and aggression thus appear to be antipodal qualities.

Previous studies concerning aggression and MMPI personality differences show no clear pattern. Magee (1964) found no difference between high and average aggressive boys on items selected from scale 4. Butcher (1965), on the other hand, found that high and low aggressive boys were more disturbed than those in the middle range of aggression. Lefkowitz (1966) found that delinquents who failed to adjust to institutionalization had significantly higher scores on scale 9 than delinquents who succeeded in adjusting. Scale 9 has been found to relate to delinquency in conjunction with scale 4.

In the present study, analyses of the 13 MMPI scales for subjects in the upper and lower quartiles of aggression at three age periods demonstrated that, although scales 4 and 9 have the largest relation to aggression, other scales were also involved. Generally, as the aggression and MMPI measures tend towards synchrony, the differences between high and low aggression groups become more pronounced. These findings are qualified by the marked negative relation of IQ to aggression. From the present analyses, therefore, it cannot be determined unequivocally whether MMPI differences are a function of differences in aggression or differences in IQ. However, the data are presented in this report as an empirical finding with the understanding that further analysis is required to control the possible effect of IQ on the MMPI scales. The literature addressed to this question (e.g., Dahlstrom and Welsh, 1960) suggests that the basic clinical scales are generally negatively related to IQ. An exception, but for males only, is the positive relation of scale 5 to IQ. Beyond an IQ of 65, the reliability of the MMPI seems to be unaffected by the intelligence of the subjects. In the current study, the relation between IQ and the MMPI scales was examined for certain of the comparisons. For the eighth-grade peer nominations, IQ is significantly higher for the low aggressive boys, but no differences at the acceptable statistical level emerge between MMPI scales. For girls, mean IQ for both groups is not different and again no MMPI differences occur. The greatest number and largest differences between groups occur when the ratings of aggression and MMPI were obtained concurrently, which is true for both boys and girls.

Evidence for the hypothesis that aggression is related to psychopathology is obtained from these data. For high as compared to low aggressive boys, scales 4, 6, 8, and 9 are significantly elevated. Scales 6, 8, and 9 are three of the four scales of the so-called psychotic tetrad designed to measure psychoticism. In addition, the level of elevation of the F-scale for this group is likely to be produced by psychotic and severely neurotic individuals (Dahlstrom and Welsh, 1960). Computation of the first two high points in the composite profile results in a 98 combination for the high aggressives. This code is often found in psychiatric populations. The 57 high points in the profile of the low aggressive boys seem clinically to be benign. For the high as compared to the low aggressive girls, the significantly elevated scales suggest that these subjects might behave in an antisocial aggressive or a sociopathic manner rather than in a psychotic fashion.

The MMPI differences between subjects who were rated consistently high or consistently low in aggression at grades three and thirteen were in the direction of the highs being significantly elevated on the scales indicating delinquent behavior or antisocial maladaptive behavior. Yet inspection of profiles within groups shows that the high aggressive boys evince a highly elevated 98 profile code suggestive of psychoticism, as compared to the 95 code of the low group. The mean and standard deviation of the F-scale for the high group suggests the presence in this group of individuals who are prone to admit to bizarre behavior. For the consistently high aggressive girls the results are similar. However the elevation of scores within profile is more within the normal range than is the case for high aggressive boys. These results are merely tentative and must be interpreted with caution because of the attenuation of the high aggressive subjects due to sampling bias (discussed in the section on method) and because of the differences in IQ.

When intellectual function as measured by school achievement is examined in relation to aggression, some evidence emerges that aggression is a maladaptive kind of behavior. This finding seems to be more salient for girls and may occur because girls are better school achievers than boys. Thus any variable which relates to achievement does so with greater strength. Although the measures of aggression were obtained prior to and after the measures of school achievement, the antecedent-consequent relationship between these two variables is difficult to determine. Obviously, high aggression could lead to low school achievement; or low achievement, as frustration, could produce high aggression. Other studies cited in Feshbach (1970) also have found that aggression is positively related to reading disability and underachievement for school children.

When the data are examined for aggressive behavior which is tangibly socially maladaptive, the evidence is only barely suggestive. Although more high aggressive boys were arrested on criminal charges than those in the low group, the conditions determining arrest are so confounded with social status, sex, population density and other variables that interpretation of these findings as support for the hypothesis is largely unwarranted. Yet it should be noted that a relation exists between third-grade aggression and residential mobility. Since the arrest data reported are exclusively for New York State, a tenable assumption is that the number of arrests in the high aggression group would be larger if data could have been obtained for those subjects who may have moved outside of New York State.

Within the limits of the restrictions on the interpretation of the data, aggression does seem to be related to maladaptive behavior. Notwithstanding the conservative evaluation of the findings, significant relationships occurred between various measures of aggression and indicators of psychopathology.

The relations discussed have appeared out of the context of a theoretically oriented study. Measures appropriate to sets of rationally selected variables were used at the three points in the subjects' lives which the investigators were able to study. In addition to making a deliberate search for relations of interest (e.g., television violence and aggressive behavior), the data speak for themselves through multivariate analytic techniques. In the current phase of this longitudinal study, as in the earlier phases, the approach which has used both deductive and inductive methods has supported and explicated the theory underlying this study.

The relevance of experience at the third grade, such as exposure to television violence, on aggressive behavior is noted not only at the age of exposure—as previously reported—but even more strongly at later ages. As a child develops his aggressive behaviors over the years, exposure to television violence seems to affect his experiences as victim and witness of aggression as well as his expression of aggression and antisocial acts. Aggression even seems to affect indices of psychopathology; e.g., MMPI scores. It also appears to relate to the subjects' educational and vocational achievements. As Berkowitz notes (1970), the expression of aggression appears to be self-stimulating: aggression may well beget further aggression.

## SUMMARY AND CONCLUSIONS

The present study is the third and final phase of a longitudinal investigation of the psychosocial development of aggressive behavior. The original study, begun in 1959-60, focused on 875 school children, the entire third grade in Columbia County, New York. The children were tested in groups in their classrooms; 713 of their mothers and 570 of their fathers were interviewed face-to-face, independently and in individual sessions. The primary goal of the study was to determine the extent of aggressive behavior at school and at home and to attempt to account for the variation in aggression by social, geographic, economic, and cultural factors. A second goal was to gain an understanding of how aggressive behavior is learned. This goal was approached by relating the ways in which children act out their aggression to the kinds of training in its expression and control they receive from various socializing agents, such as parents, teachers, and peers. A third aim was to determine the consistency of aggressive behavior across time by studying the same subjects at ages 13 and 19 in the eighth and twelfth grades, respectively. The major dependent variable was aggression as observed in the school situation, and the major class of independent variables was defined by parents' socializaton practices. This study is presented in detail in Eron et al. (1971). In accordance with the design, 252 of the original 875 children were tested in their eighth-grade classrooms in 1964-65.

Emerging from the study of the third graders was the somewhat unexpected finding that the exposure of boys to a violent television diet was related to peer nominations of aggression. A similar finding occurred for eighth graders using the same methods in another geographical region. Further exploration of these findings was a pivotal aim of the design of the ten-year followup phase.

The current project had three specific aims: to complete the longitudinal study of the psychosocial development of aggressive behavior for which data were collected in 1960 and 1965; to investigate the synchronous and longitudinal relationships between violence content in television and aggressive behavior on the part of the viewer; to examine the consequences of childhood aggression for functioning in late adolescence and young adulthood. Three hypotheses were investigated:

(1) When examined longitudinally, positive relationships obtain between violent television preferences and aggressive behavior;

(2) Early aggressive behavior is positively related to later aggressive behavior;

(3) Aggressive behavior is positively related to psychopathology.

Survey and assessment techniques were used to obtain data from as many as possible of the original 875 third-grade subjects. Current addresses were culled from various sources, and letters were sent to 735 (or 84 percent) of the original 875 subjects, inviting them to be interviewed. The letter explained the nature of the research, and each subject was offered $20 as an incentive to participate. Subjects were required to give two hours of their time: the first hour in an individual face-to-face interview and the second responding to written psychological tests.

Willingness to be interviewed was indicated by 460 former subjects. Of this number, 427 contributed data which could be compared across the ten-year span. Thus the ten-year followup sample was comprised of 211 boys and 216 girls. The modal age of this group was 19 years and the mean number of years of school completed was 12.57 ± .82. Based on current test scores the mean IQ was 109.12 ± 11.57. According to their father's occupation, the sample may be described as predominantly middle class. Sampling bias occurred in the ten-year followup phase, resulting in the attenuation of subjects in the upper quartile of third-grade aggression. Approximately twice as many subjects who were low in aggression as measured in the third grade consented to be interviewed in the thirteenth grade, as compared to subjects who were high in aggression in the third grade. In part the effect of such sampling bias was controlled statistically.

Peer nominations provided the primary measure of aggression for these thirteenth-grade subjects. With few changes, the peer nomination items were the same as used in the third- and eighth-grade studies. Self ratings and psychological tests provided secondary measures of aggression. Television diet was obtained from the interview, and the programs were rated for violence content by two judges, independently. A second violence rating developed in another study was also employed. Data on these 427 subjects were collected from six sources: peer nominations; individual face-to-face interviews; subjects' heights; psychological tests; school records yielding measures of IQ and standardized achievement test scores; and number of boys arrested in New York State who were in the upper and lower quartiles of aggression as measured in the third grade. A basic data set, comprised of 94 variables, was compiled. Included were 49 variables from the third-grade study, five variables from the eighth-grade study, and 40 variables from the current study. The data were analyzed within and across time periods by a variety of statistical procedures. Basic analyses were performed for each sex group and for the total.

The first hypothesis relating violent television programs to aggressive behavior was largely confirmed. The data suggest that a violent television diet is in fact a longitudinal antecedent of such behavior. The second hypothesis which related aggression at one stage of development to aggression at later stages was also largely confirmed. The data substantiated the hypothesis that aggression in childhood was a predictor of aggression in early and late adolescence. The third hypothesis, which stated that aggression was related to psychopathology, was only partially substantiated. High aggression impedes functioning and appears to be maladaptive. However, certain of the results were confounded with IQ and were therefore inconclusive. Further analyses of these data are required.

# Conclusions

The analyses performed on the data of the present study lead to these findings:

Aggressive behavior in early and late adolescence is predicatable from aggressive behavior in childhood. Peer nominations provide a highly reliable and valid measure of this behavior. Boys are substantially more aggressive than girls throughout the range of development. Highly aggressive girls possess "masculine" attitudes and interests. High aggression appears to be an intellectually, socially, and emotionally maladaptive form of behavior.

Early television preferences are unrelated to television preferences five and ten years later. Amount of television viewing is inversely related to measured intelligence and social educational accomplishments, whereas preferences for violent televison are unrelated to these variables. Judgment of the content of television as realistic is inversely related to measured intelligence.

Preference of boys for violent television fare at grade three, as reported by their parents, is related to the expression of aggressive behavior at that age. The relationship between aggressive behavior and preference at grade three for violent television fare is stronger longitudinally than synchronously. The relationship between violent television preference at grade three and aggressive behavior at grade 13 is moderately positive (.31), while the relationship between aggressive behavior at grade three and preference for violent television at grade 13 is near zero (.01), and the difference between these correlations is statistically significant. On the basis of these cross-lagged correlations, the most plausible single causal hypothesis would appear to be that preferring violent television fare in the third grade leads to the building of aggressive habits.

# FOOTNOTES

1. The investigators are indebted to the Surgeon General's Scientific Advisory Committee on Television and Social Behavior and to the New York State Department of Mental Hygiene for their support. Thanks are also due to Anne Karabin and Victor Pompa, New York State Department of Mental Hygiene, research assistants. Dr. Eron is on the faculty at the University of Illinois, Chicago Circle. Dr. Walder works with Behavioral Service Consultants, Inc., Greenbelt, Maryland. Dr. Huesmann is on the faculty at Yale University.
2. The original plan for followup in the twelfth grade was delayed because the investigators were unable to obtain funding until the subjects were one year older than planned.
3. The major findings of this survey of third-grade children and their parents are reported in the following papers: Eron, 1956, 1960, 1963; Eron, Banta, Walder, and Laulicht, 1961; Eron, Laulicht, Walder, Farber, and Spiegel, 1961; Eron and Walder, 1961; Eron, Walder, Toigo, and Lefkowitz, 1963; Eron et al., 1971; Lefkowitz, Walder, and Eron, 1963; Lefkowitz, 1962, 1964; Toigo, 1962, 1965; Toigo, Walder, Eron, and Lefkowitz, 1962; Walder et al., 1961; Walder, Eron, and Laulicht, 1957.
4. The investigators are indebted to Bert Pekowsky of NBC for obtaining these ratings.
5. Temporary staff consisted of two interviewers, one research assistant, and one secretary. The investigators are indebted to Marjorie Kline and Ann McAleer for their assistance in this study.
6. Thanks are due John Robinson.
7. Because of the large number of intercorrelations resulting from the analyses, only those coefficients reaching statistical significance at the .01 level of confidence or beyond for a two-tailed test were accepted as non-zero.
8. For convenience of presentation, the group of subjects tested in the ten-year followup study will be designated as thirteenth grade.
9. An attempt had been made to have the programs rated by local raters (school librarians) immediately after the data collection period. However, because of lack of resources and support previously noted, it was impossible to communicate personally with these raters or train them in the rating task. Thus we had little confidence in their ratings; indeed, superficial inspection of the ratings indicated that these raters were not familiar with the programs they rated.
10. It should be pointed out that these relations held only for boys. They do not apply to the girls in this sample, except for the relation between third-grade aggression and aggression ten years later. This correlation is even higher for girls than it is for boys.

11. The correlations reported in Table 3 and Figure 1 did not vary significantly when IQ and social status were held constant by partial correlation technique.
12. The specifics of the scores are available in Eron et al. (1971), which describes their construction in detail.

# REFERENCES

Bachman, J. G. *Youth in transition.* Institute for Social Research, University of Michigan, 1967.

Bandura, A., Ross, D., and Ross, S. A. Transmission of aggression through imitation of aggressive models. *Journal of Abnormal and Social Psychology,* 1961, **63,** 575-82.

Bandura, A., Ross, D., and Ross, S. A. Imitation of film mediated aggressive models. *Journal of Abnormal Psychology,* 1963a, **66,** 3-11.

Bandura, A., Ross, D., and Ross, S. Vicarious reinforcement and imitative learning. *Journal of Abnormal and Social Psychology,* 1963b, **67,** 601-07.

Berkowitz, L. Aggressive cues in aggressive behavior and hostility catharis, *Psychological Review,* 1964, **71,** 104-22.

Berkowitz, L. Experimental investigations of hostility catharsis. *Journal of Consulting and Clinical Psychology,* 1970, **35,** 1-7.

Berkowitz, L., Corwin, R., and Heironimus, M. Film violence and subsequent aggressive tendencies. *Public Opinion Quarterly,* 1963, **27,** 217-29.

Berkowitz, L., and Rawlings, E. Effects of film violence on inhibitions against subsequent aggression. *Journal of Abnormal and Social Psychology,* 1963, **66,** 405-12.

Bryan, J. H., and Schwartz, T. Effects of film material upon children's behavior. *Psychological Bulletin,* 1971, **75 (1),** 50-59.

Butcher, J. Manifest aggression: MMPI correlates in normal boys. *Journal of Consulting Psychology,* 1965, **29,** 446-54.

Cattell, R. B. *The scientific analysis of personality.* Baltimore: Penguin Books, 1965.

Dahlstrom, W. G., and Welsh, G. S. *An MMPI handbook.* Minneapolis: University of Minnesota Press, 1960.

Darlington, R. D. Multiple regression in psychological research and practice. *Psychological Bulletin,* 1968, **69,** 161-82.

Dollard, J., Doob, L. W., Miller, N. E., Mowrer, O. H., and Sears, R. R. *Frustration and aggression.* New Haven: Yale University Press, 1939.

Eron, L. D. Social and cultural factors in mental illness. *Proceedings of the Rip Van Winkle Clinic,* 1956, **7,** No. 2, 16-38.

Eron, L. D. *Psychosocial development of aggressive behavior.* Progress Report, Project M1726, U.S.P.H.S., May 15, 1960.

Eron, L. D. Relationship of TV viewing habits and aggressive behavior in children. *Journal of Abnormal and Social Psychology*, 1963, **67**, 193-96.

Eron, L. D., Banta, T. J., Walder, L. O., and Laulicht, J. H. Comparison of data obtained from mothers and fathers on child rearing practices and their relation to child aggression. *Child Development*, 1961, **32**, 457-72.

Eron, L. D., Laulicht, J. H., Walder, L. O., Farber, I. E., and Spiegel, J. P. Application of role and learning theories to the study of the development of aggression in children. *Psychological Reports*, 1961, **9**, 291-334, (Monograph Supplement 2-V 9 1961).

Eron, L. D., and Walder, L. O. Test burning: 11. *American Psychologist*, 1963, **166**, 237-44.

Eron, L. D., Walder, L. O., and Lefkowitz, M. M. *The learning of aggression in children.* Boston: Little, Brown, 1971.

Eron, L. D., Walder, L. O., Tiogo, R., and Lefkowitz, M. M. Social class, parental punishment for aggression and child aggression. *Child Development*, 1963, **34**, 849-67.

Feshbach, S. Aggression. In P. H. Mussen (Ed.), *Carmichael's Manual of Child Psychology* (3rd Ed.), Vol. 2, New York: Wiley, 1970, Pp. 159-250.

Feshbach, S., and Singer, R. D. *Television and Aggression.* San Francisco: Jossey-Bass, 1971.

Flanagan, J. C., Davis, F. B., Dailey, J. T., Shaycoft, M. F., Orr, D. B., Goldberg, I., and Neyman, C. A. *Project Talent: The identification, development and utilization of human talents. The American high school student* (Final Report to U. S. Office of Education, Project No. 635). Pittsburgh: University of Pittsburgh Project Talent Office, 1964.

Goodenough, F., and Tyler, L. *Developmental psychology.* New York: Appleton-Century-Crofts, 1959.

Greenberg, B. S., and Gordon, T. F. Critics and public perceptions of violence in TV programs. Michigan State University: Department of Communication, 1970.

Hamburg, D. A., and Lunde, D. T. Sex hormones in the development of sex differences in human behavior. In E. E. Maccoby (ed.), *The development of sex differences.* Stanford, Calif.: Stanford University Press, 1966.

Hathaway, S. R., and McKinley, J. C. *The Minnesota Multiphasic Personality Inventory.* New York: The Psychological Corporation, 1969.

Hathaway, S. R., and Monachesi, E. D. *An atlas of juvenile MMPI profiles.* Minneapolis: University of Minnesota Press, 1961.

Hathaway, S. R., and Monachesi, E. D. *Adolescent personality and behavior.* Minneapolis: University of Minnesota Press, 1963.

Holtzman, W. H., Thorpe, J. S., Swartz, J. D., and Herron, W. E. *Ink-blot perception and personality.* Austin: University of Texas Press, 1961.

Lange, D. L., Baker, R. K., and Ball, S. J. Sampling procedures used in the Harris Poll (Appendix III-I). In *Violence and the media,* Vol. 9. A Report to the National Commision on the Causes and Prevention of Violence. Washington, D.C., United States Government Printing Office, 1969.

Lefkowitz, M. M. Some relationships between sex role preference of children and other parent child variables. *Psychological Reports,* 1962, **10,** 43-53.

Lefkowitz, M. M. Aggression and size of human figure drawings. *Psychology in the Schools,* 1964, **3,** 312-14.

Lefkowitz, M. M. MMPI scores of juvenile delinquents adjusting to institutionalization. *Psychological Reports,* 1966, **19,** 911-14.

Lefkowitz, M. M. Screening juvenile delinquents for psychopathology by use of the Z-test. *Journal of Projective Techniques & Personality Assessment,* 1968, **32,** 5, 475-78.

Lefkowitz, M. M., Walder, L. O., and Eron, L. D. Punishment, identification and aggression. *Merrill Palmer Quarterly of Behavior and Development,* 1963, **9,** 159-74.

Lorenz, K. *On aggression.* New York: Harcourt, Brace and World, 1966.

Magee, R. D. Correlates of aggressive-defiant classroom behavior in elementary school boys: A factor analytic study. *Dissertation Abstracts,* 1964, **2 (25),** 1340-41.

Montagu, M.F.A. The new litany of "innate depravity", or original sin revisited. In M.F. Ashley Montagu (Ed.), *Man and Aggression,* New York: Oxford University Press, 1968, 3-17.

Nunnally, J. C. *Psychometric theory.* New York: McGraw Hill, 1967.

Pearson, J. S., and Swenson, W. M. *A user's guide to the Mayo Clinic Automated MMPI Program.* New York: The Psychological Corporation, 1967.

Rozelle, R. M., and Campbell, D. T. More plausible rival hypotheses in the cross-lagged pause correlation technique. *Psychological Bulletin,* 1969, **71,** 74-79.

Scott, J. P. *Animal behavior.* Garden City, New York: Doubleday, 1963.

Sears, R. R. Relation of early socialization experiences to aggression in middle childhood. *Journal of Abnormal and Social Psychology,* 1961, **63,** 461-92.

Semler, I. J., and Eron, L. D. Replication Report: Relationship of aggression in third grade children to certain pupil characteristics. *Psychology in the Schools,* 1967, **4,** 356-58.

Semler, I. J., Eron, L. D., Meyerson, L. J., and Williams, J. F. Relationship of aggression in third grade children to certain pupil characteristics. *Psychology in the Schools,* 1967, **4,** 85-88.

Stroo, A. A. De relatie tussen agressie bij kinderen van ± 8 jaar en opvoedingsmethoden van moeders. Doctoraaiscriptie, Vrije Universiteit, Amsterdam, 1970.

Toigo, R. Parental social status as a contextual and individual determinant of aggressive behavior among third-grade children in the classroom situation. Unpublished doctoral dissertation, Columbia University, 1962.

Toigo, R. Social status and schoolroom aggression in third-grade children. *Genetic Psychology Monographs*, 1965, **71**, 221-63.

Toigo, R., Walder, L. O., Eron, L. D., and Lefkowitz, M. M. Examiner effect in the use of a near sociometric procedure in the third grade classroom. *Psychological Reports*, 1962, **11**, 785-90.

Walder, L. O., Abelson, R., Eron, L. D., Banta, T. J., and Laulicht, J. H. Development of a peer-rating measure of aggression. *Psychological Reports*, 1961, **9**, 497-556, (Monographs Supplement, 4-49).

Walder, L. O., Eron, L. D., and Laulicht, J. H. Manual of procedures in study of aggression. *Proceedings of the Rip Van Winkle Clinic*, 1957, **8**, 1-30.

Walters, R. H., and Zak, M. S. Validation studies of an aggression scale. *Journal of Psychology*, 1959, **47**, 209-18.

Warner, W. L., Meeker, M., and Eells, K. *Social class in America*. New York: Harcourt Brace, 1960.

Williams, J. F., Meyerson, L. J., Eron, L. D., and Semler, I. J. Peer-rated aggression and aggressive responses elicited in an experimental situation. *Child Development*, 1967, **38**, 181-90.

Winer, B. J. *Statistical principles in experimental design*. New York: McGraw-Hill, 1962.

Zulliger, H. *The Zulliger Individual and Group Test*. New York: International Universities Press, 1969.

# Appendix A:
# Invitational Letters

## 1.　Letter to superintendents

May 1970

Dear

You may recall that in 1960 the Rip Van Winkle Foundation, then located in Hudson, New York, began a longitudinal study of the psychosocial development of aggressive behavior of all third grade school children in Columbia County. (The results of this research will shortly be published by Little, Brown & Co. in a book entitled "The Learning of Aggression in Children.") A ten year follow-up in two phases was anticipated and in 1965 the research team again collected data from these children in a number of the schools in the county. Completion of the final phase of the study is planned for this year.

The subjects of this study are now approximately 19 years old and no longer in the public school system. The research team, comprised of Leonard Eron, Leopold Walder, and myself as Principal Investigator, plans to interview as many of the original subjects as possible. Carried out under the aegis of the New York State Department of Mental Hygiene, this last phase of the project is supported by the Surgeon General's Scientific Advisory Committee on Television and Social Behavior of the United States Department of Health Education and Welfare.

Appreciative of your full cooperation in the past, we would like, once again, to enlist your aid in bringing this longitudinal study to completion. Our immediate needs are for address lists of these former students, class rosters, and certain information from school records. As in our past research, the anonymity of all subjects is guaranteed—our sole interest being the statistical relationships among groups. I would like to plan a visit with you in the near future to discuss the final phase of this project in greater detail and will call you soon to arrange for an appointment.

Sincerely,

Monroe M. Lefkowitz, Ph. D.
Principal Research Scientist

# 2.   Initial letter to subjects

May 1970

Dear

About ten years ago you were in the third grade in Columbia County. At that time you participated in a study on the development of behavior conducted by the Rip Van Winkle Foundation. The study was intended as a ten year follow-up and it is now time for completion. An interview with you is required to complete the study. We estimate the interview will take about two hours of your time. Within a week after the interview you will receive a check for $20 from our business office. The $20 will pay for the time you have devoted to this important scientific study. The interview will be conducted at our field office in Hudson, New York, at 414 Union Street (across from Court Square and next to the post office).

Briefly the interview will deal with background material on yourself, television preferences, and questions about your behavior and attitudes. This is a study of developing behavior in young people. It has been deemed of vital importance by the United States Surgeon General's Office and is supported by the National Institute of Mental Health. We are asking for your continued participation.

We would greatly appreciate it if you would complete the enclosed form and return it in the stamped addressed envelope indicating your intention to participate. Please return the form even if you do not wish to participate. Should you have any further questions, please call or write to me at the numbers or address below.

Sincerely,

Monroe M. Lefkowitz, Ph. D.
Principal Investigator

# 3.   Followup letter to subjects

July 1970

Dear

Several weeks ago we wrote to you about a study in which you participated when you were in the third grade. In that letter we stated that this study was intended as a ten-year follow-up of how behavior develops and that an interview with you was required to complete the study.

Since we have not heard from you—perhaps the original letter did not come to your attention—we would like to offer you a second invitation to appear for an interview. We estimate the interview will take about two hours of your time. Within a week after the interview, you will receive a check for $20 from our business office. The $20 will pay for the time you have devoted to this important scientific study. The interview will be conducted at our Field Office in Hudson, New York, at 414 Union Street (across from Court House Square and next to the Post Office).

We would greatly appreciate it if you would complete the enclosed form and return it in the stamped, addressed envelope indicating your intention to participate. It is important that you return the form even if you do not wish to participate so that we can close our records.

Sincerely yours,

Monroe M. Lefkowitz, Ph.D.
Principal Investigator

# 4.   Subject's response form

# _____

I am interested in participating

_____                    _____
Yes                                           No

### Please Print

Name:

Address:

Phone:

Today's date:

Best time to be called for appointment _____

## PLEASE RETURN THIS FORM EVEN IF YOU DO NOT WISH TO PARTICIPATE

Hudson Field Unit Office
414 Union Street
Hudson, New York   12534
Tel: 828-3707 or 828-3860

# 5.  Second request

\#  _____

I am interested in participating

_____          _____

Yes                          No

Please Print

Name:

Address:

Phone:

Today's date:

Best time to be called for appointment _____

### PLEASE RETURN THIS FORM EVEN IF YOU DO NOT WISH TO PARTICIPATE

Hudson Field Unit Office
414 Union Street
Hudson, New York   12534
Tel: 828-3707 or 828-3860

# Appendix B: Interview

## 1970 Questionnaire: Follow Up Study of Behavior in Columbia County, New York
## FACE SHEET

Name _____

          Last                 First            Middle

If married woman, maiden name _____

Address _____

Phone_____

Date of Interview _____

                Month           Day          Year

Interviewer _____

Time started _____

## Peer Rating Questions

What schools did you attend for each of the grades after grade 3?

| Grade | School | |
|-------|--------|---|
| 4 | _____ | _____ |
| 5 | _____ | _____ |
| 6 | _____ | _____ |
| 7 | _____ | _____ |
| 8 | _____ | _____ |
| 9 | _____ | _____ |
| 10 | _____ | _____ |
| 11 | _____ | _____ |
| 12 | _____ | _____ |

Any other schooling?

_____     _____

_____     _____

_____     _____

GIVE *S* THE LISTS (FROM FEEDER SCHOOLS) OF THE LAST COLUMBIA COUNTY SCHOOL HE ATTENDED

"Ten years ago, when you were in the third grade, you answered a series of questions about yourself and about your classmates. I would like your cooperation in answering a similar series of questions.

"I have lists of people who might have gone to school with you. GIVE FEEDER SCHOOL LISTS TO S Put a check in the box next to the names of the people you know well enough to answer some questions about. Generally, these would be people who had been in class with you. You might remember the way they acted in school.

"S MARKS NAMES. IF S SAYS "I DON'T KNOW ANYONE," CHECK ANSWERS TO PAGE 2 AND THE APPROPRIATENESS OF THE PACKET OF FEEDER SCHOOLS

"I shall ask you questions, one at a time. For each question, tell me the identification numbers of all those people who fit that question. Do not name yourself for any of these questions. You may name any number of people for each question. Notice that to these questions there are no answers that are right for everybody. Base your answers on what you last knew of each person from personal observation and contact.

"START WITH 03. IF S RESPONDS WITH ONLY ONE NAME, SAY You may give any number of answers. You may check more names if you think of them as I ask the questions."

## Peer Rating Record Form

00. Whom do you know? _____

03. Whom did you like to sit next to in class? _____

04. Who did not listen to the teacher? _____

09. Who was very quiet? _____

11. Who did things that bothered others? _____

19. Who used to say "excuse me" even when they did not do anything bad? _____

12. Who started fights over nothing? _____

21. Who would never fight even when picked on? _____

14. Who was always getting into trouble? _____

82. Who made up stories and lies to get other students into trouble? ____

16. Who used to say mean things? _____

35. Who pushed or shoved students? _____

36. Who took other students' things without asking? _____

87. Who gave dirty looks or made unfriendly gestures to other students? _____

88. Who was a leader of a club or a group? _____

37. Who were the students that you would like to have had for your best friends? _____

PR 1. Who are the students who have moved out of the School District? For each, tell me where they have moved to.

<u>SUBJECT NUMBER</u>        <u>TO WHERE MOVED</u>

IND. 3. What is your birthdate? _____

                           month       day       year

FAS 4. What is your marital status?
1. single
2. married
3. separated
4. annulled
5. divorced
6. widowed
7. other (specify)

FAS 5. (IF MARRIED) How Long have you been married?
0. less than 1 year
1. 1 to 2 years
2. 2 to 3 years
3. more than 3 years
99. DNA

FAS 6. (IF MARRIED) Do you have any children?
0. none
1. one
2. two
3. three
4. more than 3
99. DNA

ASP 7. What is the greatest amount of education you expect to have during your life?
1. less than high school
2. completion of high school
3. vocational or business school
4. junior college
5. 4 year college degree
6. graduate education

ASP  8.  How well off financially do you  1. barely able to make a
         expect to be in your lifetime?        living
                                            2. able to provide the
         READ ALTERNATIVES                      necessities
                                            3. comfortable
                                            4. well-to-do
                                            5. wealthy
                                            6. extremely wealthy


ASP  9.  What kind of work do you
         expect to be doing ten years
         from now? OBTAIN SPECIF-
         IC OCCUPATION, E.G.,
         TEACHER, TRUCKDRIV-
         ER, SMALL BUSINESS
         OWNER, ETC.

HOC 10.  How many people live in the    2. two
         home in which you grew up?      3. three
         Include yourself, brothers,     4. four
         sisters, parents, relatives,    5. five
         boarders, roomers, servants,    6. six
         etc.                            7. seven
                                         8. eight
                                         9. nine
                                        10. ten
                                        11. eleven
                                        12. twelve
                                        13. thirteen or more


ISS  12.  What kind of work do you do in your full time occupation?
          (Do not include summer-only jobs.) OBTAIN SPECIFIC
          OCCUPATION, E.G., TEACHER, TRUCKDRIVER,
          SMALL BUSINESS OWNER, ETC. E WRITES DETAILS
          OF OCCUPATION AND CODES LATER


                                            _____
                                                        CODE


ISS  13.  What kind of work does your father (or male head of house-
          hold) do in his major occupation? If he works (or has
          worked) on more than one job, tell me the one on which he
          spends (or spent) most of his time? OBTAIN SPECIFIC
          OCCUPATION, E.G., TEACHER, TRUCKDRIVER,

SMALL BUSINESS OWNER, ETC. *E* WRITES DETAILS OF OCCUPATION AND CODES LATER.

CODE

ISS 14. What kind of work does your mother (or female head of household) do in her major occupation? If she is a housewife in addition to outside work, tell me about her outside work. IN THIS CASE, *E* CODES ONLY THE OUTSIDE WORK. If she works on more than one outside job, tell me the most important one. If she is now out of work, or if she is retired or not living, tell me the one she did last. OBTAIN SPECIFIC OCCUPATION. E.G., TEACHER, TRUCKDRIVER, SMALL BUSINESS OWNER, ETC. *E* WRITES DETAILS OF OCCUPATION AND CODES LATER.

CODE

ISS 16. Which of the following best describes your family's finances?

READ ALTERNATIVES

1. barely able to make a living
2. have the necessities
3. comfortable
4. well-to-do
5. wealthy
6. extremely wealthy

ISS 17. How many books are in your home?

READ ALTERNATIVES

1. none, or very few (0-10)
2. a few books (11-25)
3. one bookcase full (26-100)
4. two bookcases full (101-250)
5. three or four bookcases full (251-500)
6. a room full - a library (501 or more)

ISS 18. How many rooms are in your home? Count all rooms; bedrooms, bathrooms, kitchen, living room, dining room, recreation room, enclosed porch, etc.

_____ (please write in)

REL 19. How often do you attend church?

0. never
1. a few times a year
2. about once a month
3. few times a month
4. once a week
5. more than once a week

REL 20. Would you mind telling me your religion?

(write response)_____

1. Protestant
2. Catholic
3. Jewish
4. Greek Orthodox
5. Greek Catholic
6. Other

## IN PUN ITEMS SEX OF ADULT AND OF CHILD IS SAME AS SEX OF S.

"We would like to learn something about your ideas for raising children. Imagine that you are the father (mother) of an eight year old boy (girl) and try to answer the following questions accordingly."

PUN 21. If you saw your son (daughter) grab things from another child, would you tell him (her) that young men (ladies) don't do this sort of thing?

0. no
1. yes
98. DK

PUN 22. If you saw your son (daughter) grab things from another child, would you say, "I would like to be proud of you."?

0. no
1. yes
98. DK

PUN 23. Would you make your son (daughter) apologize if he (she) grabbed things from another child?

0. no
1. yes
98. DK

PUN 24. Would you tell your son (daughter) you don't love him (her) for grabbing things from another child?

0. no
1. yes
98. DK

PUN 25. Would you point out how some close friend of his (hers) behaves better than your son (daughter) does, if he (she) grabbed things from another child?

0. no
1. yes
98. DK

PUN 26. If you saw your son (daughter) grab things from another child, would you *not* let him (her) play with his (her) friends for two days?

0. no
1. yes
98. DK

*INSTRUCTIONS TO RESPONDENT:* "I am going to read a number of statements to you. For each one I would like you to tell me if you agree or disagree."

RAG 27. There are two kinds of people in this world: the weak and the strong.

1. disagree
2. agree

RAG 28. Dealing with policemen and government officials is always unpleasant.

1. disagree
2. agree

RAG 29. Most people get killed in accidents because of their own reckless driving.

1. disagree
2. agree

RAG 30. Horses that don't pull should be beaten and kicked.

1. disagree
2. agree

RAG　31.　At times we enjoy being hurt by those we love.

1. disagree
2. agree

RAG　32.　Many a decent fellow becomes a crook or a criminal because he can't stand to be pushed around so much.

1. disagree
2. agree

RAG　33.　I easily lose patience with people.

1. disagree
2. agree

RAG　34.　I often do things that I regret afterwards.

1. disagree
2. agree

RAG　35.　It makes me mad when I can't do things for myself the way I like to.

1. disagree
2. agree

RAG　36.　Occasionally I was in trouble with the police or law.

1. disagree
2. agree

RAG　37.　I almost never dare to express anger toward people for fear I may lose their love or approval.

1. disagree
2. agree

RAG　38.　As a young kid I often mixed with the wrong crowd.

1. disagree
2. agree

VAG　39.　Have you ever been slapped or kicked by another person?

0. No or not sure

IF YES: How many times would you estimate that this has happened to you?

1. once
2. twice
3. three times
4. four or more times
98. not sure

VAG   40.   Have you ever been punched            0. No or not
            or beaten by another person?       sure

            IF YES: How many times             1. once
            would you estimate that this       2. twice
            has happened to you?               3. three times
                                               4. four or more times
                                              98. Not sure

VAG   41.   Have you ever been choked            0. No or not
            by another person?                 sure

            IF YES: How many times             1. once
            would you estimate that this       2. twice
            has happened to you?               3. three times
                                               4. four or more times
                                              98. Not sure

VAG   42.   Have you ever been threat-           0. No or not
            ened or actually cut by some-      sure
            body using a knife?

            IF YES: How many times             1. once
            would you estimate that this       2. twice
            has happened to you?               3. three times
                                               4. four or more times
                                              98. not sure

VAG   43.   Have you ever been threat-           0. No or not
            ened with a gun or shot at?        sure

            IF YES: How many times             1. once
            would you estimate that this       2. twice
            has happened to you?               3. three times
                                               4. four or more times
                                              98. not sure

WAG   44.   Have you ever seen another person slapped or kicked?

0. No or not sure

IF YES: How many times would you estimate that you have seen another person slapped or kicked?

1. once
2. twice
3. three times
4. four or more times
98. not sure

WAG   45.   Have you ever seen another person punched or beaten?

0. No or not sure

IF YES: How many times would you estimate that you have seen another person punched or beaten?

1. once
2. twice
3. three times
4. four or more times
98. not sure

WAG   46.   Have you ever seen another person choked:

0. No or not sure

IF YES: How many times would you estimate that you have seen another person choked?

1. once
2. twice
3. three times
4. four or more times
98. not sure

WAG   47.   Have you ever seen another person threatened or actually cut with a knife?

0. No or not sure

IF YES: How many times would you estimate that you have seen another threatened or actually cut with a knife?

1. once
2. twice
3. three times
4. four or more times
98. not sure

WAG   48.   Have you ever seen another person threatened with a gun or shot at?

0. No or not sure

IF YES: How many times would you estimate that you have seen another person threatened by a gun or shot at?

1. once
2. twice
3. three times
4. four or more times
98. not sure

## IN PUN ITEMS SEX OF ADULT AND OF CHILD IS SAME AS SEX OF S.

"Imagine again that you are the father (mother) of an eight year old boy (girl) and try to answer the following questions accordingly."

PUN 49. If you heard your son (daughter) say mean things to another child, would you tell him (her) in a nice way to act differently?

0. no
1. yes
98. DK

PUN 50. If you heard your son (daughter) say mean things to another child, would you say, "Get on that chair and don't move until you apologize."?

0. no
1. yes
98. DK

PUN 51. Would you *not* let your son (daughter) play with his (her) friends for two days if you heard him (her) say mean things to another child?

0. no
1. yes
98. DK

PUN 52. If you heard your son (daughter) say mean things to another child, would you point out how some close friends of his (her) behave better than he (she) does?

0. no
1. yes
98. DK

PUN 53. If you heard your son (daughter) say mean things to another child, would you wash out his (her) mouth with soap?

0. no
1. yes
98. DK

PUN   54.   If you heard your son
            (daughter) say mean things to
            another child, would you
            say, "I would like to be
            proud of you."?

0. no
1. yes
98. DK


RAG   55.   Have you ever spanked a
            child?

0. No or not sure

            IF YES: How many times
            would you estimate that you
            have done this?

1. once
2. twice
3. three times
4. four or more times
98. not sure


RAG   56.   Have you ever slapped or
            kicked another person?

0. No or not sure

            IF YES: How many times
            would you estimate that you
            have done this?

1. once
2. twice
3. three times
4. four or more times
98. not sure


RAG   57.   Have you ever punched or
            beaten another person?

0. No or not sure

            IF YES: How many times
            would you estimate that you
            have done this?

1. once
2. twice
3. three times
4. four or more times
98. not sure


Getting ahead in your job or place in the community sometimes means
that you have to do certain things you may not like. How willing would
you be to do each of the following things in order to get ahead?

ASP 58. How willing would you be to
learn new skills in order to get
ahead?
READ ALTERNATIVES TO *S*

1. not at all willing
2. a little willing
3. somewhat willing
4. very willing
98. DK

ASP 59. How willing would you be to
leave your friends to get
ahead?

READ ALTERNATIVES TO *S*

1. not at all willing
2. a little willing
3. somewhat willing
4. very willing
98. DK

ASP 60. How willing would you be to
move around the country a lot to get
ahead?

READ ALTERNATIVES TO *S*

1. not at all willing
2. a little willing
3. somewhat willing
4. very willing
98. DK

ASP 61. How willing would you be to
take on more responsibility in
order to get ahead?

READ ALTERNATIVES TO *S*

1. not at all willing
2. a little willing
3. somewhat willing
4. very willing
98. DK

ASP 62. How willing would you be to
give up spare time in order to
get ahead?

READ ALTERNATIVES TO *S*

1. not at all willing
2. a little willing
3. somewhat willing
4. very willing
98. DK

IN PUN ITEMS SEX OF ADULT AND OF CHILD IS SAME AS SEX
OF *S*.

"Imagine again that you are the father (mother) of an eight year old
boy (girl) and try to answer the following questions accordingly."

PUN 63. If your son (daughter) were rude to you, would you tell him (her), "I will give you something you like if you act differently."?

0. no
1. yes
98. DK

PUN 64. If your son (daughter) were rude to you, would you wash out his (her) mouth with soap?

0. no
2. yes
98. DK

PUN 65. Would you remind your son (daughter) of what others will think of him (her) if he (she) were rude to you?

0. no
1. yes
98. DK

PUN 66. If your son (daughter) were rude to you, would you say, "Get on that chair and don't move until you apologize."?

0. no
1. yes
98. DK

PUN 67. Would you tell your son (daughter) that young men (ladies) don't do this sort of thing—if he (she) were rude to you?

0. no
1. yes
98. DK

PUN 68. Would you spank your son (daughter) until he (she) cries —if he (she) were rude to you?

0. no
1. yes
98. DK

## PROFILE IDENTIFICATION - PID - INSTRUCTIONS

REMOVE THIS PAGE AND HAND QUESTIONNAIRE TO *S*

We are interested in finding out how you do certain things such as walking, talking, and so forth. On the sheet of paper before you is a list of things described by sets of opposite words. Between each pair of words are five steps, or grades, ranging from one way of doing something to its opposite. I would like you to rate yourself for each type of activity, such as walking, talking, etc., by placing a check mark on one of the steps on each line. Notice that the closer you place your check mark to either of the opposite words, the more it means you act the way the word says.

Please try the example. If I were to ask you how you like your coffee, how would you place your check marks?

IF *S* GIVES ONLY EXTREME RESPONSES ON EXAMPLES, SAY:

You showed that you liked your coffee very hot/cold. How would you place your check mark if you wanted your coffee just a little less hot/cold?

*(AFTER EXAMPLE IS COMPLETED)* Thank you, would you please complete the list.

SCAN PID FOR COMPLETION OF EACH ITEM AND THEN RE-TRIEVE QUESTIONNAIRE.

| PID | | I walk | | | |
|---|---|---|---|---|---|
| fast | —— | —— | —— | —— | slow |
| loud | —— | —— | —— | —— | soft |
| often | —— | —— | —— | —— | not often |

| | | I talk | | | |
|---|---|---|---|---|---|
| slow | •—— | —— | —— | —— | fast |
| soft | —— | —— | —— | —— | loud |
| not often | —— | —— | —— | —— | often |

| | | I stand | | | |
|---|---|---|---|---|---|
| straight | —— | —— | —— | —— | lean forward |
| at ease | —— | —— | —— | —— | firm |

| | | I eat | | | |
|---|---|---|---|---|---|
| much | —— | —— | —— | —— | little |
| fast | —— | —— | —— | —— | slow |

| | | I write | | | |
|---|---|---|---|---|---|
| slow | —— | —— | —— | —— | fast |
| small | —— | —— | —— | —— | large |
| heavy | —— | —— | —— | —— | light |

| | | My body is | | | |
|---|---|---|---|---|---|
| light | —— | —— | —— | —— | dark |
| tall | —— | —— | —— | —— | short |
| thick | —— | —— | —— | —— | thin |
| hard | —— | —— | —— | —— | soft |
| strong | —— | —— | —— | —— | weak |

| | | I like coffee | | | |
|---|---|---|---|---|---|
| hot | —— | —— | —— | —— | cold |
| light | —— | —— | —— | —— | dark |
| sweet | —— | —— | —— | —— | not sweet |

PRESENT TO S

TEL 69. Here is a list of possible reasons for watching television. When you watch T. V., how often does each of these reasons apply to you? Is it USUALLY one of your reasons, OCCASIONALLY a reason, RARELY, or NEVER?

| REASON | Check the appropriate box for each reason | | | |
|---|---|---|---|---|
| | 3 USUALLY | 2 OCCASION-ALLY | 1 RARELY | 0 NEVER |
| .01 I watch to see a special program I've heard a lot about | | | | |
| .02 I watch because there is nothing else to do at the time | | | | |
| .03 I watch to get away from the ordinary cares and problems of the day | | | | |
| .04 I turn on the set just to "keep me company" when I'm alone | | | | |
| .05 I watch because I think I can learn something | | | | |
| .06 I watch because I'm afraid I might be missing something good | | | | |
| .07 I watch so I can talk later to my friends about the show | | | | |
| .08 I start on one show and can't leave the T.V. for the rest of the evening | | | | |
| .09 I watch just for "background" while I am doing something else | | | | |
| .10 I watch mainly to be sociable when others are watching | | | | |
| .11 I watch to see a specific program that I enjoy very much | | | | |

PRESENT TO *S*

TEL  70.  Here is a list of weekly programs that are on network television during the evening.

Circle each program that you have seen all the way through TEN times or more since January 1, 1970. (Each program has been on about 15 weeks.)

Monday

| | | |
|---|---|---|
| *Gunsmoke* | *My World/Welcome* | *It Takes a Thief* |
| *Here's Lucy* | *Laugh-In* | *ABC Monday Movie* |
| *Mayberry RFD* | *Monday Movies* | |
| *Doris Day* | | |
| *Carol Burnett* | | |

Tuesday

| | | |
|---|---|---|
| *Lancer* | *I Dream of Jeannie* | *Mod Squad* |
| *Red Skelton* | *Debbie Reynolds* | *Movie of the Week* |
| *Governor and J.J.* | *Julia* | *Marcus Welby, M.D.* |
| *Sixty Minutes* | *Tuesday Movies* | |

Wednesday

| | | |
|---|---|---|
| *Hee Haw* | *The Virginian* | *Nanny and the Professor* |
| *Beverly Hillbillies* | *Kraft Music Hall* | *Courtship of Eddie's Father* |
| *Medical Center* | *Then Came Bronson* | *Room 222* |
| *Hawaii Five-O* | | *Johnny Cash* |
| | | *Engelbert Humperdinck* |

Thursday

| | | |
|---|---|---|
| *Family Affair* | *Daniel Boone* | *Pat Paulson 1/2 Comedy Hour* |
| *Jim Nabors* | *Ironside* | *That Girl* |
| *Thursday Movie* | *Dragnet* | *Betwitched* |
| | *Dean Martin* | *Tom Jones* |
| | | *Paris 7000* |

Friday

| | | |
|---|---|---|
| *Get Smart* | *High Chaparral* | *Flying Nun* |
| *Tim Conway* | *Name of the Game* | *Brady Bunch* |
| *Hogan's Heroes* | *Bracken's World* | *Ghost and Mrs. Muir* |
| *Friday Movie* | | *Here Come the Brides* |
| | | *Love, American Style* |

Saturday

| | | |
|---|---|---|
| *Jackie Gleason* | *Andy Williams* | *Let's Make a Deal* |
| *My Three Sons* | *Adam-12* | *Newlywed Game* |
| *Green Acres* | *Saturday Movie* | *Lawrence Welk* |
| *Petticoat Junction* | | *Hollywood Palace* |
| *Mannix* | | *Cesar's World* |

Sunday

| | | |
|---|---|---|
| *Lassie* | *Marlin Perkins* | *Land of the Giants* |
| *To Rome with Love* | *Walt Disney* | *The FBI* |
| *Ed Sullivan* | *Bill Cosby* | *Sunday Movie* |
| *Glen Campbell* | *Bonanza* | |
| *Mission: Impossible* | *Bold Ones* | |

TEL 71.  How many hours altogether on Saturday and (PLUS) Sunday do you watch TV?

_____ hours

TEL 72.  What is the total number of hours during the rest of the week (Monday through Friday) do you watch TV:

_____ hours

TEL 73.  How many hours did you watch yesterday?

_____ hours

TEL 74.  How many T.V. sets (that work) do you have in your home?

black & white                _____ color

TEL 75.  If in real life you could be like some T.V. character, which one would you like to be?

TEL 75.2 How many hours do you personally spend watching TV per day?

_____

_____

TEL  76.  Would you agree or disagree
          with these complaints about
          T.V.?

          1. too much sex                    1. agree
                                             2. disagree
                                            98. DK

          2. Not enough information           1. agree
          programs?                          2. disagree
                                            98. DK

          3. Too many commercials             1. agree
                                             2. disagree
                                            98. DK

          4. Too much violence                1. agree
                                             2. disagree
                                            98. DK

          5. Not enough comedy pro-           1. agree
          grams                              2. disagree
                                            98. DK

          6. Too many news programs           1. agree
                                             2. disagree
                                            98. DK

          7. Not enough programs              1. agree
          showing life as it really is       2. disagree
                                            98. DK

          8. Not enough violence              1. agree
                                             2. disagree
                                            98. DK

TEL  77.  All things considered, would       1. from T.V.
          you say you have learned            2. in school
          more things                         3. both equally
                                            98. DK

          READ ALTERNATIVES

TEL  78.  Do you ever watch the net-          0. no
          work news programs, like
          Walter Cronkite, Huntley-
          Brinkley, or Frank Rey-
          nolds?

          IF YES, How often do you            4. every night
          watch these network news            3. two or three/week
          programs?                           2. once/week
                                              1. less often than
                                                 once/week

TEL  79.  Some people say that these          3. too much
          shows have given *too much*         2. right amount
          attention to violence, while        1. not enough
          others say there is *not enough*
          attention to violence in news
          shows. How do you feel?

We're also interested in sports you watch on television. Of the following
sports events which have been on television, how many have you
watched this last year?

TEL  80.  Football games
                                              4. most
                                              3. about half
                                              2. some
                                              1. none

TEL  81.  Hockey
                                              4. most
                                              3. about half
                                              2. some
                                              1. none

TEL  82.  Boxing
                                              4. most
                                              3. about half
                                              2. some
                                              1. none

TEL  83.  Wrestling
                                              4. most
                                              3. about half
                                              2. some
                                              1. none

TEL   83a.   What are your four favorite programs on television, the
             ones you try to watch every time they are on the air?

             a. _____

             b. _____

             c. _____

             d. _____


MED   84.   And   what   about   movies?          0.  none (go to next)
            Since January 1, about how            1.  one
            many movies would you say             2.  two to four
            you've gone to see?                   3.  five to ten
                                                  4.  more than ten

            IF YES: Which movie was
            your favorite? (IF *ONE*,
            which movie did you see?) _____

We're also interested in things you like in the other mass media: newspapers, magazines, comics, and radio.

MED   85.   What newspapers do you
            read? _____
            _____

MED   86.   How often do you read the             4.  every day
            newspapers you read most?             3.  3 or 4 times/week
                                                  2.  once a week
                                                  1.  less than that

What kinds of things interest you in the paper? Do you usually read each
of these parts of the paper *all the way through, just read a little of it, or
skip over it?*

MED   87.   Sports                                2.  all
                                                  1.  little
                                                  0.  skip over


MED   88.   Stories about politics                2.  all
                                                  1.  little
                                                  0.  skip over

MED 89. Stories about murders and robberies

2. all
1. little
0. skip over

MED 90. Stories about the fighting in Vietnam

2. all
1. little
0. skip over

MED 91. Stories about riots and bombings

2. all
1. little
0. skip over

MED 92. Comics

2. all
1. little
0. skip over

MED 93. What are your four favorite magazines?

Most favorite: .1 _____
.2 _____
.3 _____
4th favorite: .4 _____

MED 94. We'd like you to tell us some things about different kinds of T.V. shows. First of all, here is a list of Westerns. How realistic do you think these programs are in telling about how life in the West really was? (Put an X in the correct position.)

| | 3<br>Exactly like<br>it was | 2<br>More real<br>than fake | 1<br>More fake<br>than real | 98<br><br>Don't know |
|---|---|---|---|---|
| Gunsmoke | _____ | _____ | _____ | _____ |
| Bonanza | _____ | _____ | _____ | _____ |
| Lancer | _____ | _____ | _____ | _____ |
| High Chaparral | _____ | _____ | _____ | _____ |
| The Virginian | _____ | _____ | _____ | _____ |

MED 95. We'd like to ask you the same questions but about shows that tell about police and government work. How realistic would you say these programs are in showing what police work is really like? (Put an X in the correct position.)

|  | 3<br>Exactly like<br>it is | 2<br>More real<br>than fake | 1<br>More fake<br>than real | 98<br>Don't know |
|---|---|---|---|---|
| Mod Squad | _____ | _____ | _____ | _____ |
| Hawaii Five-O | _____ | _____ | _____ | _____ |
| Dragnet | _____ | _____ | _____ | _____ |
| It Takes a Thief | _____ | _____ | _____ | _____ |
| Name of the Game | _____ | _____ | _____ | _____ |
| Mannix | _____ | _____ | _____ | _____ |
| Adam-12 | _____ | _____ | _____ | _____ |
| The FBI | _____ | _____ | _____ | _____ |
| Mission: Impossible | _____ | _____ | _____ | _____ |

MED 96. Now I would like to get your judgment on some questions concerning the possible effect of television violence (REPEAT BEFORE EACH STATEMENT BELOW: "HOW LIKELY IS IT THAT T.V. VIOLENCE: IS IT LIKELY, POSSIBLE, OR UNLIKELY?")

.1 Plays a part in making America a violent society?

3. likely
2. possible
1. unlikely

.2 Allows viewers to blow off steam by watching violence, thus decreasing the likelihood of their being violent?

3. likely
2. possible
1. unlikely

.3 Makes people insensitive to real acts of violence that they hear about or see?

3. likely
2. possible
1. unlikely

.4 Provides entertainment and relaxation without harmful or bad effects?

3. likely
2. possible
1. unlikely

.5 Triggers violent acts from people who are maladjusted or mentally unstable?

3. likely
2. possible
1. unlikely

.6 Supports and strengthens traditional American values?

3. likely
2. possible
1. unlikely

MED  97.  How do you feel about the amount of violence portrayed in television programs today, not including news programs—do you think that there is too much, a reasonable amount, or very little violence?

3. too much
2. a reasonable amount
1. very little
98. not sure

MED  98.  Apart from the amount of violence, do you generally approve or disapprove of the kind of violence that is portrayed on T.V.?

1. approve
2. disapprove
98. not sure

## IN PUN ITEMS SEX OF ADULT AND OF CHILD IS SAME AS SEX OF S

"Imagine again that you are the father (mother) of an eight year old boy (girl) and try to answer the following questions accordingly."

PUN  99.  If your son (daughter) got very mad at you, would you get angry with him (her)?

0. no
1. yes
98. DK

PUN  100.  If your son (daughter) got very mad at you, would you slap him (her) in the face?

0. no
1. yes
98. DK

PUN  101.  Would you say, "That isn't a nice thing to do," if your son (daughter) got very mad at you?

0. no
1. yes
98. DK

PUN  102.  Would you tell your son (daughter) you don't love him (her) for getting very mad at you?

     0. no
     1. yes
    98. DK

PUN  103.  Would you tell your son (daughter) in a nice way how to act differently if he (she) got very mad at you?

     0. no
     1. yes
    98. DK

PUN  104.  If your son (daughter) got very mad at you, would you send him (her) to another room where he (she) would be alone and without toys?

     0. no
     1. yes
    98. DK

IAG  105.  Please put a checkmark for each statement in the box which best expresses your feeling.

|  | 4<br>Almost<br>Always<br>true | 3<br>Often<br>true | 2<br>Some-<br>times<br>true | 1<br>Seldom<br>true | 0<br>Never<br>true |
|---|---|---|---|---|---|
| .1 I feel like swearing |  |  |  |  |  |
| .2 I feel like losing my temper at people |  |  |  |  |  |
| .3 I feel like being a little rude to people· |  |  |  |  |  |
| .4 I feel like picking a fight or arguing with people |  |  |  |  |  |

OAG  106.  Please put a checkmark for each statement in the box which best describes how you act.

|  | 4<br>Almost<br>Always<br>true | 3<br>Often<br>true | 2<br>Some-<br>times<br>true | 1<br>Seldom<br>true | 0<br>Never<br>true |
|---|---|---|---|---|---|
| .1 I get angry and smash things |  |  |  |  |  |
| .2 I am a little rude to people |  |  |  |  |  |
| .3 I lose my temper at people |  |  |  |  |  |

HAND THIS AND NEXT PAGE TO *S*.

BEH   107.   Here are a number of things which you might do that could get you into trouble. Please tell us how many times you have done these things in the last three years. For each question, put a check in the box next to the answer that is true.

Number of times

| In the last three years how many times have you done this? | 5 or more | 4 | 3 | 2 | 1 | 0 |
|---|---|---|---|---|---|---|
| .01  Stayed out later than parents said you should | | | | | | |
| .02  Got into a serious fight with a student in school | | | | | | |
| .03  Run away from home | | | | | | |
| .04  Taken something not belonging to you worth under $50 | | | | | | |
| .05  Went onto someone's land or into some house or building when you weren't supposed to be there | | | | | | |
| .06  Set fire to someone else's property on purpose | | | | | | |
| .07  Been suspended or expelled from school | | | | | | |
| .08  Got something by telling a person something bad would happen to him if you did not get what you wanted | | | | | | |
| .09  Argued or had a fight with either of your parents | | | | | | |
| .10  Got into trouble with the police because of something you did | | | | | | |
| .11  Hurt someone badly enough to need bandages or a doctor | | | | | | |
| .12  Damaged school property on purpose | | | | | | |
| .13  Taken something from a store without paying for it | | | | | | |

Number of times

| | 5 or more | 4 | 3 | 2 | 1 | 0 |
|---|---|---|---|---|---|---|
| .14 Hit a teacher | | | | | | |
| .15 Drunk beer or liquor without parents' permission | | | | | | |
| .16 Smoked in school (against the rules) | | | | | | |
| .17 Hit your father | | | | | | |
| .18 Taken a car that didn't belong to someone in your family without permission of the owner | | | | | | |
| .19 Taken an expensive part of a car without the permission of the owner | | | | | | |
| .20 Taken part in a fight where a bunch of your friends are against another bunch | | | | | | |
| .21 Hit your mother | | | | | | |
| .22 Taken something not belonging to you worth over $50 | | | | | | |
| .23 Had to bring your parents to school because of something you did | | | | | | |
| .24 Taken an inexpensive part of a car without permission of the owner | | | | | | |
| .25 Skipped a day of school without a real excuse | | | | | | |
| .26 Used a knife or gun or some other thing (like a club) to get something from a person | | | | | | |

## Z 108. ADMINISTER THE Z TEST

There are a few other things to do before we are finished. One is a measure of your height. Another is a True-False questionnaire about your attitudes and feelings. The last is to give you your voucher for $20 when you complete the questionnaire. Let's go to the office so that the secretary can measure your height, but before we do I would like to have the height of your parents. (Did you say they are both alive?)

ANT 109. How tall is (was) your father?

‾‾‾ ‾‾‾
feet   inches

ANT 110. How tall is (was) your mother?

‾‾‾ ‾‾‾
feet   inches

## TAKE S TO SECRETARY

ANT 111. S's HEIGHT

‾‾‾ ‾‾‾
feet   inches

MMP 112. TAKE S TO MMPI AND GIVE S MMPI INSTRUCTIONS.

If you have any questions after I leave, ask the secretary or some other staff person who's in this room. When finished with this test, give it to the secretary and she will give you your voucher.

SECRETARY CHECKS FOR THE NUMBER OF UNANSWERED QUESTIONS(?) TO DETERMINE THAT THE MMPI IS SCORABLE BEFORE GIVING VOUCHER. IF TOO MANY UNANSWERED QUESTIONS (?) THE SECRETARY ASKS S TO ANSWER MORE OF THE QUESTIONS BEFORE GIVING VOUCHER.


FATHER ALIVE?  1. YES _____
               0. NO  _____

MOTHER ALIVE?  1. YES _____
               0. NO  _____

INT 113. WAS THE INTERVIEW AN EASY JOB?  1. YES
                  2. NO

INT 114. WAS THERE MUCH DISSIMULATION?  1. YES
                  2. NO

INT 115. ANYTHING UNUSUAL ABOUT THE  1. YES
    INTERVIEW?           2. NO

INT 116. IF YES, EXPLAIN _____

_____

_____

_____

_____

_____

_____

NOTES: _____

_____

_____

_____

_____

_____

Time ended _____

# Appendix C:
# Variables derived from interview schedule

1. Respondents' Aggression

a. *Respondent as object of aggression (VAG)*. This score is the sum of five items, questions 39 through 43. The higher the score, the more frequently respondent says he has been the victim of aggression.

b. *Respondent as witness of aggression (WAG)*. This score is the sum of five items, questions 44 through 48. The higher the score, the more frequently the respondent says he has observed aggression towards others.

c. *Aggressive habit - A (AHA)*. This score is the sum of three items, questions 55 through 57. The higher the score, the more often the respondent says he carried out physical aggression against another person.

d. *Aggressive habit - B (AHB)*. This score is the sum of three items, questions 106.1 through 106.3. The higher the score, the more frequently does the respondent say he vents his hostility.

e. *Total aggressive habit (TAH)*. This score is the sum of three other scores: AHA + AHB + ASB. The higher the score, the more the respondent admits thats that he displays aggressive behavior.

f. *Antisocial Behavior (ASB)*. This score is the sum of 26 items, questions 107.1 through 107.26. The higher the score, the more the subject admits to past delinquent behaviors.

g. *Aggressive Drive (AGD)*: This score is the sum of four items, questions 105.1 through 105.4. The higher the score, the more often the subject says he would like to express aggression.

h. *Total Aggressive Environment (TAG)*. This score is the sum of five other scores: VAG + WAG + AHA + ASB + AGD. The higher the score, the more often has the subject been exposed to the expression or experience of aggression.

i. *Personal Opinion Inventory (WAZ)*. This score is the sum of 12 items, questions 27 through 38 with 1 being the item score for "disagree" and 2 being the item score for "agree". This scale was adopted from Walters and Zak (1959) and is identical to the one administered to the subjects' parents ten years earlier. The higher the score, the more aggression.

j. *Potential Punishment for Aggression (PUN-TOP)*. This score is the weighted sum of 24 items, question 21 through 26, 49 through 54, 63 through 68, and 99 through 104. The weights are as follows:

| | Response | |
|---|---|---|
| Question | No or Don't Know | Yes |
| 21 | 0 | 1 |
| 22 | 0 | 1 |
| 23 | 0 | 2 |
| 24 | 0 | 3 |
| 25 | 0 | 2 |
| 26 | 0 | 3 |
| 49 | 0 | 1 |
| 50 | 0 | 2 |
| 51 | 0 | 3 |
| 52 | 0 | 2 |
| 53 | 0 | 3 |
| 54 | 0 | 1 |
| 63 | 0 | 1 |
| 64 | 0 | 3 |
| 65 | 0 | 2 |
| 66 | 0 | 2 |
| 67 | 0 | 1 |
| 68 | 0 | 3 |
| 99 | 0 | 2 |
| 100 | 0 | 3 |
| 101 | 0 | 1 |
| 102 | 0 | 3 |
| 103 | 0 | 1 |
| 104 | 0 | 3 |

The higher the score, the more punishment the respondent would administer were he the parent of an eight-year-old child. These items were identical to those asked of the subjects' parents ten years earlier.

2.   Social status factors

a.   Social Status of Family (ISS). This category of variables is a set of 4 scores. They are:
(1) *Number of books (NOB)*, question 17. The higher the number, the higher the social status.
(2) *Occupation of father (FOC)*, question 13 (or head of household) or 14, coded into 7 categories (Warner et al., 1960). The higher the score, the lower the social status.
(3) *Total number of rooms.*
(4) *Composite social status index (CIS)*. These responses were converted into 4 standard scores and combined as follows: questions 16 + 17 - 13 18. The higher the score, the higher the social status.

b.   Current occupational status of respondent (CSR). This category is a set of two scores. They are:

(1) *Occupation of respondent (ROC)*. Question 12 coded into 7 categories (Warner et al., 1960). The higher the score, the lower the social status.
(2) *Education of respondent (EDR)*. The higher the score, the higher the social status. These two scores were not combined into a composite.

c.   Mobility aspirations (ASP). This category is a set of two scores. They are:
(1) *Total aspiration (TAS)*. Questions 7, 8, and 9 are combined in the following manner:

(7-Q7) + (7-Q8) + Q9. The higher the score, the higher the aspiration.
(2) *Mobility orientation (MOO)*. The sum of 5 items, questions 58 through 62. The higher the score, the higher the aspiration.

d.   Church attendance (REL-RAT). Question 19 yields the stated frequency of church attendance. The higher the score, the more frequent the stated church attendance.

3.   Psychopathology

a. Minnesota Multiphasic Personality Inventory (MMPI), Form R (Hathaway & McKinley, 1969). This pencil-and-paper test provided three scores:

(1) *MMPI-49*. Elevation of scales 4 and 9 scored in the following manner:

if 4 and 9 not the two highest of 11 "clinical" scales,* score = 0; if both 4 and 9 $\geq$ 70, score = 4;

if only one of the two $\geq$ 70 or if both 4 and 9 $\geq$ 60, score = 3;

if only one of the two $\geq$ 60, score = 2;

if neither 4 nor 9 $\geq$ 60, score = 1.

(2) *MMPI-49S.* Sum of T scores on scales 4 and 9. For both of the foregoing MMPI scores, the higher the score, the more likely is the person to act out in an antisocial manner.

(3) *MMPI-T.* This score is the number of clinical scales (11 scales, K corrected) greater than T = 70. The greater the number, the more the likelihood of psychopathology.

b. The Z-Test (Zulliger, 1969). This is a 3-card inkblot technique for which scoring categories were adopted from Holtzman, Thorpe, Swartz, and Herron (1961) as modified by Lefkowitz (1968). Two scores were computed:

(1) *Hostility (Z-HOS-2).* This is a binary score in which zero signifies the absence and 1 the presence of hostility.

(2) *Psychopathology (Z-SUM).* This score is computed by summing four binary scores: hostility, anxiety, movement, and pathognomonic verbalization. The higher the score, the greater the psychopathology.

4. TV Variables

a. *Hours of watching TV (TV-HW-A).* This score is the sum of questions 71 and 72, total number of hours TV is watched by subject per week. If one of the questions was not answered, then the response to the other question was multiplied by 2.

b. *TV Violence—Hudson (TV-VIOL-H).* Ratings of violence by two judges were computed from question 83a. Each program (see appendix C) was categorized as nonviolent = 0, uncertain = 1, violent = 2. A subject's score was the average rating of the programs mentioned multiplied by 10. The higher the score the more violent the mentioned programs.

c. *TV Violence—Greenberg (TV-VIOL-G).* Ratings of violence on question 83a. The average violence ratings for the subject's four favorite TV programs based on the "Public" violence ratings as determined by Greenberg and Gordon (1970). If the

---

*The K-Scale was inadvertently included in the clinical scales by the computer program.

program mentioned had not been noted by these authors, it was assigned a rating of 1.5 which approximated the mean rating. The higher the score, the more violent the programs.

    d.    *Sports Programs on TV (TV-SPT).* This score was comprised of questions 80-83. The higher the score, the more contact sports watched (football, hockey, boxing, and wrestling).

    e.    *Realism of TV (ROT).* The sum of ratings 1, 2, or 3, for each of 14 programs contained in questions 94 and 95. The lower the score, the more realistic is the subject, i.e., the more he states that these TV programs are "fake" or "phony".

5.  Height

    a.    *Height of subject (SHT).* Question 111. Standing height in inches obtained by reading from a tape measure fixed to the wall. Girls removed their shoes. Subject's height in inches was multiplied by 10.

    b.    *Discrepancy between Subject's Height and Average of Mother's and Father's Height (DAH).* The average of questions 109 and 110 minus subject's height, plus 100. When score is above 100, subject is shorter than average of his parents; when score is below 100, subject is taller than average of his parents.

6.  School Records

    a.    *Achievement (ACH).* Mean of all 12th grade achievement tests for which the subject had percentile scores. The mean was multiplied by 10.

    b.    *IQ.* Obtained from 12th grade school records.

    c.    *Times Tardy (TARDY).* Obtained from 12th grade school records. Does not include subjects who were never tardy.

7.  Number of arrests

Boys in the third grade study were classified within the upper and lower quartiles of aggression. The New York State Identification and Intelligence Service was asked to furnish aggregate data on the number of arrests in New York State within each group. The criterion data were collected when modal age of subjects was 19 years.

# Appendix D: Classification according to violence of TV programs in ten-year followup

## Violent

Avengers
Bold Ones
Bonanza
Daniel Boone
Dark Shadows
Dragnet
FBI
Get Smart
Gunsmoke
Hawaii Five-0
High Chapparal
I Spy
Invaders
Ironsides

It Takes a Thief
Lancer
Land of the Giants
Man From Uncle
Mannix
Mission: Impossible
Mod Squad
Name of the Game
Prisoner
Superman
Then Came Bronson
Three Stooges
Virginian
Wild, Wild West

## Nonviolent

Adam 12
Adams Family
American Bandstand
Andy Williams
Another World
Art Linkletter
Auto Racing
Banana Splits
Basketball
Beverly Hillbillies
Bewitched
Big Valley
Bill Cosby
Bracken's World
Brady Bunch
Bullwinkle
Burke's Law
Cartoons
Carol Burnett
Comedy Shows

Comedy Tonight
Courtship of Eddie's Father
David Frost
David Susskind
Days of our Lives
Dean Martin
Debbie Reynolds
Dick Cavett
Doris Day
Ed Sullivan
Engelbert Humperdinck
Evening With the Pops
Family Affair
First Tuesday
Football
Fugitive
Galloping Gourmet
Ghost and Mrs. Muir
Glen Campbell
Gomer Pyle, U.S.M.C.

## Nonviolent

| | |
|---|---|
| Governor and J.J. | Mike Douglas |
| Green Acres | Monkeys |
| Hullaballoo | My Favorite Martian |
| He & She | My Three Sons |
| Hee Haw | N.E.T. Playhouse |
| Here Come the Brides | News Programs |
| Hogan's Heroes | Pat Paulsen Show |
| Honeymooners | Perry Mason |
| Huntley-Brinkley | Petticoat Junction |
| I Dream of Jeannie | Quiz Shows |
| I Love Lucy | Ray Stevens |
| Jack Benny | Red Skelton |
| Jeopardy | Room 222 |
| Jim Nabors | Science Shows |
| Johnny Carson | Sesame Street |
| Johnny Cash | Sixty Minutes |
| Julia | Soap Operas |
| Kraft Music Hall | Smothers Brothers |
| Lassie | Star Trek |
| Laugh-In | Stock Car Races |
| Leonard Bernstein | That Girl |
| Let's Make a Deal | The Doctors |
| Love, American Style | The Show |
| Love Is a Many Splendored Thing | To Rome With Love |
| Love Stories | Tom Jones |
| Marcus Welby, M.D. | Undersea World of Jaques Cousteau |
| Mayberry, R.F.D. | Walt Disney |
| Medical Center | Walter Cronkite |
| Meet the Press | White Paper |
| Merv Griffin | Wide World of Sports |

## Cannot be coded—don't know

| | |
|---|---|
| Laredo | Specials |
| Outer Limits | T.V. Movies |

# Appendix E: Code manual for data set of 95 variables

| Matrix # | Variable # | Mnemonic | Description | Card | Field | Grade |
|---|---|---|---|---|---|---|
| 1 | 1 | N513 | aggression | 1 | 1 | 3 |
| 2 | 2 | N533 | aggression anxiety | 1 | 2 | 3 |
| 3 | 3 | N543 | popularity | 1 | 3 | 3 |
| 4 | 6 | MBGA | boys games | 1 | 6 | 3 |
| 5 | 7 | MGGA | girls games | 1 | 7 | 3 |
| 6 | 8 | LFFR | frequency aggression | 1 | 8 | 3 |
| 7 | 9 | LMFR | frequency aggression | 1 | 9 | 3 |
| 8 | 12 | LFEA | educational aspiration | 1 | 12 | 3 |
| 9 | 13 | LMEA | educational aspiration | 1 | 13 | 3 |
| 10 | 14 | LFWZ | Walters-Zaks | 1 | 14 | 3 |
| 11 | 15 | LMWZ | Walters-Zaks | 1 | 15 | 3 |
| 12 | 16 | LFRO | respondents occupation | 1 | 16 | 3 |
| 13 | 18 | LFRJ | rejection | 1 | 18 | 3 |
| 14 | 19 | LMRJ | rejection | 1 | 19 | 3 |
| 15 | 20 | LFRA | recency aggression | 1 | 20 | 3 |
| 16 | 21 | LMRA | recency aggression | 1 | 21 | 3 |
| 17 | 22 | LFNU | nurturance | 2 | 1 | 3 |
| 18 | 23 | LMNU | nurturance | 2 | 2 | 3 |
| 19 | 24 | LFPD | parental disharmony | 2 | 3 | 3 |
| 20 | 25 | LMPD | parental disharmony | 2 | 4 | 3 |
| 21 | 27 | LMCI | confessing | 2 | 6 | 3 |
| 22 | 36 | LFPU | punishment | 2 | 16 | 3 |
| 23 | 37 | LMPU | punishment | 2 | 17 | 3 |
| 24 | 38 | LFRM | residential mobility | 2 | 17 | 3 |
| 25 | 42 | LFGL | generational level | 2 | 21 | 3 |
| 26 | | SU | subject number | | | 3 |
| 27 | 44 | LFJP | judgment punishment | 3 | 2 | 3 |
| 28 | 45 | LMJP | judgment punishment | 3 | 3 | 3 |
| 29 | 46 | LFPI | profile identification | 3 | 4 | 3 |
| 30 | 47 | LMPI | profile identification | 3 | 5 | 3 |
| 31 | 58 | LFGI | guilt | 3 | 16 | 3 |
| 32 | 59 | LMGI | guilt | 3 | 17 | 3 |
| 33 | 97 | LFOA | occupational aspiration | 5 | 13 | 3 |
| 34 | 98 | LMOA | occupational aspiration | 5 | 14 | 3 |
| 35 | 109 | LFRG | religiosity | 6 | 4 | 3 |
| 36 | 110 | LMRG | religiosity | 6 | 5 | 3 |
| 37 | 121 | LFMO | mobility orientation | 6 | 16 | 3 |
| 38 | 122 | LMMO | mobility orientation | 6 | 17 | 3 |
| 39 | 136 | LFFP | F-scale acquiescence | 7 | 10 | 3 |
| 40 | 137 | LMFP | F-scale acquiescence | 7 | 11 | 3 |
| 41 | 139 | LMEN | enuresis | 7 | 13 | 3 |
| 42 | 141 | LFED | parent education | 7 | 15 | 3 |
| 43 | 142 | LMED | parent education | 7 | 16 | 3 |
| 44 | 150 | LFTV | hours TV watched | 8 | 3 | 3 |
| 45 | 151 | LMTV | hours TV watched | 8 | 4 | 3 |
| 46 | 201 | MDAP | first picture drawn | 10 | 12 | 3 |
| 47 | 8 | IQ | IQ | 16 | 1 | 3 |
| 48 | 9 | TVVLF | TV violence | 16 | 2 | 3 |
| 49 | 10 | TVVLM | TV violence | 16 | 3 | 3 |
| 50 | 11 | SEX | sex of subject | 16 | 4 | 3 |
| 51 | 12 | ROT | TV realism | 16 | 5 | 13 |
| 52 | 13 | JET | effect TV violence | 16 | 6 | 13 |
| 53 | 6 | ISS-NOB | number of books | 17 | 6 | 13 |

| Matrix # | Variable # | Mnemonic | Description | Card | Field | Grade |
|----------|-----------|----------|-------------|------|-------|-------|
| 54 | 8 | ISS-FOC | fathers occupation | 17 | 8 | 13 |
| 55 | 9 | ISS-CIS | composite social status | 17 | 9 | 13 |
| 56 | 10 | CSR-ROC | respondents occupation | 17 | 10 | 13 |
| 57 | 11 | CSR-EDR | respondents education | 17 | 11 | 13 |
| 58 | 16 | ASP-TAS | total aspiration | 17 | 16 | 13 |
| 59 | 17 | ASP-MOO | mobility orientation | 17 | 17 | 13 |
| 60 | 18 | REL-RAT | religiosity | 17 | 18 | 13 |
| 61 | 20 | PUN-TOP | punishment total | 17 | 20 | 13 |
| 62 | 25 | RAG-WAZ | Walters-Zaks | 18 | 4 | 13 |
| 63 | 26 | RAG-AHA | spank, slap, punch | 18 | 5 | 13 |
| 64 | 27 | RAG-AHB | smash, rude, temper | 18 | 6 | 13 |
| 65 | 28 | RAG-ASB | delinquent behavior | 18 | 7 | 13 |
| 66 | 29 | RAG-TAH | Total aggressive habit | 18 | 8 | 13 |
| 67 | 30 | RAG-AGD | aggressive drive | 18 | 9 | 13 |
| 68 | 31 | VAG | victim-aggression | 18 | 10 | 13 |
| 69 | 32 | WAG | witness-aggression | 18 | 11 | 13 |
| 70 | 33 | TAG | Total aggressive environment | 18 | 12 | 13 |
| 71 | 34 | PER-AGG | numerator-aggression | 18 | 13 | 13 |
| 72 | 35 | PER-ANX | anxiety-aggression | 18 | 14 | 13 |
| 73 | 36 | PER-POP | popularity | 18 | 15 | 13 |
| 74 | 38 | HGT-SHT | subjects height | 18 | 17 | 13 |
| 75 | 40 | HGT-DAH | height deviation | 18 | 19 | 13 |
| 76 | 42 | Z-HOS-2 | hostility | 18 | 21 | 13 |
| 77 | 46 | Z-SUM | psychopathology | 19 | 4 | 13 |
| 78 | 47 | MMPI-49 | 4, 9 above 70 T | 19 | 5 | 13 |
| 79 | 48 | ACH | achievement | 19 | 6 | 13 |
| 80 | 49 | I Q | I Q | 19 | 7 | 13 |
| 81 | 50 | TARDY | TARDY | 19 | 8 | 13 |
| 82 | 51 | TV-HW-A | TV hours watched | 19 | 9 | 13 |
| 83 | 55 | TV-SPT | TV sports | 19 | 13 | 13 |
| 84 | 56 | TV-VIOL-H | Violence-Hudson raters | 19 | 14 | 13 |
| 85 | 57 | TV-VIOL-G | Violence-Greenberg | 19 | 15 | 13 |
| 86 | 58 | MMPI-T | Clin. scales > 70 T | 19 | 16 | 13 |
| 87 | 59 | MMPI-49S | sum 4 + 9 | 19 | 17 | 13 |
| 88 | 61 | PER-LED | peer leader | 19 | 19 | 13 |
| 89 | 62 | PER-WKY | who knows you | 19 | 20 | 13 |
| 90 | 63 | PER-AGG/WKY | aggression | 19 | 21 | 13 |
| 91 | 1 | PER-AGG | 9 items | 20 | 1 | 8 |
| 92 | 2 | PER-AGG 2 | item aggression score | 20 | 2 | 8 |
| 93 | 3 | PER-POP | popularity | 20 | 3 | 8 |
| 94 | 4 | TV-VIOL-I | violence rating | 20 | 4 | 8 |
| 95 | 5 | TV-VIOL-JH | violence rating | 20 | 5 | 8 |

# Two Comments on Cross-lagged Correlation

## Threats to the Internal Validity of Cross-Lagged Panel Inference, as Related to "Television Violence and Child Aggression: A Followup Study"

David A. Kenny

*Northwestern University*

Panel or longitudinal studies allow the researcher to study important variables in their naturalistic setting. However, since panel studies lack both the experimental and statistical controls present in experimental research, there are greater threats to the validity of an inference made from a panel study. A major threat to the validity of an inference in a panel study is the problem of differential reliability of measurement. This problem has been repeatedly emphasized by Campbell and his students (Campbell and Clayton, 1961; Campbell, 1963; Rozelle and Campbell, 1969; Crano, Kenny, and Campbell, 1971).

In its simplest form cross-lagged panel correlation (CLPC) involves a simple comparison of cross-lagged correlations. However, such a model assumes that the reliability of each variable stays constant over time. As Campbell (1963) points out: "A variable which increases in reliability from Time 1 to Time 2 will, *ceteris paribus*, show up as an effect rather than a cause" (p. 240). A second and related threat to the validity of an inference from panel data refers to true factorial structure of the variables. As Kenny (1971) points out, what distinguishes CLPC model from path models elucidated by Duncan (1969) and Heise (1970) is the assumption that there are factors that cause both variables in the panel. The logic of CLPC assumes that the factorial structure of each variable is stationary over time. Rozelle and Campbell (1969) suggest a test of this assumption by comparing the two synchronous correlations over time. If the two are not equal, then it is not plausible to assume a stationary factor structure. Kenny has devised a more general test of the stationarity assumption for the multivariate case.

Keeping these threats to the validity of a CLPC inference in mind, let us turn our attention to "Television violence and child aggression: a followup study" (1971). Using CLPC the authors conclude that viewing television violence (TVVL) causes aggression (AGG). The relevant cross-lagged correlations are reproduced from the study in Figure 1. The authors base their argument that TVVL3 causes AGG13 on:

1. $r_{\text{TVVL3 AGG13}} > r_{\text{TVVL13 AGG3}}$

2. $r_{\text{TVVL3 AGG13}} > r_{\text{TVVL3 AGG3}}$.

An examination of Figure 1 reveals that none of the variables significantly correlates with the TVVL13 measure. Given this failure to correlate, one or both of the following is true: 1) The TVVL13 is very unreliable. This seems plausible since it has near-zero correlations with all variables, including TVVL3. 2) A common factor that causes the other three variables causes TVVL13 in the opposite direction. Since either one of the two of the above are true, and since both are threats to the validity of a CLPC inference, a simple comparison of cross-lagged correlations is not valid in this case. Given unreliability or unstationarity, the cross-lagged asymmetry can be explained without resorting to causation. (The author attempted to find a variable that caused TVVL13 negatively and TVVL3, AGG3, and AGG13 positively, but no such variable was found. In fact, intelligence, achievement, and subjects' mobility aspirations correlated in the same direction with all four variables.)

The results would be completely uninterpretable if it were not for the fact that $r_{\text{TVVL3 AGG13}}$ is greater than $r_{\text{TVVL3 AGG3}}$. If TVVL did not cause AGG, then the cross-lagged correlation should be smaller than the synchronous correlation, *ceteris paribus*. There are two important aspects that determine exactly how much difference the two correlations should be: 1) the relationship of the reliability of AGG3 to AGG13; and

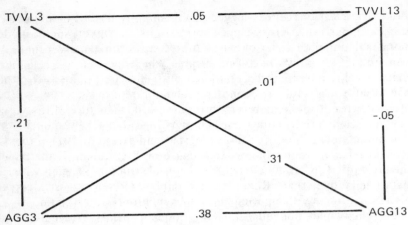

Figure 1:  The correlations between television violence and aggression for 211 boys over a ten-year lag

2) the temporal erosion or attenuation rate of the common causes of AGG and TVVL.

If the reliability of the AGG3 measure was lower than the AGG13 measure, the inequality of the cross-lagged and synchronous correlations could be partly explained. Differential reliability over time is an omnipresent threat to the validity of panel inferences. There are no measures of internal consistency of peer aggression, but it is possible to indirectly obtain evidence of the reliability of the AGG3 and AGG13 measures by the test-retest correlations and the correlation of aggression with other variables.

Since there are three waves, it is possible to estimate reliability coefficients for the middle measure (cf. Humphreys, 1960; Werts, Jöreskog, and Linn, 1971). Such an estimate is simply $^r$AGG3 AGG8$^r$AGG8 AGG13$^{/r}$AGG3AGG13. The obtained reliability is a respectable .82. The reliability for the first or last measure is not determined or identified. However, we can get a rough idea of the reliability of the variables by examining the test-retest correlations with the eighth grade measure. The 3-8 correlation is .48 and the 8-13 correlation is .65. At first glance this suggests that the 13 measure is more reliable, but other considerations lessen such a possibility. It is reasonable to expect aggression to be more stable over the 8-13 time period than 3-8. If such is the case, the correlations are not equal because of differential temporal erosion of the aggression trait and not because of reliability. Also the grade 13 measure is not actually a thirteenth grade measure but a retrospective measure. It is actually a twelfth or eleventh grade measure. Thus we should expect a $^r$8 11.5 correlation to be greater than $^r$3 8. So the test-retest correlations fail to indicate that the third grade measure is less reliable than the thirteenth grade measure of aggression.

A second and stronger test of reliability stability has been suggested (Kenny, 1971; Crano, Kenny, and Campbell, 1971). This "communality adjustment" involves an examination of the ratio of time one synchronous correlations of a variable with all other variables over the comparable time two synchronous correlations. Unfortunately for the present study, few variables were repeatedly measured in the same manner. Of those that were, the correlations are rather small. However, it is possible to use correlations involving measures of intelligence at grade 3 (IQ3) and achievement at grade 13 (ACH13). Let us assume that some factor common to both IQ and ACH causes AGG *synchronously* (or vice versa). If such is the case, then the ratio of the reliability of AGG3 over the reliability AGG13 equals $^rAGG3\ IQ3^rAGG3\ ACH13^{/(r}AGG13\ IQ3\ ^rAGG13\ ACH13)$. The obtained value is 1.09. Thus, it appears that the reliability of AGG3 is just as large if not larger than AGG13, so the fact that the AGG3-TVVL3 correlation is smaller than the AGG13-TVVL3 correlation cannot be attributed to the fact of lower reliability of the AGG3 measure.

The problem now is to infer how much smaller the .21 correlation would have eroded if TVVL did not cause AGG. Basically the reasoning is like this: If AGG and TVVL are not causally related, then the .21 synchronous correlation between them is due to the fact that both are caused by some common cause. The common cause changes over time and so, *ceteris paribus*, the lagged correlations should be smaller than the synchronous correlation. The magnitude of the difference is a function of the test-retest correlation of the common cause. Rozelle and Campbell (1969) refer to this correlation as the attenuation constant, and Kenny (1971) as the temporal erosion rate. Other authors have suggested partialing AGG3 out of the correlation between TVVL3 and AGG13. Such a procedure assumes that the test-retest correlation is the temporal erosion rate, but the test-retest correlation is a gross underestimate of the rate of erosion since it is affected by both unreliability and temporal erosion (Bohrnstedt, 1969; Brewer, Crano, and Campbell, 1970). Partial correlations and multiple regression usually overestimate the strength of a relationship if the control variable is measured with error.

One estimate of the common factor erosion rate is the unattenuated test-retest correlation of the aggression measure. Earlier we stated that an estimate of reliability of the AGG8 measure is .82. If we assume that AGG3 and AGG13 have the same reliability, the unattenuated test-retest correlation is .46. But such a value is a weighted sum of *all* the erosion rates that make up the aggression measure. For instance, it is reasonable to assume that intelligence causes aggression. An estimate of the erosion rate due to intelligence can be obtained by $^rAGG13\ IQ3^{/r}AGG3\ IQ3$. This equals .75. A rough *ad hoc* estimate of the common factor erosion rate can be obtained by averaging .46 and .75. The common factor temporal erosion rate equals .605. Multiplying .605 times .21 equals .127.

Testing to see whether .127 is significantly different from .31 using a Fisher's z yields a z of 1.97 which is significant at the .05 level. It should be kept in mind that this difference is a function of the erosion rate that we have chosen and the assumption of equal reliability in the two AGG measures.

Thus, the strongly significant results that the authors originally obtained were biased by unstationarity and the use of partial correlations. The data still indicates that TVVL causes violence, but the results, though statistically significant, are somewhat marginal. Nonexperimental inference is a risky business, and a sample of 211 boys will almost undoubtedly never present us with a final answer. However, the data do suggest that watching violent television shows does cause later aggression.

## BIBLIOGRAPHY

Bohrnstedt, G.W. Observations on the measurement of change. In Edgar F. Borgatta (Ed.) *Sociological Methodology, 1969.* San Francisco: Jossey-Bass, 1969.

Brewer, M., Crano, W., and Campbell, D.T. The use of partial correlations to test hypotheses. *Sociometry,* 1970, **33**, 1-11.

Campbell, D.T. From description to experimentation: Interpreting trends as quasi-experiments. In C.W. Harris (Ed.) *Problems in measuring change.* Madison: University of Wisconsin Press, 1963.

Crano, W.D., Kenny, D.A., and Campbell, D.T. Does intelligence cause achievement? A cross-lagged panel analysis. Accepted for publication, *Journal of Educational Psychology,* 1971.

Duncan, O.D. Some linear models for two-wave, two-variable panel analysis. *Psychological Bulletin,* 1969, **70**, 177-82.

Heise, D. Causal inference from panel data. In E. Borgatta and G. Bohrnstedt (Eds.) *Sociological Methodology 1970.* Jossey-Bass: San Francisco, 1971.

Humphreys, L.G. Investigations of a simplex. *Psychometrics,* 1960, **25**, 313-23.

Lefkowitz, M., Eron, L., Walder, L., and Huesmann, L.R. Television violence and child aggression: a followup study. In *Television and Social Behavior,* Vol. 3 (this volume).

Kenny, D.A. Cross-lagged and synchronous common factors in panel data. To be published in A. Goldberger and O.D. Duncan (Eds.) *Structural Equations Models.*

Rozelle, R.M., and Campbell, D.T. More plausible rival hypotheses in the cross-lagged panel correlation technique. *Psychological Bulletin,* 1969, **71**, 74-80.

Werts, C., Jöreskog, K., and Linn, R. Comment on "The estimation of measurement error in panel data." *American Sociological Review,* 1971, **36**, 110-12.

# Comment on "Television violence and child aggression: a followup study"

John M. Neale

*State University of New York at Stony Brook*

Correlational investigations have always been prevalent in behavioral research and for some purposes can provide important information. However, two problems of interpreting an obtained correlational relationship have been viewed as major limitations on the utility of the approach. One, the *problem of directionality*, refers to the fact that a correlation between two variables tells us only that they are related or tend to covary with one another, but does not tell us whether one is caused by the other. Consider, for example, the correlation between attendance in class and obtained grades. One possible interpretation of this relationship is that greater class attendance increases the amount learned and

141

thus produces higher grades. However, a second interpretation is also available: good grades might lead the students who obtain them to attend class more frequently. Thus, in many instances the problem of directionality cannot be resolved; hence, the oft-cited dictum "correlation does not imply causation."

The second major problem in interpreting correlational data is the so-called *third variable problem*. That is, two variables may be correlated without being causally related to each other. Rather, some unknown variable may be mediating the obtained relationship. For instance, returning to the previous example, the correlation between grades and attendance may reflect the operation of a third variable—"conscientiousness." That is, students who are high in conscientiousness may both attend class regularly and work diligently to obtain high grades.

The previous example illustrates a fairly obvious instance of a relationship being produced by the operation of a third variable. However, in many instances unsuspected third variables may be operative, thus making the problem considerably more difficult to solve.

## The cross-lagged panel design

The problem of the directionality of a correlational relationship may be answered in some circumstances by employing a design in which measurements are repeated on the same individuals at two points in time —*the cross-lagged panel design* (Campbell, 1963). As an example, consider the study mentioned previously on attendance and grades. This time, however, the measurements of attendance and grades are made twice, say at the end of the first and second semesters. The two competing hypotheses of primary interest[1] are:

Hypothesis 1: higher grades cause higher attendance;

Hypothesis 2: greater attendance causes higher grades.

The design and a hypothetical pattern of results are shown in figure 1.

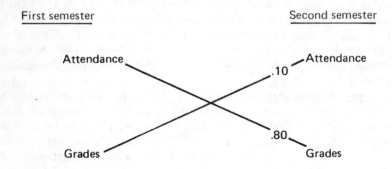

Figure 1: Cross-lagged panel design to assess the effect of attendance on grades

*Note that the most relevant correlations are those on the diagonals.*

Hypothesis 1 states that grades "cause" attendance and thus implies that the correlation between first-semester grades and second-semester attendance should be high. Conversely, Hypothesis 2 states that attendance "causes" higher grades (assuming that the subject matter of the course is cumulative over the two semesters), and thus implies that the correlations between attendance in the first semester and grades in the second semester should be relatively high. Generally, the two diagonal correlations are compared and a decision between the two hypotheses is then based on which correlation is higher.

The cross-lagged panel technique employing the diagonal correlations rests on the assumption that "causes" must precede "effects." Thus, the correlation of an effect with a prior "cause" is compared with the correlation of an effect with a "cause" which temporally came after it.

An example of a pattern of results favoring the hypothesis that good attendance causes high grades is illustrated in Figure 1. The correlation between first-semester attendance and second-semester grades is .80, while the correlation between first-semester grades and second-semester attendance is .10. Since the former correlation is significantly larger than the latter, hypothesis two is selected.

The recent study of Lefkowitz, Eron, Walder, and Huesmann (1971), a correlational study of the relationship between watching violent television fare and subsequent aggression, used the cross-lagged panel technique. In the Lefkowitz et al. study, all the children in a particular county were examined while in the third grade, and were subsequently followed up ten years later. While many variables were investigated, for the purposes of these comments only the measures relating to the viewing of violent television and rated aggressiveness need be considered. The measure of aggression in the classroom was a peer nomination technique in which the children in a particular classroom selected other children who fit particular descriptions such as: Who is always getting into trouble? Who starts a fight over nothing? The measure of the degree of violent television watched by the child was obtained by having the parents provide a list of the child's favorite programs. Ratings of the violence contained in these programs were then made independently by two raters so that the child's putative television diet could be assigned a violence rating.

Of the initial 875 subjects in the study, 427 were able to be contacted successfully ten years later. The followup sample was composed of 211 boys and 216 girls. These subjects were interviewed by a member of the research team, and during this interview data was collected both on stated preferences for television programs and on ratings of aggression. As was done with the third grade sample, the subjects' preferred television programs were independently rated for their violent content, so that a score could be assigned reflecting the degree of violence in the preferred

television shows of each subject. To obtain a rating of degree of aggressiveness, subjects were presented with lists of names of other students
and were asked which of them might fit into the various categories of
aggressive responding. The categories of aggressive responding represented a slightly modified version of the form which had been used for
the third graders. For the male subjects the major outcome of the Lefkowitz et al. investigation is presented in Figure 2.

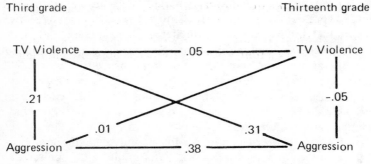

Figure 2: Results of the Lefkowitz, Eron, Walder, and Huesmann study

Within the cross-lagged technique, the critical correlations to be examined are those on the diagonals. Based on the assumption that a
"cause" must be temporally prior to an "effect," two rival hypotheses
may be pitted against each other. If aggression during the third grade
was causally related to the amount of television violence preferred ten
years later, then the correlation between these two variables should be
high. Conversely, if the amount of television violence preferred during
the third grade were causally related to the level of aggressive behavior
ten years later, then this correlation should be high. As may be seen
from Figure 2, the Lefkowitz et al. cross-lagged (on the diagonals) data
may be taken as support for the hypothesis that higher levels of violence
on preferred television programs in the third grade is causally related to
the amount of aggressive responding ten years later. That is, the correlation between preference for violent television programs in the third
grade and peer-rated aggression ten years later ($r = .31$) was significantly higher than the correlation between peer-rated aggression in the third
grade and preference for violent television fare in the thirteenth grade
($r = .01$).

## Path analysis

There may be some problems involved in utilizing the raw correlation
coefficients in attempting to interpret the results of a panel study, some
of which may be circumvented by employing the procedures of *path
analysis*. Path analysis was developed to explicate the *causal* paths accounting for a set of observed correlations. With the variables expressed

in standardized form, path coefficients are obtained from a multiple regression equation between the predictor and criterion variables. While the technique has been used more often in cases where a large number of variables are under study, Heise (1970) has applied the technique to the cross-lagged panel design. He has noted that in this application:

different measurements on the same variable are treated here as hypothetically different variables. For example, $X_1$ and $X_3$ are construed as distinct variables even though they actually are only measurements at different times on the same variable (X odd). Therefore, in the path analysis, the two-variable, two-wave situation is treated as a four-variable problem (1970, p.4).

An illustration of a four-variable problem is presented in Figure 3.

$$X_1 \qquad\qquad\qquad\qquad X_3$$

$$X_2 \qquad\qquad\qquad\qquad X_4$$

Figure 3: Path diagram for a two-variable, two-wave panel design

Of the twelve possible paths or connecting lines which could be drawn in such a four-variable problem, four can be immediately eliminated as not implicating causality. The elimination of these four paths is based on the assumption that later states can not "determine" prior states; thus, the paths $X_3 \longrightarrow X_1$, $X_3 \longrightarrow X_2$, $X_4 \longrightarrow X_2$, and $X_4 \longrightarrow X_1$ can all be eliminated. In such a design there are four causal paths of primary interest: $X_1 \longrightarrow X_3$, $X_1 \longrightarrow X_4$, $X_2 \longrightarrow X_3$ and $X_2 \longrightarrow X_4$. That is, the primary interest is in the possible causal relationships between prior and later states (the synchronous correlation, e.g. $r_{X1X2}$, provides a context in which the causal paths may be interpreted). In contrast to the usual procedures in the cross-lagged panel design, however, path analysis does *not* employ raw correlation coefficients to estimate the strength of these various possible causal relationships. Rather, *path coefficients* are employed.

With the variables expressed in standardized form, path coefficients are obtained from a multiple regression equation between the predictor and criterion variables. In the simple case with which we are now dealing, the regression equation is merely between two variables holding constant the possible influence of third variables. Thus, the path coefficients for each of the four important paths in such a study may be written as follows:

$$p_{31} = \frac{p13 - p12\, p23}{1 - p_{12}^2}$$

$$P_{32} = \frac{\rho 23 - \rho 12 \ \rho 13}{1 - \rho_{12}^2}$$

$$P_{41} = \frac{\rho 14 - \rho 12 \ \rho 24}{1 - \rho_{12}^2}$$

$$P_{42} = \frac{\rho 24 - \rho 12 \ \rho 14}{1 - \rho_{12}^2}$$

Observed correlations among variables, $r_{ij}$, are used to estimate the true correlations, $P_{ij}$. Each of these path coefficients is equivalent to a standardized partial regression coefficient; that is, $P_{31} = \beta_{31.2}$, $P_{32} = \beta_{32.1}$, $P_{41} = \beta_{41.2}$, and $P_{42} = \beta_{42.1}$.

The use of path analysis controls successfully for one important problem which might ensue were the raw correlations employed. That is, consider the path from $X_1$ to $X_4$. In addition to the direct path between these two variables, there is a less direct but nevertheless plausible means by which $X_1$ could indirectly influence $X_4$. This possibility is diagrammed in Figure 4. For example, a high correlation between first-semester attendance and second-semester grades could be mediated by: 1) a high correlation between grades and attendance in the first semester, and 2) a high correlation between first and second semester grades.

Figure 4: Alternate path for the $X_1 - X_4$ relationship

More formally, the synchronous correlation between $X_1$ and $X_2$ plus a high $X_2 - X_4$ correlation could "explain" the $X_1$ to $X_4$ relationship. Path analysis circumvents this problem by employing standard partial regression coefficients rather than the raw correlations.

Heise (1970) has also examined some important properties of path analysis of panel data by employing computer simulation procedures. In one important series, he investigated the influence of low reliabilities of the measurements (i.e., reliabilities of .50 to .64). His conclusion was as follows:

There appears to be a close parallelism between the estimated values and the true values of the system parameters, and, in fact

the product-moment correlation between the two sets of coefficients is .99. This suggests that even though the two-wave model does not yield the actual values of the system parameters
when measurements are imprecise, it might give a set of numbers which could be used for causal inference (p.15).

For the aforementioned reasons, it seems both important and appropriate to apply the procedures of path analysis to the Lefkowitz et al. data
generated. The results of this analysis are displayed in Figure 5.

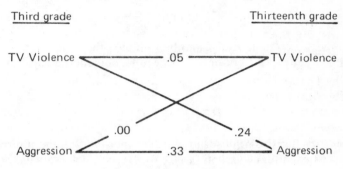

Figure 5:  Path analysis of the Lefkowitz et al. data

As may be seen, the results of the path analysis do not contradict and,
in fact, add further support to the conclusion of Lefkowitz et al. concerning the influence of violent television in the third grade upon subsequent aggressive behavior in early adulthood. The path coefficient for
the relationship between television violence in the third grade and subsequent aggressive behavior was .24, while the path coefficient for the relationship between aggression in the third grade and subsequent preference for violent television fare was 0.00. The most plausible interpretation of these results is that a preference for violent television in the third
grade is causally related to aggressive behavior ten years later.

Two further points merit discussion. First, while the path analysis
does not require that the same variables be measured at each of the two
times, the introduction of different measures does raise the issue of possible changes in reliability and thus provides a possible challenge to the
interpretation of the results of the cross-lagged design. As Campbell
(1963) has noted, a variable which increases in reliability from time one
to time two will, ceteris paribus, show up as an "effect" rather than as a
cause. However, a case can be made that both the measure of preference for violent television programs and peer-rated aggressiveness may
have been more reliable in the thirteenth grade (see Chaffee, 1971).
Thus, since no compelling evidence is available that only one of the variables increased in reliability, the change-in-reliability interpretation of
the Lefkowitz et al. data becomes less plausible. Second, within the

context of the logic of panel designs, the possibility remains that the relationship between viewing violent television fare and subsequent levels of aggression is mediated by a third variable. However, other correlational and experimental research has ruled out many plausible third variables. Thus, the most parsimonious interpretation of the Lefkowitz et al. data seems to be that favored by the investigators themselves—namely, that preference for violent television programs in the third grade is causally related to subsequent aggressive behavior.

## FOOTNOTES

1. As noted by Rozelle and Campbell (1969), there are actually four possible hypotheses, but only two need be considered for illustrative purposes.

## REFERENCES

Campbell, D. T. From description to experimentation: interpreting trends as quasi-experiments. In C. W. Haris (Ed.) *Problems in measuring change*. Madison: University of Wisconsin Press, 1963.

Chaffee, S. J. Television and adolescent aggressiveness. In *Television and social behavior*, Vol. 3 (this volume).

Heise, D. R. Causal inference from panel data. In E. F. Borgatta and G. W. Bohrnstedt (Eds.) *Sociological methodology 1970*. San Francisco: Jossey-Bass, 1970.

Lefkowitz, M. M., Eron, L. D., Walder, L. O., and Huesmann, L. R. Television violence and aggression: A followup study. In *Television and social behavior*, Vol. 3 (this volume).

Rozelle, R. M., and Campbell, D. T. More plausible rival hypotheses in the cross-lagged panel correlation technique. *Psychological Bulletin*, 1969, **71**, 74-80.

# Adolescent Television Use in the Family Context

Steven H. Chaffee and Jack M. McLeod

*University of Wisconsin*

This study consists of a secondary analysis of data originally collected in a field survey of parent-adolescent communication and political socialization, under a grant to the authors by the National Science Foundation.[1] The data were gathered in 1968 in five eastern Wisconsin school districts, which had been selected to provide socioeconomic and political diversity. Since details of sampling and data collection have been described elsewhere (Chaffee, Ward, and Tipton, 1970), only those particulars that are pertinent to this study will be described here.

Adolescent viewing of two kinds of television programs that often feature violent action—spy-adventure shows and westerns—is the central dependent variable in this study. Adolescents' self-reported frequency of viewing such programs is analyzed in relation to a series of individual and parent-child interaction factors. Individual correlates include the youngster's grade level, sex, IQ, socioeconomic status (SES), dogmatism, and total use of television. Parental and interaction variables include the parent's sex, viewing of violent programs, and total use of television; parent-child communication structure; and parental sanctions in terms of affection, punishment, and restrictiveness toward the child.

## PROCEDURES AND MEASURES

# The sample

The five communities are located in the Fox River Valley and suburban Milwaukee regions of Wisconsin and ranged in population from about 18,000 to 68,000 in the 1960 census. On the basis of census occupational and income data, three communities were classified as predominantly white-collar and two as blue-collar in preliminary planning for the study. In May 1968, questionnaires were administered all seventh- and tenth-grade students in the smaller communities, and in certain schools (selected in collaboration with local school officials) in the larger cities. These questionnaires provided what will be referred to hereafter as our "spring-child" data. They also formed the basic universe for drawing the final sample.

In all, some 8,000 questionnaires were filled out in May. From these a subsample was drawn according to three criteria:

If more than a few questionnaire items had not been answered, the student was eliminated from the study.

Those who gave rural-route addresses, or who indicated they would not be in the same school district the following fall semester, were eliminated.

A sampling list was compiled randomly from the remaining questionnaires, designed to provide roughly equal Ns for each district, grade level, and sex.

This sampling list was given to interviewers of the Wisconsin Survey Research Laboratory, who interviewed one parent of each student at home in September and October. Fathers and mothers were sampled alternately, according to a predetermined schedule. These interviews provide the "parent" measures referred to in this report. At the end of each interview, the parent was asked for permission to administer a second questionnaire to the child at school. In November 1968, those children whose parents had given permission were remeasured, providing what is called "fall-child" data here. The eventual sample of 1,292 comprises more than 90 per cent of those whose parents had been interviewed in early fall.

Throughout this report, we will refer to "junior high" and "senior high" subsamples, although those labels do not necessarily coincide with the precise titles of the schools. The junior high sample consists of 641 who were seventh graders in May and eighth graders in November. The 651 senior high respondents were in the tenth grade in May and the eleventh in November.

This sample is obviously not representative of the schools, districts, or cities involved, since several nonrandom factors were involved in the sampling. The two grade-level subsamples are only roughly comparable, because junior high and middle school district boundaries are not always coterminous with senior high boundaries, and because Roman Catholic families are more likely to send their children to public senior high schools than to public junior highs.

There is nothing "typical" about these five districts, any more than any other five. Their populations are overwhelmingly white, and they are suburban and industrial communities concentrated in an agrarian region of the upper Midwest. These biases in the sample will affect the absolute level on at least some of our variables. Therefore we will concentrate on relationships between variables in our analysis. The extent to which these relationships are peculiar to this sample can be checked independently, by replication in other settings.

## Measures

This section describes the indices used in this report, beginning with the dependent variables and following with the independent variables in the order in which they are introduced in the analysis.

*Child's violence viewing.* In both spring and fall, the student was asked to indicate which kinds of television programs he watched at least "pretty often." Among the program types listed were "westerns" and "spy-adventure shows." The spring and fall data have been combined into a single three-level index for each type of program, and these indices have been further summed into a six-level measure that we will call "violence viewing" on the assumption that the programs included were fairly likely in 1968 to present scenes involving violent action. For convenience throughout the paper, we will use the label *VV* to refer to this violence viewing index and to the corresponding measure for the parent (see below).

Some important inadequacies of the *VV* measures should be mentioned. Few items, not finely graded, are involved; this means that we cannot expect better than minimal reliability of measurement. Further, the questions are not very specific; in 1968 a great variety of programs could have been loosely described by the labels "spy-adventure" and "western," including some comedy shows. No better measures are available for this study, simply because television violence was not considered a factor of importance when the original study of family communication and political socialization was planned and carried out. To compensate somewhat for unreliability, the sample size is large, and there is a rather rich variety of other variables for analysis. Rather small correlations will be statistically significant (albeit numerically unimpressive), and we will be able to control simultaneously for a number of potentially important factors.

One might reason that there is an important difference between watching television a great deal (and therefore seeing considerable violent action) and the more specific behavior of selecting violent programs to the relative exclusion of other television fare. Therefore we have analyzed not only the *absolute* VV level, but also the *relative* VV level by controlling for the child's total television time. Items in the spring and fall questionnaires asked, respectively, "About how long did you watch television yesterday?" and "On an average day, about how many hours do you usually spend watching television in the evening after 5 p.m.?" These items were summed into a single index of television time. This index bears an obvious part-whole relationship to VV (with which it correlates .29). By controlling for television time, we can examine the specific effects on VV of our independent variables, separately from their general influence on the child's overall use of television.

*Parent's television use.* The parent questionnaire included single-item measures of television time and of western and spy program viewing that were identical to the spring-child questions. These items were summed and analyzed in the same fashion as were the corresponding child items.

*Dogmatism.* Rokeach (1960) introduced this concept as an indicator of a "close-minded" personality. Four items were drawn from the Rokeach battery and included in both the parent and child (fall) questionnaires; agreement scores were summed to provide an estimate of dogmatism for each individual. The items:

a.  In this complicated world, the only way we can know what is going on is to rely on leaders or experts who can be trusted. (+)
b.  It's often good to reserve judgment about what's going on until you have heard all the opinions about it. (−)
c.  Of all the different beliefs that exist in the world, there is probably only one that is correct. (+)
d.  In most political disagreements, there is something good to be said on both sides of the question. (−)

*Socioeconomic status.* A three-item SES index was constructed from questions (asked of the parent) concerning occupation of main earner, family income, and parent's education.

*Intelligence quotient.* For approximately 90 per cent of the youngsters, school records provided estimates of IQ. Therefore analyses involving this measure will have somewhat reduced Ns. The most recent IQ score was used, regardless of the particular test involved.

*Family communication pattern.* The present data constitute the most extensive attempt to date to assess the structure of parent-child communication in a large sample of families. This line of research began in a southern Wisconsin community in 1965 (see McLeod, Chaffee, and Eswara, 1966; Chaffee, McLeod, and Wackman, 1966; McLeod, Chaffee, and Wackman, 1967); fragments of related findings have been published (McLeod, Rush, and Friederich, 1968-69; Stone and Chaffee, 1970; Chaffee, McLeod, and Atkin, 1971). These early studies provide the empirical base for a general model of coorientation (Chaffee and McLeod, 1970; McLeod and Chaffee, in press). Since the measures constitute the most original aspect of this report, we will digress somewhat here to describe their background.

In a half-dozen studies in a variety of social settings, we have consistently found by factor analysis that there are at least two dimensions of variation in the structure of parent-child communication. Although these dimensions are in some respects conceptually contradictory, we have found that empirically they are either uncorrelated or slightly positively associated. We have called these dimensions *socio-oriented* and *concept-oriented* patterns of constraint on the developing child. (In the present sample, these two measures correlate .11, which is the strongest association we have found between them in any study to date.)

The socio-oriented relation, which may be pressed on a very young child, is typified by encouraging the youngster to maintain harmonious interpersonal relations, avoid controversy, and repress his inner feelings on extrapersonal topics. Following are some sample items that were asked, with appropriate variations in wording, of both parent and child; in some cases the question asked about the *frequency* of the act, and in other question parental *emphasis* was estimated by the respondent:

> (Parent) urges (child) to give in on arguments rather than risk antagonizing others.
> (Parent) answers (child's) arguments by saying something like, "You'll know better when you grow up."
> (Parent) lets (child) know that (child) should not show anger in a group.
> (Parent) stresses that there are some things in life that are either right or wrong.
> (Parent) says that the best way to stay out of trouble is to keep away from it.
> (Parent) says that discussions are better if you keep them pleasant.

Concept-oriented communication was measured on a similar set of items, dealing with the emphasis or frequency of parental constraints on the child to express his own ideas, become exposed to controversy, and challenge the views of others. Some sample items:

> (Parent) encourages (child) to challenge (parent's) ideas and beliefs.
> (Parent) asks (child's) opinion when family is discussing something.
> (Parent and child) have family talks about topics like politics or religion, where some persons take different sides from others.
> (Parent) says that (child) should always look at both sides of an issue before making up (child's) mind.
> (Parent) argues about things like politics or religion when visiting with friends or relatives, when (child) is present.

The socio-orientation decreases during adolescence. Concept-orientation changes very little from junior to senior high school. At both grade levels, about as many families stress *both* or *neither* orientation as stress one or the other (Chaffee, McLeod and Atkin, 1971).

Although it is possible to treat each of these dimensions as a separate independent variable, we have found in some studies that the two interact, producing structural patterns that are not simply the sums of their two constituent functions. Therefore we will treat family communication at later points in this report in terms of four types:

a. *Laissez faire* families, which emphasize neither type of relation. Children are not prohibited from challenging parental views but neither are they exposed to the world of independent and contending ideas.

b. *Protective* families, which stress socio-relations only. The child is encouraged to get along with others, at the expense of concept-relations that would expose him to the controversial world of ideas. Not only is he prohibited from expressing dissent, but he is given little chance to encounter information on which he might base his own views.

c. *Pluralistic* families, which emphasize the development of strong and varied concept-relations in an environment comparatively free of social restraints. The child is encouraged to explore new ideas and is exposed to controversial material; he can make up his own mind without fear of endangering social relations with his parents.

d. *Consensual* families, which attempt to stress both orientations. While the child is exposed to controversy, and told he should enter into it, he is (paradoxically) constrained to develop concepts that are consonant with existing socio-relations. That is, he is in effect encouraged to learn his parents' ideas and adopt their values.

*Affection, punishment, and restrictiveness.* In addition to socializing their children via family communication patterns, parents can exercise a number of direct sanctions over their children's behavior. We constructed four indices representing different kinds of sanctions: parental affection, physical punishment, verbal punishment, and restrictiveness.

Affection is based on three items in the spring-child questionnaire. The first two were separate indicators for father and mother, in response to the question, "How often do you feel your parents show they love you?" The third item consisted of the number of different ways of demonstrating affection that the child indicated in response to the question, "How do you think your parents show you they love you?"

Physical Punishment is a four-item index, consisting of two questions, each asked separately of parent and child (spring). The first question asked how often (parent) punished (child) physically when (child) was younger. The second asked how often (parent) punishes child "now" by "spanking." (Appropriate variations in wording were used in the respective questionnaires.)

Verbal Punishment is a six-item index, consisting of three questions, each asked separately of parent and child (spring). The items asked how often (parent) punishes (child) by three methods: by yelling at (child);

by trying to make (child) feel bad; and by lecturing (child) or talking to (child) about it.

Restrictiveness is a six-item sum based on three items, each of which was asked of both parent and child (spring). Two of these items asked how often (parent) punishes (child) by taking away privileges and/or by "grounding" (child). The third item asked how many different kinds of (child's) activities the parents had "definite rules" for; a checklist of eight possible areas for rules was offered. On the assumption that the youngster's perception of a rule was functionally more important for our purposes than the parent's perception, the parental response to this item was given only half the weight of the child's response in our index.

## FINDINGS

Although the selection of variables and models of analysis implies certain theoretical assumptions, the presentation of data here will not proceed on the basis of formal hypotheses. Rather, we will examine a series of complex tables, each of which shows a number of relationships, and discuss the possible theoretical import of those relationships that we find to be non-zero. Statistical significance tests are not an important element of the analysis, except as rough indicators of which relationships are strong enough to warrant further consideration. We therefore will use asterisks to indicate three conventional significance levels: * (p < .05), ** (p < .01) and *** (p < .001). For difference comparisons, these asterisks indicate the significance of the z-ratio (two-tailed). For correlations, they indicate the significance of the difference of the correlation from zero, in either direction. All correlations are Pearson product-moment coefficients (r), unless otherwise indicated.

## Overall analyses

Taking the entire sample (N = 1292) first, Tables 1-3 show various relationships between child's VV and other variables. Since the sample size is large, some quite modest correlations are asterisked as statistically significant in these tables.

Table 1 shows the raw correlations between child's VV and 12 variables, each of which is related to the criterion variable to at least some extent. The first two correlated measures are the parent's estimate of his own viewing. Clearly the specific VV measures correlate more strongly with child's VV than does the general measure of the parent's television time. However, the parent's television time measure correlates .19*** with child's television time. Correlations between parent and child on similar measures have led other authors to conclude that a process of "modeling," wherein the child fashions his viewing behavior in line with "parental example," can explain why youngsters watch television as they do (Himmelweit et al., 1958; Schramm et al., 1961). In Schramm's rather strong words, "example is the best persuader" and exercises "a very potent kind of influence" over a child's viewing (Schramm et al., 1961: 182). On the basis of several kinds of evidence, we have concluded elsewhere (Chaffee, McLeod, and Atkin, 1971) that the case for the modeling hypothesis is fairly weak, at least at the adolescent age level.

Table 1:  Correlates of child's violence viewing, total sample

| Correlated measure | Child's viewing index | | |
|---|---|---|---|
| | Westerns | Spy-adventure | *VV* sum |
| Parent's *VV*[a] | .22*** | .10*** | .13*** |
| Parent's TV time | .04 | .05 | .06* |
| Child's TV time | .23*** | .24*** | .29*** |
| Child's I.Q. | −.24*** | −.10*** | −.21*** |
| SES | −.15*** | .04 | −.08** |
| Child's dogmatism | .12*** | .03 | .10*** |
| Concept-oriented FCP | −.07** | .02 | −.04 |
| Socio-oriented FCP | .11*** | .11*** | .13*** |
| Affection | .06* | .05 | .07* |
| Physical punishment | .09*** | .05 | .09** |
| Verbal punishment | .06* | .08** | .08** |
| Restrictiveness | .10*** | .12*** | .14*** |

(N=1292)

[a]Corresponding indices were correlated (parent-western with child-western, etc.).

   *p < .05
  **p < .01
***p < .001

Table 1 also shows correlations between *VV* and several properties of the family or the child. Unsurprisingly, the child's TV time is a good predictor of his *VV*; this can be thought of as a part-whole correlation. The fact that this is the largest correlation in Table 1 is trivial substantively. (Indeed, the fact that it is no larger than .30 is evidence that both measures are little more than minimally reliable.)

The child's IQ is clearly negatively associated with *VV*, which replicates the Schramm et al. (1961) finding among adolescents. For dogmatism and SES, the correlations with *VV* are restricted to western programs; these variables are not significantly associated with spy-adventure viewing, a pattern that we find for many other predictors as well (see below). Generally, however, these variables, which are exogenous to the parent-child interaction, form a coherent pattern. The high *VV* child is more likely to be from a low SES family, to record low scores on IQ tests, and to endorse dogmatic statements on a "personality" inventory. These factors are themselves interrelated, of course; dogmatism is associated with lower IQ (r = −.26) and lower SES (r = −.11). In our later analyses, we have controlled for IQ and SES, but have dropped dogmatism from the partialing analysis because it is a minor factor and redundant to the more obvious measures of intelligence and status. (We continue to show the raw correlations between dogmatism and *VV* in various subsamples, however.) We retain SES in our partialing (below), even though it is weakly related to *VV*, because earlier studies found that SES interacts with parent-child interaction variables similar to those in this study (Maccoby, 1954; Schramm et al., 1961).

Looking next in Table 1 at family communication patterns, there is a tendency toward higher *VV* in socio-oriented homes; in the concept-oriented families the youngsters are less likely to view westerns. As indicated in our earlier discussion, we expect these two dimensions to interact somewhat; we will defer detailed comparisons among the four family types to a later point in this report.

Finally, Table 1 shows positive correlations between *VV* and the four indices of affection, punishment, and restrictiveness. The positive association with affection runs counter both to suggestions from earlier studies with younger children (e.g., Maccoby, 1954), and perhaps to "common sense." On the other hand, the general thrust of the literature would incline one to expect, if anything, stronger correlations between *VV* and the punishment and restrictiveness measures. This hypothesis has not been specifically stated, but it is certainly suggested by the emphasis on primary group and family influences on children's television use (Himmelweit et al., 1958; Schramm et al., 1961; Hess and Goldman, 1962; Maccoby, 1954; Riley and Riley, 1951, 1959; Tannenbaum and Greenberg, 1968; Ward and Wackman, 1971). Moreover, the rather low raw correlations of these four measures with *VV* could be due to response-set on the part of the child; inferences about the relationships should be deferred pending partialed analyses that would control for this factor (see below).

Table 2 presents three multivariate analyses, with and without controls for child's television time. The first of these shows that parent-child *VV* correlations stand up rather well under partialing and are independent of the time spent with television by either parent or child. The small raw correlation between parent's television time and child's *VV* (see Table 1) is accounted for by the specific correlation between the two *VV* measures.

A similar situation is found for family communication patterns in Table 2. The relationship between socio-orientation and a portion of the *VV* variance is not strengthened by adding the concept-orientation measure and using the multiple correlation.

Finally, Table 2 shows that the positive raw correlation between *VV* and the two punishment indices vanishes when the affection and restrictiveness measures are controlled. The latter two measures remain positively associated with *VV* even when child's television time is partialed out. The direction of causality (if any) remains an open issue, of course.

Table 2: Multiple regression analyses of child's _VV_, total sample

| Independent variable | Child's viewing index | | | | | |
|---|---|---|---|---|---|---|
| | Westerns | | Spy-adventure | | _VV_ sum | |
| | abs.[a] | rel.[a] | abs. | rel. | abs. | rel. |
| _Parental TV use_ | | | | | | |
| Parent's _VV_ | .23*** | .22*** | .10*** | .09*** | .12*** | .11*** |
| Parent's TV time | −.01 | −.04 | .02 | −.01 | .01 | −.04 |
| Multiple correlation[b] | .23*** | | .11*** | | .13*** | |
| _Family communication patterns_ | | | | | | |
| Concept-orientation | −.08** | −.06** | .00 | .03 | −.05 | −.02 |
| Socio-orientation | .12*** | .08** | .11*** | .07* | .14*** | .10*** |
| Multiple correlation | .14*** | | .11*** | | .14*** | |
| _Parental sanctions_ | | | | | | |
| Affection | .07* | .06* | .06* | .05 | .08** | .07* |
| Physical punishment | .05 | .05 | −.02 | −.02 | .03 | .03 |
| Verbal punishment | .01 | .02 | .04 | .04 | .03 | .04 |
| Restrictiveness | .06* | .04 | .10*** | .08** | .10*** | .07** |
| Multiple correlation | .13*** | | .14*** | | .16*** | |

(N=1292)
Note: Cell entries are partial correlations between the independent variable and the viewing index, controlling for all other independent variables in the group.
[a] Absolute viewing index (abs.) is the raw sum score. For the relative viewing index (rel.),
  child's TV time is controlled.
[b] Multiple correlation represents the total relationship with the entire group of independent
  variables.

Table 3 shows the relative predictive power of each of these independent variables for _VV_, when all the other variables are held constant. Only three independent variables statistically "survive" this stringent partialing: parent's _VV_, affection, and IQ. When child's television
time remains uncontrolled, two other variables are of borderline significance: restrictiveness and the suppressing influence of concept-oriented FCP.

# Analyses by grade level

Tables 4-7 examine the junior high and senior high subsamples separately. Table 4 replicates the Schramm et al. (1961) finding of a decline in
television time during adolescence, and shows that this trend includes
both western and spy-adventure programs. An earlier study from this
same body of data shows that this trend does not extend to news program
viewing, which increases gradually through adolescence and into adulthood (Chaffee, Ward, and Tipton, 1970).

Table 3: Grand multiple regression analysis of violence viewing, total sample

| Independent variable | Child's violence viewing | |
|---|---|---|
| | Absolute | Relative |
| Parent's _VV_ | .11*** | .10*** |
| Parent's TV time | .00 | −.04 |
| Child's TV time | | .24*** |
| Child's I.Q. | −.18*** | −.16*** |
| SES | .01 | .03 |
| Concept-oriented FCP | −.07* | −.04 |
| Socio-oriented FCP | .05 | .03 |
| Affection | .09** | .08** |
| Physical punishment | .02 | .02 |
| Verbal punishment | .03 | .04 |
| Restrictiveness | .06* | .05 |
| Multiple correlation | .29*** | |

(N=1178)

Note: Cell entries are partial correlations between the independent variable and child's _VV_, controlling for all other independent variables in the table. Total N is reduced because IQ data were not available for all students.

Table 4: Child's TV use, by grade level

| Index | Junior high | Senior high | z |
|---|---|---|---|
| Child's TV time | 5.20 | 3.93 | 12.6*** |
| Child's western viewing | 3.01 | 2.69 | 4.9*** |
| Child's spy viewing | 3.87 | 3.49 | 6.3*** |
| Child's _VV_ | 6.88 | 6.18 | 6.9*** |
| (N) | (641) | (651) | |

*** p < .001

Table 5 examines the parent-child "modeling" correlations for _VV_ separately for each grade level. These correlations are stronger at the junior high level, particularly when various control variables are partialed out. It is comparatively impressive that the junior high raw correlation between parent and child _VV_ is not reduced when variance due to IQ, SES, parent and child television time, family communication patterns, affection, punishment, and restrictiveness are all controlled. At the senior high level, these controls reduce the parent-child correlation to a nonsignificant figure.

The importance of these latter factors at each grade level is examined in Tables 6 and 7. IQ, SES, and dogmatism are associated with _VV_ to about the same extent regardless of grade. This is not true of the parent-child interaction variables, however. There appears to be a decline with age in the importance of family communication patterns and physical

Table 5: Parent-child viewing correlations, by grade level

| Index | Junior high | | Senior high | | Total sample | |
|---|---|---|---|---|---|---|
| | uncon. | cont.[d] | uncon. | cont. | uncon. | cont. |
| TV time: | | | | | | |
| Raw correlation[a] | .17*** | | .20*** | | .19*** | |
| Western viewing: | | | | | | |
| Raw correlation | .24*** | .23*** | .21*** | .18*** | .22*** | .20*** |
| Partial correlation[b] | .16*** | .18*** | .10* | .09* | .13*** | .13*** |
| Relative partial corr.[c] | .15*** | .16*** | .10* | .09* | .12*** | .13*** |
| Spy-adventure viewing: | | | | | | |
| Raw correlation | .13*** | .15*** | .07 | .04 | .10*** | .09** |
| Partial correlation | .10** | .10* | .00 | .00 | .05 | .05 |
| Relative partial corr. | .09* | .08 | .00 | .00 | .04 | .03 |
| Violence viewing (_VV_) | | | | | | |
| Raw correlation | .16*** | .20*** | .10** | .07 | .13*** | .12*** |
| Partial correlation | .17*** | .18*** | .06 | .06 | .11*** | .11*** |
| Relative partial corr. | .16*** | .16*** | .06 | .06 | .10*** | .10*** |
| (N) | (641) | (543) | (651) | (635) | (1292) | (1178) |

[a]Raw correlation is the Pearson r between parent's viewing and child's viewing, on the index listed.
[b]Partial correlation is the raw r, controlled for FCP, affection-punishment indices, and parent's TV time.
[c]Relative partial correlation is controlled for child's TV time.
[d]Controlled ("cont.") correlations are controlled for SES, IQ, and parent's TV time. Ns are somewhat smaller due to missing IQ data.

Table 6: Correlates of child's _VV_, by grade level

| Correlated measure | Grade | Child's viewing index | | | |
|---|---|---|---|---|---|
| | | Westerns | Spy-adv. | _VV_ | (N) |
| Child's IQ | jr. hi | −.23*** | −.05 | −.18*** | (543) |
| | sr. hi | −.23*** | −.11** | −.21*** | (635) |
| SES | jr. hi | −.18*** | .05 | −.09* | (641) |
| | sr. hi | −.15*** | .01 | −.09* | (651) |
| Child's dogmatism | jr. hi | .12** | −.01 | .07 | (641) |
| | sr. hi | .09* | .02 | .07 | (651) |
| Concept-orientation | jr. hi | −.13** | .00 | −.09* | (641) |
| | sr. hi | −.02 | .02 | .00 | (651) |
| Socio-orientation | jr. hi | .13** | .11* | .16*** | (641) |
| | sr. hi | .05 | .05 | .06 | (651) |
| Affection | jr. hi | .01 | −.02 | −.01 | (641) |
| | sr. hi | .06 | .06 | .07 | (651) |
| Phys. punishment | jr. hi | .10** | .03 | .09* | (641) |
| | sr. hi | .03 | .00 | .02 | (651) |
| Verbal punishment | jr. hi | .03 | .07 | .06 | (641) |
| | sr. hi | .06 | .05 | .07 | (651) |
| Restrictiveness | jr. hi | .02 | .07 | .05 | (641) |
| | sr. hi | .11** | .08* | .11** | (651) |

punishment, and contrarily an increase for affection, verbal punishment, and restrictiveness.

The data in Table 7, where each of these variables is examined with the others held constant, are consistent with those inferences—to the extent that any relationships hold up under this extensive partialing. An interesting note, in passing, is that a *negative* partial correlation between parent's television time and child's *VV* emerges in Table 7, at the junior high level. This finding is, of course, relative to many other factors in Table 7; it simply underscores the meaninglessness of the parent's total viewing, in contrast with his specific viewing of violent programs. The latter is the best predictor of child's *VV* in the junior high subsample.

Table 7: Grand multiple regression analysis of violence viewing, by grade level

| Independent variable | Child's violence viewing (VV) | | | |
| | Junior high | | Senior high | |
| | abs.[a] | rel.[a] | abs. | rel. |
|---|---|---|---|---|
| Parent's *VV* | .18*** | .16*** | .06 | .06 |
| Parent's TV time | −.08 | −.09* | .05 | .01 |
| Child's TV time | | .14** | | .24*** |
| Child's I Q | −.15*** | −.14** | −.19*** | −.16*** |
| SES | .00 | .03 | −.01 | .00 |
| Concept-oriented FCP | −.08 | −.08 | −.03 | −.01 |
| Socio-oriented FCP | .11* | .10* | −.01 | −.01 |
| Affection | .03 | .04 | .08* | .07 |
| Physical punishment | .07 | .07 | −.04 | −.02 |
| Verbal punishment | .00 | .01 | .07 | .06 |
| Restrictiveness | −.01 | −.01 | .06 | .06 |
| Multiple correlation | .31*** | | .27*** | |
| (N) | (543) | (543) | (635) | (635) |

Note: Cell entries are partial correlations between child's VV and the listed independent variable, controlling for all other variables in this table.

[a]Absolute viewing index (abs.) is the raw sum score. For the relative viewing index (rel.), child's TV time is controlled.

## Analyses by sex

Tables 8 through 12 break the analysis into subsamples according to the respondent's sex. Table 8 shows that boys spend more time with television, and watch more violent programs, than girls. The differences are stronger at the senior high level. The decline in *VV* during adolescence (see Table 4) is more marked among the girls in Table 8. In effect, girls develop more rapidly during adolescence, toward the lower adult levels of *VV*. All these trends are similar to those reported by Schramm et al. (1961).

Table 8:  Child's TV use, by sex and grade level

| Index | Grade | Females | Males | z |
|---|---|---|---|---|
| Child's TV time | jr. hi | 5.08 | 5.29 | 1.6 |
| | sr. hi | 3.78 | 4.13 | 3.0** |
| Child's western viewing | jr. hi | 2.91 | 3.10 | 2.0* |
| | sr. hi | 2.57 | 2.83 | 2.7** |
| Child's spy viewing | jr. hi | 3.76 | 3.96 | 2.5* |
| | sr. hi | 3.35 | 3.66 | 3.9*** |
| Child's *VV* | jr. hi | 6.67 | 7.06 | 3.3*** |
| | sr. hi | 5.92 | 6.49 | 4.1*** |
| (N) | jr. hi | (298) | (343) | |
| | sr. hi | (364) | (287) | |

Sex differences in *relative* violence viewing were analyzed by special correlational techniques. The point biserial correlation between child's sex and *VV* is .11** for junior high and .15*** for senior high, using the means in Table 8 as base scores. When these figures are controlled for child's television time, the partial point biserial correlations are .10** (junior high) and .13** (senior high), respectively. This means that the tendency for males to view violence more, particularly at the senior high level, holds true for relative as well as absolute viewing.

Parent-child sex comparisons are shown in Table 9. One salient feature stands out: the child's viewing correlates more strongly with the mother's than with the father's, regardless of the child's sex. This is true at both grade levels, and for each viewing index, and holds up consistently regardless of other controls introduced in the partialing analyses. There is no *VV* correlation in the father-daughter subsample. The tendency toward greater parent-child correlations for westerns than for spy-adventure programs holds up consistently across all four subsamples in Table 9 and under all statistical controls.

Table 10 shows the raw correlations within each sex-grade subsample, between *VV* and IQ, SES and dogmatism. There is a tendency toward more *VV* among low-SES boys, at both grade levels. The subsample partialing makes little difference with respect to either IQ or dogmatism.

Correlations of parent-child interaction variables with *VV* are shown separately for each sex-combination subsample in Table 11. The pattern is quite clear: each of the six variables predicts *VV* most strongly within the mother-son subsample. In fact, aside from restrictiveness, the mother-son data provide the only significant relationships in Table 11. It is as if all forms of maternal control over the son increase the likelihood of *VV* to some extent: affection, punishment, restrictiveness, and socio-oriented communication.

The same-sex (i.e., father-son, mother-daughter) data are quite weak overall, and the father-daughter relationship appears to mean nothing aside from a positive correlation between *VV* and restrictiveness.

Table 9: Parent-child viewing correlations, by sex of parent and child

| Index | Fathers | | Mothers | |
|---|---|---|---|---|
| | Sons | Daughters | Sons | Daughters |
| TV time: | | | | |
| Raw correlation | .14* | .15** | .23*** | .22*** |
| Western viewing: | | | | |
| Raw correlation | .19** | .19** | .29*** | .25*** |
| Partial correlation | .18** | .19** | .27*** | .24*** |
| Relative partial r | .18** | .17** | .26*** | .23*** |
| Spy-adventure viewing: | | | | |
| Raw correlation | .11 | .02 | .13* | .13* |
| Partial correlation | .09 | .02 | .12* | .12* |
| Relative partial r | .08 | −.01 | .10 | .11* |
| Violence viewing (VV): | | | | |
| Raw correlation | .13* | .02 | .19*** | .19*** |
| Partial correlation | .11 | .02 | .15** | .16** |
| Relative partial r | .10 | −.02 | .12* | .15** |
| (N) | (297) | (301) | (333) | (361) |

Note: For explanation of the various partialing techniques in this table, see notes to Table 5. There are no controls for IQ or SES in this table.

Table 10: Correlates of child's VV, by child's sex and grade level

| Correlated measure | Sons | | Daughters | |
|---|---|---|---|---|
| | jr. hi | sr. hi | jr. hi | sr. hi |
| Child's IQ | −.11 | −.25*** | −.25*** | −.20** |
| (N) | (291) | (282) | (252) | (353) |
| SES | −.13* | −.19** | −.08 | −.05 |
| Child's dogmatism | .04 | .12 | .10 | .02 |
| (N) | (343) | (287) | (298) | (364) |

In Table 12 these variables are examined simultaneously, within each subsample. With the other independent variables controlled, VV appears to be a function of the following:

—Mother's VV.

—Mother's affection.

—Father's restrictiveness toward daughter.

—Mother-son family communication pattern, both as a positive function of socio-orientation and as a negative function of concept-orientation.

The father-child variables predict VV less well as a group than do the mother-child variables, to judge from the multiple correlations in Table 12. The weakest data are in the father-son column, where none of the interaction variables is significantly related to child's VV. This is somewhat a surprising nonfinding on its face, and it contrasts with Clarke's

Table 11: Correlates of child's _VV_, by sex of parent and child

| Correlated measure | Fathers | | Mothers | |
|---|---|---|---|---|
| | Sons | Daughters | Sons | Daughters |
| Concept-oriented FCP | −.02 | .02 | −.10 | −.06 |
| Socio-oriented FCP | .10 | .04 | .30** | .08 |
| Affection | .09 | .05 | .11* | .09 |
| Physical punishment | .08 | −.03 | .11* | .08 |
| Verbal punishment | .10 | −.03 | .17** | .08 |
| Restrictiveness | .08 | .12* | .18** | .10* |
| (N) | (297) | (301) | (333) | (363) |

(1969) finding that the father-son relationship is a sensitive factor in accounting for teenage magazine reading. Other analyses (not shown) indicate that child's _VV_ is associated with mother's punishment and restrictiveness, in the junior high sample, only when coupled with a high degree of affection.

Table 12: Grand multiple regression analysis of child's _VV_, by sex of parent and child

| Independent variable | partial r | Fathers | | Mothers | |
|---|---|---|---|---|---|
| | | Sons | Daughters | Sons | Daughters |
| Parent's _VV_ | abs. | .11 | .02 | .15** | .16** |
| | rel. | .10 | −.02 | .12* | .15** |
| Child's TV time | rel. | .19** | .38*** | .27*** | .18*** |
| Concept-oriented FCP | abs. | −.07 | −.01 | −.20*** | −.08 |
| | rel. | −.04 | .05 | −.17** | −.05 |
| Socio-oriented FCP | abs. | .05 | .02 | .23*** | .03 |
| | rel. | .03 | −.04 | .21*** | .00 |
| Affection | abs. | .10 | .04 | .14* | .13* |
| | rel. | .07 | −.04 | .13* | .13* |
| Physical punishment | abs. | .04 | −.08 | −.06 | .02 |
| | rel. | .04 | −.07 | −.05 | .02 |
| Verbal punishment | abs. | .05 | −.07 | .05 | .04 |
| | rel. | .05 | −.06 | .05 | .06 |
| Restrictiveness | abs. | .00 | .15* | .08 | .06 |
| | rel. | .01 | .12* | .07 | .05 |
| Multiple r | abs. | .20*** | .17** | .39*** | .25*** |
| (N) | | (297) | (301) | (333) | (363) |

Note: For explanations of the various entries in this table, see notes to Table 7.

Our data also show that the mothers spend more time watching television daily than the fathers, but that the fathers report higher _VV_ levels. The absence of significant father-child "modeling" correlations thus cannot be ascribed to a low level of _VV_ by the father; nor can the significant mother-child "modeling" data be accounted for by her high general viewing—since parent's television time is uncorrelated with child's *VV*. All of this suggests that it is at least plausible to hypothesize that the youngsters influence their mothers to watch violent programs, rather than *vice versa*. We have discussed this "reverse modeling" hypothesis elsewhere (Chaffee, McLeod, and Atkin, 1971), and it is supported by studies showing that parents more frequently ask their teenagers for television program advice than *vice versa* (Clarke, 1963; Bottorff, 1970).

## Analyses by family communication patterns

For our last set of detailed analyses, we turn to the fourfold breakdown by family communication types, in Tables 13-15. Table 13 shows differences among the four FCP types in terms of standard scores. For parents, these scores are standardized on the overall mean across the four types. For the youngsters, the scores are standardized across eight categories—two grade levels for each of four FCP types. Thus the child data show developmental differences within, as well as differences between, the four family types.

Looking first in Table 13 at the television time measures, the highest scores within each line, for both parent and child, are found in the protective families, and the lowest in the pluralistic homes. For *VV* the protectives are again highest, but the laissez-faire scores are somewhat lower than the pluralistics.

Table 13: Parent's and child's TV use (standard scores), by family communication pattern

| Index | Laissez-faire | Pluralistic | Protective | Consensual |
|---|---|---|---|---|
| | Parent's TV use | | | |
| Parent's TV time | −09 | −16* | +22** | +06 |
| Parent's *VV* | −14* | −04 | +16* | +05 |
| (N) | (345) | (317) | (277) | (353) |
| | Child's TV use | | | |
| Child's TV time | | | | |
| jr. hi | +34*** | −02 | +71*** | +36*** |
| sr. hi | −27*** | −51*** | −15 | −42*** |
| Child's *VV* | | | | |
| jr. hi | +09 | +09 | +36*** | +24** |
| sr. hi | −29*** | −25** | −02 | −15 |
| (N) | | | | |
| jr. hi | (160) | (138) | (146) | (197) |
| sr. hi | (185) | (179) | (131) | (156) |

Note: Standard scores represent each cell mean, calculated as a deviation from the overall mean on the listed index, divided by the overall standard deviation. Scores have been multiplied by 100 to eliminate decimals. A negative score indicates the cell mean is below the overall mean for the index. Asterisks indicate the cell mean is significantly different from the overall mean for remaining cells.

In terms of junior-to-senior high net change, the pluralistic youngsters show the least shift during adolescence in the reduction of their total television time, but this is mainly because they do not watch TV a great deal even in junior high school. Conversely, the protectives show the greatest net change, but mostly because in junior high they spend so much more time with television than the other groups. (If more age levels were included in the sample, they might well show that the adolescent trend toward less television occurs first for pluralistics and latest among protectives.) For VV, however, the four types of children are about equal in the degree to which they reduce this behavior during adolescence. (These inferences would be much more solid if they were supported by longitudinal data from the same cohort, rather than semicomparable samples from different cohorts as is the case here.)

Table 14:  Parent-child viewing correlations, by family communication pattern

| Index | Grade | Laissez-faire | Pluralistic | Protective | Consensual |
|---|---|---|---|---|---|
| TV time | jr. hi | .13 | .11 | .01 | .27*** |
|  | sr. hi | .13 | .22** | .29*** | .17* |
| Western viewing | jr. hi | .26** | .11 | .23** | .28*** |
|  | sr. hi | .27** | .23** | .13 | .18* |
| Spy viewing | jr. hi | .14 | −.09 | .11 | .28*** |
|  | sr. hi | .07 | .06 | .06 | .04 |
| Violence viewing (VV) | jr. hi | .20* | −.03 | .15* | .25*** |
|  | sr. hi | .11 | .11 | .07 | .08 |
| (N) | jr. hi | (160) | (138) | (146) | (197) |
|  | sr. hi | (185) | (179) | (131) | (156) |

Table 14 presents the parent-child "modeling" correlations for each FCP type. They tend to be stronger at the junior high level for VV and at the senior high level for television time. The most consistent evidence for the modeling hypothesis is found in the consensual families, for the junior high subsample; this finding is consistent with the general proposition that within-family agreement on values is most likely to be found in the consensual home. The pluralistic homes appear to provide the least parent-child similarity in violence viewing, at least at the junior high level; similar findings have been reported elsewhere for television news and for news reading (Chaffee, McLeod, and Atkin, 1971).

Parental control variables associated with violence viewing, within FCP types, are examined in Table 15. Generally speaking, there are few significant correlations, and they follow no obvious pattern. This is perhaps to be expected, since earlier (Table 7) we found that these indices show little relationship with VV when grade level and FCP orientations are controlled.

Table 15: Correlates of child's *VV*, by family communication pattern

| Correlated measure | Grade | Laissez-faire | Pluralistic | Protective | Consensual |
|---|---|---|---|---|---|
| Affection | jr. hi | −.30*** | .08 | −.10 | .08 |
| | sr. hi | .01 | .04 | .20* | .11 |
| Physical punishment | jr. hi | −.01 | .10 | .08 | .07 |
| | sr. hi | .02 | −.02 | −.03 | .03 |
| Verbal punishment | jr. hi | −.11 | .19* | −.08 | .09 |
| | sr. hi | .07 | .04 | −.03 | .05 |
| Restrictiveness | jr. hi | −.02 | .06 | −.01 | .02 |
| | sr. hi | .19** | .07 | .06 | .03 |
| (N) | jr. hi | (160) | (138) | (146) | (197) |
| | sr. hi | (185) | (179) | (131) | (156) |

# CONCLUSIONS

With the full range of evidence before us, we can now consider the possible roles played by various elements of parent-child interaction in fostering *VV* by adolescents. Our inferences can be made without being challenged on the basis of the following variables, which have been controlled in our analyses:

a. IQ, which is strongly, and negatively, related to *VV* viewing.
b. Socioeconomic status, which has a mild negative relationship with *VV* that vanishes when other variables are controlled.
c. Age, which in adolescence is negatively related to *VV*.
d. Sex, which is related to *VV* in that boys watch programs of this type more than girls do.
e. Child's television time, which has a part-whole relationship with *VV*.

We will consider three classes of independent variables: parent's television use, parent-child communication patterns, and parental controls and sanctions regarding the child's behavior.

*Parent's television use.* The amount of time spent watching television by the parent is unrelated to the adolescent's violence viewing. Specific viewing of westerns by the parent is associated with similar viewing by the child; for spy-adventure programs there is a similar, though weaker, correlation. The correlations are stronger in early adolescence and where the parent involved is the mother.

Is this evidence that adolescents "model" their viewing of violent programs after "parental example"? Undoubtedly there are some instances in which parent viewing of violence encourages an adolescent to watch the program too. But a general hypothesis of child-to-parent modeling is scarcely necessary to account for the correlations we find.

To begin with, it should be noted that "parental example" can be either positive or negative. It seems more likely that parents, who watch violent programs far less than their adolescent children, would set a "negative example" by not watching. (Further, by not watching, the parents are more likely to involve the family in alternative activities.) This negative-effect inference is strengthened by the finding that the mother's viewing correlates more strongly with the child's than does the father's. If "modeling" were truly operating with any frequency, we should expect a teenage son to emulate his father. Moreover, the father tends to watch violent programs more often than the mother, although he spends less total time with television; if "modeling" were occurring, he would seem the more likely model, insofar as violence viewing is concerned.

Perhaps an even more plausible hypothesis, as we have mentioned earlier, is that the correlations are caused by "reverse modeling," from child to parent. Adolescents are, after all, the "TV experts" in the home, and we have cited evidence that parents often ask them for viewing advice (see also Chaffee, McLeod, and Atkin, 1971).

Another explanation for the parent-child correlations could be that two people living in the same house will be exposed to the same television shows to some extent, simply because it is not easy for one resident to avoid seeing a show that another has tuned in. Elsewhere we have rejected this "opportunity" hypothesis at least tentatively, because we were unable to find any difference between one-set and multiple-set homes in the degree of parent-child viewing correlation (Chaffee, McLeod, and Atkin, 1970); we reasoned that forced exposure to another's program selection would be more likely in single-set homes.

Finally, of course, there remains the possibility that exogenous factors that we have not incorporated into this study might independently "cause" members of the same family to use television in similar ways. We have controlled for some factors on which parent and child will be similar (IQ, television time, family communication pattern) or identical (SES). These controls have not eliminated the parent-child correlations, but it is conceivable that other variables might.

During adolescence the youngster's television use, including his viewing of violent programs, gradually decreases, approaching an adult level. But the similarity of his viewing to that of his parents decreases in this maturing period. It is quite unlikely, then, that "modeling" plays a major role in this phase of the developing person's life. Earlier authors, who were perhaps more concerned with younger children, appear to have relied too much on raw correlations without considering other hypotheses and external variables.

*Family communication patterns.* One factor that appears to account for a portion of the parent-child similarity in violence viewing is the habitual structure of family communication. The socio-orientation in particular accounts for large differences among the youngsters, and these differences remain fairly constant during adolescence. Similar, though less pronounced, patterns of difference are found among the parents in these families. Violence viewing is especially high in the "protective" home, where the parents stress the socio-orientation but not the concept-orientation in their child rearing communication.

These findings are roughly consistent with earlier studies, in which we found that the use of mass media for public affairs content is mainly associated with the concept-orientation, but entertainment media use follows the socio-orientation (Chaffee, McLeod, and Wackman, 1966; McLeod, Chaffee, and Wackman, 1967; Chaffee, McLeod, and Atkin, 1971).

We do not find here, however, that partialing out the family communication typology eliminates the parent-child correlations; nor does it help us much in specifying the conditions under which these correlations will be stronger. An earlier report showed greater parent-child television use correlations in socio-oriented homes (Chaffee, McLeod, and Atkin, 1971). This finding does not appear to hold for violence viewing specifically.

*Parental sanctions.* The most disappointing set of predictor variables in this study are the indices of parental affection, physical and verbal punishment, and restrictiveness. Neither punishment measure correlates with violence viewing at all. The "influence" of restrictiveness appears to be restricted to the father-daughter relationship and the senior high level. Only parental affection (as perceived by the child) is associated with violence viewing, and this finding holds mainly for the mother and senior high children.

Our measures are scarcely optimal, of course, and the question of a relationship between punishment and violence viewing should remain open pending more elaborate attempts to investigate it. Physical punishment is, after all, rare for adolescents, and verbal punishment may be something of a "constant" that is common to all parent-adolescent relationships. With a younger sample, or more reliable measures, the expectable correlations might yet be found.

The association we find between maternal affection and violence viewing by the child is neither intuitively satisfying nor consistent with what little "literature" exists on the topic. Because this correlation has withstood some rather stringent statistical partialing tests here, however, it is difficult to ignore. Maccoby (1954) found that upper-middle-class children who are not treated warmly at home spent more time watching television. Schramm et al. (1961) concluded that the Maccoby inference was basically sound, after examination of data based on a measure of parent-child conflict over aspirations for the child. The measures, time frames, ages, and locales of those studies are not necessarily comparable to ours, but in a loose conceptual fashion there is some discrepancy between the conclusions invited by our data and theirs.

The positive correlation between restrictiveness and violence viewing is clearly more in line with earlier inferences. It is not decreased appreciably by controlling for the child's television time, so it cannot be attributed to the fact that a "grounded" or restricted adolescent has more opportunity to stay home and watch television. On the other hand, it is not a strong correlation, all things considered. As with our other parental sanction variables, conclusive inferences (null or otherwise) should be withheld pending much fuller investigation than has been possible here.

*Violence viewing in the family context.* If there is one general conclusion to be reached from this study, it would be that family context variables do not make as much difference in adolescent violence viewing as earlier writers have suggested. Watching television (violent and otherwise) appears to be a "cultural universal" in early adolescence, and the period in which the developing child withdraws from heavy television use is also the period in which he becomes progressively less influenced by his parents. Parental viewing preferences are probably a minor, mostly negative, factor. Sex role differences account for some divergence among the adolescents, but do not account for similarities between them and their parents. Parental controls on the child make little difference, and neither does the family's socioeconomic status. There is evidence that long-range patterns of family communication help to shape the use the adolescent will make of television (and other media), but it is likely that these patterns are firmly established by early adolescence.

All of this begs the pressing policy question of effects of television violence on the youngster. Does the adolescent who watches violent programming in an affectionate or concept-oriented home environment react differently to it than, say, another youngster in a punitive or socio-oriented home? Is a boy's possible "modeling" of violent television action in any way related to the viewing or other behavior of his parents? We cannot deal with such questions with the limited data here. Hopefully, however, this study can help future researchers select important variables and fruitful hypotheses for more detailed study of television violence and the family environment.

## FOOTNOTES

1. This technical report describes research pursuant to Contract No. HSM 42-70-30 with the National Institute of Mental Health, Health Services and Mental Health Administration, U.S. Department of Health, Education, and Welfare. Charles K. Atkin (now at Michigan State University) was the primary project assistant. Others aiding in the data analysis included George Pasdirtz, William Elliott, Garrett O'Keefe Jr., and Selwyn Edwards.

# REFERENCES

Bottorff, A. Television, respect, and the older adolescent. Unpublished master's thesis, University of Wisconsin, 1970.

Chaffee, S.H., and McLeod, J.M. Coorientation and the structure of family communication. Paper presented at the meeting of the International Communication Association, Minneapolis, May, 1970.

Chaffee, S.H., McLeod, J.M., and Atkin, C.K. Parent-adolescent similarities in television use. Paper presented at the meeting of the Association for Education in Journalism, Washington, D.C., August, 1970.

Chaffee, S.H., McLeod, J.M., and Atkin, C.K. Parental influences on adolescent media use. *American Behavioral Scientist*, 1971, **14**, 323-40.

Chaffee, S.H., McLeod, J.M., and Wackman, D.B. Family communication and political socialization. Paper presented at the meeting of the Association for Education in Journalism, Iowa City, Ia., August, 1966.

Chaffee, S.H., Ward, L.S., and Tipton, L.P. Mass communication and political socialization. *Journalism Quarterly*, 1970, **47**, 647-59.

Clarke, P. An experiment to increase the audience for educational television. Unpublished doctoral dissertation, University of Minnesota, 1963.

Clarke, P. Identification with father and father-son similarities in reading behavior. Paper presented at the meeting of the Association for Education in Journalism, Berkeley, Calif., August, 1969.

Hess, R., and Goldman, H. Parents' views of the effects of TV on their children. *Child Development*, 1962, **33**, 411-26.

Himmelweit, H., Oppenheim, A., and Vince, P. *Television and the child*. London: Oxford University Press, 1958.

McLeod, J.M., and Chaffee, S.H. The construction of social reality. In J. Tedeschi (Ed.) *The social influence processes*. Chicago: Aldine, in press.

McLeod, J.M., Chaffee, S.H., and Eswara, H. Family communication patterns and communication research. Paper presented at the meeting of the Association for Education in Journalism, Iowa City, Ia., August, 1966.

McLeod, J.M., Chaffee, S.H., and Wackman, D.B. Family communication: An updated report. Paper presented at the meeting of the Association for Education in Journalism, Boulder, Colo., August, 1967.

McLeod, J.M., Rush, R.R., and Friederich, K.H. The mass media and political information in Quito, Ecuador. *Public Opinion Quarterly*, 1968-69, **32**, 575-87.

Riley, J.W., and Riley, M.W. Mass communication and the social system. In R.K. Merton, L. Broom, L.S. Cottrell (Eds.) *Sociology Today*. New York: Basic Books, 1959.

Riley, M.W., and Riley, J.W. A sociological approach to communications research. *Public Opinion Quarterly*, 1951, **15**, 445-60.

Rokeach, M. *The open and closed mind*. New York: Basic Books, 1960.

Schramm, W., Lyle, J., and Parker, E.B. *Television in the lives of our children*. Stanford, Calif.: Stanford University Press, 1961.

Stone, V.A., and Chaffee, S.H. Family communication patterns and source-message orientation. *Journalism Quarterly*, 1970, **47**, 239-46.

Tannenbaum, P.H., and Greenberg, B.S. Mass communication. *Annual Review of Psychology*, 1968, **19**, 351-86.

Ward, S., and Wackman, D. Family and media influences on adolescent consumer learning. *American Behavioral Scientist*, 1971, **14**, 415-27.

# Adolescents, Parents, and Television Use: Adolescent Self-report Measures from Maryland and Wisconsin Samples

Jack M. McLeod, Charles K. Atkin, and Steven H. Chaffee

*University of Wisconsin*

This is a report of two nonexperimental studies of the relationships among three sets of variables: adolescent aggression, television viewing behavior, and structural attributes of family social environment.[1] The first study examines questionnaire data obtained from 473 adolescents in Prince Georges County, Maryland. Data for the second study were gathered from 151 adolescents in Middleton, Wisconsin. This report contains data comparable between the two samples; a final report will include additional data available only from the Wisconsin sample.

Various self-report measures of aggression are treated as the ultimate dependent variable, although specification of the direction of causality is precluded by the lack of experimental control and panel design. The aggression measures are related to indices of self-reported frequency of viewing specific television programs and to cognitive reactions to violent television content. The aggression and viewing variables are studied in association with various aspects of the family social environment: parental punishment, affection, control over television viewing, nonaggression training, and social status.

Our analysis begins with an examination of each of the major sets of variables taken singly. We then take pairs of variable sets in their bivariate relationships, and conclude by investigating various multivariate combinations.

## PROCEDURES AND MEASURES

# Sampling

During April of 1970, questionnaires were completed by 229 seventh graders and 244 tenth graders in eight public schools in Prince Georges County, Maryland. This county, contiguous with the eastern half of Washington, D.C., was included to provide geographical and socioeconomic balance to our ongoing Wisconsin research. The sample selection, supervised by Dr. Jennie McIntyre of the University of Maryland, was coordinated with other studies conducted for the Television and Social Behavior program.

The Wisconsin data were gathered in Middleton, a community of approximately 7,000 that serves both as a bedroom suburb of Madison and as a trading center for the surrounding area. In October of 1969, 225 adolescents, comprising the entire school population in two grades, completed questionnaires in the city's two schools. During the same month, personal interviews were conducted with the mothers of these children. One year later, interviewers returned to the homes to reinterview 151 of the mothers and to administer questionnaires to 68 of the then seventh graders and to 83 adolescents now in the tenth grade. Move-outs accounted for the largest portion of the attrition from the original population.

Neither sample should be thought of as "typical" of the larger U.S. populations because opportunity was involved in the selection of both research sites. The Maryland sample was closer to the national average in some respects—as, for example, in its having 15 percent black students, contrasted with the all-white Wisconsin group. In other ways, however, both samples are atypical in being somewhat higher than average on various measures of socioeconomic status. For example, the proportion of mothers attending college was 33 percent for Maryland and 37 percent for Wisconsin. On all such measures, the Wisconsin families are slightly higher in social status. While the effect of bias in each sample cannot be known, it is likely that these effects would alter the absolute level on at least some of the variables. For that reason, standard scores rather than means are shown in our tables. We will also concentrate on relationships between variables in our analysis. The generalizability of these relationships can be known with certainty only through replication in other settings.

In keeping with our other research on adolescents, throughout this report we refer to "junior high" and "senior high" subsamples, although those labels do not necessarily coincide with the precise titles of schools. The Maryland junior high students were in seventh grade and those in senior high were in tenth grade. The Wisconsin groups were a grade lower in each case when the first questionnaire was administered and at those grade levels when they were studied for the second time.

The two grade levels are only roughly comparable, because the junior and senior high boundaries are not always coterminous and because Roman Catholic families are more likely to send their children to public senior high schools than to public junior highs.

# Measures: adolescent aggression

This section describes the various indices of self-reported adolescent aggression. The sections following describe our measures of television viewing behavior, structural attributes of the family social environment, and cognitive reactions to violent television programming. The description of each index will include a limited number of examples of items; a full listing for each index is included in Appendix A.

*Manifest physical aggression.* The adolescents were asked to judge a battery of 17 items and to indicate whether each was "not like me," "a little like me," or "a lot like me." This "like me" scale is taken from Greenberg and Dominick (1968). Item analysis and factor analysis indicated a grouping of six of these items having a common emphasis on the display of physical aggression. Three of the items are adapted from the assault aggression subscale of the Buss-Durkee (1957) aggression-hostility inventory, although these authors use a different underlying response scale.

The items:
- a. Whoever insults me or my family is asking for a fight.
- b. If somebody hits me first, I let him have it.
- c. When I lose my temper at someone, once in a while I actually hit them.

Three other items were devised for this research:
- d. When I am mad at someone, I sometimes fight with them instead of talking about the problem.
- e. When I was younger, I used to act like a bully sometimes.
- f. I don't feel it is wrong for me to hit other kids who deserve it.

*Aggressive behavioral delinquency.* Three items that involve overt aggressive acts were taken from the 23-item delinquency scale of Short and Nye (1957-58, 1958; Nye and Short, 1957). The student was asked to indicate the frequency with which he had been involved in each on a five-step scale ranging from "never" to "more than five times." Because of time limitations, these items were among the questions eliminated from the questionnaire given Wisconsin junior high students. The items:

a. Been in fights with several people on each side.
b. Hurt someone on purpose to get back for something they had done to you.
c. Got into a serious fight with another student at school.

*Zaks-Walters aggression.* Seven items were chosen from the Zaks-Walters 12-item inventory of generalized aggression. Although the manifest content of their items less clearly deals with overt aggressiveness, Walters and Zaks (1959) report predictive validity in discriminating between assaultive and nonassaultive prisoners to be greater than other more obvious self-report measures. They show similar validation results for other criterion groups. While the original scale involves a simple agree-disagree dichotomy, for certain items we used the three-choice "a lot like me" category system described above for manifest physical aggression. For most items, we used a five-step scale ranging from "agree strongly" to "disagree strongly" through the middle "no opinion." A sample of items:

a. I often do things which I regret after. ("a lot like me" scale)
b. I am very patient with people. ("a lot like me" scale, reversed scoring)
c. There are two kinds of people in this world: the weak and the strong. (agreement scale)

The combination of two underlying scales was justified by a satisfactory level of internal consistency and discriminant validity.

*Hypothetical aggressive reactions.* Adolescents were presented with four hypothetical conflict situations and asked to choose among three or four alternatives the thing they were most likely to do. The chosen responses were coded according to their degree of aggressiveness and summed across the four items. Two sample items:

a. What if someone cut in front of you in a long line. What would you do to them? (Shove them out, yell at them, just let it go)
b. Suppose someone played a real dirty trick on you. What would you do? (Hit them, yell at them, ignore them, laugh at them)

In the above examples, shoving and hitting were coded as highest in aggression, with yelling as an intermediate aggressive response. Letting it go, ignoring, and laughing at them were scored as equally low.

*Overall aggression sum.* By following the assumption that self-report measurement of adolescent aggression is best approached by surrounding the concept with a variety of items and scales, we combined the four indices described above into a single "best" measure of overall aggression. The combination of the 20 items makes a potential range of 64 scale positions for this "best estimate". For convenience, we will refer to this sum as *OAS* throughout this report.

*Buss-Durkee assault aggression.* This measure is comprised of the three Buss-Durkee items among the six described above for manifest physical aggression plus the following:

a. I can't think of any good reason for hitting anyone. (reversed scoring)

All items use the "a lot like me" three-category system for measurement.

*Buss-Durkee irritability.* More covert internal responses were measured by grouping three Buss-Durkee items with the "a lot like me" underlying scale:

a. I lose my temper easily.

b. It really makes me mad when somebody makes fun of me.

c. If someone doesn't treat me right, I don't let it bother me (reversed scoring).

*Approval of aggression.* Two items, rated on a five-step agree strongly-disagree strongly scale, comprised the approval of aggression measure. Neither item refers to the adolescents' overt aggression, but rather they tap the sanctioning of aggression as a means of solving conflict. The measures:

a. It's all right to hurt an enemy if you are mad at him.

b. In order to get revenge, it's all right to hurt an enemy.

Both are judged on a five-point agree-disagree scale.

# Measures: adolescent television viewing levels

Adolescents were given a list of 65 prime time programs organized by night of the week shown. Each show was checked according to frequency of viewing: *almost always* (nearly every week); *often* (at least half the time); *sometimes* (at least once or twice); and *never*. The shows were then grouped according to their manifest content into six categories. Frequency ratings for each adolescent were then summed across all shows in each category.

*Program categories.* The six program categories, the most popular shows in each, and the number of shows in the category were:

a. Crime-detective: *Mod Squad, Adam 12, Mannix* (11 shows).

b. Westerns: *Here Come the Brides, Bonanza, Daniel Boone* (7 shows).

c. Adventure-drama: *Hogan's Heroes, Land of the Giants, Marcus Welby* (6 shows).

d. Comedy-variety: *Laugh-in, Tom Jones, Glen Campbell* (14 shows).

    e. Situation comedy: *Bill Cosby, Room 222, Eddie's Father* (25 shows).

    f. Game shows: *Let's Make a Deal, Newlywed Game* (2 shows).

*Overall violence viewing.* Although the first three program types are associated with violent content and the last three with lesser levels, there is considerable variation within categories. As a result, it was desirable to index the level of violent content for each show individually to produce the best indicator of total exposure—overall violence viewing, or *OVV* as we shall call it for the remainder of the report.

This index was constructed from the ratings of the amount of violent content in individual television programs, obtained from three different samples: Minneapolis high school students (Murray, Cole, and Fedler, 1970); a probability sample of the Detroit adult public (Greenberg and Gordon, 1970), and a selected sample of television critics (Greenberg and Gordon, 1970). Each judge rated each program along a five-step scale ranging from 1 (least violent) to 5 (most violent). For each set of judges, the programs were rank ordered into twelve groupings, using natural breaks in the distribution of mean ratings. These ranks were then summed across the three sets of judges to provide an overall rank order of programs. An overall mean rating across all judges was also computed for each program, yielding the same ordering of programs. Actually, there was a very high level of agreement among the three sets of judges across the 65 programs (see Appendix B).

Natural breaks in the mean/rank order data were used to cut the programs into eight levels of violence, with weighting ranging from 0 (low violence) to 7 (high violence). Amount of viewing for each program for each adolescent was given a weight ranging from 0 (never watch) to 4 (almost always watch). Thus, the *OVV* for each individual is the sum of the products of the violence and exposure weights across 65 programs.

*News-public affairs programs.* The frequency of viewing of four types of shows—national news, local news, current event shows, and interview shows—were summed to get a news-public affairs index. Response categories for these shows were "never," "sometimes," and "often."

*Saturday morning programs.* Adolescents were asked how many hours they spent watching television before noon on an average Saturday. They filled in estimates of hours and minutes.

*Total viewing time.* Estimates of the adolescents' total television viewing were obtained by combining the responses to three questions regarding time spent viewing yesterday, the day before yesterday, and on an average day after 5 p.m. It is particularly important to devise a good index of viewing time because it does double duty as a control variable and as an independent variable. It serves to control our exposure in analyzing inferences about the associations of specific program-type viewing and the aggression measures. It will also be considered an independent variable because much of the previous literature on effects of television has used simple exposure time rather than specific programming.

*Violent television movies.* Five movies shown on television during the weeks preceding our data collection were used to determine the viewing of violent movies. The students were asked to indicate whether or not they had seen each of the five movies that varied in level of violent content according to analysis by judges. Their exposure to the more violent films relative to the less violent ones constituted the index.

## Measures: family environment

A wide variety of family environment indicators were used, ranging from specific parental regulation of television viewing to more general treatment variables of affection and punishment. Also included were structural aspects of the environment, number of siblings, and social status.

*Parental control over television.* The extent to which the parents control the extent of adolescent television viewing was measured by summing responses to six items with a variety of underlying scales. Included were:

a. Who has the most to say about what you watch on television? (self or sibling, either self or parent, parent)
b. Do your parents always know what programs you are watching on TV? (no, yes)
c. Are there certain programs that your parents sometimes do not let you watch? (no, yes)

The "parent" and the two "yes" responses are scored as high control. Additional points were added if the parent specifically prohibited either "crime shows," "westerns," or "violent shows."

*Parental emphasis on nonaggression.* Teaching of nonviolence was indexed by four items:

a. Do your parents punish you if you are mean to other kids? (no, I'm never mean, yes)
b. Do your parents want you to fight back if other kids pick on you? (yes, no)
c. How important does your mother think it is for you to learn to defend yourself? (very important, somewhat important, not important)
d. How often did your parents say you shouldn't do the bad things people do on TV? (never, sometimes, often)

In each case, the last response indicated is scored as nonaggressive.

*Parental interpretation of television violence.* Parental attempts to immunize their children against television violence were indexed by asking the adolescent how frequently (never, sometimes, often) their parents said each of five things to them, interpreting violent television content. Some of these are:

  a. Told you that things are not like this in real life.
  b. Said that these stories are "just pretend."
  c. Explained that there are better ways than violence to solve problems.

*Parental punishment: physical, verbal, and restrictive.* Adolescents were given a list of parental behaviors an asked to indicate whether their parents did each "very often," "fairly often," "not too often," or "never." The single item indicating physical punishment was, "punish you physically when you were younger."

Verbal punishment was indexed by two items: a) Punish you by yelling at you; b) Punish you by lecturing you.

Restrictive punishment was measured by: a) Punish you by "grounding" you; b) Punish you by taking away your privileges.

The intercorrelation of items justified the separation of parental punishment into these three components.

*Parental affection.* On the same frequency scale used for the punishment items Parental Affection was indexed by the single item: "show that they love you."

*Structural aspects.* The number of siblings and two measures of social status, father's occupation and mother's education, provided three structural indicators. Duncan's socioeconomic status scale was used to classify the occupation of the father.

In addition, school performance will be used as a control variable in the later sections of this report.

# Measures: cognitive reactions to television violence

Cognitive reactions of adolescents to violent television content may be thought of as qualitative dimensions parallel to the quantity of content to which they are exposed. Five types of responses are examined.

*Perceived learning of aggression.* It is reasonable to expect that any association between violent television viewing and aggressive reactions would be higher among adolescents who feel that television presents opportunities for learning of antisocial behavior. A five-item index was constructed to tap this dimension using the three-step "a lot like me" scale. Some items:

  a. These programs show me how to get back at people who make me angry.
  b. Sometimes I copy the things I see people doing on these shows.
  c. Some programs give me ideas on how to get away with something without getting caught.

*Linkage of violent television to real life.* Perception of a close similarity between the world portrayed on violent television programs and everyday reality should also tend to facilitate the relation between the extent of violent viewing and aggression. Following the work of Greenberg and Dominick (1968) and Berkowitz (1962), four items were developed using the "a lot like me" scale. The items:

a. Action and adventure shows tell about life the way it really is.
b. The people I see in adventure stories are just like the people I meet in real life.
c. Some stories remind me of frustrating things that have happened to me.
d. Some characters remind me of people who have made me mad.

*Involvement in violent programming.* To measure the degree of psychological involvement with the characters and stories of action-adventure shows, a six-item index was developed. Once more, the "a lot like me" scale was used. An examination of item intercorrelations provided justification for separating involvement and the two preceding cognitive indices. Some examples of involvement items:

a. I am so involved in some programs that I get carried away with the story.
b. I get upset when my favorite star is yelled at or threatened.
c. I sometimes forget that characters in these shows are just actors.

*Identification with violent characters.* Adolescents were asked to name the one person on television they would most like to be. They were also given a list of six male actors and asked to pick the one they most like to see at the movies. The characters chosen in each case were rated by the amount of violent action typically involved in the actor's portrayal. The two ratings were combined to form an index of identification with violent characters.

*Perceived efficacy of violent characters.* A series of descriptive statements about what happens on action and adventure shows were listed. The students indicated the frequency (often, sometimes, never) with which each happens on shows they watch. Three highly correlated items were grouped because each indicates the effectiveness of violence for the aggressing character:

a. The hero's friends think it is OK if he hurts the bad guy.
b. The guy who gets rough gets his way.
c. The bad guy deserves the beating he gets.

## FINDINGS

Our analysis is divided into three segments: levels and internal consistency of the major sets of variables; bivariate relationships between sets of variables; and multivariate predictors of adolescent aggression.

For each part of the analysis, there will be successive parallel tables, the first for Maryland and the second for Wisconsin.

Although the selection of variables and modes of analysis imply certain theoretical perspectives, the presentation of data will not formally test hypotheses. Rather we will examine a series of complex tables, each of which shows a number of relationships, and discuss the possible theoretical import of those relationships that we find to be non-zero. Statistical significance tests are not an important element of the analysis, except as rough indicators of which relationships are strong enough to warrant further consideration. We therefore use asterisks to indicate two conventional significance levels: * (p < .05), ** (p < .01). For comparison of levels of standardized means across sex and age categories, these asterisks indicate the significance of the particular cell mean from the mean of all other cells combined. For correlations, they indicate the significance of the difference of the correlation from zero, in either direction. All correlations are Pearson product-moment correlations (r).

## Single variable analyses

The standardized levels and interindex correlations are shown for each of four sets of variables in Tables 1-16: adolescent aggression, television viewing, family environment, and cognitive reactions to television. (All tables are in Appendix C.)

*Standardized levels of adolescent aggression.* Two very clear generalizations can be made from the data in Tables 1 and 2: that boys show considerably higher levels on most aggression measures than do girls, and that there is a considerable decline in aggression level from junior to senior high on most indices. The lowered senior high levels are found for both boys and girls. While the sex differences should surprise nobody, the magnitude of the age differences across the three-year period is perhaps less obvious. This developmental pattern is not well recognized in the research literature.

The Zaks-Walters scales show no definite pattern, the lack of difference between sexes being consistent with previous work (Walters and Zaks, 1959). The mixture of attitudinal with behavioral items in the Zaks-Walters scales may partially account for the lack of difference between groups.

An exception to the general pattern is the nonbehavioral Buss-Durkee Irritability index, which deals with covert internal responses. Girls are higher than boys, and there are inconsistent findings for age groups. The reversal is perhaps not surprising since four of the seven studies cited by Buss (1961) show females with higher irritability levels than males. The conceptual definition offered by Buss, "a readiness to explode at the slightest provocation. . .including quick temper, grouchiness, exasperation, and rudeness" (p. 169), certainly fits the female stereotype better than does the overt aggression implied in other of our indices.

Two other findings regarding adolescent aggression levels should be mentioned. (Data for neither finding are shown in our tables.) The distribution on all indices proved to be satisfactory, with the raw means on all eight for each sample falling not further than one-half of a standard deviation from the mean that would have been obtained if all respondents had checked the middle position on a given scale (e.g., "somewhat" on the "like me" scale). Although all means except those on Zaks-Walters Aggression are somewhat below this "theoretical mean," the degree of skewness on no index is so severe as to seriously attenuate the correlations in subsequent analyses. Another comforting finding is that the means of our two samples are remarkably similar. Only in the hypothetical aggressive reactions index, where Maryland is significantly higher, do differences occur.

*Internal consistency of adolescent aggression indices.* Tables 3 and 4 contain the intercorrelations of the aggressions in the two samples. It should be noted that the *overall sum* (OAS) is a combination of the first four indices, producing several strong part-whole correlations. In addition, *assault* has three items in common with *physical* aggression; since these two indices are quite similar, only the physical aggression index will be subjected to further analysis. Of the remaining 36 independent cells in the two matrices, all correlations except two are positive, although most are low to moderate in magnitude.

The two indices lowest in internal consistency are the same two that showed deviant patterns on the sex and grade level comparisons. Zaks-Walters and Buss-Durkee Irritability have the lowest average correlation with other independent indices (+.20 and +.15 respectively), perhaps reflecting the lesser concern with overt behavior in these measures than elsewhere.

*Standardized levels of adolescent television viewing.* Adolescent boys watch considerably more violent television fare than girls as evidenced by higher levels on crime-detective programs, overall violence viewing (OVV), and violent television movies. These differences are shown for the two samples in Tables 5 and 6. These findings are consistent with the data reported by Chaffee, McLeod, and Atkin (1970) and Chaffee and McLeod (1971), which show sex differences for westerns and spy-adventure programs. The Maryland data also show greater male viewing of westerns and adventure-drama, although the Wisconsin pattern is somewhat inconsistent. The present data also show Wisconsin boys higher on viewing time among seniors only, while Maryland sex differences are negligible.

Finally, Chaffee et al. found that boys exceeded girls in public affairs viewing at both grade levels. In varying degrees, our data support this finding. For both our Maryland and Wisconsin samples, girls watch more situation comedy and game programs than do boys.

A sharp decline in adolescent viewing from junior to senior high for virtually every program category except news-public affairs and violent television movies is shown in Tables 5 and 6. The drop is particularly sharp for situation comedy and Saturday morning shows and includes all three high violence categories and the *OVV* index. The violence viewing results are consistent with Chaffee and McLeod, who found similar trends for both western and spy-adventure programs; using the same data, Chaffee, Ward, and Tipton (1970) also found that viewing of news and public affairs programming increases through adolescence and into adulthood.

Table 5 for Maryland also replicates findings of a general decrease in time spent with television during adolescence, reported by Schramm, Lyle, and Parker (1961), Chaffee and McLeod, and Chaffee et al. The Wisconsin girls' subsample also follows this trend, but the boys show a surprising increase. One possible explanation is that the Wisconsin questionnaires were given out during October at a time when football (including the nearby Green Bay Packers) was occupying some 12 hours of air time per week. A good share of the senior high boys' television time may have been devoted to this programming, since they are the subgroup most interested in sports. The Maryland data, having been gathered during April, showed no such bulge for the senior boys.

*Intercorrelation among television viewing indices.* Some justification for using the label "violence viewing" is found in Tables 7 and 8. Without evidence that crime, westerns, and adventure shows correlate as an actual syndrome of adolescent viewing behavior, it might be argued that such a label is merely a fiction of the researcher. Across the two samples, the three "violent" program types do have a higher average inter-correlation with each other (+.59 and +.34 for the two samples) than with the "less violent" categories of comedy-variety, situation comedy, game shows, and news (+.40 and +.22). The fit is less than perfect, however, for in the Maryland sample the comedy-variety and situation comedy indices are more highly associated with the three violent categories than with game shows or news. News does not correlate highly with anything in either sample.

Additional evidence for violence viewing as a syndrome is shown in the correlation of overall violence (*OVV*) with the specific program types. It correlates much more highly with the three violent program types (average r of +.82 and +.75 for the two samples) than with the four less violent categories (+.49 and +.23). Of course, the raters of violence may have been aware of these subject matter categories when they rated the shows and thereby unconsciously biased their judgments.

*Standardized levels of family environment variables.* Tables 9 and 10 show considerable variation between subgroups and inconsistency among samples on the family environment standardized levels. In terms of parental attempts to influence the adolescents' viewing behavior, there is a consistent pattern for parents to interpret (e.g., to say things on television are not like that in real life) more for boys and for younger children generally than for girls and older children. Younger children also reported more parental control over viewing and more emphasis on nonaggression.

Punishment and affection levels showed considerable inconsistency between samples, but there was a nonsurprising pattern of boys reporting more physical punishment and less affection than girls. Between the junior and senior high age groups, there is a trend toward greater parental use of verbal punishment and less restrictive punishment and display of affection. Senior high students in both samples also report a decidedly lower level of education for their mothers. It cannot be ascertained if this is a real difference or merely misreporting among the younger children.

*Intercorrelation among family environment indices.* Tables 11 and 12 reveal moderate correlations within areas (attempts to influence viewing, punishment, and social structure) and very low correlations across these areas. Attempts to control are more closely related to affection than to punishment, although neither association is large. Affection is negatively related to punishment, but again the correlations are low. Perhaps the most interesting finding in these tables is the independence of measures of punishment and attempted influence from the social status measures. Mothers' education and affection show only a slight positive relation in both samples.

*Standardized levels of cognitive reactions to television.* Boys are more likely to see opportunities for learning antisocial behavior and to identify with violent characters while girls report higher levels of involvement in programming, according to Tables 13 and 14. This finding seems compatible with our findings in Tables 1 and 2, where boys were higher in the measures of overt aggression and lower on the more internalized responses of the irritability index.

Table 13 and 14 also show a pronounced decline from junior to senior high for all cognitive reaction indices except perceived efficacy of violent characters which has a slight increase. The drop is quite pronounced for perceived learning of aggression and for identification with violent characters, particularly among girls. The lessening of most types of cognitive reactions parallels the general decline of viewing among the older children shown for most specific program types in Tables 5 and 6.

*Intercorrelation among cognitive reactions to television.* Some suggestion that there is a general dimension of reactivity to violent television is found in the data in Tables 15 and 16. All indices except identification with violent characters show moderate to high correlations with the other reactivity measures. Identification was perhaps the weakest index in terms of reliability, perhaps accounting for its lower level of association.

# Bivariate analyses

Our analysis of bivariate relationships between sets of variables is based on the data in Tables 17-28, found in Appendix C. There are five subsections with two tables within each: aggression by violence viewing; violence viewing by family environment; aggression by family environment; cognitive reactions to television by aggression and violence viewing, and all variables by socioeconomic status and school performance.

*Violence viewing and aggressive behavior.* Any purported link between childrens' viewing of media violence and their level of aggressive behavior requires evidence that shows a positive association between these two variables. To show causality—that violence viewing leads to aggressiveness, for example—would also require evidence about the direction of influence and eliminate other alternative explanations. For the present, however, we will simply examine the evidence regarding the required positive association.

Tables 17 and 18 show the correlations between Overall Violence Viewing ( *OVV* ) and the Overall Aggressive Sum ( *OAS* ) and its four component parts. In general, there is evidence of a positive association between viewing of television violence and the indices of aggression. The key *OVV* by *OAS* correlations are substantial ( +.32 and +.30, both significant at .01 level) for all respondents combined (N=472, N=151), and for each of the sex-age subgroups except junior high boys ( +.14 and +.12). The strongest association is among the junior girls in each sample ( +.28 and +.38), followed by senior boys ( +.31 and +.23) and senior girls ( +.21 and +.23).

On the individual indices of aggressive behavior, the overall correlations are significantly positive in each case except for Zaks-Walters aggression in Maryland. Violence viewing relates most strongly with hypothetical aggressive reactions ( +.32 and +.22), followed by manifest physical aggression ( +.28 and +.17), aggressive behavioral delinquency ( +.22 and +.20), and Zaks-Walters aggression ( +.08 and +.24). Within age-sex subgroups, 31 of 38 correlations are greater than +.10, and 12 correlations are statistically significant. On the other hand, the relationship of violence viewing with irritability aggression is uniformly nonsignificant across all respondents ( −.03 and +.02), with all subgroup correlations falling between −.10 to +.10 (data not shown). Thus, this index of internal aggressiveness personality appears to be unrelated to viewing of violent programs.

The consistently positive association between behavioral aggression and violence viewing in both samples stands in contrast to the apparently inconclusive pattern of findings from experimental and field investigations of the impact of media violence on adolescent antisocial behavior. Most experimental evidence substantiates the proposition that under certain conditions the viewing of violent media content makes an aggressive response by the child more likely, but permits no more than speculation about the learning of aggressiveness as a relatively enduring disposition. For reviews of these studies, see Berkowitz (1962), Hartley (1964), Walters (1966), Flanders (1968), Goranson (1969a, 1969b), and Atkin, Murray, and Nayman (1971).

While field studies are often cited as refuting any causal link between television and aggressive behavior, a careful reading of the survey literature reveals little convincing evidence for or against the proposition that television bears some guilt for adolescent aggression. Himmelweit, Oppenheim, and Vince (1958) concluded that well-adjusted children will learn to adjust to television violence, but they presented no evidence directly bearing on this inference. They do suggest that violence viewing can precipitate aggressive behavior among those who are emotionally disturbed and predisposed to act aggressively. In addition, mothers' diaries indicated that young children often displayed aggressive play after watching television. Teacher ratings of students along an aggressive-submissive continuum were not different between samples with and without television available.

Schramm et al. found that tenth graders who preferred television to print media were significantly higher than others on an antisocial aggression scale, but no significant differences were found among sixth graders. On the other hand, sixth graders in a Canadian community with television were significantly *lower* on antisocial aggression than sixth graders in a comparison community without television; there were no differences between tenth graders in these two towns, however.

Eron (1963) reported a strong positive relationship between peer ratings of aggression and viewing of violent programs among third grade boys, but there was a negative association between aggression and overall time spent with television for these boys. There were no significant relationships for girls.

Cowden, Bassett, and Cohen (1969) found that a high level of exposure to violence portrayals was associated with emotional instability and getting into arguments and fights among institutionalized adolescent boys, but there was no relationship between violence viewing and more serious assaultive offenses.

Our research shows that among both boys and girls at two grade levels, the more the child watches violent television fare, the more aggressive he is likely to be as measured by a variety of self-report measures. Since the data are correlational, the reverse also holds: the more aggressive the child is, the more likely he is to watch high levels of violent television programming.

Since much of the writing in the field refers to the amount of time the child spends with television rather than with the specifics of violent content, it is useful to relate our measure of total viewing time to the indices of aggression. Tables 19 and 20 show these correlations. Once again, predominantly positive correlations are shown with significant associations between viewing time and *OAS* across all subjects in each sample. The magnitude of the correlations are considerably smaller than those for *OVV*, however, except for the junior boys, where the viewing time by *OAS* correlations are a respectable +.20 and +.25. Later in this report we will control viewing time in studying the *OVV* by aggression indices.

*Family environment and violence viewing.* Tables 21 and 22 show the relationship of violence viewing ( *OVV* ) and ten measures of the family environment. There is an overall *positive* relationship between *OVV* and interpretation (e.g., things are not like that in real life) and a mild positive relationship between *OVV* and control of the child's viewing. While these findings suggest the ineffectiveness of such techniques to actually influence the adolescent's television viewing behavior, perhaps a more likely inference is that of reverse causation: the heavy violence viewing child influences the parent to do something to control and discount this behavior.

Bassett, Cowden, and Cohen (1968) found that among institutional-- ized delinquent boys, those who reported a high incidence of physical punishment at home were more likely to prefer violent television content. Others have stated theories with implied hypotheses regarding the relationship of violence viewing and various forms of punishment, such that we would expect a strong positive relationship (Himmelweit et al., 1958; Schramm et al., 1961; Hess and Goldman, 1962; Maccoby, 1954; Riley and Riley, 1951, 1959; Tannenbaum and Greenberg, 1968; Ward and Wackman, 1971). On the other hand, Chaffee and McLeod (1971), using almost identical punishment measures to ours with a different sample, found only low correlations with violence viewing (+.09 with physical punishment, +.08 with verbal punishment, and +.14 with restrictive punishment).

The present data in Tables 21 and 22 are close to those of Chaffee and McLeod in showing a larger positive correlation for restrictive punishment overall (+.14 and +.24) than for physical or verbal punishment. The data for physical and verbal punishment show no relationship to *OVV* in Maryland and mild positive correlations in Wisconsin.

Contrary to Maccoby (1954), who found a negative relationship between affection and "escapist" television viewing, we find essentially no relationship in either sample using the violence viewing index. In fact, the direction is slightly positive (+.03 and +.04). This is also in keeping with the Chaffee and McLeod +.07 correlation with similar measures.

Tables 21 and 22 also show a slight tendency for children in larger families to watch more violent programming. In part, this may be due to a negative relationship between size of family and social status. The measures of social status, fathers' occupations, and mothers' educations do show the expected negative association with $OVV$, but the education relationship is not consistently large. It does indicate, however, that social status controls are desirable in our later multivariate tables.

*Family environment and aggressive behavior.* It is apparent from Tables 23 and 24 that parental attempts to influence the child's violence viewing behavior and aggressive behavior are not associated with lower levels of adolescent aggression. The correlations are inconsistent and generally low. Of course, this does not mean that such parental attempts are ineffective. The possibility of interactive effects will be examined in the multivariate section of this report.

There is an extensive though not totally consistent literature suggesting that we should expect a positive relationship between punishment and aggressive behavior. Sears et al. (1953) found a positive relationship between maternal punitiveness and overt aggression at school among boys and a curvilinear function for girls. Becker et al. (1962) replicated Sears et al. and also found that aggression in the home was positively correlated with mothers' punitiveness for both sexes. Similar supportive findings for various measures and samples are shown by Eron et al. (1961), Sears et al. (1957), and Lefkowitz et al. (1963). Other data suggest that use of power-assertive techniques over time may inhibit the more overt forms of aggression. Sears (1961) found in a panel design that early punishment by the mother lost its positive association with aggression between ages five and twelve and tended to relate to inhibited or deflected forms of aggression. McCord et al. (1959) found that criminal acts were less likely when both mother and father were consistently punitive.

Our data show the expected positive relationship between all three forms of punishment and the $OAS$ measure for both boys and girls in senior high school only (Tables 23 and 24). The junior high correlations are low and inconsistent. The interaction of punishment and age-grade for $OAS$ contrasts with earlier results for punishment and violence viewing where the correlations were almost equal in size for each grade level. Likewise, all forms of punishment predict aggression about equally while restrictive punishment was clearly the best predictor of violence viewing.

The stronger findings for senior high also carries over to the affection variable where we obtain the expected negative relationship for the older group only. Both the punishment and affection interaction findings are surprising because of the purported decline of family influence during late adolescence.

Social status does not seem to be related to aggression in any clear and consistent way. This does not support the popular and stereotype of high levels of aggressive behavior among working-class children.

*Cognitive reactions to television and aggressive behavior.* A close inspection of the data from the two samples in Table 25 reveals considerable discrepancy. In general, there are stronger ties between cognitive reactions and aggressive behavior in the Maryland sample, and among girls in both groups. The strongest association is found for the first index, where those perceiving learning from the violent content are clearly the most aggressive adolescents. Among girls at least, those seeing a tie between television violence and real life and those reporting the highest levels of involvement are also high in aggressive behavior.

While the logical status of these variables is in question because they in a sense presume viewing of violence, they will be useful as additional variables in our later regression analyses.

*Cognitive reactions to television and violence viewing.* Table 26 shows a generally positive correlation between cognitive reactions to television and the level of violence viewing. The magnitude of these correlations are somewhat lower than in the previous table, perhaps indicating that reactivity is more closely tied to the adolescent's aggressive behavior than to his viewing habits. The two reactions with the strongest relationships to violence viewing are perceived learning and linkage to real life. The causal question can be raised whether frequent viewing leads to perceiving learning and reality in television violence or whether such perceptions lead the adolescent to seek out the more violent content.

*Social status, school performance, and other variables.* Tables 27 and 28 show the correlation of two control variables, socioeconomic status and school performance, with all other variables. As shown in part earlier, social status is generally unrelated to adolescent aggression. Only for approval of aggression do we find a semblance of a relationship, and these correlations are quite small. As also has been discussed earlier, the fathers' occupational status is related negatively to every program category except news-public affairs and violent television movies, and is unrelated or inconsistently related to other variables in our analysis.

It appears likely that school performance has a somewhat different meaning in each of our samples. While it is negatively related to all aggression measures except irritability in our Maryland sample, our Wisconsin group shows substantial negative correlations only for the Zaks-Walters and approval of aggression measures. The OAS correlations show a wide discrepancy ($-.29$ and $+.07$) between samples. It should be noted that the measures differed slightly between the two school systems; while the students self-reported school grades on an identical item, school reports of student performance were based on teacher ratings along a four-step scale in Wisconsin and a three-level track assignment in Maryland.

While the two samples show greater consistency in violence viewing in that the low school performers tend to watch more violence, the correlations are higher for Maryland. The low performers in each sample also tend to be low on news-public affairs viewing, and, consistent with previous research (Schramm et al., 1961; Himmelweit et al., 1958; Scott,

1956), they tend to spend more time with television. For entertainment of various types, however, the high users tend to be adolescents with low grades in Maryland and with high grades in Wisconsin.

Parents who emphasize nonaggression and those displaying affection tend to have high performance children. For other forms of parental influence and punishment, there appears to be no consistent difference in performance.

Although the correlations are not large, low school performance tends to be associated with the adolescents' perceiving learning from violent content, with seeing a linkage to real life, and in identifying with violent television characters.

## Multivariate analyses

Adolescent aggressive behavior will be the key criterion variable for our multivariate analysis. We will begin by examining the basic relationships between violence viewing and aggression, partialing out three control variables, and then examine more complex regression analyses.

*Violence viewing and aggressive behavior: partial correlations.* Tables 29 and 30 show the raw zero-order correlations of violence viewing ($OVV$) by various aggression measures, together with the partial correlations removing the effects of total television viewing time. The partials represent the associations for viewing of violent content *per se*, apart from the sheer time spent with television. In this way, it represents choice behavior rather than simple exposure.

Partialing out viewing time slightly reduces the positive correlations of violence viewing and aggressive behavior in most cases, but the basic result is the same as for the raw correlations. With only one exception, the statistically raw correlations for all students within each sample remain significant for the partials. The key $OVV$ by $OAS$ correlation for all respondents drops from +.32 to +.28 for the partial in Maryland and from +.30 to +.24 in Wisconsin.

Similarly, the partialing out of socioeconomic status and school performance does not alter the basic pattern of the raw correlations (Tables 31 and 32). There was essentially no effect of partialing out SES and only a minor decline (from +.32 to +.26) in one sample for the school performance partial.

We may conclude, then, that adolescents viewing high levels of violent content on television tend to have high levels of aggressive behavior, regardless of television viewing time, socioeconomic status or school performance. These partials appear to rule out as alternative explanations simple television exposure, social status, and general competence as a student.

*Viewing of program types by aggressive behavior.* Table 33 attempts to measure the contribution of each of seven specific program types to

OAS by partialing out the effects of each of the other six types. Data for both samples are presented in the same table. Since Tables 7 and 8 revealed that virtually each program type is related positively with all other program types, it is obvious that the partial here should act to reduce all positive raw correlations.

Crime-detective and Saturday morning programs retain their significant positive associations with aggression level after the viewing of other program types is removed. The adventure-drama correlations, though considerably diminished, remain low positive and statistically significant in the Maryland sample.

Perhaps the most interesting feature of Table 33 is the finding that the moderate to low positive associations for westerns by OAS (+.20 and +.12) become negative (−.01 and −.07) after removing the effects of viewing of other shows. Situation comedy viewing becomes rather strongly negative through a similar process in the Wisconsin sample.

*Multiple predictors of aggressive behavior.* The objective of the analyses shown in Tables 34 and 35 is to see to what degree the different variables can improve on the prediction of aggressive behavior ( OAS ) by our violence viewing index ( OVV ). The key to understanding the table, then, is to compare the zero-order OAS by OVV correlations shown in the top rows to the multiple correlations produced by each of the third variables. The larger the difference from the zero-order correlation, the more the third variable contributes to predicting aggressive behavior over and above that of violence viewing.

Across the two samples, perceived learning of aggression from violent television programs makes the largest independent contribution to the OVV-OAS relationship (from +.32 to +.56 and from +.30 to +.40). Thus, the quantitative and qualitative aspects of violence viewing combine to produce a substantially larger multiple correlation with aggressive behavior than either singly. Similarly, irritability combines with violence viewing to augment the correlation (to +.42 and +.41). The other factors are less consistent or relatively unimportant in accounting for additional aggressive behavior. Among senior high students, higher levels of physical punishment and lower levels of affection tend to make mild contributions to the relationship, but the junior high pattern is mixed.

*Multiple regression: aggressive behavior by violence viewing and family predictors.* Tables 36 and 37 show the results of a multiple regression analysis using the OAS index as the criterion variable and the OVV index, punishment, and affection as the three predictor variables. We felt the relatively high intercorrelation of punishment items and the consistency of direction in their predictions justified the combination of all three punishment types (physical, verbal, and restrictive) into a single index for regression purposes. Admittedly, this is a *post hoc* procedure, but our efforts here are not hypothesis-testing, but hypothesis-building for future research.

The cell entries for each of the three predictor variables represent the correlation of that variable and *OAS*, partialing out the effects of the other two predictor variables. In both samples, the violence viewing index for all subjects combined has the highest partial correlation coefficient. This appears to be largely a function of a relatively weak prediction by punishment in the junior high sample. Both violence viewing and punishment contribute considerably more than does affection, which shows a weak negative overall partial and positive coefficients for three of the eight sub-group cells.

The multiple correlations of the variables on *OAS* is shown in the fourth row of Tables 36 and 37. The three variables together account for 17.6 percent of the variance in *OAS* in Maryland and for 12.2 percent in Wisconsin. The multiple correlation coefficients tend to be somewhat larger for senior high than for junior high students.

*Multiple regression: aggressive behavior by five key predictor variables.* Two more strong correlates of aggressive behavior—perceived aggression learning and Buss-Durkee irritability, are added in Tables 38 and 39. These two variables, one a cognitive reaction to violent television content and the other a presumed internal response, become important independent predictors of *OAS*, with partials equal to or greater than those of *OVV* in most comparisons.

Nevertheless, the addition of these two variables does not decrease the partial coefficients of *OVV* by *OAS* to any marked degree. The partials for the punishment index are diminished, and its predictive power (as well as that of affection) is largely confined to the senior high respondents.

The combination of these five variables provides for a substantial multiple correlation with the overall aggression sum in each sample (.62 and .51, both significant at .01 level). These factors account for 38.5 percent of the *OAS* variance in Maryland and 26.0 percent in Wisconsin. Within the age-sex subgroups, the multiple correlations range from .46 to .69; seven out of eight are statistically significant.

We may conclude that the level of violence viewing remains an important predictor of aggression when a series of other variables are controlled, but we may also say that by taking into account the adolescent's perceptions of learning and his level of irritability, we can increase our power to predict considerably.

*Violence viewing by aggressive behavior within levels of nonaggressive emphasis.* The parental attempts at emphasizing nonaggression was shown to have little consistent association with either violence viewing (Tables 21 and 22) or aggressive behavior (Tables 23 and 24). In our *post hoc* probing, we treated this variable as a possible factor interacting with level of violence viewing. To do this, we divided the nonaggressive teaching attempts into high and low groups and ran *OVV* by *OAS* correlations within the two levels. The results are shown in Tables 40 and 41.

There is a distinct tendency for the correlations to be lower for those reporting that their parents emphasize nonaggression and higher where less parental concern is expressed, although the pattern of results is somewhat inconsistent in the Wisconsin cells with few respondents. This tendency holds for the physical aggression and hypothetical aggression indices as well as for *OAS*. The differences are more uniform across measures and across sex and age categories for the larger Maryland sample than in Wisconsin. An analysis of variance on *OAS* using high *vs.* low nonaggression emphasis and high *vs.* low violence viewing yields a significant interaction for all Maryland respondents ($p < .01$, F test).

To some degree, then, there is evidence that parental emphasis on nonaggressive behavior has some effect, not directly either on violence viewing or on aggressive behavior, but indirectly in reducing the relationship between these two factors.

An examination of interactive relationships with other third variables did not show any significant conditional differences in the basic *OVV-OAS* correlations.

## CONCLUSIONS

Our findings for the internal consistency of various indices of aggression (Tables 3 and 4) and television viewing behavior (Tables 7 and 8) provide some justification for our use of the terms "aggressive behavior" and "violence viewing." With the exception of the Buss-Durkee Irritability scale, all other indices of self-reported aggression showed moderate to high intercorrelations. Since irritability is the only measure which involves internal feelings rather than overt behavior, we grouped four of the remaining indices using the term "aggressive behavior." The sum of the four indices became our key criterion variable, the overall aggression sum ( *OAS* ).

Similarly, the three "violent" program types (crime-detective, westerns, and adventure-drama) among the seven categories, tended to form a highly intercorrelated cluster of adolescent viewing preferences. Each correlated more highly than did the less violent program types with the sum of violence viewing based on our ratings of the amount of violent content in each of 65 programs. This helped to justify our use of the latter measure, overall violence viewing ( *OVV* ), as a key variable in our analysis.

One comforting conclusion that can be drawn from our analysis of standardized means is that both of our key measures, the *OAS* and the *OVV* indices, along with adolescents' reactivity to violent television, decline in level from junior to senior high school. This may be a function of the general maturation of the child and also of the specific competition from other more socially approved activities in later adolescence.

The crucial finding in this report, however, is that there is a clear if moderate positive association between the adolescents' level of violence viewing and their level of self-reported aggression. This finding holds across most indices of aggression, and for both sexes and age levels in two samples of adolescents. The average correlation between the overall aggression ( OAS ) and violence viewing ( OVV ) indices is + .24 within sex-age groups and + .31 for all respondents combined.

A variety of causal inferences could be drawn from these bivariate findings. First, the long-term viewing of violence may lead the adolescent to perform aggressive acts. Of at least equal plausibility is the second possible inference—that the aggressive child may seek out the more violent programs while viewing television. Finally, some third variable or set of variables may be causing the level of both aggressive behavior and violence viewing to be high or low. Without further evidence, we cannot choose among these inferences. We have at least shown that there is concomitant variation between the two variables, to the extent the correlations are very unlikely to be simply chance fluctuations.

Two other factors are necessary to move beyond the statement of a positive relationship: some evidence must be shown regarding time order of the variables in order to rule out reverse causation, and other alternative explanations must be eliminated. While our research design did not contain the desirable attribute of having a panel with a long interval intervening between successive measurement, we will present some limited analyses of the time-order question in our next report. In this report, we present evidence only for the last of the requirements, elimination of alternative explanations through control.

Our nonexperimental design, lacking in the ability to randomly assign people to manipulated conditions, implies that we would have to check an infinite list of alternative explanations, whereas only a limited number of such checks are available with the data we have gathered. We are able to say that we have tested out several dozen variables as potential alternatives. This was accomplished by partialing their effects from the basic violence viewing-aggressive behavior correlations. Although these zero-order correlations are not overwhelmingly large, none of the third variables taken singly or in combination with other variables reduces the magnitude of the basic correlations in a fundamental way.

Prior to examining our data, it might have been expected that several of our control variables would be likely to be highly correlated with both violence viewing and aggressive behavior and thus, when partialed out would markedly lower the key OVV by OAS correlations. For example, socioeconomic status is such a potential alternative explanation. Previous research has indicated that lower-status adolescents watch more entertainment television, and the conventional wisdom attributes higher levels of aggression to them as well. While our data show the expected relationship with violent content, socioeconomic status is unrelated to aggressive behavior. Thus, the status control does not affect the violence viewing-aggressive behavior correlation. Similarly, various tables in this report show little or no effect on the basic *OVV* by *OAS* relationship when these variables are controlled: sex, age, school performance, punishment, affection, and irritability. Many other variables not shown in the tables produce a similar result. Somewhat greater reduction results from controlling television viewing time and the various cognitive reaction measures, but the basic finding remains intact. We must conclude that, after introducing a wide variety of variables as controls, the relationship between violence viewing and aggressive behavior is robust.

*Correlates of violence viewing and aggressive behavior.* Conclusions about the correlates of aggressive behavior and violence viewing must be tempered by the admission that the results for family environment variables are characterized more by a lack of relationship than by strong findings. Parental attempts to influence produce no clear and consistent association with either variable, and other parental treatment variables of punishment and affection show relationships only for certain subgroups. The situation is disappointing from both a theoretical and a practical standpoint.

A summary of all variables found to be related to either aggressive behavior or to violence viewing is shown below:

Type of relationship to:

| Variable | Aggressive behavior (OAS) | Violence viewing (OVV) |
|---|---|---|
| *Social structural* | | |
| Sex of child | Boys higher | Boys higher |
| Age of child | Younger higher | Younger higher |
| Socioeconomic status | No relationship | Negative |
| School performance | Negative, but inconsistent | Negative |
| *Parental treatment* | | |
| Physical punishment | Positive, older children only | No relationship |

| Variable | Aggressive behavior (OAS) | Violence Viewing (OVV) |
|---|---|---|
| Verbal punishment | Positive, older children only | No relationship |
| Restrictive punishment | Positive, older children only | Positive |
| Affection | Negative, older children only | No relationship |
| *Cognitive reactions* | | |
| Learning of aggression | Positive | Positive |
| Linkage to real life | Positive | Positive, girls only |
| Involvement | Positive | Positive, girls only |
| Identification | Positive | Slight, boys only |
| *Personality* | | |
| Irritability | Positive | No relationship |

The emergence of cognitive reactions to television as the most consistent set of variables related to both *OAS* and *OVV* raises questions about the logical status of these variables. In a sense, they imply both aggression and television use. Perhaps they are best conceptualized as intervening variables operating as contributory conditions increasing the strength of the violence viewing-aggressive behavior relationship when reactivity is high and decreasing it under lower activity.

Despite the disappointing results for the parental treatment variables, we cannot conclude that parents have little influence on their childrens' television viewing and the aggressiveness of behavior. We did find relatively low levels of violence viewing among children reporting less frequent use of restrictive punishment and, among senior high school adolescents at least, those less often punished and more often given affection were lower on self-reports of aggressive behavior. We also found a considerably lower violence viewing-aggressive behavior correlations among adolescents who reported that their parents stress nonaggression by such techniques as telling the child not to fight back, not to copy things on television, and so forth. Greater attention should be paid to the effectiveness of these "immunizing" techniques in future research.

We should add that we have by no means exhausted the possibilities for studying family variables. In our next report, we shall consider the role of the child's modeling of his mother's television viewing and her self-reported aggressive behavior. Dimensions of parent-child interaction will also be considered. Doubtless there are other variables that other investigators will examine. Our main advice to them based on the studies reported here concerns the measurement of television behavior. We have found that it improves the precision of prediction of measurement to go from simple amount of viewing time to watching of specific shows, and finally to the level of violence in those specific programs. We also suggest that the child's reaction to violent television is as important an attribute to consider as his exposure to programs.

## CONTENTS OF FORTHCOMING REPORT

The present report describes data gathered from both the Maryland and the Wisconsin samples. Additional findings will be presented in a second report (McLeod, Atkin, and Chaffee, also in this volume) that will deal with the two-year Wisconsin investigation. The reports have been kept separate because rather different kinds of data are involved. For example, the second report will examine longitudinal data from both adolescents and their mothers across a greater number of variables, with more extensive measurement of variables from the first report.

First, we will examine mother-child modeling of television viewing behavior and of aggressive behavior and values. Both mother and child separately completed identical scales of program viewing and 20 aggression items indexing five types of aggression.

The mother also reported the level of aggressive behavior of the child; teacher and peer reports of the child's aggressive behavior were also obtained to provide additional independent sources of aggression data. The second report will describe the relationships among the child's self-report and the three external sources, and relate them to his television viewing behavior.

Both the mother and child completed ratings on the interpersonal communication environment within the home; these family communication patterns will be examined in their relation to the viewing and aggression measures. Parent-child coorientational agreement, accuracy, and congruency on various values will also be studied. Another key independent variable is the child's peer relations, as reported by himself and his mother.

Longitudinal data on 1969 to 1970 differences on certain aggression measures, television viewing, and attitudes about television will be analyzed. For many variables in the first report, the two-wave Wisconsin study obtained additional measures, providing improved indices. Twice as many items will enter into the Buss-Durkee and behavioral delinquency indices. Supplementary data from the mother is available for the indices of punishment, affection and other measures.

New data from the child will include a violence viewing index relating to viewing behavior three to four years earlier, selectivity in television viewing choices and differences in involvement, reality linkage, and aggression learning from westerns *vs.* crime-detective programs. The report will also include multivariate analyses of violence viewing and cognitive reactions to television as criterion variables, examining the relative contribution of various family variables to these behaviors.

## FOOTNOTES

1. This technical report describes research pursuant to Contract No. HSM 42-70-77 with the National Institute of Mental Health, Health Services and Mental Health Administration, U.S. Department of Health, Education, and Welfare. Jack McLeod and Steven Chaffee were co-principal investigators. Charles Atkin, now at Michigan State University, was the study director. Others aiding in the data analysis were William Elliott, William Engels, Kenneth Sheinkopf, and Catherine Willette.

## REFERENCES

Atkin, C.K., Murray, J.P., and Nayman, O.B. (Eds.) *Television and social behavior: an annotated bibliography of research focusing on television's impact on children.* Rockville, Md.: Public Health Service Publication No. 2099, National Institute of Mental Health, 1971.

Bassett, T., Cowden, J., and Cohen, M. The audio-visual viewing habits of selected subgroups of delinquents. *Journal of Genetic Psychology,* 1968, **112,** 37-41.

Becker, W.C., Peterson, D.R., Luria, Z., Shoemaker, D.J., and Hellmer, L.A. Relations of factors derived from parent-interview ratings to behavior problems of five-year-olds. *Child Development,* 1962, **33,** 509-35.

Berkowitz, L. *Aggression: a social psychological analysis.* New York: McGraw-Hill, 1962.

Buss, A.H. Aggression and hostility inventories. *The psychology of aggression.* New York: Wiley, 1961.

Buss, A.H., and Durkee, A. An inventory for assessing different kinds of hostility. *Journal of Consulting Psychology,* 1957, **21,** 343-49.

Chaffee, S.H., and McLeod, J.M. Adolescent television use in the family context. In *Television and social behavior* Vol. 4. *Television in day-to-day life.* Washington, D.C.: U.S. Government Printing Office, 1971.

Chaffee, S.H., McLeod, J.M., and Atkin, C.K. Parent-adolescent similarities in television use. Paper presented at the meeting of the Association for Education in Journalism, Washington, D.C., August, 1970.

Chaffee, S.H., McLeod, J.M., and Atkin, C.K. Parental influences on adolescent media use. *American Behavioral Scientist*, 1971, **14**, 323-40.

Chaffee, S.H., Ward, L.S., and Tipton, L.P. Mass communication and political socialization. *Journalism Quarterly*, 1970, **47**, 647-59.

Cowden, J., Bassett, H.T., and Cohen, M. An analysis of some relationships between fantasy-aggressive and aggressive behavior among institutionalized delinquents. *Journal of Genetic Psychology*, 1969, **114**, 179-83.

Eron, L. Relationship of TV viewing habits and aggressive behavior in children. *Journal of Abnormal and Social Psychology*, 1963, **67** (2), 193-96.

Eron, L., Banta, T., Walder, L., and Laulicht, J. Comparison of data obtained from mothers and fathers on childrearing practices and their relation to child aggression. *Child Development*, 1961, **32**, 457-72.

Flanders, J.P. A review of imitative behavior. *Psychological Bulletin*, 1968, **69**, 316-37.

Goranson, R.E. The catharsis effect: two opposing views. In Baker, R., and Ball, S. *Violence and the media: A report to the National Commission on the Causes and Prevention of Violence.* Washington D.C.: U.S. Government Printing Office, 1969.

Goranson, R.E. A review of recent literature on psychological effects of media portrayals of violence. In Baker and Ball, *Violence and the media.*

Greenberg, B.S., and Dominick, J.R. Television usage, attitude, and functions for low-income and middle-class teenagers. Report #4, *Communication among the urban poor.* East Lansing, Mich.: Department of Communication, Michigan State University, 1968.

Greenberg, B.S., and Gordon, T.F. Perceptions of violence in television programs: critics and the public. In *Television and social behavior*, Vol. 1. Washington, D.C.: U.S. Government Printing Office, 1971.

Hartley, R.L. *The impact of viewing "aggression": studies and problems of extrapolation.* New York: Columbia Broadcasting System Office of Social Research, 1964.

Hess, R., and Goldman, H. Parents' views of the effects of TV on their children. *Child Development*, 1962, **33**, 411-26.

Himmelweit, H., Oppenheim, A., and Vince, P. *Television and the child.* London: Oxford University Press, 1958.

Lefkowitz, M.M., Walder, L.O., and Eron, L.D. Punishment, identification, and aggression. *Merrill-Palmer Quarterly*, 1963, **9**, 159-74.

Maccoby, E.E. Why do children watch television? *Public Opinion Quarterly*, 1954, **18**, 239-44.

McCord, W., McCord, J., and Zola, I. *Origins of crime*. New York: Columbia University Press, 1959.

Murray, R., Cole, R., and Fedler, F. Teenagers and TV violence: how they rate and view it. *Journalism Quarterly*, 1970, **47**, 247-55.

Nye, F.I., and Short, J. Scaling delinquent behavior. *American Sociological Review*, 1957, **22**, 326-31.

Riley, J.W., and Riley, M.W. Mass communication and the social system. In R.K. Merton, L. Broom and L.S. Cottrell (Eds.) *Sociology today*. New York: Basic Books, 1959.

Riley, M.W., and Riley, J.W. A sociological approach to communications research. *Public Opinion Quarterly*, 1951, **14**, 445-60.

Schramm, W., Lyle, J., and Parker, E.B. *Television in the lives of our children*. Stanford, Calif.: Stanford University Press, 1961.

Scott, L.F. Television and school achievement. *Phi Delta Kappa*, 1956, **38**, 25-28.

Sears, R. The relation of early socialization experiences to aggression in middle childhood. *Journal of Abnormal and Social Psychology*, 1961, **63**, 466-92.

Sears, R., Whiting, J., Nowlis, V., and Sears, P. Some child-rearing antecedents of aggression and dependency in young children. *Genetic Psychological Monographs*, 1953, **47**, 135-236.

Short, J., and F. Nye. Extent of unrecorded delinquency, tentative conclusions. *Journal of Criminal Law, Criminology, and Police Science*, 1958, **49**, 196-302.

Short, J., and F. Nye. Reported behavior as a criterion of deviant behavior. *Social Problems*, 1957-58, 207-13.

Tannenbaum, P.H., and Greenberg, B.S. Mass communication. *Annual Review of Psychology*, 1968, **19**, 351-86.

Walters, R. Implications of laboratory studies of aggression for the control and regulation of violence. *Annals of the American Academy of Political and Social Science*, 1966, **364**, 60-72.

Walters, R., and Zaks, M. Validation studies on an aggression scale. *Journal of Psychology*, 1959, **47**, 209-18.

Ward, L.S., and Wackman, D. Family and media influences on adolescent consumer learning. *American Behavioral Scientist*, 1971, **14**, 415-27.

Zaks, M., and Walters, R. First steps in the construction of a scale for the measurement of aggression. *Journal of Psychology*, 1959, **47**, 199-208.

# Appendix A: Complete listing of questionnaire items comprising each index

*Aggression indices*

*Manifest physical aggression:* "Here are some things other students say about getting along with people. How much is each statement like you?"

Whoever insults me or my family is asking for a fight.
If somebody hits me first, I let him have it.
When I lose my temper at someone, once in a while I actually hit them.
When I am mad at someone, I sometimes fight with them instead of talking about the problem.
When I was younger, I used to act like a bully sometimes.
I don't feel it is wrong for me to hit other kids who deserve it.

Scoring—"a lot like me" (2), "a little like me" (1), "not like me" (0)


*Aggressive behavioral delinquency:* "Here is a list of things that kids at other schools say they have done. How often have you done these things in the last three years?"

Been in fights with several people on each side.
Hurt someone on purpose to get back for something they had done to you.
Got into a serious fight with another student at school.

Scoring—"more than 5 times" (4), "4 or 5 times" (3), "2 or 3 times" (2), "one time" (1), "never" (0)


*Zaks-Walters aggression:* "How much do you agree or disagree with these statements?"

There are two kinds of people in this world: the weak and the strong.
Dealings with policemen and government officials are usually pleasant. (reversed)
Many good people become crooks or criminals because they can't stand to be pushed around so much.


"Here are some things other students say about getting along with people. How much is each statement like you?"

I often do things which I regret after.
I am very patient with people. (reversed)
It makes me mad when I can't do things for myself the way I like to.
When I was younger, I often hung around with the wrong kind of kids.

Scoring—"a lot like me" (2), "a little like me" (1), "not like me" (0)

*Hypothetical aggressive reactions:*

What if someone cut in front of you in a long line. What would you do to them? "shove them out" (4), "yell at them" (2), "just let it go" (0)

Suppose someone played a real dirty trick on you. What would you do? "hit them" (4), "yell at them" (2), "laugh at them" (0), "ignore them" (0)

What if somebody picks a fight with you on the way home from school. What would you do about this? "fight" (3), "back out of it" (1), "try to discuss the problem" (0)

Suppose you saw some guys fighting each other after school one day. What do you think you would do in this situation? "cheer on the fighters" (2), "watch the fight" (1), "break it up" (1), "ignore it" (0)

*Buss-Durkee assault aggression:* "Here are some things other students say about getting along with people. How much is each statement like you?"

Whoever insults me or my family is asking for a fight.
If somebody hits me first, I let him have it.
When I lose my temper at someone, once in a while I actually hit them.
I can't think of any good reason for hitting anyone. (reversed)

Scoring—"a lot like me" (2), "a little like me" (1), "not like me" (0)

*Buss-Durkee irritability:* "Here are some things other students say about getting along with people. How much is each statement like you?"

I lose my temper easily.
It really makes me mad when somebody makes fun of me.
If someone doesn't treat me right, I don't let it bother me. (reversed)

Scoring—"a lot like me" (2), "a little like me" (1), "not like me" (0)

*Approval of aggression:* "How much do you agree or disagree with these statements?"

It's all right to hurt an enemy if you are mad at him.
In order to get revenge, it's all right to hurt an enemy.

Scoring—"agree strongly" (5), "agree somewhat" (4), "no opinion" (3), "disagree somewhat" (2), "disagree strongly" (1)

*Overall aggression sum:* Unweighted sum of first 20 items, including Manifest physical aggression, Aggressive behavioral delinquency, Zaks-Walters aggression, and Hypothetical aggressive reactions, ranging from low (0) to high (50).

## Television viewing indices

"Here is a list of some programs that have been on television this year. About how often have you really watched each of these shows? For each program, make one check showing whether you watched it: *Almost always* (nearly every week) or *Often* (at least half the time) or *Sometimes* (at least once or twice) or *Never*."

Scoring—"almost always" (4), "often" (3), "sometimes" (2), "never" (0)

**Crime-detective programs:**

Mod Squad
Hawaii Five-O
Ironside
Dragnet
It Takes a Thief
Get Smart
Name of the Game
Mission Impossible
The FBI
Adam-12
Mannix

**Western programs:**

Gunsmoke
Lancer
Virginian
Daniel Boone
High Chapparal
Here Come the Brides
Bonanza

**Adventure-drama programs:**

Marcus Welby, M.D.
Medical Center
Then Came Bronson
Hogan's Heroes
World of Disney
Land of the Giants

**Comedy-variety programs:**

Red Skelton
Laugh-in
Carol Burnett
Pat Paulsen
Hee Haw
Johnny Cash
Glen Campbell
Jim Nabors
Dean Martin
Lawrence Welk
Tom Jones
Ed Sullivan
Jackie Gleason
Andy Williams

Here's Lucy
Mayberry RFD
Doris Day
Beverly Hillbillies
Green Acres
Julia
To Rome with Love
I Dream of Jeannie
Flying Nun
Eddie's Father
My World
Room 222
Bill Cosby
Family Affair
Bewitched

**Situation comedy programs:**

Debbie Reynolds
Governor and J.J.
Tim Conway
Petticoat Junction
Brady Bunch
Nanny and Professor
That Girl
Love American Style
Ghost and Mrs. Muir
My Three Sons

**Game programs:**

Let's Make a Deal
Newlywed Game

*Overall violence viewing:* Weighted sum of previous 65 programs, ranging from most violent (7) to least violent (0), as indicated in Appendix B. The sum across all 65 programs ranges from low violence viewing (0) to high violence viewing (436).

*News-public affairs programs:* "How often do you watch news and public affairs shows on television?"

National news broadcasts (like Walter Cronkite)
Current events shows (like 60 Minutes)
Local news broadcasts (like Six O'Clock reports)
Interview shows (like Meet the Press)

Scoring—"often" (2), "sometimes" (1), "never" (0)

*Saturday morning programs:* "On an average Saturday morning, about how many hours do you usually spend watching TV before noon?"

_____hours _____minutes

Scoring—(8) 4 hours 40 minutes or more
(7) 3 hours 40 minutes — 4 hours 39 minutes
(6) 2 hours 40 minutes — 3 hours 39 minutes
(5) 2 hours 10 minutes — 2 hours 39 minutes
(4) 1 hour  40 minutes — 2 hours  9 minutes
(3) 1 hour  10 minutes — 1 hour  39 minutes
(2) 1 hour  40 minutes —  1 hour   9 minutes
(1) less than 40 minutes
(0) None

*Total viewing time:* sum of three items, using same scoring system as above.

On an average weekday, about how many hours do you personally spend watching TV?

_____ hours _____minutes

Now we would like to find out about your television viewing in the last few days. Think of all the programs you saw yesterday and the day before, and figure out *exactly* how much time you spent watching TV programs each day.

Yesterday:_____ hours_____minutes
       (what day was it)

Day Before
Yesterday: _____ hours _____minutes
       (what day was it)

*Violent television movies:* "Did you watch any of these movies shown on TV this year?"

| Maryland | Wisconsin |
|---|---|
| San Francisco International | Countess from Hong Kong |
| Tony Rome* | Guns of Navarone* |
| Casino Royale* | Spy Who Came in from the Cold* |
| The Family Jewels | Georgy Girl |
| The Dirty Dozen* | Fall of the Roman Empire* |

Scoring—One point each for starred movies; if all five watched, 2 points.

### Family Environment Indices

*Parental control over television:*

Who has the most to say about what you watch on television? "mother" (2), "father" (2), "either mother or me" (1), "brothers or sisters" (0), "me" (0)

Do your parents always know what programs you are watching on TV? "yes" (1), "no" (0)

"Are there certain programs that your parents sometimes do not let you watch?

| No | Yes:   (mark as many as you have to) | |
|---|---|---|
| | Westerns* | TV movies |
| | Scary shows | Crime shows* |
| | Cartoons | Violent shows* |
| | Sexy shows | Adult shows |

Scoring—"yes" (1), "no" (0), plus 1 point each for starred program types.

*Parental emphasis on non-aggression:*

Do your parents punish you if you are mean to other kids? "yes" (2), "I'm never mean" (1), "no" (0)

Do your parents want you to fight back if other kids pick on you? "no" (1), "yes" (0)

How important does your mother think it is for you to learn to defend yourself? "not important" (2), "somewhat important" (1), "very important" (0)

How often did your parents say you shouldn't do the bad things people do on TV? "often" (2), "sometimes" (1), "never" (0)

*Parental interpretation of TV violence:* "When you watched action-adventure shows with your parents, how often did they used to say these things if someone in the story was hurt badly, during westerns and crime shows?"

Told you that things are not like this in real life.
Said that these stories are "just pretend."
Explained that there are better ways than violence to solve problems.
Said you shouldn't do the bad things people do on TV.
Reminded you that the people on TV are just actors and not really getting hurt.

Scoring—"often" (2), "sometimes" (1), "never" (0)

*Parental punishment:* "How often do your parents do these things with you?"

Punish you by grounding you.
Punish you by taking away your privileges.
Punish you by yelling at you.
Punish you by lecturing you.
Punish you physically when you were younger.

Scoring—"very often" (3), "fairly often" (2), "not too often" (1), "never" (0)

*Parental affection:* "How often do your parents do these things with you?"

Show that they love you. "very often" (3), "fairly often" (2), "not too often" (1), "never" (0)

*Number of siblings:*

How many brothers do you have?___ How many are older than you?____
How many sisters do you have?_____ How many are older than you?____

*Father occupation:*

What kind of work does your father (or stepfather) do for a living? What is his job called, what kind of business or industry does he work in and *what does he do?* For example: "Sales clerk, waits on customers in a department store" or "Weaver, operates a loom in a cotton textile mill."

Scoring—Coded according to Duncan Socio-Economic Index, ranging from "Osteopath" (96) to "Textile Mill Laborer" (01)

*Mother education:*

How much education did your mother have? "college graduate" (5), "some college" (4), "high school graduate" (3), "some high school" (2), "grade school only" (1)

## Cognitive Reactions

*Perceived learning of aggression:* "Here are some things other students say about TV programs with lots of action and adventure, like Westerns and crime shows. We want to know how much each statement is *like you:* how well does each statement describe your feelings about this kind of program?"

These programs show me how to get back at people who make me angry.

Sometimes I copy the things I see people doing on these shows.

Some programs give me ideas on how to get away with something without getting caught.

When someone attacks another person and isn't punished, I sometimes feel I can get away with it too.

When the bad guy gets a beating he deserves, I sometimes feel like getting even with people who have bothered me.

Scoring—"a lot like me" (2), "a little like me" (1), "not like me" (0)

*Linkage of TV violence to real life:* "Here are some things other students say about TV programs with lots of action and adventure, like Westerns and crime shows. We want to know how much each statement is *like you:* how well does each statement describe your feelings about this kind of program?"

Action and adventure shows tell about life the way it really is.

The people I see in adventure stories are just like the people I meet in real life.

Some stories remind me of frustrating things that have happened to me.

Some characters remind me of people who have made me mad.

*Involvement in violent TV programming:* "Here are some things other students say about TV programs with lots of action and adventure, like Westerns and crime shows. We want to know how much each statement is *like you:* how well does each statement describe your feelings about this kind of program?"

I am so involved in some programs that I get carried away with the story.

I get upset when my favorite star is yelled at or threatened.

I sometimes forget that characters in these shows are just actors playing roles.

I get excited when I watch these programs.

Once in a while I feel like things that happen to my hero are really happening to me.

I pay close attention to these shows.

Scoring—"a lot like me" (2), "a little like me" (1), "not like me" (0)

*Identification with violent characters:*

Name the one person on television who you would most like to be. Mentioned violent male (2), mentioned aggressive female (1), mentioned other character (0)

Which actors do you most like to see at the movies? "John Wayne" (2), "Jim Brown" (2), "Clint Eastwood" (2), "Sidney Poitier" (1), "Paul Newman" (1), "Dustin Hoffman" (0).

*Perceived efficacy of violent characters:* "Here are some descriptions of what happens on action and adventure programs. How often does each of these things happen on the shows that you watch?"

The hero's friends think it is O.K. if he hurts the bad guy.
The guy who gets rough gets his way.
The bad guy deserves the beating he gets.

Scoring—"often" (2), "sometimes" (1), "never" (0)

*School Performance:*

What are your average grades in school? "A's" (5), "A's" and B's" (4), "B's" (3), "B's and C's" (2), "C's" (1), "less than C's" (0)

Maryland: Track in school (Teacher report). "above average" (3), "average" (2), "below average" (1)

Wisconsin: Ability estimate (Teacher report). Please estimate the overall scholastic ability of this student. "superior" (4), "above average (3), "average" (2), "below average" (1), "poor" (0)

# Appendix B: Mean violence ratings of individual television programs by three sets of judges

| Assigned weight* | Violent programs | Public (N=303) | Students (N=41) | Critics (N=37) |
|---|---|---|---|---|
| 7 | Mannix | 3.37 | 3.26 | 3.91 |
| 7 | The F. B. I. | 3.19 | 3.41 | 3.79 |
| 7 | Mod Squad | 3.56 | 3.05 | 3.65 |
| 7 | Hawaii Five-O | 3.24 | 3.31 | 3.81 |
| 6 | Mission Impossible | 3.35 | 3.06 | 3.55 |
| 6 | Gunsmoke | 3.16 | 3.09 | 3.49 |
| 6 | It Takes a Thief | 3.23 | 2.94 | 3.39 |
| 5 | The Virginian | 2.88 | 3.13 | 3.19 |
| 5 | Ironside | 2.95 | 3.00 | 3.00 |
| 5 | Bonanza | 2.90 | 2.91 | 3.11 |
| 5 | The Name of the Game | 2.77 | 3.00 | 3.05 |
| 5 | Land of the Giants | 2.69 | 2.83 | 3.47 |
| 5 | High Chapparal | 2.98 | 2.78 | 3.46 |
| 5 | Lancer | 2.67 | 2.82 | 3.32 |
| 5 | Dragnet | 2.98 | 2.83 | 2.78 |
| 4 | Daniel Boone | 2.43 | 2.82 | 2.91 |
| 4 | Adam 12 | — | 2.72 | — |
| 4 | Then Came Bronson | 2.51 | 2.50 | 2.65 |
| 3 | Get Smart | 2.27 | 2.76 | 2.24 |
| 2 | Here Come the Brides | 1.85 | 2.03 | 2.32 |
| 2 | Hogan's Heroes | 1.81 | 2.19 | 2.07 |
| 1 | Room 222 | 1.87 | 1.61 | 1.49 |
| 1 | Marcus Welby, M.D. | 1.61 | 1.87 | 1.91 |
| 1 | World of Disney | 1.56 | 1.62 | 2.04 |
| 1 | Medical Center | — | 2.27 | — |
| 1 | Laugh-In | 1.33 | 1.79 | 1.79 |

Note: Table values are mean ratings of each program along a five-step scale, ranging from 5 (a lot of violence) to 1 (none at all).

*Assigned weight: In computing the Overall Violence Viewing Index, each of these programs was assigned the indicated weighting of violent content, based on the average weighting across the three sets of judges.

| Nonviolent programs | Public (N=303) | Students (N=41) | Critics (N=37) |
|---|---|---|---|
| *Love, American Style* | 1.40 | 1.41 | 1.39 |
| *Lassie* | 1.34 | — | 1.88 |
| *Red Skelton* | 1.24 | 1.50 | 1.51 |
| *Jackie Gleason* | 1.22 | 1.56 | 1.38 |
| *Let's Make a Deal* | — | 1.38 | — |
| *The Newlywed Game* | — | 1.59 | — |
| *My World and Welcome to It* | 1.36 | 1.38 | 1.09 |
| *Bill Cosby* | 1.33 | 1.52 | 1.12 |
| *Dean Martin* | 1.30 | 1.46 | 1.28 |
| *The Ghost and Mrs. Muir* | 1.28 | 1.53 | 1.20 |
| *Tim Conway* | 1.26 | — | 1.24 |
| *The Governor and J.J.* | 1.24 | — | 1.11 |
| *Beverly Hillbillies* | 1.23 | 1.70 | 1.25 |
| *Pat Paulsen* | 1.22 | — | 1.26 |
| *Nanny and the Professor* | 1.20 | — | 1.12 |
| *Here's Lucy* | 1.18 | 1.46 | 1.30 |
| *I Dream of Jeannie* | 1.16 | 1.46 | 1.46 |
| *To Rome With Love* | 1.35 | 1.24 | 1.07 |
| *The Flying Nun* | 1.18 | 1.50 | 1.17 |
| *Debbie Reynolds* | 1.18 | 1.24 | 1.39 |
| *Bewitched* | 1.17 | 1.42 | 1.15 |
| *Tom Jones* | 1.17 | 1.43 | 1.07 |
| *Brady Bunch* | 1.17 | 1.50 | 1.14 |
| *That Girl* | 1.15 | 1.44 | 1.14 |
| *Mayberry R.F.D.* | 1.27 | 1.26 | 1.08 |
| *Petticoat Junction* | 1.13 | 1.44 | 1.16 |
| *Hee Haw* | 1.07 | — | 1.31 |
| *Julia* | 1.18 | 1.28 | 1.14 |
| *Green Acres* | 1.14 | 1.45 | 1.14 |
| *Johnny Cash* | 1.12 | — | 1.07 |
| *Jim Nabors* | 1.11 | 1.28 | 1.13 |
| *Glen Campbell* | 1.10 | 1.35 | 1.05 |
| *Eddie's Father* | 1.09 | 1.25 | 1.02 |
| *Carol Burnett* | 1.09 | 1.26 | 1.29 |
| *My Three Sons* | 1.07 | 1.26 | 1.02 |
| *Andy Williams* | 1.07 | 1.36 | 1.19 |
| *Family Affair* | 1.06 | 1.21 | 1.02 |

Note: Above programs are all assigned a weighting of 0.

# Appendix C: Tables

Table 1: Standardized adolescent aggression levels, by age and sex: Maryland data

| Aggression measure | Grade | Boys | Girls |
|---|---|---|---|
| Manifest physical aggression | jr. hi | +45** | −02 |
| (6 item index) | sr. hi | +13 | −44** |
| Aggressive behavioral delinquency | jr. hi | +50** | −29** |
| (3 item index) | sr. hi | +26** | −37** |
| Zaks-Walters aggression | jr. hi | +01 | +02 |
| (7 item index) | sr. hi | −08 | +05 |
| Hypothetical aggressive reactions | jr. hi | +69** | −16 |
| (4 item index) | sr. hi | +27** | −63** |
| Overall aggression sum | jr. hi | +60** | −16 |
| (20 item index) | sr. hi | +21* | −51** |
| Buss-Durkee assault aggression | jr. hi | +37** | +01 |
| (4 item index) | sr. hi | +19* | −40** |
| Buss-Durkee irritability | jr. hi | −20* | +08 |
| (3 item index) | sr. hi | −02 | +12 |
| Approval of aggression | jr. hi | +27** | +18 |
| (2 item index) | sr. hi | +12 | −44** |
| (N) | jr. hi | (122) | (108) |
| | sr. hi | (107) | (136) |

Note: Standard scores represent each cell mean, calculated as a positive or negative deviation from the overall mean on the listed index, divided by the overall standard deviation. Scores have been multiplied by 100 to eliminate decimals. Asterisks indicate the cell mean is significantly different from the overall mean for the remaining cells.

*p < .05
**p < .01

Table 2: Standardized adolescent aggression levels, by age and sex: Wisconsin data

| Aggression measure | Grade | Boys | Girls |
|---|---|---|---|
| Manifest physical aggression | jr. hi | +30* | +21 |
| (6 item index) | sr. hi | +24 | −70** |
| Aggressive behavioral delinquency | jr. hi[a] | − − | − − |
| (3 item index) | sr. hi | +21 | −23 |
| Zaks-Walters aggression | jr. hi | +11 | −06 |
| (7 item index) | sr. hi | +09 | −16 |
| Hypothetical aggressive reactions | jr. hi | +62** | +04 |
| (4 item index) | sr. hi | +18 | −82** |
| Overall aggression sum | jr. hi | +52** | +11 |
| (20 item index) | sr. hi | +24 | −84** |
| Buss-Durkee assault aggression | jr. hi | +19 | +13 |
| (4 item index) | sr. hi | +38** | −68** |
| Buss-Durkee irritability | jr. hi | +05 | +44** |
| (3 item index) | sr. hi | −19 | −17 |
| Approval of aggression | jr. hi | +39** | +02 |
| (2 item index) | sr. hi | +24 | −65** |
| (N) | jr. hi | (38) | (30) |
|  | sr. hi | (43) | (40) |

[a]Not measured for junior high students.

Table 3: Intercorrelations among aggression indices: Maryland data

| Aggression measure | Correlations, all respondents | | | | | | |
|---|---|---|---|---|---|---|---|
| Physical | − − | | | | | | |
| Delinquency | .56 | − − | | | | | |
| Zaks-Walters | .31 | .22 | − − | | | | |
| Hypothetical | .59 | .54 | .17 | − − | | | |
| Overall sum | .84 | .79 | .50 | .83 | − − | | |
| Assault | .87 | .49 | .24 | .53 | .73 | − − | |
| Irritability | .30 | .16 | .31 | .07 | .27 | .28 | − − |
| Approval | .42 | .29 | .14 | .40 | .38 | .42 | .12 |
| (N = 473) | Physical | Delinquency | Zaks-Walters | Hypothetical | Overall sum | Assault | Irritability |

Note: Cell entries are zero-order Pearsonian r correlation coefficients.

For $r \gtreqless .09$, $p < .05$
$r \gtreqless .12$, $p < .01$

Table 4: Intercorrelations among aggression indices: Wisconsin data

| Aggression measure | Correlations, all respondents | | | | | | |
|---|---|---|---|---|---|---|---|
| Physical | – – | | | | | | |
| Delinquency | .26 | – – | | | | | |
| Zaks-Walters | .13 | .32 | – – | | | | |
| Hypothetical | .33 | .25 | .10 | – – | | | |
| Overall sum | .74 | .62 | .46 | .76 | – – | | |
| Assault | .83 | .30 | .10 | .38 | .69 | – – | |
| Irritability | .34 | –.02 | .05 | .22 | .29 | .29 | – – |
| Approval | .27 | .12 | .29 | .36 | .44 | .24 | –.06 |
| (N = 151) | Physical | Delinquency | Zaks-Walters | Hypothetical | Overall sum | Assault | Irritability |

Note: Cell entries are zero-order Pearsonian r correlation coefficients.

For $r \geqq .16, p < .05$
$r \geqq .21, p < .01$

Table 5: Standardized adolescent television viewing levels,
by age and sex: Maryland data

| TV viewing measure | Grade | Boys | Girls |
|---|---|---|---|
| Crime-detective programs | jr. hi | +40** | –05 |
| (11 show index) | sr. hi | +05 | –36** |
| Western programs | jr. hi | +33** | +09 |
| (7 show index) | sr. hi | –14 | –29** |
| Adventure-drama programs | jr. hi | +34** | +03 |
| (6 show index) | sr. hi | –08 | –27** |
| Comedy-variety programs | jr. hi | +29** | +18 |
| (14 show index) | sr. hi | –11 | –30** |
| Situation comedy programs | jr. hi | +20* | +63** |
| (25 show index) | sr. hi | –66** | –15 |
| Game programs | jr. hi | +17 | +51** |
| (2 show index) | sr. hi | –46** | –20* |
| Overall violence viewing | jr. hi | +38** | +01 |
| (65 show index) | sr. hi | –00 | –35** |
| News-public affairs programs | jr. hi | +31** | –33** |
| (4 item index) | sr. hi | +15 | –13 |
| Saturday morning programs | jr. hi | +50** | +47** |
| (number of hours) | sr. hi | –40** | –47** |
| Total viewing time | jr. hi | +17 | +17 |
| (3 item index) | sr. hi | –13 | –17* |
| Violent TV movies | jr. hi | +34** | –35** |
| (5 item index) | sr. hi | +38** | –33** |
| (N) | jr. hi | (122) | (108) |
| | sr. hi | (107) | (136) |

Table 6:  Standardized adolescent television viewing levels,
by age and sex: Wisconsin data

| TV viewing measure | Grade | Boys | Girls |
|---|---|---|---|
| Crime-detective programs | jr. hi | +24 | +13 |
| (11 show index) | sr. hi | +12 | −45** |
| Western programs | jr. hi | +21 | +06 |
| (7 show index) | sr. hi | −15 | −08 |
| Adventure-drama programs | jr. hi | +06 | +19 |
| (6 show index) | sr. hi | −10 | −10 |
| Comedy-variety programs | jr. hi | −00 | +36* |
| (14 show index) | sr. hi | −07 | −19 |
| Situation comedy programs | jr. hi | +04 | +74** |
| (25 show index) | sr. hi | −46** | −14 |
| Game programs | jr. hi | −13 | +48** |
| (2 show index) | sr. hi | −21 | −01 |
| Overall violence viewing | jr. hi | +22 | +09 |
| (65 show index) | sr. hi | +05 | −33* |
| News-public affairs programs | jr. hi | −07 | −14 |
| (4 item index) | sr. hi | +16 | 00 |
| Saturday morning programs | jr. hi | +28* | +77** |
| (number of hours) | sr. hi | −24 | −59** |
| Total viewing time | jr. hi | +06 | +29 |
| (3 item index) | sr. hi | +24 | −54** |
| Violent TV movies | jr. hi | −18 | −32* |
| (5 item index) | sr. hi | +57** | −18 |
| (N) | jr. hi | (38) | (30) |
| | sr. hi | (43) | (40) |

Table 7: Intercorrelations among television viewing indices: Maryland data

| TV viewing measure | Correlations, all respondents | | | | | | | | | |
|---|---|---|---|---|---|---|---|---|---|---|
| Crime-detective | – – | | | | | | | | | |
| Western | .56 | – – | | | | | | | | |
| Adventure-drama | .69 | .52 | – – | | | | | | | |
| Comedy-variety | .53 | .43 | .54 | – – | | | | | | |
| Situation comedy | .47 | .44 | .58 | .48 | – – | | | | | |
| Game | .33 | .30 | .34 | .31 | .57 | – – | | | | |
| Overall violence | .94 | .77 | .76 | .56 | .53 | .37 | – – | | | |
| News | .17 | .09 | .15 | .22 | .01 | .03 | .16 | – – | | |
| Saturday morning | .30 | .34 | .32 | .28 | .42 | .32 | .35 | -.02 | – – | |
| Total time | .34 | .27 | .39 | .33 | .41 | .29 | .37 | -.02 | .33 | – – |
| TV movies | .31 | .23 | .25 | .16 | .01 | .01 | .32 | .18 | .07 | .18 |
| (N = 473) | Crime-detective | Western | Adventure-drama | Comedy-variety | Situation comedy | Game | Overall violence | News | Saturday morning | Total time |

For $r \geqq .09$, p < .05

$r \geqq .12$, p < .01

Table 8: Intercorrelations among television viewing indices: Wisconsin data

| TV viewing measure | Correlations, all respondents | | | | | | | | | |
|---|---|---|---|---|---|---|---|---|---|---|
| Crime-detective | – – | | | | | | | | | |
| Western | .45 | – – | | | | | | | | |
| Adventure-drama | .48 | .38 | – – | | | | | | | |
| Comedy-variety | .23 | .20 | .37 | – – | | | | | | |
| Situation comedy | .31 | .23 | .49 | .54 | – – | | | | | |
| Game | .15 | .07 | .40 | .32 | .55 | – – | | | | |
| Overall violence | .92 | .73 | .61 | .29 | .36 | .18 | – – | | | |
| News | .06 | .10 | .07 | .19 | .08 | -.10 | .08 | – – | | |
| Saturday morning | .19 | .26 | .29 | .18 | .31 | .11 | .25 | .09 | – – | |
| Total time | .25 | .30 | .24 | .37 | .22 | .07 | .32 | .15 | .34 | – – |
| TV movies | .18 | -.02 | .06 | .04 | -.06 | -.03 | .12 | .20 | -.03 | .16 |
| (N = 151) | Crime-detective | Western | Adventure-drama | Comedy-variety | Situation comedy | Game | Overall violence | News | Saturday morning | Total time |

For $r \geqq .16$, p < .05

$r \geqq .21$, p < .01

Table 9: Standardized adolescent family variable levels, by age and sex: Maryland data

| Family variable measure | Grade | Boys | Girls |
|---|---|---|---|
| Parental control over TV viewing (6 item index) | jr. hi | +29** | +29** |
| | sr. hi | −23* | −29** |
| Parental emphasis on non-aggression (4 item index) | jr. hi | +19* | +09 |
| | sr. hi | −08 | −16 |
| Parental interpretation of TV violence (5 item index) | jr. hi | +21* | +26** |
| | sr. hi | −31** | −14 |
| Parental physical punishment when younger (1 item) | jr. hi | +04 | −19* |
| | sr. hi | +32** | −14 |
| Parental verbal punishment (2 item index) | jr. hi | −20* | −14 |
| | sr. hi | +22* | +10 |
| Parental restrictive punishment (2 item index) | jr. hi | +35** | −10 |
| | sr. hi | −02 | −18* |
| Parental affection (1 item) | jr. hi | +26** | +27** |
| | sr. hi | −55** | +05 |
| Number of siblings | jr. hi | +01 | +25** |
| | sr. hi | −11 | −12 |
| Father occupation (Duncan SES scale) | jr. hi | +07 | −21* |
| | sr. hi | +15 | −03 |
| Mother education (Number of years) | jr. hi | +21* | +30** |
| | sr. hi | −25** | −21* |
| (N) | jr. hi | (122) | (108) |
| | sr. hi | (107) | (136) |

Table 10: Standardized adolescent family variable levels, by age and sex: Wisconsin data

| Family variable measure | Grade | Boys | Girls |
|---|---|---|---|
| Parental control over T V viewing (6 item index) | jr. hi | +20 | +44** |
|  | sr. hi | −43** | −09 |
| Parental emphasis on non-aggression (4 item index) | jr. hi | +16 | +35* |
|  | sr. hi | −23 | −12 |
| Parental interpretation of TV violence (5 item index) | jr. hi | +17 | +39* |
|  | sr. hi | −37** | −06 |
| Parental physical punishment when younger (1 item) | jr. hi | +47** | −41* |
|  | sr. hi | +12 | −25 |
| Parental verbal punishment (2 item index) | jr. hi | −15 | +22 |
|  | sr. hi | 00 | −03 |
| Parental restrictive punishment (2 item index) | jr. hi | +09 | +16 |
|  | sr. hi | +11 | −31* |
| Parental affection (1 item) | jr. hi | −04 | +28 |
|  | sr. hi | −13 | −03 |
| Number of siblings | jr. hi | −13 | +04 |
|  | sr. hi | +20 | −13 |
| Father occupation (Duncan SES scale) | jr. hi | +14 | +08 |
|  | sr. hi | −12 | −07 |
| Mother education (Number of years) | jr. hi | +28* | +27 |
|  | sr. hi | −19 | −26* |
| (N) | jr. hi | (38) | (30) |
|  | sr. hi | (43) | (40) |

Table 11: Intercorrelations among family variable indices: Maryland data

| Family variable measure | Correlations, all respondents | | | | | | | | |
|---|---|---|---|---|---|---|---|---|---|
|  | Control over TV | Nonaggressive emphasis | TV interpretation | Physical punishment | Verbal punishment | Restrictive punishment | Affection | Number of siblings | Father occupation |
| Control over TV | − − | | | | | | | | |
| Nonaggression emphasis | .12 | − − | | | | | | | |
| TV interpretation | .09 | .39 | − − | | | | | | |
| Physical punishment | .11 | .04 | −.04 | − − | | | | | |
| Verbal punishment | .04 | .02 | .02 | .32 | − − | | | | |
| Restrictive punishment | .13 | .16 | .15 | .27 | .25 | − − | | | |
| Affection | .11 | .11 | .14 | −.18 | −.17 | −.12 | − − | | |
| Number of siblings | .09 | .01 | .07 | −.01 | −.04 | −.09 | −.05 | − − | |
| Father occupation | −.04 | .04 | −.08 | .03 | .02 | .04 | .03 | −.11 | − − |
| Mother education | .07 | .18 | .05 | .02 | .01 | .02 | .13 | −.03 | .18 |

(N = 473)

For r ≥ .09, p < .05

r ≥ .12, p < .01

Table 12: Intercorrelations among family variable indices: Wisconsin data

| Family variable measure | Control over TV | Nonaggressive emphasis | TV interpretation | Physical punishment | Verbal punishment | Restrictive punishment | Affection | Number of siblings | Father occupation |
|---|---|---|---|---|---|---|---|---|---|
| Control over TV | – – | | | | | | | | |
| Nonaggression emphasis | .23 | – – | | | | | | | |
| TV interpretation | .29 | .45 | – – | | | | | | |
| Physical punishment | –.03 | –.02 | –.14 | – – | | | | | |
| Verbal punishment | –.06 | –.02 | –.05 | .24 | – – | | | | |
| Restrictive punishment | .05 | .02 | 00 | .24 | .40 | – – | | | |
| Affection | .17 | .04 | .21 | –.14 | –.07 | –.06 | – – | | |
| Number of siblings | .10 | .10 | –.07 | –.11 | –.04 | .05 | –.15 | – – | |
| Father occupation | –.05 | .08 | .07 | –.03 | .06 | –.07 | .14 | –.11 | – – |
| Mother education | –.03 | .14 | .04 | .06 | .16 | .12 | .13 | –.29 | .41 |

Correlations, all respondents

(N = 151)

For $r \geqq .16$, $p < .05$

$r \geqq .21$, $p < .01$

Table 13: Standardized adolescent levels of cognitive reaction to television violence, by age and sex: Maryland data

| Reaction measure | Grade | Boys | Girls |
|---|---|---|---|
| Perceived learning of aggression (5=item index) | sr. hi | +31** +04 | +17 –42** |
| Linkage of violent TV content to real life (4=item index) | jr. hi sr. hi | +08 –05 | +14 –14 |
| Involvement in violent programming (6=item index) | jr. hi sr. hi | –14 –36** | +27** +18* |
| Identification with violent characters (2=item index) | jr. hi sr. hi | +61** +45** | –17 –60** |
| Perceived efficacy of violent characters (3=item index) | jr. hi sr. hi | –05 +18* | –07 –04 |
| (N) | jr. hi sr. hi | (122) (107) | (108) (136) |

For $r \geqq .09$, $p < .05$

$r \geqq .12$, $p < .01$

Table 14: Standardized adolescent levels of cognitive reaction to television violence, by age and sex:  Wisconsin data

| Reaction measure | Grade | Boys | Girls |
|---|---|---|---|
| Perceived learning of aggression | jr. hi | +52** | +25 |
| (5=item index) | sr. hi | 00 | −68** |
| Linkage of violent TV content to real life | jr. hi | +33* | +05 |
| (4=item index) | sr. hi | −07 | −27* |
| Involvement in violent programming | jr. hi | +05 | +25 |
| (6=item index) | sr. hi | −21 | 00 |
| Identification with violent characters | jr. hi | +47** | −17 |
| (2=item index) | sr. hi | +20 | −53** |
| Perceived efficacy of violent characters | jr. hi | +01 | −06 |
| (3=item index) | sr. hi | −01 | +06 |
| (N) | jr. hi | (38) | (30) |
| | sr. hi | (43) | (40) |

For r ≥ .16, p<.05

r = .21, p<.01

Table 15:  Intercorrelations among cognitive reaction indices:  Maryland data

| Reaction measure | Correlations, all respondents | | | |
|---|---|---|---|---|
| Learning | − − | | | |
| Linkage | .50 | − − | | |
| Involvement | .24 | .38 | − − | |
| Identification | .17 | .01 | .06 | − − |
| Efficacy | .16 | .22 | .15 | .06 |
| (N = 473) | Learning | Linkage | Involvement | Identification |

For r ≥ .09, p<.05

r ≥ .12, p<.01

Table 16:  Intercorrelations among cognitive reaction indices:  Wisconsin data

| Reaction measure | Correlations, all respondents | | | |
|---|---|---|---|---|
| Learning | − − | | | |
| Linkage | .45 | − − | | |
| Involvement | .36 | .39 | − − | |
| Identification | .29 | .18 | .10 | − − |
| Efficacy | .30 | .19 | .35 | .00 |
| (N = 151) | Learning | Linkage | Involvement | Identification |

For r ≥ .16, p<.05

r ≥ .21, p<.01

Table 17:  Correlations between level of violence viewing and level of aggressive behavior:  Maryland data

| Aggression measure | Grade | Boys | Girls | Overall |
|---|---|---|---|---|
| Manifest physical aggression | jr. hi | +.17* | +.33** | +.28** |
|  | sr. hi | +.23* | +.15 |  |
| Aggressive behavioral delinquency | jr. hi | +.08 | +.13 | +.22** |
|  | sr. hi | +.23* | +.16 |  |
| Zaks-Walters aggression | jr. hi | −.02 | +.15 | +.08 |
|  | sr. hi | +.15 | +.04 |  |
| Hypothetical aggressive reactions | jr. hi | +.12 | +.20* | +.32** |
|  | sr. hi | +.33** | +.26** |  |
| OVERALL AGGRESSION SUM | jr. hi | +.14 | +.28** | +.32** |
|  | sr. hi | +.31** | +.21** |  |
| (N) | jr. hi | (122) | (108) | (473) |
|  | sr. hi | (107) | (136) |  |

Note:  Cell entries are zero-order correlation coefficients between each aggression variable and the Violence Viewing Index.

Table 18:  Correlations between level of violence viewing and level of aggressive behavior:  Wisconsin data

| Aggression measure | Grade | Boys | Girls | Overall |
|---|---|---|---|---|
| Manifest physical aggression | jr. hi | +.13 | +.29 | +.17* |
|  | sr. hi | +.06 | −.06 |  |
| Aggressive behavioral delinquency | jr. hi | − − | − − | +.20* |
|  | sr. hi | +.12 | +.21 |  |
| Zaks-Walters aggression | jr. hi | +.19 | +.14 | +.24** |
|  | sr. hi | +.11 | +.45** |  |
| Hypothetical aggressive reactions | jr. hi | −.02 | +.24 | +.22** |
|  | sr. hi | +.28 | +.06 |  |
| OVERALL AGGRESSION SUM | jr. hi | +.12 | +.38* | +.30** |
|  | sr. hi | +.23 | +.23 |  |
| (N) | jr. hi | (38) | (30) | (151) |
|  | sr. hi | (43) | (40) |  |

Note:  Cell entries are zero-order correlation coefficients between each aggression variable and the Violence Viewing Index.

Table 19: Correlations between total viewing time and level of aggressive
behavior: Maryland data

| Aggression measure | Grade | Boys | Girls | Overall |
|---|---|---|---|---|
| Manifest physical aggression | jr. hi | +.16 | −.02 | +.14** |
| | sr. hi | +.14 | +.18* | |
| Aggressive behavioral delinquency | jr. hi | +.12 | −.07 | +.08 |
| | sr. hi | .00 | +.20* | |
| Zaks-Walters aggression | jr. hi | −.06 | +.11 | +.04 |
| | sr. hi | +.04 | +.03 | |
| Hypothetical aggressive reactions | jr. hi | +.26** | +.10 | +.21** |
| | sr. hi | +.22* | +.20* | |
| OVERALL AGGRESSION SUM | jr. hi | +.20* | +.04 | +.17** |
| | sr. hi | +.14 | +.21** | |
| (N) | jr. hi | (122) | (108) | (473) |
| | sr. hi | (107) | (136) | |

Note: Cell entries are zero-order correlation coefficients between each
aggression variable and the Total Viewing Time Index.

Table 20: Correlations between total viewing time and level of aggressive
behavior: Wisconsin data

| Aggression measure | Grade | Boys | Girls | Overall |
|---|---|---|---|---|
| Manifest physical aggression | jr. hi | +.18 | −.15 | +.16* |
| | sr. hi | +.17 | −.08 | |
| Aggressive behavioral delinquency | jr. hi | − − | − − | +.19* |
| | sr. hi | +.15 | +.11 | |
| Zaks-Walters aggression | jr. hi | +.55** | +.27 | +.27** |
| | sr. hi | +.15 | +.08 | |
| Hypothetical aggressive reactions | jr. hi | −.07 | −.17 | +.09 |
| | sr. hi | −.06 | +.04 | |
| OVERALL AGGRESSION SUM | jr. hi | +.25 | −.13 | +.23** |
| | sr. hi | +.14 | +.04 | |
| (N) | jr. hi | (38) | (30) | (151) |
| | sr. hi | (43) | (40) | |

Note: Cell entries are zero-order correlation coefficients between each
aggression variable and the Total Viewing Time Index.

Table 21:  Correlations between level of violence viewing and
family variables:  Maryland data

| Family variable measure | Grade | Boys | Girls | Overall |
|---|---|---|---|---|
| Parental control over TV viewing | jr. hi | −.08 | −.06 | +.05 |
| | sr. hi | +.16 | .00 | |
| Parental emphasis on nonaggression | jr. hi | −.21* | −.15 | −.07 |
| | sr. hi | −.04 | −.04 | |
| Parental interpretation of TV violence | jr. hi | +.13 | +.09 | +.15** |
| | sr. hi | +.06 | +.23** | |
| Parental physical punishment | jr. hi | −.04 | −.09 | −.02 |
| | sr. hi | +.02 | −.06 | |
| Parental verbal punishment | jr. hi | −.02 | −.04 | −.01 |
| | sr. hi | .00 | +.11 | |
| Parental restrictive punishment | jr. hi | −.04 | +.08 | +.14** |
| | sr. hi | +.15 | +.09 | |
| Parental affection | jr. hi | +.04 | +.07 | +.03 |
| | sr. hi | +.13 | −.14 | |
| Number of siblings | jr. hi | +.06 | +.21* | +.12** |
| | sr. hi | +.24* | −.01 | |
| Father occupation | jr. hi | −.15 | −.03 | −.17** |
| | sr. hi | −.37** | −.16 | |
| Mother education | jr. hi | −.19* | +.03 | −.03 |
| | sr. hi | −.06 | −.05 | |
| (N) | jr. hi | (122) | (108) | (473) |
| | sr. hi | (107) | (136) | |

Note:  Cell entries are zero-order correlation coefficients between each family
variable and the Violence Viewing Index.

Table 22:  Correlations between level of violence viewing and
family variables:  Wisconsin data

| Family variable measure | Grade | Boys | Girls | Overall |
|---|---|---|---|---|
| Parental control over TV viewing | jr. hi | +.09 | −.08 | +.10 |
| | sr. hi | +.29 | +.04 | |
| Parental emphasis on nonaggression | jr. hi | −.17 | +.08 | +.01 |
| | sr. hi | −.03 | +.11 | |
| Parental interpretation of TV violence | jr. hi | −.08 | +.23 | +.09 |
| | sr. hi | +.12 | +.08 | |
| Parental physical punishment | jr. hi | +.18 | +.21 | +.18* |
| | sr. hi | +.15 | +.06 | |
| Parental verbal punishment | jr. hi | +.11 | +.07 | +.11 |
| | sr. hi | +.02 | +.20 | |
| Parental restrictive punishment | jr. hi | +.29 | +.02 | +.24** |
| | sr. hi | +.05 | +.41** | |
| Parental affection | jr. hi | +.04 | −.05 | +.04 |
| | sr. hi | +.12 | +.01 | |
| Number of siblings | jr. hi | −.17 | +.27 | +.10 |
| | sr. hi | +.11 | +.20 | |
| Father occupation | jr. hi | −.46** | −.38* | −.25** |
| | sr. hi | −.29 | .00 | |
| Mother education | jr. hi | −.47** | −.25 | −.11 |
| | sr. hi | −.04 | −.04 | |
| (N) | jr. hi | (38) | (30) | (151) |
| | sr. hi | (43) | (40) | |

Note:  Cell entires are zero-order correlation coefficients between each family
variable and the Violence Viewing Index.

Table 23: Correlations between level of overall aggression and
family variables: Maryland data

| Family variable measure | Grade | Boys | Girls | Overall |
|---|---|---|---|---|
| Parental control over TV viewing | jr. hi | −.15 | +.04 | +.02 |
| | sr. hi | +.02 | −.05 | |
| Parental emphasis on nonaggression | jr. hi | −.23** | −.16 | −.09* |
| | sr. hi | −.01 | −.21* | |
| Parental interpretation of TV violence | jr. hi | +.05 | +.15 | +.07 |
| | sr. hi | −.07 | +.13 | |
| Parental physical punishment | jr. hi | −.08 | −.03 | +.12** |
| | sr. hi | +.22* | +.19 | |
| Parental verbal punishment | jr. hi | +.12 | −.01 | +.17** |
| | sr. hi | +.36** | +.38** | |
| Parental restrictive punishment | jr. hi | +.22* | +.20* | +.26** |
| | sr. hi | +.12 | +.30** | |
| Parental affection | jr. hi | −.15 | +.06 | −.17** |
| | sr. hi | −.21* | −.36** | |
| Number of siblings | jr. hi | +.02 | +.03 | +.07 |
| | sr. hi | +.16 | +.10 | |
| Father occupation | jr. hi | +.01 | +.03 | +.02 |
| | sr. hi | .00 | −.12 | |
| Mother education | jr. hi | −.04 | +.04 | .00 |
| | sr. hi | −.14 | −.01 | |
| (N) | jr. hi | (122) | (108) | (473) |
| | sr. hi | (107) | (136) | |

Note: Cell entires are zero-order correlation coefficients between each family
variable and the Overall Aggression Index.

Table 24: Correlations between level of overall aggression and
family variables: Wisconsin data

| Family variable measure | Grade | Boys | Girls | Overall |
|---|---|---|---|---|
| Parental control over TV viewing | jr. hi | +.15 | +.08 | +.02 |
| | sr. hi | −.01 | −.24 | |
| Parental emphasis on nonaggression | jr. hi | −.02 | +.16 | +.08 |
| | sr. hi | +.03 | +.11 | |
| Parental interpretation of TV violence | jr. hi | −.08 | +.08 | −.08 |
| | sr. hi | −.28 | −.08 | |
| Parental physical punishment | jr. hi | +.11 | +.21 | +.30** |
| | sr. hi | +.26 | +.31* | |
| Parental verbal punishment | jr. hi | +.13 | −.07 | +.09 |
| | sr. hi | +.14 | +.25 | |
| Parental restrictive punishment | jr. hi | +.09 | −.08 | +.19* |
| | sr. hi | +.25 | +.17 | |
| Parental affection | jr. hi | +.22 | −.14 | −.09 |
| | sr. hi | −.38** | −.06 | |
| Number of siblings | jr. hi | −.33* | +.23 | +.08 |
| | sr. hi | +.21 | +.12 | |
| Father occupation | jr. hi | +.09 | −.20 | .00 |
| | sr. hi | −.09 | +.04 | |
| Mother education | jr. hi | +.03 | −.29 | +.09 |
| | sr. hi | −.04 | +.13 | |
| (N) | jr. hi | (38) | (30) | (151) |
| | sr. hi | (43) | (40) | |

Note: Cell entries are zero-order correlation coefficients between each family
variable and the Overall Aggression Index.

Table 25: Correlations between level of overall aggression and cognitive reaction variables: Maryland and Wisconsin data

| Cognitive reaction measure: Maryland | Grade | Boys | Girls | Overall |
|---|---|---|---|---|
| Perceived learning of aggression | jr. hi | +.40** | +.52** | +.53** |
| | sr. hi | +.56** | +.41** | |
| Linkage of TV violence to real life | jr. hi | +.32** | +.31** | +.31** |
| | sr. hi | +.38** | +.30** | |
| Involvement in violent TV programming | jr. hi | +.27** | +.28** | +.12** |
| | sr. hi | +.13 | +.24** | |
| Identification with violent characters | jr. hi | −.17* | −.11 | +.22** |
| | sr. hi | +.25** | +.05 | |
| Perceived efficacy of violent characters | jr. hi | −.09 | +.10 | +.13** |
| | sr. hi | +.22* | +.21* | |
| (N) | jr. hi | (122) | (108) | (473) |
| | sr. hi | (107) | (136) | |

| Cognitive reaction measure: Wisconsin | Grade | Boys | Girls | Overall |
|---|---|---|---|---|
| Perceived learning of aggression | jr. hi | +.01 | +.31 | +.33** |
| | sr. hi | +.14 | +.14 | |
| Linkage of TV violence to real life | jr. hi | −.03 | +.11 | +.13 |
| | sr. hi | +.02 | +.12 | |
| Involvement in violent TV programming | jr. hi | +.12 | +.29 | +.08 |
| | sr. hi | −.15 | +.32* | |
| Identification with violent characters | jr. hi | −.01 | +.33 | +.31** |
| | sr. hi | +.04 | +.31* | |
| Perceived efficacy of violent characters | jr. hi | +.06 | +.34 | +.12 |
| | sr. hi | +.04 | +.28 | |
| (N) | jr. hi | (38) | (30) | (151) |
| | sr. hi | (43) | (40) | |

Note: Cell entires are zero-order correlation coefficients between each cognitive reaction variable and the Overall Aggression Sum.

Table 26:  Correlations between level of violence viewing and cognitive reaction
variables:  Maryland and Wisconsin data

| Cognitive reaction measure:  Maryland | Grade | Boys | Girls | Overall |
|---|---|---|---|---|
| Perceived learning of aggression | jr. hi | +.19* | +.25** | +.24** |
| | sr. hi | +.09 | +.18* | |
| Linkage of TV violence to real life | jr. hi | +.34** | +.30** | +.27** |
| | sr. hi | +.08 | +.31** | |
| Involvement in violent TV programming | jr. hi | +.16 | +.19* | +.14** |
| | sr. hi | +.13 | +.25** | |
| Identification with violent characters | jr. hi | +.16 | +.01 | +.21** |
| | sr. hi | +.16 | +.17* | |
| Perceived efficacy of violent characters | jr. hi | +.09 | +.03 | +.10* |
| | sr. hi | +.11 | +.10 | |
| (N) | jr. hi | (122) | (108) | (473) |
| | sr. hi | (107) | (136) | |
| Cognitive reaction measure:  Wisconsin | Grade | Boys | Girls | Overall |
| Perceived learning of aggression | jr. hi | +.12 | +.29 | +.21** |
| | sr. hi | +.08 | +.10 | |
| Linkage of TV violence to real life | jr. hi | +.17 | +.18 | +.21** |
| | sr. hi | +.12 | +.25 | |
| Involvement in violent TV programming | jr. hi | −.05 | +.31 | +.10 |
| | sr. hi | +.07 | +.08 | |
| Identification with violent characters | jr. hi | +.06 | +.07 | +.15 |
| | sr. hi | +.23 | −.03 | |
| Perceived efficacy of violent characters | jr. hi | +.16 | +.16 | +.03 |
| | sr. hi | .00 | −.15 | |
| (N) | jr. hi | (38) | (30) | (151) |
| | sr. hi | (43) | (40) | |

Note:  Cell entires are zero-order correlation coefficients between each cognitive
reaction variable and the Violence Viewing Index.

Table 27: Correlations with socioeconomic status and
school performance: Maryland data

| Measure | r with SES | r with SP |
|---|---|---|
| Manifest physical aggression | −.01 | −.30** |
| Aggressive behavioral delinquency | −.01 | −.26** |
| Zaks-Walters aggression | −.03 | −.11* |
| Hypothetical aggressive reactions | −.01 | −.34** |
| Overall aggression sum | −.02 | −.35** |
| Buss-Durkee assault aggression | +.01 | −.29** |
| Buss-Durkee irritability | +.06 | +.02 |
| Approval of aggression | −.09* | −.35** |
| Crime-detective programs | −.12** | −.25** |
| Western programs | −.22** | −.18** |
| Adventure-drama programs | −.13** | −.15** |
| Comedy-variety programs | −.16** | −.14** |
| Situation comedy programs | −.21** | −.23** |
| Game programs | −.17** | −.17** |
| Overall violence viewing index | −.17** | −.24** |
| News-public affairs programs | +.12** | +.13** |
| Saturday morning programs | −.12** | −.21** |
| Total viewing time | −.12** | −.14** |
| Violent TV movies | +.06 | −.03 |
| Parental control over TV viewing | −.04 | +.01 |
| Parental emphasis on nonaggression | +.04 | +.15** |
| Parental interpretation of TV violence | −.08 | −.15** |
| Parental physical punishment | +.03 | +.06 |
| Parental verbal punishment | +.02 | +.02 |
| Parental restrictive punishment | +.04 | −.06 |
| Parental affection | +.03 | +.05 |
| Number of siblings | −.11* | −.20** |
| Mother education | +.18** | +.02 |
| Perceived learning of aggression | −.14** | −.25** |
| Linkage of TV violence to real life | −.08 | −.14** |
| Involvement in violent programming | −.04 | +.09* |
| Identification with violent characters | +.09* | −.15** |
| Perceived efficacy of violent characters | −.04 | .00 |

(N = 473)

Table 28: Correlations with socioeconomic status and
school performance: Wisconsin data

| Measure | r with SES | r with SP |
|---|---|---|
| Manifest physical aggression | −.04 | +.11 |
| Aggressive behavioral delinquency | +.08 | −.02 |
| Zaks-Walters aggression | −.15 | −.16* |
| Hypothetical aggressive reactions | +.08 | +.12 |
| Overall aggression sum | .00 | +.07 |
| Buss-Durkee assault aggression | −.01 | +.13 |
| Buss-Durkee irritability | +.05 | +.05 |
| Approval of aggression | −.13 | −.17* |
| Crime-detective programs | −.16* | −.08 |
| Western programs | −.26** | −.13 |
| Adventure-drama programs | −.22** | −.03 |
| Comedy-variety programs | −.29** | +.06 |
| Situation comedy programs | −.04 | +.17* |
| Game programs | −.09 | +.04 |
| Overall violence viewing index | −.25** | −.12 |
| News-public affairs programs | +.04 | +.16* |
| Saturday morning programs | −.10 | +.15 |
| Total viewing time | −.29* | −.13 |
| Violent TV movies | +.06 | −.14 |
| Parental control over TV viewing | −.05 | +.18* |
| Parental emphasis on nonaggression | +.08 | +.23** |
| Parental interpretation of TV violence | +.07 | +.02 |
| Parental physical punishment | −.03 | +.02 |
| Parental verbal punishment | +.06 | −.04 |
| Parental restrictive punishment | −.07 | −.06 |
| Parental affection | +.14 | +.26** |
| Number of siblings | −.11 | −.02 |
| Mother education | +.41** | +.26** |
| Perceived learning of aggression | −.02 | −.18* |
| Linkage of TV violence to real life | −.14 | −.18* |
| Involvement in violent programming | +.01 | +.02 |
| Identification with violent characters | −.16* | −.21** |
| Perceived efficacy of violent character | +.03 | .00 |

(N = 151)

Table 29: Partial correlations between level of violence viewing and level of aggressive behavior, controlling total television viewing time: Maryland data

| Aggression measure | Grade | Boys | | Girls | | Overall | |
|---|---|---|---|---|---|---|---|
| | | raw r | partial: TV time | raw r | partial: TV time | raw r | partial: TV time |
| Physical | jr. hi | +.17 | +.13 | +.33 | +.33** | +.28 | +.26** |
| | sr. hi | +.23 | +.20* | +.15 | +.08 | | |
| Delinquency | jr. hi | +.08 | +.04 | +.13 | +.14 | +.22 | +.21** |
| | sr. hi | +.23 | +.25** | +.16 | +.08 | | |
| Zaks-Walters | jr. hi | −.02 | −.02 | +.15 | +.14 | +.08 | +.08 |
| | sr. hi | +.15 | +.15 | +.04 | +.03 | | |
| Hypothetical | jr. hi | +.12 | +.03 | +.20 | +.19* | +.32 | +.26** |
| | sr. hi | +.33 | +.28** | +.26 | +.20 | | |
| OVERALL SUM | jr. hi | +.18 | +.12 | +.28 | +.28** | +.32 | +.28** |
| | sr. hi | +.31 | +.29** | +.21 | +.14 | | |
| (N) | jr. hi | (122) | | (108) | | (473) | |
| | sr. hi | (107) | | (136) | | | |

Note: Cell entries in *raw r* columns are zero-order correlation coefficients between the Violence Viewing Index and each aggression measure. Cell entries in *partial: TV time* columns are partial r correlation coefficients between the Violence Viewing Index and each aggression measure, controlling for the Total TV Time Index. Significance levels are indicated for partial correlations only.

Table 30: Partial correlations between level of violence viewing and level of aggressive behavior, controlling total television viewing time: Wisconsin data

| Aggression measure | Grade | Boys | | Girls | | Overall | |
|---|---|---|---|---|---|---|---|
| | | raw r | partial: TV time | raw r | partial: TV time | raw r | partial: TV time |
| Physical | jr. hi | +.13 | +.08 | +.29 | +.37* | +.17 | +.12 |
| | sr. hi | +.06 | −.01 | −.06 | −.05 | | |
| Delinquency | jr. hi | − − | − − | − − | − − | +.20 | +.17* |
| | sr. hi | +.12 | +.06 | +.21 | +.20 | | |
| Zaks-Walters | jr. hi | +.19 | +.06 | +.14 | +.05 | +.24 | +.17* |
| | sr. hi | +.11 | +.06 | +.45 | +.44** | | |
| Hypothetical | jr. hi | −.02 | .00 | +.24 | +.33 | +.22 | +.20* |
| | sr. hi | +.28 | +.33* | +.06 | +.05 | | |
| OVERALL SUM | jr. hi | +.12 | +.06 | +.38 | +.47** | +.30 | +.24** |
| | sr. hi | +.23 | +.19 | +.23 | +.23 | | |
| (N) | jr. hi | (38) | | (30) | | (151) | |
| | sr. hi | (43) | | (40) | | | |

Note: Cell entries in *raw r* columns are zero-order correlation coefficients between the Violence Viewing Index and each aggression measure. Cell entries in *partial: TV time* columns are partial r correlation coefficients between the Violence Viewing Index and each aggression measure, controlling for the Total TV Time Index. Significance levels are indicated for partial correlations only.

Table 31: Partial correlations between level of violence viewing and level of aggressive behavior, controlling socioeconomic status and school performance:  Maryland data

| Aggression measure | Grade | Boys | | | Girls | | | Overall | | |
|---|---|---|---|---|---|---|---|---|---|---|
| | | raw r | partial: SES | SP | raw r | partial: SES | SP | raw r | partial: SES | SP |
| Physical | jr. hi | +.17 | +.17* | +.17* | +.33 | +.33** | +.31** | +.28 | +.28** | +.23** |
| | sr. hi | +.23 | +.27** | +.16 | +.15 | +.13 | +.10 | | | |
| Delinquency | jr. hi | +.08 | +.08 | +.06 | +.13 | +.13 | +.11 | +.22 | +.22** | +.17** |
| | sr. hi | +.23 | +.21* | +.13 | +.16 | +.14 | +.12 | | | |
| Zaks-Walters | jr. hi | −.02 | −.02 | .00 | +.15 | +.16 | +.15 | +.08 | +.07 | +.06 |
| | sr. hi | +.15 | +.15 | +.09 | +.04 | +.04 | +.02 | | | |
| Hypothetical | jr. hi | +.12 | +.11 | +.10 | +.20 | +.20* | +.19* | +.32 | +.32** | +.26** |
| | sr. hi | +.33 | +.35** | +.25** | +.26 | +.25** | +.20* | | | |
| OVERALL SUM | jr. hi | +.14 | +.14 | +.11 | +.28 | +.28** | +.26** | +.32 | +.32* | +.26** |
| SUM | sr. hi | +.31 | +.33** | +.21* | +.21 | +.19* | +.16 | | | |
| (N) | jr. hi | (122) | | | (108) | | | (473) | | |
| | sr. hi | (107) | | | (136) | | | | | |

Note:  Cell entries in *raw r* columns are zero-order correlation coefficients between the Violence Viewing Index and each aggression measure. Cell entries in *partial : SES* columns are partial r correlation coefficients between the Violence Viewing Index and each aggression measure, controlling for Father Occupation (Duncan SES Scale). Cell entries in *partial: SP* columns are partial r correlation coefficients controlling for the School Performance Index. Each control variable is partialled out separately in this analysis. Significance levels are indicated for partial correlations only.

Table 32: Partial correlations between level of violence viewing and level of aggressive behavior, controlling socioeconomic status and school performance: Wisconsin data

| Aggression measure | Grade | Boys | | | Girls | | | Overall | | |
|---|---|---|---|---|---|---|---|---|---|---|
| | | raw r | partial: SES | SP | raw r | partial: SES | SP | raw r | partial: SES | SP |
| Physical | jr. hi | +.13 | +.17 | +.21 | +.29 | +.29 | +.32 | +.17 | +.16* | +.18* |
| | sr. hi | +.06 | −.02 | +.06 | −.06 | −.06 | −.08 | | | |
| Delinquency | jr. hi | − − | − − | − − | − − | − − | − − | +.20 | +.23** | +.20* |
| | sr. hi | +.12 | +.21 | +.11 | +.21 | +.21 | +.20 | | | |
| Zaks-Walters | jr. hi | +.19 | +.10 | +.14 | +.14 | −.03 | +.11 | +.24 | +.22* | +.23** |
| | sr. hi | +.11 | +.09 | +.12 | +.45 | +.45** | +.44** | | | |
| Hypothetical | jr. hi | −.02 | +.10 | +.04 | +.24 | +.23 | +.25 | +.22 | +.25** | +.24** |
| | sr. hi | +.28 | +.28 | +.28 | +.06 | +.06 | +.04 | | | |
| OVERALL SUM | jr. hi | +.12 | +.18 | +.18 | +.38 | +.34 | +.40* | +.30 | +.31** | +.31** |
| SUM | sr. hi | +.23 | +.21 | +.23 | +.23 | +.23 | +.21 | | | |
| (N) | jr. hi | (38) | | | (30) | | | (151) | | |
| | sr. hi | (43) | | | (40) | | | | | |

Note:  Cell entries in *raw r* columns are zero-order correlation coefficients between the Violence Viewing Index and each aggression measure. Cell entries in *partial: SES* columns are partial r correlation coefficients between the Violence Viewing Index and each aggression measure, controlling for Father Occupation (Duncan SES Scale). Cell entries in *partial: SP* columns are partial r correlation coefficients controlling for the School Performance Index. Each control variable is partialled out separately in this analysis. Significance levels are indicated for partial correlations only.

Table 33: Partial correlations between level of aggressive behavior and viewing of seven types of television programming

| Viewing measure | All respondents, Maryland | | All respondents, Wisconsin | |
|---|---|---|---|---|
| | raw r | partial r | raw r | partial r |
| Crime-detective programs | +.32 | +.16** | +.33 | +.30** |
| Adventure-drama programs | +.30 | +.11* | +.19 | +.08 |
| Saturday morning programs | +.19 | +.09* | +.22 | +.23** |
| Game programs | +.18 | +.07 | +.02 | +.06 |
| Western programs | +.20 | −.01 | +.12 | −.07 |
| Comedy-variety programs | +.17 | −.03 | +.08 | +.09 |
| Situation comedy programs | +.18 | −.05 | −.05 | −.26** |
| (N) | (473) | | (151) | |

Note: Cell entries are partial correlation coefficients between the Overall Aggression Sum and each television viewing variable, controlling for all other television viewing variables in the set. Significance levels are indicated for partial correlations only.

Table 34: Multiple predictors of aggressive behavior: violence viewing and
selected third variables: Maryland data

| Independent variables | Grade | Boys | Girls | Overall |
|---|---|---|---|---|
| Violence viewing (OVV) | jr. hi | +.14 | +.28 | +.32 |
| (raw r) | sr. hi | +.31 | +.21 | |
| OVV and Parental emphasis on | jr. hi | .22 | .30 | .32 |
| nonaggression (multiple r) | sr. hi | .31 | .29 | |
| OVV and Buss-Durkee irritability | jr. hi | .31 | .50 | .42 |
| | sr. hi | .52 | .33 | |
| OVV and Parental physical punishment | jr. hi | .15 | .28 | .34 |
| | sr. hi | .38 | .29 | |
| OVV and Parental verbal punishment | jr. hi | .18 | .28 | .36 |
| | sr. hi | .48 | .41 | |
| OVV and Parental restrictive | jr. hi | .24 | .33 | .39 |
| punishment | sr. hi | .32 | .35 | |
| OVV and Parental affection | jr. hi | .30 | .28 | .36 |
| | sr. hi | .39 | .40 | |
| OVV and Perceived learning of aggression | jr. hi | .37 | .54 | .56 |
| | sr. hi | .62 | .43 | |
| OVV and linkage of TV violence to real | jr. hi | .29 | .36 | .39 |
| life | sr. hi | .48 | .33 | |
| OVV and Involvement in violent TV | jr. hi | .26 | .37 | .33 |
| programming | sr. hi | .32 | .29 | |
| OVV and Identification with violent | jr. hi | .14 | .30 | .35 |
| characters | sr. hi | .38 | .21 | |
| OVV and Father occupation SES | jr. hi | .14 | .28 | .32 |
| | sr. hi | .31 | .21 | |
| OVV and School performance | jr. hi | .32 | .34 | .43 |
| | sr. hi | .45 | .38 | |
| (N) | jr. hi | (122) | (108) | (473) |
| | sr. hi | (107) | (136) | |

Note: Cell entries are multiple correlation coefficients between the Overall Aggression
Sum and the Violence Viewing Index and each third variable, one at a time. Multiple
correlations greater than the raw correlation indicate the added contribution of the
family and TV reaction variables to the relationship between aggression and viewing.
Significance levels are not indicated.

Table 35: Multiple predictors of aggressive behavior: violence viewing and selected third variables: Wisconsin data

| Independent variables | Grade | Boys | Girls | Overall |
|---|---|---|---|---|
| Violence viewing (OVV) (raw r) | jr. hi | +.12 | +.38 | +.30 |
| | sr. hi | +.23 | +.23 | |
| OVV and Parental emphasis on nonaggression (multiple r) | jr. hi | .12 | .40 | .31 |
| | sr. hi | .23 | .24 | |
| OVV and Buss-Durkee irritability | jr. hi | .65 | .41 | .41 |
| | sr. hi | .23 | .48 | |
| OVV and Parental physical punishment | jr. hi | .15 | .41 | .39 |
| | sr. hi | .33 | .38 | |
| OVV and Parental verbal punishment | jr. hi | .17 | .40 | .30 |
| | sr. hi | .27 | .31 | |
| OVV and Parental restrictive punishment | jr. hi | .13 | .39 | .32 |
| | sr. hi | .33 | .24 | |
| OVV and Parental affection | jr. hi | .25 | .40 | .31 |
| | sr. hi | .47 | .24 | |
| OVV and Perceived learning of aggression | jr. hi | .12 | .43 | .40 |
| | sr. hi | .26 | .26 | |
| OVV and Linkage of TV violence to real life | jr. hi | .13 | .39 | .30 |
| | sr. hi | .23 | .24 | |
| OVV and Involvement in violent TV programming | jr. hi | .18 | .42 | .30 |
| | sr. hi | .28 | .38 | |
| OVV and Identification with violent characters | jr. hi | .12 | .49 | .40 |
| | sr. hi | .23 | .39 | |
| OVV and Father occupation SES | jr. hi | .20 | .39 | .31 |
| | sr. hi | .23 | .23 | |
| OVV and School performance | jr. hi | .26 | .40 | .31 |
| | sr. hi | .24 | .24 | |
| (N) | jr. hi | (38) | (30) | (151) |
| | sr. hi | (43) | (40) | |

Note: Cell entries are multiple correlation coefficients between the Overall Aggression Sum and the Violence Viewing Index and each third variable, one at a time. Multiple correlations greater than the raw correlation indicate the added contribution of the family and TV reaction variables to the relationship between aggression and viewing. Significance levels are not indicated.

Table 36: Multiple regression analysis of aggressive behavior, by violence viewing, parental punishment and affection: Maryland data

| Independent variable | Grade | Boys | Girls | Overall |
|---|---|---|---|---|
| Violence viewing index | jr. hi | +.19* | +.27** | +.32** |
|  | sr. hi | +.30** | +.17* |  |
| Parental punishment sum | jr. hi | +.14 | +.10 | +.23** |
|  | sr. hi | +.29** | +.30** |  |
| Parental affection | jr. hi | −.15 | +.05 | −.14** |
|  | sr. hi | −.23* | −.24** |  |
| <u>Multiple correlation</u> | jr. hi | .27 | .30* | .42** |
|  | sr. hi | .46** | .49** |  |
| (N) | jr. hi | (122) | (108) | (473) |
|  | sr. hi | (107) | (136) |  |

Note: Cell entries are partial correlation coefficients between the Overall Aggression Sum and each family and viewing variable, controlling for all other independent variables. The Multiple correlation entries represent the total relationship with the entire set of independent variables.

Table 37: Multiple regression analysis of aggressive behavior, by violence viewing, parental punishment and affection: Wisconsin data

| Independent variable | Grade | Boys | Girls | Overall |
|---|---|---|---|---|
| Violence viewing index | jr. hi | +.05 | +.37 | +.27** |
|  | sr. hi | +.27 | +.16 |  |
| Parental punishment sum | jr. hi | +.24 | +.04 | +.17* |
|  | sr. hi | +.29 | +.30 |  |
| Parental affection | jr. hi | +.30 | −.13 | −.07 |
|  | sr. hi | −.42** | +.09 |  |
| <u>Multiple correlation</u> | jr. hi | .34 | .40 | .35** |
|  | sr. hi | .53** | .38 |  |
| (N) | jr. hi | (38) | (30) | (151) |
|  | sr. hi | (43) | (40) |  |

Note: Cell entries are partial correlation coefficients between the Overall Aggression Sum and each family and viewing variable, controlling for all other independent variables. The Multiple correlation entries represent the total relationship with the entire set of independent variables.

Table 38: Grand multiple regression analysis of aggressive behavior, by violence viewing parental affection and punishment, child's irritability, and child's perceived learning of aggression from television: Maryland data

| Independent variable | Grade | Boys | Girls | Overall |
|---|---|---|---|---|
| Violence viewing index | jr. hi | +.14 | +.22* | +.26** |
| | sr. hi | +.29** | +.15 | |
| Perceived learning of aggression | jr. hi | +.29** | +.46** | +.45** |
| | sr. hi | +.46** | +.34** | |
| Buss-Durkee irritability | jr. hi | +.21* | +.41** | +.22** |
| | sr. hi | +.34** | +.16 | |
| Parental punishment sum | jr. hi | +.11 | +.03 | +.18** |
| | sr. hi | +.16 | +.27** | |
| Parental affection | jr. hi | −.09 | .00 | −.09* |
| | sr. hi | −.18 | −.18* | |
| Multiple correlation | jr. hi | .48** | .64** | .62** |
| | sr. hi | .69** | .58** | |
| (N) | jr. hi | (122) | (107) | (473) |
| | sr. hi | (107) | (136) | |

Note: Cell entries are partial correlation coefficients between the Overall Aggression Sum and each independent variable, controlling all other independent variables. The multiple correlation entries represent the total relationship with the entire set of independent variables.

Table 39: Grand multiple regression analysis of aggressive behavior, by violence viewing, parental affection and punishment, child's irritability, and child's perceived learning of aggression from television: Wisconsin data

| Independent variable | Grade | Boys | Girls | Overall |
|---|---|---|---|---|
| Violence viewing index | jr. hi | +.16 | +.33 | +.24** |
| | sr. hi | +.27 | +.20 | |
| Perceived learning of aggression | jr. hi | +.06 | +.21 | +.28** |
| | sr. hi | +.07 | +.12 | |
| Buss-Durkee irritability | jr. hi | +.60** | +.12 | +.28** |
| | sr. hi | −.02 | +.44** | |
| Parental punishment sum | jr. hi | +.09 | −.01 | +.11 |
| | sr. hi | +.29 | +.27 | |
| Parental affection | jr. hi | −.01 | −.09 | −.11 |
| | sr. hi | −.40* | +.11 | |
| Multiple correlation | jr. hi | .66** | .46 | .51** |
| | sr. hi | .53** | .56* | |
| (N) | jr. hi | (38) | (30) | (151) |
| | sr. hi | (43) | (40) | |

Note: Cell entries are partial correlation coefficients between the Overall Aggression Sum and each independent variable, controlling all other independent variables. The multiple correlation entries represent the total relationship with the entire set of independent variables.

Table 40: Correlations between level of violence viewing and level of aggressive behavior, at high vs. low parental emphasis on nonaggressive behavior: Maryland data

| Aggression measure | Grade | Boys | | Girls | | Overall | |
|---|---|---|---|---|---|---|---|
| | | Low | High | Low | High | Low | High |
| Physical | jr. hi | +.16 | +.21 | +.52 | +.05 | +.37 | +.19 |
| | sr. hi | +.34 | +.10 | +.07 | +.19 | | |
| Delinquency | jr. hi | +.09 | +.04 | +.20 | +.02 | +.30 | +.12 |
| | sr. hi | +.46 | +.13 | +.19 | +.11 | | |
| Zaks-Walters | jr. hi | +.09 | −.01 | +.31 | −.07 | +.16 | −.05 |
| | sr. hi | +.42 | −.02 | +.24 | −.09 | | |
| Hypothetical | jr. hi | +.25 | +.09 | +.23 | +.08 | +.44 | +.18 |
| | sr. hi | +.40 | +.28 | +.35 | +.11 | | |
| OVERALL SUM | jr. hi | +.21 | +.11 | +.45 | +.03 | +.43 | +.17 |
| | sr. hi | +.54 | +.17 | +.30 | +.11 | | |
| (N) | jr. hi | (45) | (50) | (49) | (42) | (185) | (238) |
| | sr. hi | (38) | (64) | (53) | (82) | | |

Note: Cell entries are zero-order correlation coefficients between the Violence Viewing Index and each aggression measure. Respondents were sorted into High vs. Low groups on the Parental Emphasis on Nonaggression Index by cutting at the midpoint within each grade level. For the junior high group, Low = 0-3 and High = 4-8; for the senior high group. Low = 0-2 and High = 3-8. Higher scores indicate a greater parental stress on non-violent responses to social conflict situations.

Table 41: Correlations between level of violence viewing and level of aggressive behavior, at high vs. low parental emphasis on nonaggressive behavior: Wisconsin data

| Aggression measure | Grade | Boys | | Girls | | Overall | |
|---|---|---|---|---|---|---|---|
| | | Low | High | Low | High | Low | High |
| Physical | jr. hi | +.22 | −.17 | +.25 | +.35 | +.22 | +.07 |
| | sr. hi | −.10 | +.22 | +.11 | −.33 | | |
| Delinquency | jr. hi | − − | − − | − − | − − | −.09 | +.49 |
| | sr. hi | −.44 | +.64 | +.13 | +.41 | | |
| Zaks-Walters | jr. hi | +.09 | +.32 | +.30 | −.22 | +.19 | +.33 |
| | sr. hi | −.10 | +.32 | +.26 | +.66 | | |
| Hypothetical | jr. hi | +.02 | −.08 | +.39 | +.05 | +.33 | +.02 |
| | sr. hi | +.19 | +.40 | +.32 | −.21 | | |
| OVERALL SUM | jr. hi | +.15 | +.03 | +.42 | +.31 | +.34 | +.23 |
| | sr. hi | −.12 | +.56 | +.30 | +.10 | | |
| (N) | jr. hi | (22) | (15) | (15) | (14) | (82) | (65) |
| | sr. hi | (23) | (19) | (22) | (17) | | |

Note: Cell entries are zero-order correlation coefficients between the Violence Viewing Index and each aggression measure. Respondents were sorted into High vs. Low groups on the Parental Emphasis on Nonaggression Index by cutting at the midpoint within each grade level. For the junior high group, Low = 0-3 and High = 4-8; for the senior high group. Low = 0-2 and High = 3-8. Higher scores indicate a greater parental stress on non-violent responses to social conflict situations.

# Adolescents, Parents, and Television Use: Self-report and Other-report Measures from the Wisconsin Sample

Jack M. McLeod, Charles K. Atkin, and Steven H. Chaffee

*University of Wisconsin*

This is the second and final report of research into the relationships among three sets of variables: adolescent aggression, television viewing behavior, and structural attributes of family social environment.[1] This report contains data gathered from 151 adolescents and their mothers in Middleton, Wisconsin. Our previous report contained data comparable between the Wisconsin sample and a second sample of 473 adolescents in Prince Georges County, Maryland.

The following topics are included in this final report: an analysis of modeling or mother-child similarity in both aggressive behavior and violence viewing; the relationship of self-report measures of aggression to the ratings by mothers, peers and teachers; mother-child communication as a family environment variable; the association of violence viewing and self-report and other-report measures of aggressive behavior; and the relationship of the family environment to other variables.

The report goes on to examine the role of peers; mother-child coorientation and its connection with aggressive behavior and violence viewing; the time-order problem and causal inferences; and the differential associations of westerns and other types of violent programming. The report concludes with a series of multivariate analyses, using violence viewing, cognitive reactivity to television violence, approval of aggression, and aggressive behavior as criteria.

This second report introduces many variables that were measured only in the Wisconsin surveys. In addition, a number of the previously discussed indices have been expanded to include data from the parental interviews. In all other cases, the original child self-report indices from the Maryland-Wisconsin study are carried over into the present analyses to provide for maximum comparability to the earlier findings.

## PROCEDURES AND MEASURES

## Sampling

Since the details of the sampling procedures were given in the first report (McLeod, Atkin, and Chaffee, 1971), we shall only briefly sketch the Wisconsin sampling here. In October of 1969, 225 adolescents completed questionnaires in two schools in Middleton, Wisconsin. During the same month, personal interviews were conducted with the mothers of these children. One year later, a different set of interviewers returned to reinterview 151 of the mothers and to administer questionnaires to 68 seventh graders and 83 tenth graders. We will refer to these groups as the "junior high" and "senior high" subsamples.

## Measures: adolescent self-report of aggression

Most measures of self-reported adolescent aggression were the same for both our Wisconsin and Maryland samples. These measures were discussed in our first report (this volume) and listed in full in Appendix A of that paper. Here we will simply mention the measures used earlier and concentrate on indices unique to the Wisconsin sample and introduced here for the first time.

*Overall aggression sum.* Our best single measure of adolescent aggressive behavior is the overall aggression sum (*OAS*). It is a 20-item index made up of the following subindices: manifest physical aggression (six items); aggressive behavioral delinquency (three items); Zaks-Walters aggression (seven items); and hypothetical aggressive reactions (four items). The same items were used in the first report.

*Buss-Durkee assault aggression.* The four-item index of assault aggression, adapted from Buss and Durkee (1957), was also used in our earlier report.

*Buss-Durkee verbal aggression.* Data from our measures of verbal aggression have not been reported previously. Four Buss-Durkee items were adapted by using the "a lot like me" response scale:

   a. I demand that people respect my rights.
   b. When people yell at me, I yell back.
   c. When people disagree with me, I can't help getting into arguments.
   d. I would rather give in than argue about something. (reversed scoring).

*Buss-Durkee irritability.* The three items indexing irritability were the same Buss-Durkee items as used previously.

*Buss-Durkee overall sum.* The three indices using the 11 Buss-Durkee items were combined in this report for the mother-child modeling analyses.

*Approval of aggression.* Two items relating to the sanctioning of aggression as a means of resolving conflict are repeated from our first report.

*Aggressive attitudes.* An index extending the approval of aggression index is used here for the first time. Five new items are added, all rated along a five-step agreement scale:

   a. The most successful people are the ones who use violence.
   b. It upsets me when I see someone beating up another kid. (reversed scoring).
   c. The rising amount of crime and violence in this country really doesn't bother me very much.
   d. If a student is fed up with his government these days, he is somewhat justified if he sets off a bomb in an empty Army building.
   e. During the American Revolution, blowing up British buildings was completely justified.

# Measures: mother self-report of aggression

It is obvious that it would be inappropriate to ask the mother questions from such indices as behavioral delinquency and the hypothetical situations. In all, 20 of the 31 adolescent aggression items were used for the mother. The following indices were formed: (a) Buss-Durkee Assault Aggression (4 items); (b) Buss-Durkee Verbal Aggression (4 items); (c) Buss-Durkee Irritability (3 items); (d) Buss-Durkee Overall Sum (11 items, sum of three indices above); (e) Approval of Aggression (2 items); and (f) Zaks-Walters Aggression (7 items).

# Measures: other-ratings of adolescent aggression

In order to cross-validate our adolescent self-report measures, we obtained ratings of aggression for each child from three sets of others: peers, teachers, and the child's mother. While none of the three is a very precise measurement source, we feel the three other-reports combined produces a more solid basis of comparison to the self-report measures.

*Peers.* Each adolescent in the Wisconsin sample was given a list of ten classmates and was asked to rate each on three items representing the Buss-Durkee irritability, assault, and verbal dimensions:

   a. Is patient with others. (reverse-scored for irritability)
   b. When loses temper, hits other people. (assault aggression)
   c. Yells back when yelled at. (verbal aggression)

The rating was done on a three-point scale of "often," "sometimes," and "never." The total score for each adolescent was averaged for each dimension of aggression by dividing by the number of people rating him (approximately ten raters). Most children were known by almost all raters; however, anyone not well known enough to be rated received "?" and this was not counted in averaging the ratings.

*Teachers.* Because only the sixth-grade teachers taught a given student more than one period each day, teacher ratings of aggression were not obtained for the tenth graders. Each student was rated on a four-point scale with these anchors: highly aggressive-hostile, troublemaker; more aggressive-hostile than average; average; and very passive, gets along well, submissive.

*Mothers.* A four-item index is used for the mother's report of her child's aggressive behavior. All questions were asked in the 1969 interview with the mother. The items:

   a. Does (name of child) seem to get into more fights than other children his age, fewer fights, or about the same amount of fights? (fewer=0, same=1, more=2)
   b. When (name of child) was younger, how often did (he, she) do mean things to other children while playing? Would you say often, sometimes, or never? (never=0, sometimes=1, often=2)
   c. When (he, she) was younger, how often did (he, she) show aggressive behavior toward other children? Would you say often, sometimes, or never? (never=0, sometimes=1, often=2)
   d. If your child had an argument with (his,her) best friend, how would (he,she) normally go about settling it? (nonaggressive response=0, physical aggression=2)

# Measures: adolescent television viewing levels

Both the Wisconsin mothers and their children were asked to indicate how frequently each watched various prime time television shows. Each show was checked according to a four-step scale of frequency. The 47 shows on the list in the 1969 survey for both mother and child were grouped into six manifest content categories for the mother-child modeling analyses. The categories and number of shows in each were: (a) Crime-detective (eight shows); (b) Westerns (seven shows); (c) Adventure-drama (eight shows); (d) Comedy-variety (nine shows); (e) Situation comedy (ten shows); (f) News (four shows).

*Overall violence viewing.* The same 65 program index of violence viewing (*OVV*) that was used in the first report is also used for the adolescents' television behavior here. The violence weighting for each show is based on the ratings of samples of high school students (Murray, Cole, and Fedler, 1970) and of adults and television critics (Greenberg and Gordon, 1970).

*Total viewing time.* The earlier estimates of adolescents' total television viewing time were supplemented by mother reports of the number of hours the child viewed television on an average day and on the day preceding the interview. The child provided data regarding time spent yesterday, the day before yesterday, and on an average day.

*Television violence viewing when younger.* In the 1970 questionnaire, the Wisconsin adolescents were asked how frequently they had watched each of 13 shows that were on television three or four years ago. None is still on the air. The shows were weighted according to their level of violence by the research team. A violence viewing index for this era was obtained by summing the child's viewing level for each show weighted by the show's level of violent content. The violent content groupings:

| Very high violence | High violence | Low violence |
|---|---|---|
| Combat | I Spy | Gilligan's Island |
| Man from UNCLE | Felony Squad | Dr. Kildare |
| Rat Patrol | Big Valley | Gentle Ben |
| Rawhide | The Fugitive | Donna Reed |
| | | Patty Duke |

# Measures: mothers' television viewing levels

In addition to giving the frequency with which they viewed the 47 specific television programs, the mothers also estimated their total viewing time on an average day and the day before the interview.

# Measures: family environment

By including data from the mother, much more reliable and probably valid assessment of the family environment was made possible for the

Wisconsin sample. This also allowed us to compare the views of the adolescents and their mothers through the coorientational measures of accuracy and agreement.

*Parental control over television.* The six items used in the first report to index the degree of parental control over the child's viewing were increased to 28 with the repeating of items, inclusion of new items, and data from the mother on most items. Some new items:

   a. Do (your parents, you) set limits on the amount of time (you, he) watches television? (yes, no)

   b. (Mother only) How strict are you in controlling what your child is viewing (very lenient, fairly lenient, average, fairly strict, very strict)

*Parental emphasis on nonaggression.* Repetition of items in both years, new items, and responses from mothers served to increase the measurement of parental nonaggression emphasis from four to 18 items. Included as new items were the mothers' desired behavior for their children in two of the situations used in the hypothetical aggressive reaction index for the child.

*Parental interpretation of television violence.* The five items referring to parental interpretation of television's "unreality" were also asked of the mother, thus doubling the number of items in that index.

*Parental punishment.* The five items indexing physical, verbal, and restrictive punishment were also asked of the mother. Thus, physical punishment has two items in this sample, while verbal and restrictive punishment have four each.

*Parental affection.* The single measure of affection used earlier was considerably improved by adding two items and adding in the mothers' responses to all three items. Again, a four-step scale of frequency was used. The new items:

   a. Show (their, your) affection by hugging and kissing (you, him).

   b. Tell (you, him) that (they, you) love (you, him).

*Family communication patterns.* The measurement of the structure of parent-child communication, which was not included in the first report, requires a more extensive explanation because it differs markedly in conceptualization and complexity of measurement from other variables. The measures have been developed in a series of studies where the dependent variables were various aspects of political socialization (McLeod, Chaffee, and Eswara, 1966; Chaffee, McLeod, and Wackman, 1966; McLeod, Chaffee, and Wackman, 1967; McLeod, Rush, and Friederich, 1968-69; Stone and Chaffee, 1970; and Chaffee, McLeod, and Atkin, 1971). Their relation to violence viewing has been explored by Chaffee and McLeod (1971).

In these various studies in a variety of social settings, we have found that there are at least two dimensions in the structure of parent-child communication. The two dimensions, which are either uncorrelated or slightly positively related, are called *socio-oriented* and *concept-oriented* constraints on the developing child.

The socio-oriented emphasis is typified by encouraging the youngster to maintain harmonious interpersonal relations, avoid controversy, and suppress his inner feelings. Five items, asked of both the mother and her child, index this dimension. Some of the questions ask about the *frequency* of the act, while others ask for an estimate of the degree of *emphasis*. The questions, with slight variations in wording for mother and child:

a. (Parent) says (child) shouldn't argue with adults.
b. (Parent) says (parent's) ideas are correct, and (child) shouldn't argue with them.
c. (Parent) answers (child's) arguments by saying, "You'll know better when you grow up."
d. (Parent) says that you should give in on arguments, rather than making people angry.
e. (Parent) says there are some things that just shouldn't be talked about.

Concept-oriented communication items deal with the frequency or emphasis of parental constraints on the child to express his own ideas, become exposed to controversy, and challenge others. The five items:

a. (Parent) says that every member of your family should have some say in family decisions.
b. (Parent) admits that kids know more about some things than adults do.
c. (Parent) says (child) should always look at both sides of an issue.
d. (Parent) says that getting (child's) ideas across is important, even if others don't like it.
e. (Parent) asks for (child's) opinion when the family is discussing something.

Although it is possible to treat each of these dimensions as a separate independent variable, we have found in some studies that the two interact, producing structural patterns that are not simply the sums of their two constituent functions. Therefore we treat family communication in terms of the following four types:

a. *Laissez-faire* families, which emphasize neither type of relation. Children are not prohibited from challenging parental views but neither are they exposed to the world of independent and contending ideas.
b. *Protective* families, which stress socio-relations only. The child is encouraged to get along with others, at the expense of concept-relations that would expose him to the controversial world of ideas. Not only is he prohibited from expressing dissent, but he is given little chance to encounter information on which he might base his own views.

    c. *Pluralistic* families, which emphasize the development of strong
and varied concept-relations in an environment comparatively
free of social restraints. The child is encouraged to explore new
ideas and is exposed to controversial material; he can make up
his own mind without fear of endangering social relations with
his parents.

    d. *Consensual* families, which attempt to stress both orientations.
While the child is exposed to controversy, and told he should
enter into it, he is (paradoxically) constrained to develop concepts that are consonant with existing socio-relations. That is, he
is in effect encouraged to learn his parents' ideas and adopt their
values.

*Socioeconomic status.* While the same measures of fathers' occupation and mothers' education were used for both reports, a more complex
scale of socioeconomic status has been added. The occupational and
education measures are combined in approximately equal weighting to
two other items, family income, and subjective social class.

## Measures: mother-child coorientational variables

Our studies of family communication have also provided an empirical
basis for a general model of coorientation (Chaffee and McLeod, 1970;
McLeod and Chaffee, in press). This model also implies that we gather
data about topics of mutual importance from both the mother and her
child. The data include not only the measurement of the person's own
view (perceptions, attitudes, values, etc.), but also the mother's estimate of the child's view and *vice versa*. Thus, four sets of views are
involved, two for the mother and two for the child.

The four sets of views are combined into three coorientational
measures:

*Agreement.* A comparison of the difference between the child's own
view and the mother's own view is called agreement. Obviously, there is
only a single measure of agreement common to the mother and child.
The smaller the difference, the greater is the agreement.

*Accuracy.* The mother's estimate of the child's view compared with
the child's own view forms the index of mother accuracy. The second
measure, child accuracy, is taken from the child's estimate of mother's
view compared to the mother's actual position. The smaller the discrepancy, the greater is the accuracy.

*Congruency.* Each person's own view compared with his estimate of
that of the other family member is called congruency. Independent measures for the child and the mother are available; once more, the smaller
the discrepancy, the greater the congruency. Strictly speaking, congruency is not a coorientational measure since it involves the views and

estimates of only one person at a time. Since it is part of the general coorientational model, we will keep congruency under the rubric of coorientation.

Ideally, we would use a wide variety of important topics to obtain the judgments and estimates needed for the coorientational measures. In this case, limited time and space on our questionnaires forced us to settle on a single topic—the relative importance of various attributes the child might derive from his school experience. Fortunately, we were able to increase the reliability of measurement by using the same items in both years of the Wisconsin study. The mother and child were independently asked to rank four attributes to their importance (for your child to do, for yourself): (a) making new friends who share (child's) interests; (b) being part of school activities and social life; (c) learning new ideas and different ways of thinking; and (d) preparing to earn a living.

After giving their own views, the mother and child estimated how the other would rank these same attributes. For each pair of measures, a difference score was computed for each year. The resulting sum over two years could range from zero (high) to 16 (low).

# Measures: cognitive reactions to television violence

Three indices of cognitive reactions of adolescents to television violence are included in this report. While all are measured identically to our explanation in our first report, we have added a new combined sum of these three measures.

*Perceived learning of aggression.* The degree to which the adolescent feels television offers opportunity for him to learn antisocial behavior is again indexed by five items using the "a lot like me" underlying scale.

*Linkage of violent television to real life.* Four items are used to measure the perception of similarity between the world portrayed on violent television programs and everyday reality.

*Involvement in violent programming.* The final cognitive reaction index used here is a six-item index of psychological involvement with the characters and stories of action-adventure shows.

*Total cognitive reactivity.* Perceived learning, reality linkage, and involvement are combined into a 15-item index of total cognitive reactivity. It will be used as a criterion variable in the last section of this report dealing with multiple regression analyses.

# Measure: peer integration.

Riley and Riley (1951) found that the child's lack of primary group ties with his peers is associated with a preference for violent media content. We have measured this with a five-item index of peer integration:

   a. Number of close friends (none, one or two, three to five, six to ten, more than ten)

b. Do you have a bunch of friends that you usually hang around with? (no, yes)

c. Compared with the rest of the kids you know, would you say you have more friends, less friends, or about the same number of friends? (less, same number, more)

d. How do you prefer to spend your time: alone, or in the company of friends? (usually like to be by myself, sometimes with friends and sometimes by myself, usually like to be with friends)

e. Does your child have a group of friends he usually goes around with? (Mother report: no, yes)

## FINDINGS

In keeping with our first report, the presentation of data here will not attempt to test a set of formal hypotheses. Statistical tests should be taken as rough indicators of which relationships look most promising and warrant further consideration. Caution should be used in generalizing from these findings, because our Wisconsin sample is small and we lack the Maryland sample for the replication that was present in our first study. We will use asterisks to indicate significance levels: * ($p < .05$), ** ($p < .01$). For correlations, these asterisks indicate the difference of the correlation from zero, in either direction. All correlations are Pearson product-moment coefficients (r). For tables showing standardized levels, the asterisks indicate the cell mean is significantly different from the overall mean for the remaining cells.

## Modeling analyses

Among the many possible explanations of children's behavior, modeling, or the child's imitation of the parent's behavior, is the most direct and has apparent simplicity. The simplicity is more apparent than real, however. As we shall discuss later, the presence of a correlation between the behavior of mother and child allows for a variety of alternative inferences. For the present, we will take up the question of the degree of mother-child similarity in aggressive behavior and television use.

*Modeling of aggression.* Varying degrees of evidence for modeling are shown in Table 1. (All tables are in Appendix B.) Consistent similarity between mother and child is shown for assault and verbal aggression, while irritability, a more covert attribute, shows no evidence for modeling. Assuming that irritability is more closely tied with physiological functioning, then we have little evidence that this attribute is passed on through genetic transmission. We do have evidence that more overt behavioral manifestations of aggression are passed on, presumably through environmental processes.

If modeling involves the learning of appropriate adult sex roles by the adolescent, then we would expect considerably higher mother-daughter correlations than those for mother and son. This is the case for almost all comparisons in Table 1, clearly reversing only for approval of aggression among the junior high group. Among boys, the similarity to the aggression level of the mother tends to lessen from junior to senior high.

The sharp increase in mother-daughter similarity on assault aggression, from +.17 in junior high to a remarkable +.57 in senior high, suggests a possible inference that nonaggression rather than aggression is being modeled. As will be shown in Table 4, assault aggression declines very sharply for girls during the same year the level of "modeling" is going up. It might be argued, then, that the most likely change is that of the daughter learning the relatively nonaggressive role of the mother.

Some additional evidence that the modeling correlations of Table 1, though mostly modest in magnitude, are not spurious comes from examination of the full correlation matrix of mother and child indices. These data are not shown in our tables, but they do indicate generally higher mother-child correlations on the corresponding indices (e.g., mothers' verbal aggression by daughters' verbal aggression) than on the cross-index comparisons (e.g., mothers' verbal aggression by daughters' assault aggression). Overall, the average cross-index correlation is +.04, compared to an average correlation of +.14 for corresponding indices. In particular, there is a much stronger association between mother assault and child assault (+.23) and mother verbal and child verbal (+.23) than between mother assault and child verbal (+.01) and mother verbal and child assault (+.09).

This reduces the likelihood that the modeling correlations are simply an artifact of their joint association with some third variable. If this were the case, then a given aggression measure for mother would have correlations more equal in magnitude for all child aggression measures.

*Modeling of television behavior.* Table 2 shows that the mother-child correlations for television viewing behavior are almost all positive. It is clear that the modeling correlations for types of shows are generally greater than those for time spent viewing television. Substantial correlations are also shown for the seven shows with the highest violence ratings.

The pattern of modeling correlations parallels those from our previous research (Chaffee, McLeod, and Atkin, 1971; Chaffee and McLeod, 1971) using a different and considerably larger sample of adolescents. Such correlations have led other researchers to infer that this is evidence for "positive modeling," wherein the child imitates the viewing behavior of the example set by the parent (Himmelweit et al., 1958; Schramm et al., 1961). We have argued in our earlier work (Chaffee et al.; Chaffee and McLeod) that this inference is not necessarily implied by the data, a point we shall return to in our conclusions.

Table 2 also shows that, while girls' modeling correlations for the various program types remains substantial for both age comparisons, there is a noticeable decline in mother-son similarity in the older group for viewing time as well as for several program types. The considerably higher modeling of western viewing for girls, a result expected from sex-role learning, is somewhat in contrast to the Chaffee and McLeod findings of no difference between sexes for this type of programming.

Table 3 tests a possible alternative inference that the modeling correlations are a spurious artifact of the fact that mother and child are similar in general television viewing time. The within-category figures are the average correlations within programs of a given types. The across-category figures are the average correlations of programs of the given type with all programs of other types. The difference between the two sets of correlations, then, is the "pure" or specific modeling of that type of program with general viewing removed.

It appears that modeling of westerns remains high after removing the effects of general viewing. All program types remain positive, although the within-category across-category differences are rather small for adventure-drama and situation comedies. Of course, this analysis removes only one alternative explanation and leaves a variety of other possible inferences open.

## Self-report vs. other-report of aggression

In all analyses up to this point, aggression findings have been based upon self-report measures. Our previous report analyzed the sex and age patterns for these measures and came to the conclusions that boys show considerably higher levels than girls on most aggression measures and that there is a marked decline in aggression from junior to senior high. Table 4 shows the sex and age category standardized levels for reports from peers, teachers, and the mothers of the adolescents, together with some corresponding self-report measures.

The peer report data show a pattern rather similar to the self-report results, with boys rated more aggressive than girls and with the decline for older children on the assault aggression measure. Peer-reported verbal aggression, however, departs somewhat from this pattern with a slightly higher level for girls at the junior high level. Both self- and other-reports of verbal aggression show a slight increase at the senior high level for boys. The two reports of irritability resemble each other for girls, but peer reports diverge, with a higher level for older boys.

Teacher reports, available only for the junior high sample, indicate an inconsistency with self-reports in that girls show slightly, though nonsignificantly, higher levels of aggression. The parent data are also inconsistent, with senior high mothers reporting more aggression for their sons than did the junior high mothers.

Table 5 shows the correlations among the various aggression measures. Low positive correlations are shown among the first three supposedly parallel other-report measures (average r = +.18). Even less correspondence is shown for the teacher and mother reports with the overall self-report measure (+.15 and +.09, respectively). Perhaps the lack of correlation of the teacher ratings with any other aggression index is understandable because it is only a one-item measure; however, the disappointing results for the mother reports with four items is less understandable.

Some encouragement is provided by the substantial correlation between peer reports and self-reports for the assault aggression index (+.40). The association for verbal aggression is more modest (+.17), and peer report of irritability is unrelated to self-report of irritability. However, the peer report of irritability is positively related to self-reports of assault and verbal aggression; perhaps the judgment of irritability is so difficult to make that it is made indirectly through an individual's more observable traits such as verbal and physical aggression. The adolescent's attitude toward aggression presents an anomaly, in that it correlates more highly with the peer measures than with the self-report measures (except for approval of aggression with which it has a part-whole relationship and hence is meaningless).

## Measures of family environment

Table 6 shows standardized levels of family environment indices improved for the second report by the addition of mothers' reports on these items and from some new items. New measures of mother-child communication are also introduced.

The addition of the mothers' view reveals sharpened results for parental control over adolescent television viewing, with considerably more restriction for the junior high families and slightly more for girls than for boys. A somewhat similar pattern is shown for parental affection, while physical punishment reverses with higher levels for boys. Restrictive punishment is largely characterized by very low levels for senior high girls.

Socio-orientation, as shown in Table 6, declines sharply with age and is greater among the families with girls. Concept-orientation has a less clear pattern, with the highest levels for junior boys and senior girls. The socio-orientation findings follow our theory and previous research, but we would have anticipated an increase in concept-orientation for boys as well as for girls. The improved socioeconomic status measure used here evens out from the earlier pattern, although the junior high families with boys retain their unexplained high status.

The correlations among the various family environment indices used in the first report are rather similar to those resulting in Table 7 from the introduction of more reliable measures. The two new measures, socio-orientation and concept-orientation, are unrelated. Socio-orientation shows positive correlations with all forms of parental control, with verbal and restrictive punishment, and with affection. Concept-orientation has positive associations with control over television, with interpretation of television violence, and with affection. Socioeconomic status is related to both new measures, −.25 with socio-orientation and +.41 with concept-orientation.

## Television viewing and aggression

The crucial correlations between adolescent television viewing and the new other-reports of aggression are shown in Tables 8 and 9. The level of violence viewing ($OVV$) used in the earlier report and the expanded measure of total viewing time are used as predictor variables. Three peer measures—a teacher report, a mother report, and an overall sum of the three other-reports—are used as criterion variables. Buss-Durkee verbal aggression, approval of aggression, and aggressive attitudes are self-reports also used as criterion variables here.

*Overall violence viewing and aggression.* While the large majority of correlations between violence viewing ($OVV$) and other-report measures of aggression shown in Table 8 are positive, the size of these correlations tends to be somewhat less than the corresponding associations for $OVV$ and the self-report measures of aggression shown in the first report (McLeod et al., 1971, Table 18). The overall correlation between $OVV$ and the peer report of aggression is +.20, and the teacher report of aggression also correlates +.20 with $OVV$. The lower correlations for the other-report sum appears to be largely a function of the mother report data, which show a −.29 correlation with $OVV$ for junior boys and a −.06 correlation overall.

Among the new self-report measures in Table 8, Buss-Durkee verbal aggression has no clear pattern of association with $OVV$, while aggressive attitudes shows low to moderate positive correlations.

*Television viewing time and aggression.* The television viewing time correlations with other-reports of aggression in Table 9 are fairly similar to those for $OVV$ by aggressive behavior, in that most correlations are positive and low. The only exception is among junior girls, where slight negative correlations are shown on most other-report measures.

Self-reported verbal aggression is unrelated to viewing time for most sex-grade subgroups, while aggressive attitudes has a positive relationship to viewing time among girls only.

## Family environment and other variables

Tables 10, 11, and 12 present the correlations of the new family environment measures with violence viewing and the self- and other-reports of aggression.

*Family environment and violence viewing.* Attempts to control the adolescent's television viewing and to interpret violent content are associated with generally *higher* levels of violence viewing (Table 10). While this suggests the ineffectiveness of such measures, a more likely explanation is that parents whose children are "addicted" to violent fare are likely to take measures to modify that addiction. More direct attempts to affect aggression by emphasizing nonaggression are also positively related to violence viewing, but only among families with girls.

The results for our new measures of physical, verbal, and restrictive punishment that include reports from the mother as well as from the child are very little changed from the child-only punishment measures of our first report. Low to moderate positive correlations are shown for all comparisons in Table 10. This is consistent with findings of previous research by Bassett, Cowden, and Cohen (1968) regarding physical punishment and with Chaffee and McLeod (1971) for all three punishment measures. Our correlations are considerably larger on all measures than those reported by Chaffee and McLeod, however. The fact that the punishment measures were identical for both studies suggests that the differences might be due to the fact that the present research had a more reliable measurement of violence viewing (a 65-show index as opposed to two summary items).

The tendency toward a positive relationship between the parent's giving of affection and the child's level of violence viewing noted in the first report is somewhat strengthened here. The overall correlation of +.12 is close to the comparable +.07 found by Chaffee and McLeod and is contrary to the Maccoby (1954) finding of a negative association between affection and "escapist" television viewing.

Table 10 shows rather strong positive correlations between socio-orientation and violence viewing in all groups except the junior boys. Families that emphasize harmony and suppress the child's feelings have adolescents who watch more violent television than the more egalitarian families. This is consistent with earlier work showing that socio-orientation was related to entertainment media use (Chaffee, McLeod, and Wackman, 1966; McLeod, Chaffee, and Wackman, 1967; Chaffee, McLeod, and Atkin, 1971) and with violence viewing (Chaffee and McLeod, 1971). The very slight negative relationship (−.05 overall) between concept-orientation and violence viewing also bears a close resemblance to the Chaffee and McLeod data (−.04). An analysis of these two dimensions by the four family types they form will be presented later in the report.

There is also evidence in Table 10 of the expected negative relationship whereby children in lower status families watch more violent television. This association is fairly strong for all but the senior high girls. The overall correlation (−.17) is somewhat stronger than the comparable figure from the Chaffee and McLeod report (−.08).

*Family environment and self-report aggression.* Table 11 indicates an overall *positive* correlation between parental control and self-report aggression level; however this correlation is large only among junior girls. Direct parental emphasis on nonaggression tends to be slightly related to lower aggressive behavior among boys, but it is inconsistent for girls. The conditional interaction of this variable with the viewing-aggression relationship will be discussed later.

Our first report summarized the literature that would lead us to expect a positive relationship between punishment and aggressive behavior. The addition of data from the mother does little to change our conclusions from that report. A positive relationship between all three forms of punishment and self-report aggression is shown for senior high children only (Table 11). The junior high correlations are low and inconsistent. This contrasts with the findings for punishment and violence viewing discussed earlier, where equivalent levels of association were shown for each grade level.

The results for parental affection are inconclusive (Table 11). Two moderate correlations are shown, but one is positive and the other is negative. Of the two, the $-.23$ for senior boys resembles the corresponding figure for the Maryland data in our first report.

Table 11 shows that there is a tendency toward aggression in socio-oriented homes. The results are strong for boys only, however. The other family communication dimension, concept-orientation, has a negative correlation overall, but this relationship is strong only among senior high boys ($-.39$); senior girls show a slight positive relationship. The combinations of these two dimensions will be shown later in this report.

Our expanded measure of socioeconomic status is not related to self-report aggression in a systematic fashion. Two of the correlations are positive while the other two are negative. Although the two negative correlations are larger, the overall correlation is slightly positive ($+.05$).

*Family environment and self-report aggression.* Table 12 corresponds to the previous table in showing the relationship of the family environment variable to aggression. In this table, however, other-report rather than self-report is used as the criterion aggression variable. Once again, there is no clear and consistent pattern for the parental-attempts-to-influence variable. For interpretation of television violence, for example, two of the sex-age groups show moderate positive correlations, while the two others have negative ones.

All three punishment variables are positively correlated with other-report aggression in a pattern that closely resembles the results for the self-report comparisons. The overall correlations range from $+.18$ for verbal punishment to $+.41$ for restrictive punishment, with somewhat higher associations for senior high boys than for other groups.

Contrary to prior theoretical expectations, a small *positive* relationship between affection and aggression is shown for senior high boys and girls in Table 12. We should note that we did not find this pattern for self-report aggression either in Wisconsin or in Maryland. But nowhere did we find the expected negative relationship.

Very strong results are shown for both boys and girls in senior high for socio-orientation. Families emphasizing harmony and suppression of feelings are more likely than others to have aggressive children. However, very little association is found in the junior high homes. Concept-orientation has no consistent relationship with other-report aggression.

Finally, socioeconomic status is negatively related to other-report aggression at the senior high level, but there is no relationship over all adolescents.

*Family communication patterns and other variables.* Table 13 shows the standardized levels of the four family communication types on the major viewing and aggression variables.

*Protectives*, the children whose families emphasize harmonious and hierarchical socio-relations but do not stress exposure to controversy or expression of ideas, are the heaviest television viewers and are also quite high in viewing of violence and Saturday morning fare. They see the possibilities of learning from violent programming, but curiously they are about average in involvement and in linking television to real life. Their parents are apt to control how much they watch and to place emphasis on nonaggression. They are high on all but the verbal aspects of self-report aggression and peers rate them as high on both assault and verbal aggression. Interestingly, their mothers do not see them as aggressive.

*Consensual* adolescents, whose parents emphasize both socio- and concept-orientations, are rather similar to the protectives in being very high on violence viewing and are above average in total television time. They are the most likely to see a linkage to reality in the television content, and their parents are the highest on all forms of control over their viewing. Despite heavy parental emphasis on nonaggression, peers, teachers, and their mothers are apt to describe these youngsters as aggressive. Yet the consensual children themselves are only about average on the self-report aggression measures.

*Laissez-faire* families, where neither socio- nor concept-orientation is stressed, tend to produce relatively low users of television and of violent content. The children are unlikely to see a reality linkage but do report heavier involvement in the programming. In keeping with their communication behavior, laissez-faire parents are unlikely to control viewing, interpret content, or emphasize nonaggression. Regarding aggression, the adolescents from this type of family are slightly above average in self-report aggression but slightly below average in the reports from peers and teachers.

*Pluralistic* adolescents, who receive concept-orientation but not a socio-emphasis in the home, are very low users of television and violent content and are also below average on cognitive reaction to television. Their parents are not likely to control television or teach nonaggression, but perhaps they do not have to. Their children are clearly the lowest group on both self-report and other-report measures of aggression.

## Peer integration

Previous research leads to the expectation that the more closely the adolescent is tied to a group of peers, the less frequent will be his television viewing generally and his watching of violence in particular (Schramm, Lyle, and Parker, 1961; Himmelweit, Oppenheim, and Vince 1958; Riley and Riley, 1951). The relevant data, shown in Table 14, provide little support for the expectation. The overall relationship to violence viewing is only slightly negative ($-.07$) and that with viewing time is actually positive ($+.04$). Then, too, the more popular adolescents show a slight tendency to report more (rather than less) reactivity to violence on television.

Peer integration shows a weak but consistent overall relationship to the aggression measures in Table 14; most of the correlations are positive, and strongly so in the peer reports for the junior high boys. For the most part, peer integration does not seem to be a strong predictor variable.

Data from the Maryland sample (not shown) yield more consistently positive overall correlations between peer integration and measures of aggressive behavior ($+.24$ with *OAS*). Contrary to expectations, there is also a positive overall association between integration and total television viewing time ($+.16$) and violence viewing ($+.17$); these relationships are stronger for boys than for girls.

## Coorientation of mother and child

The general expectation from previous research and theorizing is that all three coorientational measures—agreement, congruency, and accuracy—would be negatively related to violence viewing and aggression. Regarding viewing, Schramm et al. (1961) found children who disagreed with parents over aspirations spent more time with "fantasy" television. One version of this formulation assumes that lack of agreement with the parent frustrates the child, which in turn leads the child to "escape" television fare and to aggressive outlets for motive states resulting from frustration.

Table 15 shows some support for the above expectation, although in general the negative correlations are not strong. Perhaps this is due to the relatively weak measurement of the coorientation variables in that only one situation was involved, and a rank order of fixed categories was used.

It is interesting to note that for both overall violence viewing (*OVV*) and for self-report aggression (*OAS*), the key measure was accuracy (which involves a comparison of the mother's and the child's view), rather than congruency (the comparison using exclusively the child's data of his view and his estimate for his mother). Simple response set would have made the child's congruency the best predictor. This happens for mother-reported aggression, where mother congruency has the highest correlation (+.25) among the five measures.

## Past violence viewing and aggression

We would very much have liked to have used a long-term panel design to check on the crucial question of time-order or causal sequence of our variables. Because we lacked this design, we introduced what should be considered a weak substitute, in the form of a question about the frequency with which the adolescent watched various programs three or four years ago. From this, we built an index of past violence viewing that is roughly comparable to *OVV*, the current violence viewing index.

If the past viewing predicts to aggression better than current viewing, then it can be argued that the violence viewing-to-aggression direction is made more tenable. On the other hand, better prediction for the current *OVV* would make aggression-to-violence viewing more likely. Pitting the two viewing measures directly is somewhat unfair to the past viewing measure, however. The number of shows (13), compared to the 65 shows in the current index, implies that greater reliability of the latter would make better prediction more likely. The greater difficulty of recall of past behavior also operates as a handicap to the past viewing measure.

Table 16 shows the predictive power of the current and past violence viewing indices. The two measures, intercorrelated +.35, reveal very similar aggression correlations with the overall advantage going to the past measure. For reasons discussed above, this is rather surprising and argues for the violence viewing-to-aggression interpretation.

It also appears that past viewing tends to be the more strongly related to aggression for boys and for junior high children, while current viewing has the advantage among girls and the older adolescents.

## Crime-detective versus westerns: cognitive reactions

One of the more perplexing findings presented in our first report (McLeod et al., 1971) involved differential predictions of aggression for westerns and for other types of violent programs when the viewing of all other types of programs are partialed out (Table 33). Among the seven program types, the correlations of crime-detective, adventure-drama, and Saturday morning viewing with aggression level (*OAS*) remained positive when controlling for all other types of watching. The initial positive correlations of westerns and *OAS* (+.20 and +.12), however, became negative (−.01 and −.07) when the controls were introduced.

Table 17 explores the possibility that westerns are different because a different set of cognitive reactions are associated with them than with the other types of violent shows. Crime-detective shows were used as a comparison with westerns on twelve cognitive reaction items. Adolescents were asked if these were more likely to be their reactions during crime shows or during westerns, or whether they were equally likely (or unlikely) for both program types.

It is very clear that westerns are seen as less closely tied to real life than crime shows. For example, 46 percent of the adolescents felt crime shows were more likely to ". . .tell about life the way it really is"; only eight percent reported that westerns were more likely to do so. Respondents tended to see crime programs as more involving. Only a slight plurality perceived greater learning of aggression from crime shows, and most adolescents saw no differences on this attribute.

# Multivariate analyses

In the remaining tables, we examine the relationship of two or more variables in predicting various new criterion variables: other-reports of aggressive behavior, violence viewing, overall cognitive reactions, approval of aggression, and the combined index of self- and other-reports of aggressive behavior. For those regression analyses that are parallel to the models examined in the first report, we use the identical independent variable measures based on the adolescent data only.

*Violence viewing and other-reports of aggressive behavior.* Tables 18-22 present various partial and multiple correlations for the relationship between violence viewing and the other-ratings of aggression from peers, teachers, and mothers.

The control for television viewing time does not alter the raw correlations to any marked degree (Table 18). It tends to reduce the correlations for boys slightly, while reducing some comparisons for girls and increasing others to a minor degree. The partials for peer and teacher reports are only slightly lower than those found for self-reports (Table 30, first report), while the relationship to mother reports remains inconsistent and clearly negative for junior boys.

Table 19 shows that partialing on socioeconomic status and school performance leaves the overall raw correlations virtually unchanged.

*Multiple predictors of aggressive behavior.* Table 20 presents the multiple correlations for other-report aggression with violence viewing and key third variables taken one at a time. This technique shows the extent to which different variables can improve the prediction of aggression beyond its raw correlation with the $OVV$ index. The strongest contribution is made by the child's perceived learning of aggression from violent television programs (from $+.17$ to $+.35$ overall), replicating the findings with self-reported aggression (Tables 34 and 35, first report). On the other hand, the addition of irritability did not produce the sizable increase found in the case of self-report aggression. Socio-orientation combined with $OVV$ to produce substantial multiple correlations among seniors (from $+.22$ to $+.53$ for boys and from $+.09$ to $+.35$ for girls) but had no impact on the relationship for juniors. Moderate contributions were made by reality linkage, restrictive punishment, and physical punishment, particularly for senior high students.

The combination of violence viewing, parental punishment, and parental affection as predictors of the other-report aggression sum is shown in Table 21. Multiple correlations ranging from .20 to .31 are produced—considerably less than the comparable .34 to .53 range for self-report aggression (Table 37, first report). While the other-report multiple coefficients are relatively similar, the magnitude of the partials for each of the three predictors varies considerably between sex-grade categories. Punishment is the only predictor for junior boys, while violence viewing and punishment partials are high for senior boys. Punishment also shows strong partials for girls in both grades, while affection is negative for junior girls and positive for senior girls. With the exception of the senior boys, the $OVV$ index partials are considerably lower than was the case for self-report aggression.

Table 22, using five variables as a regression on other-reported aggression, is comparable to Table 38 of the first report that used the same predictor variables for self-report aggression. The .39 multiple coefficient is considerably lower than the .51 found previously for self-report aggression, the difference being particularly great among boys. Perceived learning of aggression has the highest overall partial in both cases ($+.30$ for other-report, $+.28$ for self-report), and punishment retains the low positive partial correlation it had for self-report data. On the other hand, both violence viewing and irritability show much smaller partials for other-reported aggression. Each enters as a substantial predictor for only one sex-grade comparison—violence viewing for senior boys and irritability for senior girls.

*Multiple predictors of violence viewing.* The multiple regression analyses of violence viewing are shown in Table 23. Predictor variables here are based on responses of both the mother and child to facilitate comparison with the Chaffee and McLeod results. Moderate multiple correlation coefficients are indicated for the family communication variables for all but junior boys. Socio-orientation accounts for almost all of the predictive power in this regression analysis, but Table 13 has previously shown that concept-orientation cannot be ignored because it clearly interacts with socio-orientation in its relation to violence viewing.

Affection and the three punishment variables produce moderate multiple predictions of violence viewing for all four sex-age groups (Table 23). The partials help to make restrictive punishment the strongest overall predictor of the affection-punishment set of variables, although its partial is essentially zero for junior girls and senior boys.

We have also run the multiple regression analyses for the affection-punishment variables for the Maryland data (Table 24). The family communication measures were not available for this sample, nor were mother reports of affection and punishment. The multiple coefficients are clearly lower than those in Wisconsin, but the general pattern is similar.

The overall Wisconsin results plus comparable statistics from Chaffee and McLeod (1971) using a different sample of parents and children are shown below:

Overall Correlations with Violence Viewing

| Independent var. | Absolute (zero-order) | | Relative (partials) | |
|---|---|---|---|---|
| | Wisconsin | Chaffee-McLeod | Wisconsin | Chaffee-McLeod |
| Concept-orientation | −.05 | −.05 | −.05 | −.02 |
| Socio-orientation | +.28 | +.14 | +.18 | +.10 |
| Multiple correlation | .28 | .14 | | |
| Affection | +.10 | +.08 | +.06 | +.07 |
| Physical punishment | +.07 | +.03 | +.10 | +.03 |
| Verbal punishment | +.14 | +.03 | +.09 | +.04 |
| Restrictive punishment | +.16 | +.10 | +.15 | +.07 |
| Multiple correlation | .33 | .16 | | |

The results for the samples appear quite similar in pattern, although most of the partials are small and somewhat stronger predictions are found in the Wisconsin sample. It should be noted that the Maryland results also indicate that restrictive punishment is the strongest predictor of violence viewing.

Table 25 presents a regression analysis of violence viewing with eight predictor variables for the Wisconsin sample. Multiple correlation coefficients over .50 are shown for all sex-age subgroups. Some rather odd partial coefficients are created, however, in that none of the eight predictor variables has consistently all-positive or all-negative sets of partial correlations for all four comparisons. This is doubtless the result of using so many predictor variables with such small subgroup samples. In the partials where all adolescents are combined, no one variable stands out as a dominant predictor.

The corresponding regression analysis for the Maryland sample is shown in Table 26. Six rather than eight predictor variables are used, because the family communication measures were not available, and each measure is based on child reports only. Here, the multiple correlations are considerably less and the partials for the variables change considerably from the Wisconsin sample. School performance becomes a good predictor with negative partials, perhaps comparable to the similar pattern found for I Q in the Chaffee and McLeod (1971) data. Affection and physical and verbal punishment become negligible predictors, while restrictive punishment retains the only consistent positive partial correlations with violence viewing.

*Multiple predictors of cognitive reactions to television violence.* Tables 27-30 present multiple regression analyses of cognitive reactions to television. Multiple correlation coefficients ranging from .27 to .46 are shown for the family communication dimensions in Table 27. Socio-orientation has substantial positive partials for girls, but the boys' data are inconsistent with a negative partial shown at the junior high level. Concept-orientation is inconsistent with a −.06 overall, but with positive partials for three of the four subgroups.

Affection, restrictive punishment, and physical punishment tend to be fairly good positive predictors of cognitive reactivity. For girls, verbal punishment has a negative partial and is negative overall. In general, the Wisconsin data show better prediction of cognitive reactivity for both the family communication and parental treatment variables for girls than for boys.

The Maryland data in Table 28, based on child-report predictors, show cognitive reactivity results considerably different from the Wisconsin findings. Restrictive punishment remains a good predictor of reactivity among girls, but affection and physical punishment partials are negligible overall, and verbal punishment, which has negative partials in Wisconsin, has positive coefficients in Maryland.

When the parental treatment and family communication measures are combined with school performance and socioeconomic status in Table 29 for Wisconsin, considerably higher multiples ranging from .42 to .65 are produced. Low school performance and frequent parental affection are the best and most consistent predictors of cognitive reactivity in Wisconsin. Adolescents raised in concept-oriented homes are less likely to be reactive. For girls only, reactivity is related to high physical and restrictive punishment and to low verbal punishment.

The six-variable multiple regression on cognitive reactivity in Maryland is shown in Table 30. School performance is generally negative as in Wisconsin, but the partials are much reduced. Father occupation is negative in contrast to the generally positive partials for socio-economic status in Wisconsin. Affection is inconsistent and slightly negative rather than clearly positive, physical punishment shows no clear pattern, and verbal punishment reverses by revealing positive partials. Only restrictive punishment is consistent across samples by remaining clearly positive for girls. In general, there is too much inconsistency in findings across samples and regression analyses to say much about the prediction of cognitive reactivity.

*Multiple predictors of combined self- and other-reports of aggression.*
The aggressive behavior reports by self and others are summed into a
combined index for analyses presented in Tables 31-34. The multiple
correlations of $OVV$, parental punishment, and affection with the combined aggression index shown in Table 31 range widely from $+.29$ for
junior boys to $+.49$ for senior boys—slightly lower than the multiples
using self-report aggression alone (see Table 37, first report). The $+.29$
overall zero-order correlation between $OVV$ and the combined aggression index declines slightly to $+.26$ with the family variables controlled.
On this omnibus aggression index, the parental punishment sum shows a
solid positive partial correlation of $+.20$. On the other hand, parental
affection yields a mixed pattern across subgroups.

Table 32 adds the child's irritability and perceived learning of aggression to the regression analysis. These five predictors produce more similar multiple correlations, from $+.49$ to $+.57$ across the four subgroups.
Thus, this set of predictors accounts for one-quarter to one-third of the
aggression variance. Overall violence viewing, perceived learning of
aggression, and irritability have strong positive overall correlations after
all other independent variables are controlled. Each predicts well for
girls of both grade levels, while violence viewing is weak among junior
boys and learning and irritability are slightly negative among senior
boys. The sum of the three types of parental punishment shows consistently positive partials, somewhat higher for senior high. Affection is
inconsistent with a strong negative partial among the senior high boys.

To demonstrate the total contribution of television viewing variables
alone, the set of predictors in Table 33 includes only measures of exposure and reactions to television violence. The combination of current
violence viewing, past violence viewing, and cognitive aggression learning accounts for one-fourth of the overall variance on the combined self-
and other-report aggression index, with subgroup multiples ranging from
$+.32$ to $+.51$. The partial correlations for $OVV$ and past violence viewing are quite similar, and the perceived learning measure is considerably
stronger than either exposure variable.

Although the measure of past violence viewing was not available for
the Maryland sample, the combination of $OVV$ and perceived aggression learning yields multiple correlations of a comparable magnitude
(see Table 34, first report). In the overall Maryland sample, these two
viewing factors accounted for almost one-third of the variance on the
self-report aggression index. The subgroup multiple correlations vary
from $+.37$ to $+.62$.

These data indicate that a large portion of the aggressive behavior variance can be accounted for solely by viewing variables, without any
supplementary contribution from family factors or internal aggressiveness states such as irritability.

*Violence viewing by aggressive behavior within levels of nonaggres-
sion emphasis.* Table 34 describes the conditional association of $OAS$

with the self-report, other-report, and combined indices of aggression. Results presented earlier indicate that parental attempts at emphasizing nonaggression were inconsistently related to aggressive behavior in Wisconsin (Table 12; Table 24, first report).

Respondents were divided into high and low groups on the continuum of nonaggression teaching, and zero-order viewing-aggression correlations were run at each level. New data on the association of violence viewing and other-report aggressive behavior show strong differences across high and low levels of parental nonaggression emphasis. Where parents stress nonaggressive behavior, there tends to be a slightly negative relationship, particularly for girls. Where there is a lesser emphasis, the correlations are uniformly positive. The magnitude of this distinction is much stronger for the other-report index than for the self-report index.

When the combined sum of these aggression indices is examined, the overall correlation with $OVV$ is $+.15$ in the high emphasis condition and $+.39$ in the low condition. For three of the four subgroups, there is a zero relationship where parents emphasize nonaggressive responses. The senior boys present a reversal to this general trend, however, with a $+.45$ viewing-aggression correlation under high parental emphasis. It should be noted that there are only 19 respondents in this cell.

*Multiple predictors of aggressive attitudes.* The Wisconsin seven-item index of aggressive attitudes included two items dealing specifically with approval of aggression that were also used with the Maryland sample. This pair of items was originally inserted as a test of the Berkowitz (1962) notion that violence portrayals may teach that aggression is acceptable if it can be justified. However, we found no consistent differences in the correlations between violence viewing and approval of hurting an enemy "in order to get revenge" vs approval of hurting an enemy merely "if you are mad at him."

These two items were summed to form a minimal aggression approval index in common for both samples. Tables 35 and 36 display the regression analyses for Wisconsin and Maryland. The overall and subgroup multiple correlations tend to fall in the $+.30$ to $+.40$ range, somewhat lower than the behavioral aggression multiples. In analyses not shown, the more extensive seven-item index produced substantially larger multiple correlations using these same independent variables, indicating that low reliability and limited variance may have dampened any relationships with the two-item index.

Among the four predictors of aggression approval, there is a consistent tendency for perceived learning of aggression to relate positively and for parental affection to relate negatively when other variables are controlled. The partial correlations for $OVV$ are modest in Maryland and negligible in Wisconsin, while punishment shows no clear relationship.

Table 37 presents a six variable regression on the full seven-item aggressive attitudes index in Wisconsin. These predictors account for one-fourth of the variance overall, and subgroup multiple correlations vary from +.41 to +.62. Again, the strongest partial correlations are found for perceived learning of aggression (mainly among junior boys) and parental affection (moderate-to-strong negative correlations for all subgroups). In addition, concept-oriented family communication is negatively related to approval of aggression, while socio-orientation relates positively for the junior high students. The partial correlation for $OVV$ is positive among seniors and negative among juniors.

## CONCLUSIONS

The purpose of our research is to examine the structure within and the relationships between three sets of variables: adolescent aggression, adolescent television viewing, and the family environment. We will take each of these in turn to discuss the implications of both the new data from this report and the findings presented in our earlier report.

# Adolescent aggression

Our conceptualization divided aggression into four components: aggressive behavior, verbal aggression, irritability, and attitudes toward aggression. In addition to the adolescents' self-reports on the four components, the Wisconsin sample included peer ratings on the first three and teachers' and mothers' ratings on aggressive behavior.

*Aggressive behavior.* Four subindices were combined into the 20-item index of self-reported aggressive behavior ($OAS$): manifest physical aggression (six items); aggressive behavioral delinquency (three items); Zaks-Walters aggression (11 items); and hypothetical aggressive reactions (four items). These four indices were combined because their manifest content involved overt behavior, and their intercorrelations averaged +.36 in Maryland and +.20 in Wisconsin. The addition of peer ratings of aggressive behavior in Wisconsin also helped justify the overall index with a correlation of +.42 with $OAS$.

Other empirical findings, however, raise doubts about the wisdom of isolating aggressive behavior from other forms of aggression. The Wisconsin self-report, $OAS$, showed an average correlation of +.42 with verbal aggression, irritability, and aggressive attitudes. This far exceeds the average internal subindex correlation of +.20. Then too, the peer rating of aggressive behavior has an average correlation of +.65 with peer ratings of verbal aggression and irritability, well above its +.44 correlation with overall self-report aggressive behavior. Finally, the teacher report, the mother report, and the self-report of aggressive behavior show only low positive intercorrelations.

Clearly, the self-report and the other-reports are measuring something, because the interitem correlations of the subindices are high and the test-retest reliabilities are adequate. But the views of the child, his peers, his teacher, and particularly his mother are quite different in what they are measuring.

This is in keeping with the Sears (1961) suggestion that self-report data should be supplemented by reports from all three of these outside sources, since each provides a unique perspective due to its systematically different stimulus significance to the youg adolescent. The data also indicate that the child and his peers are apparently generalizing or stereotyping across our conceptual dimensions.

We have opted for a strategy of retaining dimensions for the possibility that they will have different relationships with our television viewing and family environment variables. In addition, we have summed these individual indices into overall indices for some analyses.

*Verbal aggression.* Verbal aggression may be seen as a kind of alternative to more direct physical aggression; therefore we considered it a distinctly different type of behavior. Empirically, however, its self-report and peer report versions correlate only +.17, and the self-report correlates more highly with the own-view irritability (+.28) while the peer report is more closely associated with peer ratings of aggressive behavior (+.70) and irritability (+.60). Verbal aggression has some different properties from other forms of aggression: it does not decline among boys from junior to senior high, and it is unrelated to viewing time.

*Irritability.* A more covert, and perhaps more physiologically based, measure of aggression is irritability. Perhaps because it is a covert property, there is little agreement (+.02) between self-reported and peer reported irritability. Instead, each type of report correlates more highly with other aggression measures judged by the same source. What clearly distinguishes irritability from other forms of aggression is the total lack of modeling or similarity between mother and child on that attribute.

*Aggressive attitudes.* It is clear that there is no necessary dependency between holding aggressive attitudes and other forms of aggression. An adolescent could approve of aggression as a means of solving problems without himself behaving aggressively; conversely, without favoring aggression he could behave aggressively (e.g., as a result of "behavioral contagion" in a peer-gang situation). Empirically, aggressive attitudes are rather closely related to both self-reported and peer-reported aggressive behavior, and they are associated with various viewing and family variables in a manner similar to the measures of aggressive behavior.

## Adolescent television viewing

Four sets of adolescent viewing variables were included in our first report: viewing of specific program types, overall violence viewing, time spent with television, and cognitive reactions to television violence.

Here we added a final Wisconsin viewing variable—past violence viewing, the extent of violence in programs watched three or four years ago.

*Types of programs watched.* Crime-detective, western, and adventure-drama programs form a highly intercorrelated cluster of adolescent viewing preferences. It was shown in our first report, however, that westerns differed from the other two types in that they bear no relationship to aggressive behavior when viewing of other types of programs is controlled. Some clarification was provided here when we contrasted the cognitive reactions to westerns and crime shows. The westerns were much less likely to be linked with real life and produced less involvement in the plot.

*Overall violence viewing.* On the basis of multiple ratings of the degree of violence in 65 programs, a measure of overall violence viewing (*OVV*) was developed. This index has a positive association with both self-report and other-report aggression. The self-report correlations are substantial for all but junior boys. There is a +.30 correlation overall, with age-sex subgroup correlations averaging +.24. Other-report aggression correlations with *OVV* are considerably lower, averaging +.10 across subgroups and +.17 overall. This decrease is largely a function of one component, the mother report, which has a negative association with *OVV*. We have subjected these violence viewing-aggressive behavior correlations to partial correlation analyses controlling for a variety of third variables. While the moderate zero-order correlations are reduced, they are not eliminated except for junior boys in some analyses. The relationship between violence viewing and aggressive behavior is robust, at least for the variables considered here. Of course, some other set of variables might well eliminate the basic zero-order correlation.

*Time spent with television.* The *OVV* index is rather highly correlated with the amount of time the adolescent spends with television. It is important, then, to see to what extent the relationship to aggressive behavior is a function of the specific violence viewing or the more general television time. In general, it appears the stronger relationship is with the specific violence viewing for both self-report and other-report aggression. For both criteria, however, the junior boys violate this pattern with slightly stronger correlations for television time. Perhaps it takes boys a little longer to select out the more violent fare.

*Past violence viewing.* We attempted to get at causal direction in a limited way by asking about the adolescents' viewing three or four years ago to form a past violence viewing index. This head-to-head competition produces very similar correlations, with the advantage, if any, going to past viewing. Even this slight advantage is surprising because of the obviously greater reliability and, hence, greater predictive potential of the present *OVV* measure. Although this does not make a violence viewing-to-aggressive behavior sequence much more likely, it does seriously question the likelihood of the reverse aggressive behavior-to-violence viewing sequence.

*Cognitive reactions to violent television.* We began with five indices of cognitive reactions to violent television: opportunities for learning aggressive behavior, linkage to real life, involvement in programming, identification with violent television characters, and perceived efficacy of violent behavior on television. On the basis of relatively low correlations with other reaction items and inconsistent associations with other variables of importance, the last two indices were dropped when we formed an overall cognitive reactivity index.

Our results have shown that the cognitive reactions of children to television are important to consider along with sheer exposure to violent programming. The perceptions of antisocial learning, of a tie between the media and real life experiences, and of involvement in programs are all clearly related to aggressive behavior and, to a less extent, to the amount of violence viewing. Perceived aggression learning in particular bears a rather strong relationship to aggressive behavior independent of other aspects of viewing behavior.

## Family environment

We can categorize the host of family environment variables into four rough categories: the adolescents' personal and structural attributes, mothers' aggression and television behavior, parental treatment, and parent-child communication variables.

*Personal and structural attributes.* Perhaps the most consistent and comforting finding in our research is that virtually all indices of aggression, violence viewing, and cognitive reactivity decline from junior to senior high. Sex differences are almost as consistent, with boys higher on most measures of aggression, violence viewing, and reactivity. The exceptions are that girls tend to be higher on irritability and on involvement in violent programming.

School performance is another consistent variable: the low performers watch considerably more violent television, have stronger reactions to the content, and are more likely to approve of aggression. They are likewise more likely to behave aggressively, but the findings are not entirely consistent. It is difficult to interpret the school performance concept; it could reflect either a relatively stable personality characteristic like I Q or a learned behavior pattern shaping or reflecting viewing patterns and aggressive behavior.

Socioeconomic status is a less dominant factor than our reading of the research literature would have led us to suppose. While lower-status children do watch more violent television programming, only small and inconsistent correlations are shown for its relationship to aggression, cognitive reactivity, and attitudes approving aggression.

Finally, peer integration comparisons show a marked departure from previous literature, with the well-integrated adolescents tending to display slightly *higher* levels of violence viewing (Maryland only), aggressive behavior (mostly for boys), aggressive attitudes (seniors only), and cognitive reactions (juniors only). We would have expected the less popular youths to be higher on these indices.

*Mothers' aggression and television behavior.* Our personal interviews with Wisconsin mothers allowed us to test some assumptions about similarity between mothers' and children's behavior, or "modeling" of the mother's behavior by the child. We found evidence of mother-child similarity on the assault aggression, verbal aggression, and Zaks-Walters indices, as well as on the approval of aggression items. More important, these correlations were trait-specific with considerably higher mother-child same-index coefficients than for the cross-index comparisons. No evidence of transmission was shown for the covert irritability index. We have interpreted this as indicating that learning of overt aggression patterns is more likely than the transmission of internalized and perhaps physiologically based traits such as irritability. It is also clear that aggression modeling is greater for mother-daughter than for mother-son pairs. Whether this indicates generally greater "aggression modeling" for girls or the learning of specific and largely nonaggressive sex roles cannot be known without comparable data from the fathers.

We have also found mother-child viewing correlations that averaged +.27 for the three violent program types as well as for the three less violent categories. Is this sufficient evidence to infer that the child models his television behavior after that of his mother? Elsewhere we have argued that it is not (Chaffee et al., 1970, 1971; Chaffee and McLeod, 1971). It is possible for the "parental example" to be either positive or negative, and it seems likely that the mother, who watches violent programs far less than her children, would set a "negative example" by not watching. This alternative explanation is strengthened by the Chaffee and McLeod finding of higher "modeling" for mother than for the father among both boys and girls. The lower same-sex correlations argue against sex role learning, and the greater similarity to mother makes negative modeling more plausible.

An even more likely explanation is "reverse modeling," with the child influencing his mother. The child, as the "TV expert" in the home, is often sought for viewing advice here and in our previous research (Chaffee et al., 1971). In Wisconsin, 35 percent of the mothers said that they often happen to watch television programs just because their children are watching, while only ten percent felt that their children often watch just because *they* are viewing television. When the children were asked, 21 percent indicated that they often happen to watch because their parents are watching. It seems unlikely to us that direct modeling plays a major role in influencing the child's television behavior.

*Parental treatment.* Included under the parental treatment category are three methods parents may use to influence their child's viewing and aggressive behavior, three types of punishment, and the amount of affection shown the child.

Parental attempts to influence the child's television behavior by controlling watching and by interpreting violence apparently have little effect. They have no relation to aggressive behavior and a slight positive association with violence viewing. The latter association may be the result of the parent attempting to do something about the already heavy violence viewing by his child.

Attempt to influence by emphasizing nonaggression has only small zero-order correlations with self-report and other-report aggressive behavior. For all subgroups except senior boys in Wisconsin, however, we have found that nonaggression emphasis becomes an important contingent variable. The average correlation, for all subgroups across self- and other-reports in Wisconsin and self-report in Maryland, is +.26 in families where little stress is placed upon nonaggression; in families where such an emphasis is found, the average correlation is only +.07. Wisconsin senior boys show a sharp reversal for self-report and a slight one for other-report aggressive behavior. Except for this subgroup, the other contingencies are quite remarkable.

Despite some inconsistencies between subgroups, samples, and measures, we may conclude that physical, verbal, and restrictive punishment bear a generally positive relationship to violence viewing and aggressive behavior. When only the child's view is considered, physical and verbal punishment are essentially unrelated to violence viewing, and restrictive punishment has a clear positive relationship. The relationship becomes fairly even across the three punishment measures when the mothers' data are added. Self-report aggression is associated with high levels of all types of punishment, but only for senior high students. Other-report aggression is very strongly and positively correlated with restrictive punishment and moderately associated with the other two punishment measures. In terms of aggressive behavior, then, restrictive punishment seems to be a somewhat stronger predictor than physical and verbal punishment. This appears to have implications for explaining the punishment-aggression correlation. If simple imitation is the causal mechanism, then we would expect physical punishment to be a better predictor than restrictive punishment. Since this is clearly not the case, we must seek more indirect explanations.

While the behavioral forms of aggression are predicted by punishment, the attitudinal form of aggression is not. Approval of aggression is not consistently related to any of the three punishment measures. None of the punishment measures predicts cognitive reactivity for boys, but restrictive punishment has a consistently strong positive correlation for girls.

Our literature search led us to an oversimplified view of the function of parental affection. The conceptualization of warmth (affection) as the polar opposite of punitiveness led to the expectation of negative correlations with violence viewing and aggression. The empirical reality proved to be much more complicated than that. Affection is basically unrelated to violence viewing, although among boys the direction is clearly positive, with those receiving more affection also watching more violence. The reversal from the expected negative relationship is in line with the findings of Chaffee and McLeod.

No clear connection between affection and aggressive behavior was found. The addition of data from the mother changed the average correlation from slight negative to slight positive in the Wisconsin sample. The data for aggressive attitudes are much more clearcut, however, with a fairly strong negative relationship. No clear pattern is shown for cognitive reactivity. These findings suggest that affection may be a more complex variable than previously anticipated; it is possible that the maximum end of the affection dimension is not "high," but rather "smothering," with the optimum somewhere short of the maximum.

*Parent-child communication.* Socio-orientation appears to be a rather good predictor of both violence viewing and aggression. Children in families where the emphasis is placed on hierarchy and harmony tend to be high on violence viewing and aggressive behavior. Concept-orientation—the emphasis on expression and exposure to new ideas—has a negative association with aggressive behavior. The fact that concept-orientation is unrelated to violence viewing does not mean it is irrelevant to media behavior. Previous research has found it to be tied to the use of mass media for public affairs content, while socio-orientation has been associated with entertainment media use (Chaffee et al., 1966; McLeod et al., 1967; Chaffee et al., 1971). We need not extend our conclusions to the four parent-child communication patterns formed by dichotomizing the two dimensions, except to mention that some interaction between the dimensions was evident in our findings and bears examination with larger samples.

The final set of variables introduced in the second report were coorientational agreement, accuracy, and congruency. In a sense, these variables are outcomes of communication. We found that interpersonal agreement, rather than intrapersonal congruency, was the key variable in predicting violence viewing and aggression. Children who disagree with their parents over school goals watch more television violence and tend to display more aggressive behavior. This is congruent with previous theorizing and deserving of more concentrated investigation in future research.

## Some final questions

Although we would prefer to refrain from overgeneralizing beyond the direct findings of our data, it seems fair to discuss some of the rather difficult and perhaps almost unanswerable questions that require speculation about the implications of our research. These questions might be asked of any study of media violence and aggression.

*Do the results presented justify the conclusion that there are function-al relationships among media violence and aggression?* This is a conclusion that cannot be made from a single set of studies. It would require a concentrated and long-term series of projects conducted by many researchers using a variety of methods and research strategies. Such continuing support for research on this vital public issue has not been provided in the past by either government agencies or private foundations.

Within the limitations of our research, we have attempted to control for variables that might uncover the spuriousness of the correlation between violence viewing and aggressive behavior. These control variables included: socioeconomic status, school performance (perhaps as an index of I Q or sophistication), age, sex, television time, and regional differences. None of these controls erased the basic violence viewing-aggressive behavior correlation. Similarly, other parental treatment and communication variables examined for their association with these key variables failed to eliminate this basic correlation. While we cannot assume that other variables we did not use as controls would have no effect, we can conclude that the variables we *did* include have not indicated spuriousness.

Our analyses of other-reports of aggression also serve as checks on potential spuriousness, because of the collection of self-report data for both violence viewing and aggressiveness. While somewhat lower viewing-aggression correlations are found for other-reports than for self-reports of aggression, the basic pattern is the same for the peer and teacher reports. Only the mother report data is different in showing a slight negative viewing-aggression correlation.

*What are the causal sequences implied by the relationships found among violence viewing, aggressive behavior, and other variables? In short, what are the aggressive effects of watching media violence, if any?*

Even if we consider "other variables" as a single combination of family environment factors rather than as many single variables, an almost infinite number of potential causal sequences are formed. To list a few: violence viewing might lead to aggressive behavior; the more aggressive adolescents might select out violent content on television; the family environment might lead certain children to independently seek out violent programs and to behave aggressively with no causal relationship among the outcomes; or the family environment might lead to violence viewing but not to aggression, with violence viewing then influencing aggression (the reverse is also possible). The possibilities become even more numerous if we break each causal variable into levels and hypothesize the effect coming from a particular level (e.g., high restrictive punishment resulting in low violence viewing *vs* lack of restrictive punishment reducing the amount of viewing).

Our nonexperimental design, lacking in sequential measurement over long periods of time, simply does not enable us to disentangle causal sequences in any conclusive way. Our findings for past vs present viewing do argue for a viewing-to-aggression sequence rather than the reverse sequence, if in fact there is a causal connection one way or the other. We did find some family environmental variables that were related to both violence viewing and aggressive behavior: restrictive punishment, perhaps somewhat more than verbal or physical punishment; socio-orientation; and disagreement over goals between mother and child. In each case, however, the partialing on these variables merely reduces but does not eliminate the violence viewing-aggressive behavior correlations. As we have mentioned, a variety of control variables have also failed to show spuriousness. Whether there are other variables that would reduce the viewing-aggression association to zero cannot be ascertained here; it stands as a challenge to other researchers.

We are also left with the task of specifying the precise effects, if any, of violence viewing. At least four different types of possible effects on aggression can be distinguished: immediate aggressive responses triggered in some children under some conditions; learned internal responses later operating as personal predispositions; learned behavioral sequences or techniques used in later aggressive situations; and reduction of inhibitions to aggression in the form of values, attitudes, or cognitions.

The specification of precise effects is more appropriately answered through experimental manipulation and precise measurement of immediate and delayed effects. The work of Berkowitz and his associates (1962, 1963a, 1963b, 1965, 1966, 1967, 1969) presents evidence for the first of these effects. Our data on aggressive behavior could reflect such a process, but our measurement cannot isolate the short-term sequence. The second possible effect—the learning of internal responses—is relevant to our data on irritability, where we found it to be the only aggression index having no relationship to violence viewing. At least for this type of internal response, our findings suggest this type of effect is unlikely.

The learning of specific techniques or behavior sequences is not incompatible with our data, but on logical grounds it seems implausible that this could be very common. The specific techniques of violence are seldom shown in detail on television, and such information tends to be more readily available in places other than on television. Finally, the long-term effects of television violence on developing attitudes and cognitions favorable to violence is at once more interesting and likely, yet harder to demonstrate. We do have data of potential relevance in index of approval of aggression. It shows the same basic relationship with violence viewing as does aggressive behavior. Perhaps future researchers would do well to pay more attention to these more subtle but no less important values and cognitions about the prevalence and efficacy of aggression.

*What advice can we offer to parents who are concerned about the effects of television on their children?* Our ability to offer useful advice to concerned parents depends upon several assumptions: that they are willing to resolve the burden of proof by presuming television violence does have aggressive effects; that they are capable of altering their own behavior; and that the present viewing and/or aggressive behavior of the child is reversible or at least controllable.

We are able to say that, beyond the junior high level, both violence viewing and aggressive behavior are apt to decline in frequency. Time and maturation are on the side of the parent, but this is probably of little comfort to the parent whose child appears in imminent danger of getting into trouble. Other more positive strategies are sought.

Regarding viewing behavior, Schramm has advised parents that "example is the best persuader" and that it exercises "a very potent kind of influence" over the child's viewing (Schramm et al., 1961: 182). While our results indicate mother-child similarity of viewing particular programs, we do not feel such an inference is justified. Other more plausible explanations can be given for the presence of such a correlation. While we are skeptical about the effectiveness of the parent attempting to set a better example, at least this advice has the advantage of being reasonably easy for the concerned parent to change.

We believe "parental example" of another type—the mother's own behavior with respect to aggressiveness—may have greater impact than her own media behavior. There is a clear and trait-specific correlation between the mother and child on various aggression measures. The problem here is obviously one of the mother's being able to change her own aggressive behavior or to practice nonaggressive behavior, even if she realizes that it has consequences for the child's behavior. In addition, the assumption of reversibility of the child's behavior would have to be made. Finally, this assumes that the similar mother-child patterns are not biologically based.

One potential parental behavior that does *not* seem to be effective is the direct control over the child's television viewing behavior. Such control attempts had no direct connection with the child's aggression, nor did they operate to reduce the correlation between violence viewing and aggressive behavior. In fact, arbitrary control might serve to increase the child's frustration and make aggressive behavior more likely. Our interpretation of Feshbach (1971) suggests that "forced-feeding" of nonviolent television on institutionalized boys actually increased aggressive activity.

The control over viewing is really an indirect parental strategy, attempting to ultimately limit or reduce aggression by first limiting the child's intake of media violence. Our data suggest a more direct strategy of emphasizing nonaggression to the child. This entails telling the child not to fight back if other kids pick on him, warning him not to imitate aggressive acts seen on television, and so forth. While this emphasis will not appeal to many parents, our findings indicate that it operates as a strong contingent variable reducing the violence viewing-aggressive behavior correlation markedly.

The parent might also consider using restraint in the application of punishment. While most parents seem to realize the negative effects of physical punishment, the potential dangers of verbal and restrictive punishment are less well recognized. In particular, our data indicate that restrictive punishment ("grounding" and taking away privileges) is linked to viewing and aggression. While reverse causation could be operating, the relation is consistent and ties in with previous research.

We have also found that children in families emphasizing hierarchical and harmonious communication watch more violent television and are more aggressive. This implies that the concerned parent might attempt to avoid being "one-up" in interacting with his child and in allowing the child to bring conflict out into the open. This and the suggested restraint on restrictive punishment should not be mistaken for advocating "permissiveness." The "laissez-faire" child in our study was about average in aggressive behavior and well above average in his attitudes approving aggression. The parent can still maintain his own values while advocating the child develop his own, and he does not have to avoid communication in providing the child more room for expression.

In our discussing of parental strategies, we have extrapolated very widely from our limited source of data. Unfortunately, our evidence is no less sparse than that of researchers who have preceded us. The concerned parent at the present time has few alternatives to making his own assumptions about the effects of television and to following advice based on thin evidence and speculation. We can hope that this study will offer some suggestions to help future researchers select variables and design better and more thorough research into the complex causal connection between the family, television violence, and adolescent behavior.

## FOOTNOTES

1. This technical report describes research pursuant to Contract No. HSM 42-70-77 with the National Institute of Mental Health, Health Services and Mental Health Administration, U. S. Department of Health, Education, and Welfare. Jack McLeod and Steven Chaffee were co-principal investigators. Charles Atkin, now at Michigan State University, was the study director. Tanis Turner was responsible for typing and duplicating the report. Others aiding in data analysis were William Elliott, William Engels, Kenneth Sheinkopf, and Catherine Willette.

# REFERENCES

Bassett, T., Cowden, J., and Cohen, M. The audio-visual viewing habits of selected subgroups of delinquents. *Journal of Genetic Psychology,* 1968, **112,** 37-41.

Berkowitz, L. *Aggression: a social psychological analysis.* New York: McGraw-Hill, 1962.

Berkowitz, L. The concept of aggressive drive: some additional considerations. In Berkowitz, L. (Ed.) *Advances in Experimental Social Psychology,* Vol. 2. New York: Academic Press, 1965.

Berkowitz, L. (Ed.). *Roots of aggression: a re-examination of the frustration-aggression hypothesis.* New York: Atherton, 1969.

Berkowitz, L., Corwin, R., and Heironimus, M. Film violence and subsequent aggressive tendencies. *Public Opinion Quarterly,* 1963(a), **27,** 217-29.

Berkowitz, L., and Geen, R. G. Film violence and the cue properties of available targets. *Journal of Personality and Social Psychology,* 1966, **3**(5), 525-30.

Berkowitz, L., and Geen, R. G. Stimulus qualities of the target of aggression: a further study. *Journal of Personality and Social Psychology,* 1967, **5**(3), 364-68.

Berkowitz, L., and Rawlings, E. Effects of film violence on inhibitions against subsequent aggression. *Journal of Abnormal and Social Psychology,* 1963(b), **66**(3), 405-12.

Buss, A. H., and Durkee, A. An inventory for assessing different kinds of hostility. *Journal of Consulting Psychology,* 1957, **21,** 343-49.

Chaffee, S. H., and McLeod, J. M. Coorientation and the structure of family communication. Paper presented to meeting of the International Communication Association, Minneapolis, Minn., May 1970.

Chaffee, S. H., and McLeod, J.M. Adolescent television use in the family context. In *Television and social behavior: a report to the Surgeon General's Scientific Advisory Committee,* Vol. 4. Washington, D.C.: U. S. Government Printing Office, 1971.

Chaffee, S. H., McLeod, J.M., and Atkin, C. K. Parent-adolescent similarities in television use. Paper presented at the meeting of the Association for Education in Journalism, Washington, D.C., August, 1970.

Chaffee, S. H., McLeod, J.M., and Atkin, C.K. Parental influences on adolescent media use. *American Behavioral Scientist,* 1971, **14,** 323-40.

Chaffee, S. H., McLeod, J. M., and Wackman, D. B. Family communication and political socialization. Paper presented at the meeting of the Association for Education in Journalism, Iowa City, Iowa, 1966.

Feshbach, S., and Singer, R.D. *Television and aggression.* San Francisco: Jossey-Bass, 1971.

Greenberg, B.S., and Gordon, T.F. Perceptions of violence in television programs: critics and the public. In *Television and social behavior*, Vol. 1. Washington, D.C.: U. S. Government Printing Office, 1971.

Himmelweit, H., Oppenheim, A., and Vince, P. *Television and the child*. London: Oxford University Press, 1958.

Maccoby, E.E. Why do children watch television? *Public Opinion Quarterly*, 1954, **18**, 239-44.

McLeod, J.M., Atkin, C.K., and Chaffee, S.H. Adolescents, parents, and television use: adolescent self-report measures from Maryland and Wisconsin samples. In *Television and social behavior*, Vol. 4 (this volume).

McLeod, J.M., and Chaffee, S. H. The construction of social reality. In Tedeschi, J. (Ed.) *The Social Influence Processes*. Chicago: Aldine, in press.

McLeod, J.M., Chaffee, S. H., and Eswara, H. S. Family communication patterns and communication research. Paper presented at the meeting of the Association for Education in Journalism, Iowa City, Iowa, August, 1966.

McLeod, J.M., Chaffee, S. H., and Wackman, D. B. Family communication: an updated report. Paper presented at the meeting of the Association for Education in Journalism, Boulder, Colorado, August, 1967.

McLeod, J.M., Rush, R., and Friederich, K. The mass media and political information in Quito, Ecuador. *Public Opinion Quarterly*, 1968-69, **32**, 575-87.

Murray, R., Cole, R., and Fedler, F. Teenagers and TV violence: how they rate and view it. *Journalism Quarterly*, 1970, **47**, 247-55.

Riley, M.W., and Riley, J. W. A sociological approach to communications research. *Public Opinion Quarterly*, 1951, **15**, 445-60.

Schramm, W., Lyle, J., and Parker, E.B. *Television in the lives of our children*. Stanford, Calif.: Stanford University Press, 1961.

Sears, R. The relation of early socialization experiences to aggression in middle childhood. *Journal of Abnormal and Social Psychology*, 1961, **63**, 466-92.

Stone, V., and Chaffee, S. H. Family communication patterns and source-message orientation. *Journalism Quarterly*, 1970, **47**, 239-46.

# Appendix A: Complete listing of questionnaire items comprising each index

## Aggression Indices

*Manifest physical aggression:* same as in first report, Appendix A.

*Aggressive behavioral delinquency:* same as in first report, Appendix A.

*Zaks-Walters aggression:* (mother and child): same as in first report, Appendix A.

*Hypothetical aggressive reactions:* same as in first report, Appendix A.

*Buss-Durkee assault aggression:* (mother and child): same as in first report, Appendix A.

*Approval of aggression:* (mother and child): same as in first report, Appendix A.

*Buss-Durkee irritability:* (mother and child): same as in first report, Appendix A.

*Buss-Durkee verbal aggression:* (mother and child): "Here are some things others (students, mothers) have said about getting along with people. How much is each statement like you?"

> I demand that people respect my rights.
> When people yell at me, I yell back.
> When people disagree with me, I can't help getting into arguments.
> I would rather give in than argue about something. (reversed scoring)

Scoring—"a lot like me" (2), "a little like me" (1), "not like me" (0)

*Aggressive attitudes:* "How much do you agree or disagree with these statements?"

It's all right to hurt an enemy if you are mad at him.
In order to get revenge, it's all right to hurt an enemy.
If a student is fed up with his government these days, he is somewhat justified if he sets off a bomb in an empty Army building.
During the American Revolution, blowing up British buildings was completely justified.

The most successful people are the ones who use violence.

The rising amount of crime and violence in this country really doesn't bother me very much.

It upsets me when I see someone beating up another kid. (reversed scoring)

*Overall aggression sum:* same as in first report, Appendix A.

*Buss-Durkee overall sum:* Unweighted sum of 11 items comprising the indices of Buss-Durkee assault aggression, verbal aggression, and irritability aggression, ranging from low (0) to high (22).

*Peer ratings of aggression:* "Now we would like to know how some of the kids in your homeroom get along with other students. Everybody in the class will give ratings on the other kids in the homeroom.

Please mark a number to show whether each person does these three things *often* (2), *sometimes* (1), or *never* (0). Please try to be honest and fair, since it is important that we get an accurate idea of how students feel about each other. (If you don't know a person well enough, put a question mark in the blanks. Do not make marks for your own name, if it is on the list)."

Yells back when yelled at.

When loses temper, hits other people.

Is patient with others. (reversed scoring)

This was followed by a list of names of students in the rater's homeroom.

Scoring—"often" (2), "sometimes" (1), "never" (0), summed across all responses, divided by the number of raters, and multiplied by 10. For each type of aggression, scores range from 0 to 20.

*Teacher ratings of aggression:* "As part of the study of sixth graders' television viewing and social behavior, each teacher is being asked to make a brief rating of their students. One question concerns the level of aggressive behavior that each child displays in school. We are particularly interested in identifying the most extreme students: those who are either very well behaved, cooperative with others and their teacher, and gentle in their interpersonal relations—and the opposite type who are discipline problems, who pick on other kids, and who get into fights or loud arguments. Please assign a score to each student using this system: 4 = highly aggressive-hostile, troublemaker; 3= more aggressive-hostile than average; 2 = average; 1 = very passive, gets along well, submissive." These instructions were followed by a list of names of students in the teacher's class. Scoring as indicated in item.

*Mother ratings of aggression:*
Does (child) seem to get into more fights than other children his age, few fights, or about the same amount of fights? "more" (2), "same" (1), "fewer" (0)

When he was younger, how often did he do mean things to other children while playing? Would you say often, sometimes, or never? "often" (2), "sometimes" (1), "never" (0)

When he was younger, how often did he show aggressive behavior toward other children? Would you say often, sometimes, or never? "often" (2), "sometimes" (1), "never" (0)

If your child had an argument with his best friend, how would he normally go about settling it? physical aggression (2), non-aggressive response (0)

## Television Viewing Indices

*Program types:* (mother and child): "Here is a list of some programs that have been on television this year. About how often have you really watched each of these shows? For each program, make one check showing whether you watched it: *Almost always* (nearly every week) or *Often* (at least half the time) or *Sometimes* (at least once or twice) or *Never.*"

Scoring—"almost always" (4), "often" (3), "sometimes" (2), "never" (0).

| Crime-detective programs | Western programs: | Adventure-drama programs: |
|---|---|---|
| *Mod Squad* | *Gunsmoke* | *Medical Center* |
| *Hawaii Five-O* | *Lancer* | *Then Came Bronson* |
| *Ironside* | *Virginian* | *Hogan's Heroes* |
| *It Takes a Thief* | *Daniel Boone* | *World of Disney* |
| *Get Smart* | *High Chapparal* | *Land of the Giants* |
| *Name of the Game* | *Here Come the Brides* | *New People* |
| *Mission Impossible* | *Bonanza* | *Bracken's World* |
| *The FBI* | | *The Bold Ones* |

| Comedy-variety programs: | Situation comedy programs: | News programs: |
|---|---|---|
| *Red Skelton* | *Mayberry RFD* | *Frank Reynolds* |
| *Laugh-in* | *Julia* | *Walter Cronkite* |

| Glen Campbell | To Rome with Love | Huntley-Brinkley |
| Jim Nabors | I Dream of Jeannie | Local Evening News |
| Dean Martin | Flying Nun | |
| Lawrence Welk | Eddie's Father | |
| Ed Sullivan | Bill Cosby | |
| Leslie Uggams | Family Affair | |
| Music Hall | Bewitched | |
| | Ghost and Mrs. Muir | |

*Overall violence viewing: same as in first report, Appendix A.*

*Total viewing time:*

On an average weekday, about how many hours do you personally spend watching TV? (1969 and 1970)

_____ hours _____ minutes

Now we would like to find out about your television viewing in the last few days. Think of all the programs you saw yesterday and the day before, and figure out *exactly* how much time you spent watching TV programs each day.

Yesterday:    _____  _____ hours _____ minutes
              (what day was it)

Day Before
Yesterday:    _____  _____ hours _____ minutes
              (what day was it)

On an average weekday this fall, about how many hours does (child) spend watching TV? (Mother report)

_____ hours _____ minutes

How many hours did your child spend watching TV yesterday? (Mother report)

_____ hours _____ minutes

Scoring—(8)  4 hours 40 minutes or more
        (7)  3 hours 40 minutes—4 hours 39 minutes
        (6)  2 hours 40 minutes—3 hours 39 minutes
        (5)  2 hours 10 minutes—2 hours 39 minutes
        (4)  1 hour  40 minutes—2 hours  9 minutes

(3) 1 hour  10 minutes— 1 hour  39 minutes
(2) 1 hours 40 minutes— 1 hour   9 minutes
(1) less than 40 minutes
(0) None

*Television violence viewing when younger:* "Here is a list of programs that used to be on television several years ago. Try to remember how often you used to watch these shows when you were younger. Tell us whether you watched each show often, sometimes, or never."

| Very high violence | High violence | Low violence |
|---|---|---|
| *Combat* | *I Spy* | *Gilligan's Island* |
| *Man from UNCLE* | *Felony Squad* | *Dr. Kildare* |
| *Rat Patrol* | *Big Valley* | *Gentle Ben* |
| *Rawhide* | *The Fugitive* | *Donna Reed* |
| | | *Patty Duke* |

Scoring—"often" (2), "sometimes" (1), "never" (0). Low violence programs were reverse scored to control for overall viewing time during this period. High violence programs were double weighted. Very high violence programs were triple weighted.

*Mothers' television viewing levels:*

About how many hours do you usually spend watching TV during an average evening after 5 p.m.?

_____ hours _____ minutes

How many hours did you spend watching TV yesterday after 5 p.m.?

_____ hours _____ minutes

Scoring—same as above.

## Family Environment Indices

*Parental control over television:* For each item, reports were obtained from both the mother and child, unless otherwise indicated.

Who has the most to say about what (you, he) watch on television? (1969 and 1970) "mother" (2), "father" (2), "either mother or child" (1), "brothers or sisters" (0), "child" (0)

Do (your parents, you) always know what programs (you, he) are watching on TV? (1969 and child only 1970) "yes" (1), "no" (0)

"Are there certain programs that (your parents, you) sometimes do not let (you, him) watch?'' (1969 and 1970)

No     Yes: (mark as many as you have to)

>     Westerns*
>     Scary shows
>     Cartoons
>     Sexy shows
>     TV movies
>     Crime shows*
>     Violent shows*
>     Adult shows

Scoring—"yes" (1), "no" (0), plus 1 point each for starred program types.

As compared with most parents you know, would you say that you are very strict, fairly strict, fairly lenient, or very lenient in controlling what your child watches on television? (Mother only) "very strict" (2), "fairly strict" (2), "average" (1), "fairly lenient" (0), "very lenient" (0)

Does (your mother, you) set a limit on how much time (you, he) can spend watching TV on school days? "yes" (1), "no" (0)

"If (your mother, you) sees (you, him) watching a program that (she, you) doesn't think (you, he) should watch, what does (she, you) usually do?"

>     Order (you, him) to stop watching
>     Turn off the set or change channels
>     Suggest (you, he) do some other activity
>     Ask (you, him) nicely to stop watching

Scoring—one point for answering "often" or "sometimes" to each alternative.

*Parental emphasis on nonaggression:* For each item, reports were obtained from both the mother and child, unless otherwise indicated.

Do (your parents, you) punish (you, him) if (you, he) are mean to other kids? (1969 and 1970) "yes" (2), "never mean/don't have to" (1), "no" (0)

Do (your parents, you) want (you, him) to fight back if other kids pick on (you, him)? "no" (1), "yes" (0)

How important does (your mother, you) think it is for (you, him) to learn to defend (yourself, himself)? "not important" (2), "somewhat important" (1), "very important" (0)

How often did (your parents, you) say (you, he) shouldn't do the bad things people do on TV? "often" (2), "sometimes" (1), "never" (0)

Do (your parents, you) ever tell (you, him) not to copy the violent things that some people do on TV? "yes" (2), "don't have to" (1), "no" (0)

If someone called him a dirty name after school one day, which thing would you want him to do? (Mother only) Would you want him to yell at them, hit them, ignore them, or tell on them? "ignore" (2), "yell" (1), "tell" (1), "hit" (0)

Do you feel it is wrong for (him to hit, her to yell at) other kids who do something to deserve it? (Mother only) "yes" (1), "no" (0)

Suppose someone played a real dirty trick on him. Should he hit them, yell at them, ignore them, or laugh at them? (Mother only) "laugh" (2), "ignore" (2), "yell" (1), "hit" (0)

What if someone cut in front of him in a long line. Would you want him to yell at them, shove them out, or just let it go? (Mother only) "let it go" (2), "yell" (1), "shove" (0)

Do you think it would ever be justified if he hurt another person in order to get revenge? (Mother only) "no" (1), "yes" (0)

*Parental interpretation of TV violence:* (mother and child): same as in first report, Appendix A.

*Parental punishment:* (mother and child): same as in first report, Appendix A.

*Parental affection:* (mother and child): "How often do (your parents, you) do these things with (you, him)?"

> Show that (they, you) love (you, him).
> Show (their, your) affection by hugging and kissing (you, him).
> Tell (you, him) that (they, you) love (you, him).

Scoring—"very often" (3), "fairly often" (2), "not too often" (1), "never" (0)

*Family communication patterns:* (mother and child): "Now I would like to read a list of things parents sometimes say to their children. How often do (your parents, you) say these things to (you, him)? For each item, do (they, you) say it often, sometimes, rarely, or never."

### Socio-orientation items:

Say that (their, your) ideas are correct, and (you, he) shouldn't argue with them. (1969 and 1970)

Answer (your, their) arguments by saying, "You'll know better when you grow up." (1969 and 1970)

Say that (you, he) should give in on arguments, rather than risk making people angry. (1969 and 1970)

Say there are some things that just shouldn't be talked about. (1969 and 1970)

Say that (you, he) shouldn't argue with adults.

### Concept-orientation items:

Say that (you, he) should always look at both sides on an issue. (1969 and 1970)

Say that getting (your, his) ideas across is important, even if others don't like it. (1969 and 1970)

Ask for (your, his) opinion when the family is discussing something. (1969 and 1970)

Say that every member of your family should have some say in family decisions.

Admit that kids know more about some things than adults do.

Scoring—"often" (3), "sometimes" (2), "rarely" (1), "never" (0)

*Peer integration:*

Do you have a bunch of friends that you usually hang around with? "yes" (1), "no" (0)

Does he have a group of friends that he usually goes around with? (Mother report) "yes" (1), "no" (0)

Compared with the rest of the kids you know, would you say you have more friends, less friends, or about the same number of friends? "more" (2), "same" (1), "less" (0)

How do you prefer to spend your time: alone, or in the company of friends? "usually like to be with friends" (2), "sometimes with friends and sometimes by myself" (1), "usually like to be by myself" (0)

How many really close friends would you say you had (friends who would gladly help you if you needed help? "more than 10" (3), "6 to 10" (2), "3 to 5" (1), "1 or 2" (0), "none" (0)

*Socioeconomic status:* raw sum of four items, scored as indicated.

Mother education

1 = grade school only
2 = some high school
3 = high school graduate
4 = some college
5 = college graduate

Subjective social class:

1 = lower
2 = working
3 = lower middle
4 = middle middle
5 = upper middle
6 = upper

Father occupation:

2 = unskilled factory worker, equipment operator, household, service, police, fireman, laborer, construction
4 = craftsman, foreman, skilled, semi-skilled, farmer
6 = clerical and sales
8 = professional, managerial, executive, proprietor

Family income:

1 = under $2,000
2 = $2,000 - $3,999
3 = $4,000 - $5,999
4 = $6,000 - $7,999
5 = $8,000 - $9,999
6 = $10,000 - $14,999
7 = $15,000 - $19,999
8 = $20,000 plus

*Coorientation:* (mother and child): "Of the following four things, rate them in order of their importance for *you*. Put a "1" by the one you think is most important, a "2" by the one that is second most important, and so on. (Now I would like you to rank four things in order of their importance. Please tell me which you feel is most important for your child to do, which is second, and so on. Answer what *you* think is important, not what he might think.") (1969 and 1970)

Making new friends who share (your, his) interests.
Being part of school activities and social life.
Learning new ideas and different ways of thinking.
Preparing to earn a living.

"Which of these same four things do you think your (mother, child) feels is most important? Rank them in order of importance as you think your (mother, child) sees it." (1969 and 1970) Same items as above.

Scoring—*agreement:* sum of absolute differences between mother and child rankings of their own personal views on each item.

   *child accuracy:* sum of absolute differences between mother rankings of her personal views and child estimates of mother views on each item.

   *mother accuracy:* sum of absolute differences between child rankings of his own personal views and mother estimates of child views on each item.

Scoring—*child congruency:* sum of absolute differences between child rankings of his own personal views and his estimates of mother views on each item.

   *mother congruency:* sum of absolute differences between mother rankings of her own personal views and her estimates of child views on each item.

### Cognitive Reactions

*Perceived learning of aggression:* same as in first report, Appendix A.

*Linkage to TV violence in real life:* same as in first report, Appendix A.

*Involvement in violent TV programming:* same as in first report, Appendix A.

*Cognitive reaction sum:* sum of above indices, with perceived learning of aggression items double weighted. Scores range from low (0) to high (40).

# Appendix B: Tables

Table 1: Correlations between mother and child aggression levels: Wisconsin data

| Aggression measure | Grade | Mother-Son | Mother-Daughter | Overall |
|---|---|---|---|---|
| Buss-Durkee assault aggression | jr. hi | −.03 | +.17 | |
| (4 item index) | sr. hi | +.17 | +.57** | +.23** |
| Buss-Durkee verbal aggression | jr. hi | +.22 | +.35* | |
| (4 item index) | sr. hi | +.15 | +.28* | +.23** |
| Buss-Durkee irritability | jr. hi | +.01 | +.03 | |
| (3 item index) | sr. hi | −.16 | −.04 | −.03 |
| Buss-Durkee overall sum | jr. hi | +.14 | +.28 | |
| (11 item index) | sr. hi | −.01 | +.27* | +.18** |
| Approval of aggression | jr. hi | +.31* | +.13 | |
| (2 item index) | sr. hi | −.04 | +.22 | +.13 |
| Zaks-Walters aggression | jr. hi | +.19 | +.09 | |
| (7 item index) | sr. hi | +.09 | +.34* | +.16* |
| (N) | jr. hi | (59) | (49) | |
| | sr. hi | (60) | (59) | (225) |

Note: Cell entries are correlations between the mother's self-reported aggression and child's self-reported aggression. The basic two-wave sample of N=151 was used for the correlations between mother and child on the Zaks-Walters Aggression Index, which was measured only during the 1970 survey. All other items were administered during the 1969 survey with the full sample of N=225 mother-child pairs.

*p<.05
**p<.01

Table 2: Correlations between mother and child television viewing levels: Wisconsin data

| Viewing measure | Grade | Boys | Girls |
|---|---|---|---|
| Total television viewing time | jr. hi | +.25 | +.10 |
| | sr. hi | .00 | +.14 |
| Crime-detective programs | jr. hi | +.29* | +.30* |
| (average, 8 shows) | sr. hi | +.24 | +.21 |
| Western programs | jr. hi | +.20 | +.40** |
| (average, 7 shows) | sr. hi | +.18 | +.42** |
| Adventure-drama programs | jr. hi | +.30* | +.29 |
| (average, 8 shows) | sr. hi | +.14 | +.27* |
| Comedy-variety programs | jr. hi | +.44** | +.32* |
| (average, 9 shows) | sr. hi | +.19 | +.33* |
| Situation comedy programs | jr. hi | +.30* | +.33* |
| (average, 10 shows) | sr. hi | +.23 | +.21 |
| News programs | jr. hi | +.15 | +.28 |
| (average, 4 shows) | sr. hi | +.24 | +.29* |
| Mod Squad | jr. hi | +.49** | +.27 |
| | sr. hi | +.01 | +.16 |
| Hawaii Five-O | jr. hi | +.24 | +.30* |
| | sr. hi | +.29* | +.26 |
| Mission Impossible | jr. hi | +.29* | +.08 |
| | sr. hi | +.30** | +.27* |

Table 2 (Cont.)

| | | | |
|---|---|---|---|
| *Gunsmoke* | jr. hi | +.09 | +.59** |
| | sr. hi | +.28* | +.61** |
| *Virginian* | jr. hi | +.24 | +.53** |
| | sr. hi | +.25 | +.38** |
| *Ironside* | jr. hi | +.53** | +.47** |
| | sr. hi | +.27* | +.14 |
| *Bonanza* | jr. hi | +.29* | +.38** |
| | sr. hi | +.20 | +.51** |
| (N) | jr. hi | (59) | (47) |
| | sr. hi | (60) | (59) |

Note: Cell entries are correlations between the mother reports and child reports of viewing behavior on each measure.

Table 3: Correlations between mother and child viewing of six program categories: Wisconsin data

| Program category | Grade | Within-category r | Across-category r |
|---|---|---|---|
| Crime-detective programs | jr. hi | +.34 | +.13 |
| | sr. hi | +.30 | +.15 |
| Western programs | jr. hi | +.38 | +.16 |
| | sr. hi | +.49 | +.17 |
| Adventure-drama programs | jr. hi | +.31 | +.20 |
| | sr. hi | +.26 | +.18 |
| Comedy-variety programs | jr. hi | +.40 | +.17 |
| | sr. hi | +.29 | +.18 |
| Situation comedy programs | jr. hi | +.39 | +.18 |
| | sr. hi | +.21 | +.18 |
| News programs | jr. hi | +.29 | +.15 |
| | sr. hi | +.29 | +.08 |
| (N) | jr. hi | (106) | |
| | sr. hi | (119) | |

Note: Cell entries are mean correlations between mother reports and child reports of television program viewing. The *within-category r* represents the average mother-child correlation of all programs in that category. The *across-category r* is the average correlation of the mother's viewing of one category of program *vs.* the child's viewing of all other categories, and *vice versa*; this indicates the amount of within-category correlation that is a spurious artifact of both persons watching *any* program.

Table 4: Standardized adolescent aggression levels, by age and sex: Wisconsin data

| Aggressive measure | Grade | Boys | Girls |
|---|---|---|---|
| Peer report assault aggression (10 item index) | jr. hi | +40** | +20 |
| | sr. hi | +14 | −65** |
| Teacher report general aggression (1 item) | jr. hi | −03 | +04 |
| | sr. hi | − − | − − |
| Mother report aggression (4 item index) | jr. hi | −02 | −06 |
| | sr. hi | +16 | −12 |
| Overall other-report aggression sum (15 item index) | jr. hi | +36** | +16 |
| | sr. hi | +18 | −65** |
| Overall self-report aggression sum (20 item index) | jr. hi | +52** | +11 |
| | sr. hi | +24 | −84** |
| Self-report verbal aggression (4 item index) | jr. hi | +04 | −12 |
| | sr. hi | +22 | −18 |
| Peer report verbal aggression (10 item index) | jr. hi | +14 | +22 |
| | sr. hi | +17 | −51** |
| Self-report irritability aggression (3 item index) | jr. hi | +05 | +44** |
| | sr. hi | −19 | −17 |
| Peer report irritability aggression (10 item index) | jr. hi | +09 | +22 |
| | sr. hi | +24 | −51** |
| Self-report assault aggression (4 item index) | jr. hi | +19 | +13 |
| | sr. hi | +38** | −68** |
| Approval of aggression (2 item index) | jr. hi | +39** | +02 |
| | sr. hi | +24 | −65** |
| Aggressive attitudes (8 item index) | jr. hi | +47** | −01 |
| | sr. hi | +29* | −76** |
| (N) | jr. hi | (38) | (30) |
| | sr. hi | (43) | (40) |

Note: Standard scores represent each cell mean, calculated as a positive or negative deviation from the overall mean on the listed index, divided by the overall standard deviation. Scores have been multiplied by 100 to eliminate decimals. Asterisks indicate the cell mean is significantly different from the overall mean for the remaining cells.

*p < .05
**p < .01

Table 5: Intercorrelations among self, peer, teacher, and mother reports of aggression: Wisconsin data

| Aggression measure | Peer report | Teacher report | Mother report | Overall-other | Overall-self | Verbal-self | Verbal-peer | Irritability-self | Irritability-peer | Assault-self | Approval |
|---|---|---|---|---|---|---|---|---|---|---|---|
| | | | | | Correlations, all respondents | | | | | | |
| Peer report | – – | | | | | | | | | | |
| Teacher report | .23 | – – | | | | | | | | | |
| Mother report | .17 | .14 | – – | | | | | | | | |
| Overall-other | .95 | .50 | .45 | – – | | | | | | | |
| Overall-self | .44 | .15 | .09 | .42 | – – | | | | | | |
| Verbal-self | .10 | .08 | .06 | .12 | .46 | – – | | | | | |
| Verbal-peer | .70 | .27 | .19 | .69 | .34 | .17 | – – | | | | |
| Irritability-self | .11 | –.07 | .07 | .11 | .30 | .28 | .14 | – – | | | |
| Irritability-peer | .60 | .14 | .13 | .57 | .27 | .12 | .60 | .02 | – – | | |
| Assault-self | .40 | .02 | .03 | .32 | .76 | .41 | .26 | .29 | .22 | – – | |
| Approval | .30 | –.02 | .06 | .28 | .45 | .13 | .17 | –.06 | .23 | .28 | – – |
| Attitudes | .38 | –.03 | .13 | .37 | .50 | .11 | .23 | .00 | .29 | .28 | .79 |

(N=151)

Note: Cell entries are zero-order Pearsonian r correlation coefficients.

For $r \geq .16$, $p < .05$
$r \geq .21$, $p < .01$

Table 6: Standardized adolescent family environment levels, by age and sex: Wisconsin data

| Family environment measure | Grade | Boys | Girls |
|---|---|---|---|
| Parental control over TV viewing | jr. hi | +46** | +54** |
| (28 item index) | sr. hi | –55** | –25 |
| Parental emphasis on nonaggression | jr. hi | –06 | +13 |
| (18 item index) | sr. hi | –09 | +03 |
| Parental interpretation of TV violence | jr. hi | +16 | +09 |
| (10 item index) | sr. hi | –21 | –22 |
| Parental physical punishment | jr. hi | +34* | –44** |
| (2 item index) | jr. hi | +18 | –22 |
| Parental verbal punishment | jr. hi | 00 | +17 |
| (4 item index) | sr. hi | +05 | –18 |
| Parental restrictive punishment | jr. hi | +17 | +20 |
| (4 item index) | sr. hi | +13 | –44** |
| Parental affection | jr. hi | +22 | +55** |
| (6 item index) | sr. hi | –43** | –16 |
| Parental socio-orientation | jr. hi | +13 | +51** |
| (18 item index) | sr. hi | –27* | –21 |
| Parental concept-orientation | jr. hi | +14 | –02 |
| (16 item index) | sr. hi | –24 | +15 |
| Parental socioeconomic status | jr. hi | +36** | –06 |
| (4 item index) | sr. hi | –06 | –23 |
| (N) | jr. hi | (38) | (30) |
| | sr. hi | (43) | (40) |

Table 7: Intercorrelations among family environment variables: Wisconsin data

| Family environment measure | Correlations, all respondents | | | | | | | | |
|---|---|---|---|---|---|---|---|---|---|
| Control over TV | – – | | | | | | | | |
| Nonaggression emphasis | .29 | – – | | | | | | | |
| TV interpretation | .33 | .36 | – – | | | | | | |
| Physical punishment | .01 | –.07 | –.03 | – – | | | | | |
| Verbal punishment | .15 | .02 | .03 | .30 | – – | | | | |
| Restrictive punishment | .30 | .07 | .04 | .36 | .43 | – – | | | |
| Affection | .21 | –.01 | .12 | .01 | .03 | .08 | – – | | |
| Socio-orientation | .35 | .18 | .23 | .09 | .34 | .37 | .22 | – – | |
| Concept-orientation | .16 | –.02 | .27 | .01 | .01 | .04 | .38 | –.02 | – – |
| Socioeconomic status | –.02 | –.08 | .05 | .00 | .02 | –.08 | .16 | –.25 | .41 |
| (N=151) | Control over TV | Nonaggression emphasis | TV interpretation | Physical punishment | Verbal punishment | Restrictive punishment | Affection | Socio-orientation | Concept-orientation |

For r $\geq$ .16, p < .05

r $\geq$ .21, p < .01

Table 8: Correlations between level of violence viewing and level of aggressive behavior as reported by others: Wisconsin data

| Aggression measure | Grade | Boys | Girls | Overall |
|---|---|---|---|---|
| Peer report assault aggression | jr. hi | +.14 | +.08 | +.20* |
| | sr. hi | +.20 | +.13 | |
| Teacher report general aggression | jr. hi | +.13 | +.14 | +.20* |
| | sr. hi | – – | – – | |
| Mother report aggression | jr. hi | –.29 | +.04 | –.06 |
| | sr. hi | +.09 | –.10 | |
| OVERALL OTHER-REPORT AGGRESSION SUM | jr. hi | +.01 | +.08 | +.17* |
| | sr. hi | +.22 | +.09 | |
| Buss-Durkee verbal aggression | jr. hi | –.03 | +.24 | +.03 |
| | sr. hi | +.10 | –.14 | |
| Peer report verbal aggression | jr. hi | –.01 | +.16 | +.12 |
| | sr. hi | +.13 | +.03 | |
| Peer report irritability aggression | jr. hi | +.01 | +.12 | +.11 |
| | sr. hi | +.18 | –.07 | |
| Approval of aggression | jr. hi | +.08 | +.13 | +.09 |
| | sr. hi | +.03 | .00 | |
| Aggressive attitudes | jr. hi | +.02 | +.09 | +.17* |
| | sr. hi | +.22 | +.11 | |
| (N) | jr. hi | (38) | (30) | (151) |
| | sr. hi | (43) | (40) | |

Note: Cell entries are zero-order correlation coefficients between each aggression variable and the Violence Viewing Index.

Table 9: Correlations between total viewing time and level of aggressive behavior as reported by others: Wisconsin data

| Aggression measure | Grade | Boys | Girls | Overall |
|---|---|---|---|---|
| Peer report assault aggression | jr. hi | +.31 | −.02 | +.19* |
| | sr. hi | +.03 | +.17 | |
| Teacher report general aggression | jr. hi | +.15 | −.23 | +.04 |
| | sr. hi | − − | − − | |
| Mother report aggression | jr. hi | −.22 | −.03 | .00 |
| | sr. hi | +.12 | −.03 | |
| OVERALL OTHER-REPORT AGGRESSION SUM | jr. hi | +.22 | −.07 | +.17* |
| | sr. hi | +.06 | +.14 | |
| Buss-Durkee verbal aggression | jr. hi | +.06 | −.02 | −.01 |
| | sr. hi | −.02 | −.21 | |
| Peer report verbal aggression | jr. hi | +.10 | −.22 | +.06 |
| | sr. hi | −.03 | +.02 | |
| Peer report irritability aggression | jr. hi | −.07 | +.19 | +.15 |
| | sr. hi | +.14 | −.02 | |
| Approval of aggression | jr. hi | +.11 | +.15 | +.13 |
| | sr. hi | −.12 | +.09 | |
| Aggressive attitudes | jr. hi | +.02 | +.23 | +.10 |
| | sr. hi | −.24 | +.21 | |
| (N) | jr. hi | (38) | (30) | (151) |
| | sr. hi | (43) | (40) | |

Note: Cell entries are zero-order correlation coefficients between each aggression variable and the Total Viewing Time Index.

Table 10: Correlations between level of violence viewing and family environment variables: Wisconsin data

| Family environment measure | Grade | Boys | Girls | Overall |
|---|---|---|---|---|
| Parental control over TV viewing | jr. hi | +.07 | +.36* | |
| | sr. hi | +.13 | +.10 | +.18* |
| Parental emphasis on nonaggression | jr. hi | −.27 | +.28 | |
| | sr. hi | +.10 | +.20 | +.05 |
| Parental interpretation of TV violence | jr. hi | +.07 | +.33 | |
| | sr. hi | +.23 | +.09 | +.16* |
| Parental physical punishment | jr. hi | +.19 | +.17 | |
| | sr. hi | +.19 | +.11 | +.18* |
| Parental verbal punishment | jr. hi | +.10 | +.20 | |
| | sr. hi | +.30* | +.33* | +.25** |
| Parental restrictive punishment | jr. hi | +.30 | +.11 | |
| | sr. hi | +.14 | +.35* | +.28** |
| Parental affection | jr. hi | +.15 | −.01 | |
| | sr. hi | +.20 | +.03 | +.12 |
| Parental socio-orientation | jr. hi | +.02 | +.47** | |
| | sr. hi | +.30* | +.31 | +.28** |
| Parental concept-orientation | jr. hi | .00 | +.04 | |
| | sr. hi | −.04 | −.15 | −.05 |
| Parental socioeconomic status | jr. hi | −.33* | −.23 | |
| | sr. hi | −.29 | −.07 | −.17* |
| (N) | jr. hi | (38) | (30) | |
| | sr. hi | (43) | (40) | (151) |

Note: Cell entries are zero-order correlation coefficients between each family variable and the Violence Viewing Index.

Table 11:  Correlations between level of overall self-report aggression
and family environment variables:  Wisconsin data

| Family environment measures | Grade | Boys | Girls | Overall |
|---|---|---|---|---|
| Parental control over TV viewing | jr. hi | +.10 | +.33 | +.16* |
| | sr. hi | +.03 | −.10 | |
| Parental emphasis on nonaggression | jr. hi | −.19 | +.16 | −.07 |
| | sr. hi | −.09 | −.07 | |
| Parental interpretation of TV violence | jr. hi | −.02 | +.21 | −.03 |
| | sr. hi | −.18 | −.22 | |
| Parental physical punishment | jr. hi | +.06 | +.24 | +.27** |
| | sr. hi | +.19 | +.40** | |
| Parental verbal punishment | jr. hi | +.06 | −.13 | +.17* |
| | sr. hi | +.21 | +.40** | |
| Parental restrictive punishment | jr. hi | +.05 | −.08 | +.23** |
| | sr. hi | +.19 | +.23 | |
| Parental affection | jr. hi | +.23 | +.03 | +.07 |
| | sr. hi | −.23 | +.08 | |
| Parental socio-orientation | jr. hi | +.28 | +.04 | +.17* |
| | sr. hi | +.16 | +.06 | |
| Parental concept-orientation | jr. hi | −.09 | −.10 | −.15 |
| | sr. hi | −.39** | +.12 | |
| Parental socioeconomic status | jr. hi | +.05 | −.16 | +.05 |
| | sr. hi | −.22 | +.10 | |
| (N) | jr. hi | (38) | (30) | (151) |
| | sr. hi | (43) | (40) | |

Note:  Cell entries are zero-order correlation coefficients between each family variable
and the Overall Aggressive Sum (Self-Report).

Table 12: Correlations between level of overall other-report aggression and family environment variables: Wisconsin data

| Family environment measure | Grade | Boys | Girls | Overall |
|---|---|---|---|---|
| Parental control over TV viewing | jr. hi | −.08 | −.07 | +.04 |
| | sr. hi | −.02 | +.05 | |
| Parental emphasis on nonaggression | jr. hi | −.12 | .00 | −.08 |
| | sr. hi | −.14 | +.01 | |
| Parental interpretation of TV violence | jr. hi | −.19 | +.25 | +.02 |
| | sr. hi | +.22 | −.14 | |
| Parental physical punishment | jr. hi | +.13 | +.14 | +.28** |
| | sr. hi | +.42** | +.19 | |
| Parental verbal punishment | jr. hi | +.15 | +.11 | +.18* |
| | sr. hi | +.26 | +.05 | |
| Parental restrictive punishment | jr. hi | +.36* | +.14 | +.41** |
| | sr. hi | +.46** | +.39** | |
| Parental affection | jr. hi | +.09 | −.01 | +.13 |
| | sr. hi | +.16 | +.16 | |
| Parental socio-orientation | jr. hi | .00 | +.06 | +.28** |
| | sr. hi | +.53** | +.35* | |
| Parental concept-orientation | jr. hi | −.09 | +.23 | −.03 |
| | sr. hi | −.05 | +.05 | |
| Parental socioeconomic status | jr. hi | .00 | +.10 | .00 |
| | sr. hi | −.23 | −.06 | |
| (N) | jr. hi | (38) | (30) | (151) |
| | sr. hi | (43) | (40) | |

Note: Cell entries are zero-order correlation coefficients between each family variable and the Overall Other-Report Aggression Index.

Table 13: Standardized levels of television viewing, cognitive reactions, family environment, and aggression by family communication pattern: Wisconsin data

| Measure | Laissez-faire | Pluralistic | Protective | Consensual |
|---|---|---|---|---|
| Overall violence viewing | −14 | −41** | +25 | +32* |
| Saturday morning programs | −31* | −31** | +21 | +42** |
| Total TV viewing time | −23 | −22 | +40** | +08 |
| Learning of aggression | −04 | −29* | +19 | +14 |
| Linkage to real life | −27 | −06 | −02 | +33* |
| Program involvement | +24 | −11 | −02 | −07 |
| Control over TV viewing | −37* | −30* | +20 | +46** |
| Emphasis on nonaggression | −32* | −20 | +28 | +27* |
| Interpretation of TV violence | −42** | 00 | 00 | +36* |
| Physical aggression | +15 | −29* | +14 | +04 |
| Delinquency aggression | +10 | −20 | +16 | −03 |
| Zaks-Walters aggression | 00 | −34** | +49** | −08 |
| Hypothetical aggression | +04 | −11 | +10 | −01 |
| SELF-REPORT AGGRESSION SUM | +12 | −35** | +30* | −01 |
| Peer report aggression | −11 | −27* | +22 | +20 |
| Teacher report aggression | −16 | −22 | +20 | +18 |
| Mother report aggression | +04 | −09 | −13 | +16 |
| OTHER-REPORT AGGRESSION SUM | −11 | −29* | +18 | +24 |
| Verbal aggression | −04 | +06 | +01 | −05 |
| Peer report verbal aggression | −21 | −11 | +24 | +09 |
| Irritability aggression | −07 | −01 | +28 | −17 |
| Peer report irritability | +05 | −15 | +05 | +05 |
| Approval of aggression | +20 | −24 | +09 | −01 |
| Aggressive attitudes | +32* | −35** | +13 | −03 |
| (N) | (34) | (40) | (34) | (39) |

Note: Standard scores represent each cell mean, calculated as a positive or negative deviation from the overall mean on the listed index, divided by the overall standard deviation. Scores have been multiplied by 100 to eliminate decimals. Asterisks indicate the cell mean is significantly different from the overall mean for the remaining cells.

Table 14: Correlations between peer integration and aggression,
violence viewing, and cognitive reactions: Wisconsin data

| Measure | Grade | Boys | Girls | Overall |
|---|---|---|---|---|
| Overall violence viewing | jr. hi | −.04 | +.17 | |
| | sr. hi | −.16 | −.09 | −.07 |
| Total viewing time | jr. hi | +.18 | +.03 | |
| | sr. hi | −.05 | +.20 | +.04 |
| Cognitive reactions to TV violence sum | jr. hi | +.12 | +.25 | |
| | sr. hi | +.03 | +.08 | +.06 |
| Overall other-report aggression sum | jr. hi | +.52** | −.04 | |
| | sr. hi | +.07 | +.12 | +.11 |
| Overall self-report aggression sum | jr. hi | +.11 | +.01 | |
| | sr. hi | +.07 | +.01 | −.03 |
| Self-report verbal aggression | jr. hi | +.13 | +.08 | |
| | sr. hi | −.02 | −.09 | +.08 |
| Peer report verbal aggression | jr. hi | +.32* | +.24 | |
| | sr. hi | +.11 | −.02 | +.11 |
| Self-report irritability aggression | jr. hi | +.02 | −.17 | |
| | sr. hi | −.01 | −.20 | −.10 |
| Peer report irritability aggression | jr. hi | +.26 | +.01 | |
| | sr. hi | +.16 | +.11 | +.09 |
| Approval of aggression | jr. hi | −.19 | −.10 | |
| | sr. hi | +.23 | +.10 | −.03 |
| Aggressive attitudes | jr. hi | −.24 | +.07 | |
| | sr. hi | +.25 | +.05 | .00 |
| (N) | jr. hi | (38) | (30) | |
| | sr. hi | (43) | (40) | (151) |

Note: Cell entries are zero-order correlation coefficients between each viewing and
aggression variable and the Peer Integration Index.

Table 15: Correlations between coorientational agreement, accuracy, and congruency and television viewing, cognitive reactions, and aggression: Wisconsin data

| Measure | Agreement | Child congruency | Mother congruency | Child accuracy | Mother accuracy |
|---|---|---|---|---|---|
| Overall violence viewing | −.21 | −.07 | −.07 | −.12 | −.11 |
| Learning of aggression | −.10 | −.19 | −.12 | −.15 | −.03 |
| Linkage to real life | −.12 | −.11 | +.03 | −.19 | +.05 |
| Program involvement | +.06 | −.04 | +.08 | +.02 | +.15 |
| Physical aggression | −.19 | −.06 | +.04 | −.09 | −.11 |
| Delinquency aggression | −.19 | +.01 | +.04 | −.02 | −.11 |
| Zaks-Walters aggression | −.03 | −.14 | −.17 | −.01 | −.04 |
| Hypothetical aggression | −.12 | +.01 | −.16 | −.03 | −.04 |
| SELF-REPORT AGGRESSION SUM | −.21 | −.06 | −.11 | −.06 | −.10 |
| Peer report aggression | −.16 | −.07 | −.14 | −.14 | −.09 |
| Teacher report aggression | +.01 | +.02 | −.05 | +.06 | +.03 |
| Mother report aggression | −.02 | −.01 | −.25 | −.02 | −.02 |
| OTHER-REPORT AGGRESSION SUM | −.14 | −.07 | −.20 | −.11 | −.08 |
| Verbal aggression | −.14 | −.07 | −.10 | −.05 | .00 |
| Peer report verbal aggression | −.13 | −.03 | −.12 | −.13 | +.03 |
| Irritability aggression | +.05 | +.04 | +.07 | +.10 | +.18 |
| Peer report irritability (N = 151) | +.12 | +.10 | +.13 | +.14 | +.02 |

For $r \geqq .16$, $p < .05$

$r \geqq .21$, $p < .01$

Table 16: Correlations between current *vs* past violence viewing and
aggressive behavior: Wisconsin data

| Aggression measure | Grade | Boys | | Girls | | Overall | |
|---|---|---|---|---|---|---|---|
| | | VV Now | VV Past | VV Now | VV Past | VV Now | VV Past |
| Self: Physical | jr. hi | +.13 | +.18 | +.29 | +.20 | | |
| | sr. hi | +.06 | .00 | −.06 | −.08 | +.17 | +.16 |
| Self: Delinquency | jr. hi | − − | − − | − − | − − | | |
| | sr. hi | +.12 | +.27 | +.21 | +.13 | +.20 | +.24 |
| Self: Zaks-Walters | jr. hi | +.19 | +.23 | +.14 | −.02 | | |
| | sr. hi | +.11 | +.19 | +.45 | +.34 | +.24 | +.22 |
| Self: Hypothetical | jr. hi | −.02 | +.14 | +.24 | +.10 | | |
| | sr. hi | +.28 | +.26 | +.06 | +.13 | +.22 | +.26 |
| Self: OVERALL SUM | jr. hi | +.12 | +.26 | +.38 | +.19 | | |
| | sr. hi | +.23 | +.27 | +.23 | +.18 | +.30 | +.33 |
| Peer: Assault | jr. hi | +.14 | +.24 | +.08 | +.16 | | |
| | sr. hi | +.20 | +.01 | +.13 | +.04 | +.20 | +.17 |
| Teacher: Aggression | jr. hi | +.13 | +.22 | +.14 | +.03 | | |
| | sr. hi | − − | − − | − − | − − | +.20 | +.18 |
| Mother: Aggression | jr. hi | −.29 | −.14 | +.04 | −.13 | | |
| | sr. hi | +.09 | +.09 | −.10 | −.01 | −.06 | +.02 |
| Other: OVERALL SUM | jr. hi | +.01 | +.20 | +.08 | +.09 | | |
| | sr. hi | +.22 | +.03 | +.09 | +.04 | +.17 | +.17 |
| Self: Approval | jr. hi | +.08 | +.21 | +.13 | +.21 | | |
| | sr. hi | +.03 | +.42 | .00 | −.21 | +.09 | +.27 |
| Self: Attitudes | jr. hi | +.02 | +.06 | +.09 | +.03 | | |
| | sr. hi | +.22 | +.27 | +.11 | −.07 | +.17 | +.21 |
| (N) | jr. hi | (38) | | (30) | | | |
| | sr. hi | (43) | | (40) | | (151) | |

Note: Cell entries are zero-order correlations between each aggression variable and the
Overall Violence Viewing Index (*VV Now*) and the Violence Viewing When Younger
Index (*VV Past*). Significance levels not indicated.

Table 17: Percent reporting greater cognitive reactions to television violence on crime-detective *vs* western programs: Wisconsin data

| Cognitive reaction item | More often during crime shows | More often during westerns |
|---|---|---|
| The programs show me how to get back at people who make me angry. (L) | 18% | 11% |
| Sometimes I copy the things I see people doing on the shows. (L) | 11% | 16% |
| When someone attacks another person and isn't punished, I sometimes feel I can get away with it too. (L) | 15% | 11% |
| When the bad guy gets a beating he deserves, I sometimes feel like getting even with people who have bothered me. (L) | 18% | 15% |
| The shows tell about life the way it really is. (R) | 46% | 8% |
| The people I see on the shows are just like the people I meet in real life. (R) | 32% | 8% |
| The stories remind me of frustrating things that have happened to me. (R) | 36% | 12% |
| Some characters remind me of people who have made me mad. (R) | 44% | 19% |
| I am so involved that I get carried away with the story. (I) | 44% | 15% |
| I get upset when my favorite star is yelled at or threatened. (I) | 18% | 8% |
| Once in a while I feel like things that happen to my hero are really happening to me. (I) | 16% | 11% |
| I pay close attention to these shows. (I) | 59% | 16% |
| (N) | (151) | |

Note: Cell entries are percentages of the overall sample indicating that one type of program affected them comparatively more often than the other. In many cases, the majority of respondents marked the "don't know" category. Items labeled (L) are from the Perceived Learning of Aggression Index; those labeled (R) are from the Linkage of TV Content to Real Life Index; those labeled (I) are from the Involvement in Violent Programming Index.

Table 18: Partial correlations between violence viewing and other-reports of aggressive behavior, controlling total television viewing time: Wisconsin data

| Aggressive measure | Grade | Boys | | Girls | | Overall | |
|---|---|---|---|---|---|---|---|
| | | raw r | partial: TV time | raw r | partial: TV time | raw r | partial: TV time |
| Peer report | jr. hi | +.14 | +.01 | +.08 | +.07 | | |
| | sr. hi | +.20 | +.20 | +.13 | +.07 | +.20 | +.15 |
| Teacher report | jr. hi | +.13 | +.08 | +.14 | +.27 | | |
| | sr. hi | – – | – – | – – | – – | +.20 | +.20* |
| Mother report | jr. hi | −.29 | −.23 | +.04 | +.06 | | |
| | sr. hi | +.09 | +.06 | −.10 | −.10 | −.06 | −.06 |
| OTHER-REPORT SUM | jr. hi | +.01 | −.08 | +.08 | +.12 | | |
| | sr. hi | +.22 | +.21 | +.09 | +.05 | +.17 | +.12 |
| (N) | jr. hi | (38) | | (30) | | | |
| | sr. hi | (43) | | (40) | | (151) | |

Note: Cell entries in *raw r* columns are zero-order correlation coefficients between the Violence Viewing Index and each aggression measure. Cell entries in *partial: TV time* columns are partial r correlation coefficients between the Violence Viewing Index and each aggression measure, controlling for the Total TV Viewing Time Index. Significance levels are indicated for partial correlations only.

Table 19: Partial correlations between violence viewing and other-reports of aggressive behavior, controlling socioeconomic status and school performance: Wisconsin data

| Aggression measure | Grade | Boys | | | Girls | | | Overall | | |
|---|---|---|---|---|---|---|---|---|---|---|
| | | raw r | partial: SES | SP | raw r | partial: SES | SP | raw r | partial: SES | SP |
| Peer report | jr. hi | +.14 | +.13 | +.08 | +.08 | +.07 | −.02 | | | |
| | sr. hi | +.20 | +.15 | +.27 | +.13 | +.12 | +.02 | +.20 | +.20* | +.18* |
| Teacher report | jr. hi | +.13 | +.17 | +.09 | +.14 | +.27 | +.15 | | | |
| | sr. hi | – – | – – | – – | – – | – – | – – | +.20 | +.25* | +.18* |
| Mother report | jr. hi | −.29 | −.26 | −.30 | +.04 | +.04 | .00 | | | |
| | sr. hi | +.09 | +.09 | +.10 | −.10 | −.10 | −.11 | −.06 | −.05 | −.07 |
| OTHER-REPORT SUM | jr. hi | +.01 | .00 | −.07 | +.08 | +.11 | +.02 | | | |
| | sr. hi | +.22 | +.17 | +.26 | +.09 | +.09 | −.01 | +.17 | +.17* | +.15 |
| (N) | jr. hi | (38) | | | (30) | | | | | |
| | sr. hi | (43) | | | (40) | | | (151) | | |

Note: Cell entries in *raw r* columns are zero-order correlation coefficients between the Violence Viewing Index and each aggression measure. Cell entries in *partial: SES* columns are partial r correlations coefficients between the Violence Viewing Index and each aggression measure, controlling for the Socioeconomic Status Index. Cell entries in *partial: SP* columns are partial correlation coefficients controlling for the School Performance Index. Each control variable is partialled out separately in this analysis. Significance levels are indicated for partial correlations only.

Table 20:  Multiple predictors of other-reports of aggressive behavior:
violence viewing and selected third variables:  Wisconsin data

| Independent variables | Grade | Boys | Girls | Overall |
|---|---|---|---|---|
| Overall violence viewing (OVV) (raw r) | jr. hi<br>sr. hi | +.01<br>+.22 | +.08<br>+.09 | +.17 |
| OVV and Parental emphasis on nonaggression (multiple r) | jr. hi<br>sr. hi | .13<br>.27 | .08<br>.09 | .20 |
| OVV and Buss-Durkee irritability | jr. hi<br>sr. hi | .01<br>.22 | .23<br>.24 | .20 |
| OVV and Parental physical punishment | jr. hi<br>sr. hi | .07<br>.31 | .08<br>.20 | .31 |
| OVV and Parental verbal punishment | jr. hi<br>sr. hi | .01<br>.24 | .18<br>.13 | .22 |
| OVV and Parental restrictive punishment | jr. hi<br>sr. hi | .19<br>.28 | .09<br>.24 | .41 |
| OVV and Parental affection | jr. hi<br>sr. hi | .11<br>.25 | .13<br>.11 | .20 |
| OVV and Perceived learning of aggression | jr. hi<br>sr. hi | .35<br>.23 | .33<br>.43 | .35 |
| OVV and Linkage of TV violence to real life | jr. hi<br>sr. hi | .15<br>.36 | .14<br>.17 | .27 |
| OVV and Socio-oriented FCP | jr. hi<br>sr. hi | .01<br>.53 | .08<br>.35 | .29 |
| OVV and Concept-oriented FCP | jr. hi<br>sr. hi | .09<br>.22 | .24<br>.12 | .17 |
| OVV and Socioeconomic status | jr. hi<br>sr. hi | .01<br>.28 | .15<br>.11 | .17 |
| OVV and School performance | jr. hi<br>sr. hi | .26<br>.38 | .54<br>.39 | .29 |
| (N) | jr. hi<br>sr. hi | (38)<br>(43) | (30)<br>(40) | (151) |

Note:  Cell entries are multiple correlation coefficients between the Overall Other-Report
Aggression Sum and the Overall Violence Viewing Index and each third variable, one
at a time. Multiple correlations greater than the raw correlation indicate the added
contribution of the family and TV reaction variables to the relationship between
aggression and viewing. Significance levels are not indicated.

Table 21: Multiple regression analysis of other-reports of aggressive behavior, by violence viewing, parental punishment, and affection: Wisconsin data

| Independent variable | Grade | Boys | Girls | Overall |
|---|---|---|---|---|
| Overall violence viewing | jr. hi | −.04 | +.05 | |
| | sr. hi | +.22 | +.04 | +.14 |
| Parental punishment sum | jr. hi | +.17 | +.20 | |
| | sr. hi | +.18 | +.21 | +.17 |
| Parental affection | jr. hi | −.04 | −.16 | |
| | sr. hi | −.12 | +.15 | −.05 |
| Multiple correlation | jr. hi | .20 | .24 | |
| | sr. hi | .31 | .23 | .25* |
| (N) | jr. hi | (38) | (30) | |
| | sr. hi | (43) | (40) | (151) |

Note: Cell entries are partial correlation coefficients between the Other-Report Aggression Sum and each family and viewing variable, controlling for all other independent variables. The multiple correlation entries represent the total relationship with the entire set of independent variables. All independent variable measures are comparable to Maryland measures.

Table 22: Grand multiple regression of other-reports of aggressive behavior, by violence viewing, parental affection and punishment, child's irritability, and child's perceived learning of aggression from television: Wisconsin data

| Independent variable | Grade | Boys | Girls | Overall |
|---|---|---|---|---|
| Overall violence viewing | jr. hi | −.06 | −.04 | |
| | sr. hi | +.23 | +.05 | +.09 |
| Perceived learning of aggression | jr. hi | +.36* | +.32 | |
| | sr. hi | −.11 | +.43** | +.30** |
| Buss-Durkee irritability | jr. hi | +.07 | +.11 | |
| | sr. hi | −.04 | +.29 | +.08 |
| Parental punishment sum | jr. hi | +.12 | +.15 | |
| | sr. hi | +.18 | +.10 | +.14 |
| Parental affection | jr. hi | −.09 | −.12 | |
| | sr. hi | −.14 | +.09 | −.06 |
| Multiple correlation | jr. hi | .40 | .41 | |
| | sr. hi | .33 | .51 | .39 |
| (N) | jr. hi | (38) | (30) | |
| | sr. hi | (43) | (40) | (151) |

Note: Cell entries are partial correlation coefficients between the Other-Report Aggression Sum and each family and viewing variable, controlling for all other independent variables. The multiple correlation entries represent the total relationship with the entire set of independent variables. All independent variable measures are comparable to Maryland measures.

Table 23: Multiple regression analysis of violence viewing, by family
environment variables: Wisconsin data

| Independent variable | Grade | Boys | | Girls | | Overall | |
|---|---|---|---|---|---|---|---|
| | | abs. | rel. | abs. | rel. | abs. | rel. |
| Family Communication Patterns | | | | | | | |
| Concept-orientation | jr. hi | .00 | –.06 | –.01 | .00 | –.05 | –.05 |
| | sr. hi | –.02 | –.04 | –.08 | –.11 | | |
| Socio-orientation | jr. hi | +.02 | –.12 | +.47* | +.37* | +.28* | +.18* |
| | sr. hi | +.28 | +.25 | +.28 | +.13 | | |
| Multiple correlation | jr. hi | .02 | | .47* | | .28** | |
| | sr. hi | .30 | | .32 | | | |
| Parental Punishment and Affection | | | | | | | |
| Affection | jr. hi | +.14 | +.13 | –.04 | –.21 | +.10 | +.06 |
| | sr. hi | +.18 | +.16 | +.17 | +.15 | | |
| Physical punishment | jr. hi | +.11 | +.27 | +.13 | +.02 | +.07 | +.10 |
| | sr. hi | +.03 | +.02 | +.01 | –.01 | | |
| Verbal punishment | jr. hi | –.06 | –.18 | +.16 | +.12 | +.14 | +.09 |
| | sr. hi | +.25 | +.21 | +.33* | +.31* | | |
| Restrictive punishment | jr. hi | +.22 | +.19 | –.07 | –.01 | +.16 | +.15 |
| | sr. hi | +.01 | +.08 | +.37* | +.29 | | |
| Multiple correlation | jr. hi | .34 | | .24 | | .33** | |
| | sr. hi | .36 | | .49* | | | |
| (N) | jr. hi | (38) | | (30) | | (151) | |
| | sr. hi | (43) | | (40) | | | |

Note: Cell entries are partial correlation coefficients between each family environment
variable and the Overall Violence Viewing Index, controlling for all other independent
variables in the group. The Multiple correlation entries represent the total relationship
with the entire set of independent variables. Figures in the rel. column are predictors
of relative OVV, with the child's Total Viewing Time controlled. Figures in the abs.
column are predictors of absolute OVV.

Table 24: Multiple regression analysis of violence viewing, by parental punishment and affection: Maryland data

| Independent variable | Grade | Boys | | Girls | | Overall | |
|---|---|---|---|---|---|---|---|
| | | abs. | rel. | abs. | rel. | abs. | rel. |
| Affection | jr. hi | +.04 | +.03 | +.05 | +.05 | | |
| | sr. hi | +.11 | +.10 | −.09 | −.09 | +.02 | .00 |
| Physical punishment | jr. hi | −.04 | +.02 | −.10 | −.10 | | |
| | sr. hi | +.16 | +.11 | −.14 | −.12 | −.05 | −.01 |
| Verbal punishment | jr. hi | −.03 | −.03 | −.01 | −.01 | | |
| | sr. hi | −.06 | −.07 | +.10 | +.05 | −.03 | −.04 |
| Restrictive punsihment | jr. hi | +.07 | +.03 | +.11 | +.10 | | |
| | sr. hi | +.16 | +.15 | +.08 | +.07 | +.15** | +.12** |
| Multiple correlation | jr. hi | .08 | | .15 | | | |
| | sr. hi | .19 | | .21 | | .15* | |
| (N) | jr. hi | (122) | | (108) | | | |
| | sr. hi | (107) | | (136) | | (473) | |

Note: Cell entries are partial correlation coefficients between each family environment variable and the Overall Violence Viewing Index, controlling for all other independent variables. The multiple correlation entries represent the total relationship with the entire set of independent variables. Figures in the rel. column are predictors of relative OVV, with the child's Total Viewing Time controlled. Figures in the abs. column are predictors of absolute OVV.

Table 25: Grand multiple regression analysis of violence viewing: Wisconsin data

| Independent variable | Grade | Boys | | Girls | | Overall | |
|---|---|---|---|---|---|---|---|
| | | abs. | rel. | abs. | rel. | abs. | rel. |
| Total viewing time | jr. hi | | +.34 | | +.42* | | +.26** |
| | sr. hi | | +.21 | | +.21 | | |
| School performance | jr. hi | −.01 | +.06 | −.12 | −.01 | −.06 | −.03 |
| | sr. hi | +.05 | +.06 | −.12 | −.11 | | |
| Socioeconomic status | jr. hi | −.39* | −.30 | +.04 | +.27 | −.11 | −.06 |
| | sr. hi | −.35* | −.32 | +.04 | +.06 | | |
| Concept-oriented FCP | jr. hi | +.02 | +.07 | +.10 | +.11 | −.05 | −.05 |
| | sr. hi | −.08 | −.09 | −.15 | −.18 | | |
| Socio-oriented FCP | jr. hi | −.25 | −.32 | +.50* | +.51* | +.11 | +.06 |
| | sr. hi | −.02 | −.05 | +.01 | −.06 | | |
| Affection | jr. hi | +.30 | +.26 | −.18 | −.34 | +.11 | +.08 |
| | sr. hi | +.30 | +.29 | +.21 | +.20 | | |
| Physical punishment | jr. hi | +.11 | +.25 | +.06 | †.09 | +.09 | +.10 |
| | sr. hi | −.08 | −.09 | +.05 | +.04 | | |
| Verbal punishment | jr. hi | −.09 | −.18 | +.27 | +.25 | +.12 | +.08 |
| | sr. hi | +.34* | +.32 | +.25 | +.25 | | |
| Restrictive punishment | jr. hi | +.23 | +.25 | −.29 | −.23 | +.11 | +.12 |
| | sr. hi | .00 | +.07 | +.34* | +.30 | | |
| Multiple correlation | jr. hi | .54 | | .58 | | .40** | |
| | sr. hi | .54 | | .52 | | | |
| (N) | jr. hi | (38) | | (43) | | (151) | |
| | sr. hi | (43) | | (40) | | | |

Note: Cell entries are partial correlation coefficients between each variable and the Overall Violence Viewing Index, controlling for all other independent variables. The multiple correlation entries represent the total relationship with the entire set of independent variables. Figures in the rel. column are predictors of relative OVV, with the child's Total Viewing Time controlled. Figures in the abs. column are predictors of absolute OVV.

Table 26: Grand multiple regression analysis of violence viewing: Maryland data

| Independent variable | Grade | Boys | | Girls | | Overall | |
|---|---|---|---|---|---|---|---|
| | | abs. | rel. | abs. | rel. | abs. | rel. |
| Total viewing time | jr. hi | | +.30 | | +.08 | | |
| | sr. hi | | +.37** | | +.43** | | +.31** |
| School performance | jr. hi | −.11 | −.09 | −.11 | −.12 | | |
| | sr. hi | −.28** | −.26** | −.14 | −.06 | −.20** | −.17** |
| Father occupation | jr. hi | −.09 | −.07 | +.09 | +.09 | | |
| | sr. hi | −.36** | −.33 | −.11 | −.04 | −.10* | −.07 |
| Affection | jr. hi | +.07 | +.05 | +.05 | +.04 | | |
| | sr. hi | +.17 | +.17 | −.07 | −.08 | +.03 | +.02 |
| Physical punishment | jr. hi | −.04 | +.02 | −.09 | −.09 | | |
| | sr. hi | +.10 | +.16 | −.14 | −.12 | −.03 | .00 |
| Verbal punishment | jr. hi | −.01 | −.01 | −.01 | −.01 | | |
| | sr. hi | −.12 | −.12 | +.09 | +.04 | −.02 | −.03 |
| Restrictive punishment | jr. hi | +.09 | +.05 | +.11 | +.10 | | |
| | sr. hi | +.15 | +.15 | +.08 | +.06 | +.14** | +.12** |
| Multiple correlation | jr. hi | .17 | | .20 | | | |
| | sr. hi | .50** | | .29 | | .28** | |
| (N) | jr. hi | (122) | | (108) | | | |
| | sr. hi | (107) | | (136) | | (473) | |

Note: Cell entries are partial correlation coefficietns between each variable and the Overall Violence Viewing Index, controlling for all other independent variables. The multiple correlation entries represent the total relationship with the entire set of independent variables. Figures in the rel. column are predictors of relative OVV, with the child's Total Viewing Time controlled. Figures in the abs. column are predictors of absolute OVV.

Table 27: Multiple regression analysis of cognitive reactions to television violence, by family environment variables: Wisconsin data

| Independent variable | Grade | Boys | Girls | Overall |
|---|---|---|---|---|
| Family Communication Patterns | | | | |
| Concept-orientation | jr. hi | +.02 | +.08 | −.06 |
| | sr. hi | −.27 | +.14 | |
| Socio-orientation | jr. hi | −.27 | +.29 | +.19* |
| | sr. hi | +.09 | +.46** | |
| Multiple correlation | jr. hi | .27 | .30 | .20 |
| | sr. hi | .28 | .46* | |
| Parental Punishment and Affection | | | | |
| Affection | jr. hi | +.30 | +.14 | +.20* |
| | sr. hi | −.10 | +.23 | |
| Physical punishment | jr. hi | +.19 | +.21 | +.12 |
| | sr. hi | +.05 | +.28 | |
| Verbal punishment | jr. hi | −.05 | −.38* | −.11 |
| | sr. hi | +.06 | −.12 | |
| Restrictive punishment | jr. hi | −.16 | +.33 | +.17* |
| | sr. hi | +.06 | +.42** | |
| Multiple correlation | jr. hi | .34 | .48 | .31** |
| | sr. hi | .18 | .51* | |
| (N) | jr. hi | (38) | (30) | (151) |
| | sr. hi | (43) | (40) | |

Note: Cell entries are partial correlation coefficients between each family environment variable and the Overall Cognitive Reaction Sum, controlling for all other independent variables in the group. The multiple correlation entries represent the total relationship with the entire set of independent variables.

Table 28: Multiple regression analysis of cognitive reactions to television violence, by parental affection and punishment: Maryland data

| Independent variable | Grade | Boys | Girls | Overall |
|---|---|---|---|---|
| Affection | jr. hi | −.15 | +.15 | −.03 |
| | sr. hi | −.19 | −.06 | |
| Physical punishment | jr. hi | −.04 | −.01 | −.05 |
| | sr. hi | +.01 | −.14 | |
| Verbal punishment | jr. hi | +.10 | .00 | +.11* |
| | sr. hi | +.34* | +.15 | |
| Restrictive punishment | jr. hi | +.12 | +.21* | +.18** |
| | sr. hi | +.01 | +.22* | |
| Multiple correlation | jr. hi | .25 | .25 | .23** |
| | sr. hi | .41** | .31* | |
| (N) | jr. hi | (122) | (108) | (473) |
| | sr. hi | (107) | (136) | |

Note: Cell entries are partial correlation coefficients between each family environment variable and the Overall Cognitive Reaction Sum, controlling for all other independent variables. The multiple correlation entries represent the total relationship with the entire set of independent variables.

Table 29: Grand multiple regression analysis of cognitive reactions
to television violence: Wisconsin data

| Independent variable | Grade | Boys | Girls | Overall |
|---|---|---|---|---|
| School performance | jr. hi | −.40* | −.15 | |
| | sr. hi | −.21 | −.20 | −.19* |
| Socioeconomic status | jr. hi | +.07 | +.19 | |
| | sr. hi | −.18 | +.11 | +.15 |
| Concept-oriented FCP | jr. hi | −.10 | −.13 | |
| | sr. hi | −.23 | −.03 | −.19* |
| Socio-oriented FCP | jr. hi | −.24 | +.19 | |
| | sr. hi | −.09 | +.38* | +.13 |
| Affection | jr. hi | +.37* | +.11 | |
| | sr. hi | +.10 | +.26 | +.23** |
| Physical punishment | jr. hi | +.08 | +.21 | |
| | sr. hi | −.03 | +.30 | +.13 |
| Verbal punishment | jr. hi | −.03 | −.37 | |
| | sr. hi | +.20 | −.32 | −.15 |
| Restrictive punishment | jr. hi | −.12 | +.28 | |
| | sr. hi | +.03 | +.28 | +.13 |
| Multiple correlation | jr. hi | .59 | .53 | |
| | sr. hi | .42 | .65* | .41** |
| (N) | jr. hi | (38) | (30) | |
| | sr. hi | (43) | (40) | (151) |

Note: Cell entries are partial correlation coefficients between each variable and the
Overall Cognitive Reaction Sum, controlling for all other independent variables. The
multiple correlation entries represent the total relationship with the entire set of
independent variables.

Table 30:  Grand multiple regression analysis of cognitive reactions to
television violence:  Maryland data

| Independent variable | Grade | Boys | Girls | Overall |
|---|---|---|---|---|
| School performance | jr. hi | −.02 | −.20 | −.12* |
| | sr. hi | +.04 | −.04 | |
| Father occupation | jr. hi | −.10 | −.19 | −.09 |
| | sr. hi | −.10 | −.05 | |
| Affection | jr. hi | −.13 | +.14 | −.02 |
| | sr. hi | −.19 | −.05 | |
| Physical punishment | jr. hi | −.04 | +.03 | −.03 |
| | sr. hi | +.02 | +.14 | |
| Verbal punishment | jr. hi | +.11 | .00 | +.11* |
| | sr. hi | +.35** | +.14 | |
| Restrictive punishment | jr. hi | +.14 | +.22* | +.17** |
| | sr. hi | .00 | +.21* | |
| Multiple correlation | jr. hi | .27 | .38* | .28** |
| | sr. hi | .42** | .32* | |
| (N) | jr. hi | (122) | (108) | (473) |
| | sr. hi | (107) | (136) | |

Note:  Cell entries are partial correlation coefficients between each variable and the
Overall Cognitive Reaction Sum, controlling for all other independent variables.
The multiple correlation entries represent the total relationship with the entire
set of independent variables.

Table 31:  Multiple regression analysis of combined self- and other-reports of aggressive
behavior, by violence viewing, parental punishment and affection:  Wisconsin data

| Independent variable | Grade | Boys | Girls | Overall |
|---|---|---|---|---|
| Overall violence viewing | jr. hi | +.01 | +.34 | +.26** |
| | sr. hi | +.29 | +.13 | |
| Parental punishment sum | jr. hi | +.27 | +.17 | +.20* |
| | sr. hi | +.28 | +.30 | |
| Parental affection | jr. hi | +.18 | −.21 | −.07 |
| | sr. hi | −.33* | +.14 | |
| Multiple correlation | jr. hi | .29 | .42 | .36** |
| | sr. hi | .49* | .36 | |
| (N) | jr. hi | (38) | (30) | (151) |
| | sr. hi | (43) | (40) | |

Note:  Cell entries are partial correlation coefficients between the Combined Aggression
Sum and each family and viewing variable, controlling for all other independent variables. The multiple correlation entries represent the total relationship with the entire
set of independent variables. All independent variable measures are comparable to
Maryland measures.

Table 32: Grand multiple regression analysis of combined self- and other-reports of aggressive behavior, by violence viewing, parental affection and punishment, child's irritability, and child's perceived learning of aggression from television: Wisconsin data

| Independent variable | Grade | Boys | Girls | Overall |
|---|---|---|---|---|
| Overall violence viewing | jr. hi | +.05 | +.27 | |
| | sr. hi | +.29 | +.16 | +.22 ** |
| Perceived learning of aggression | jr. hi | +.28 | +.38 * | |
| | sr. hi | −.02 | +.28 | +.36 ** |
| Buss-Durkee irritability | jr. hi | +.45 ** | +.18 | |
| | sr. hi | −.03 | +.44 * | +.25 ** |
| Parental punishment sum | jr. hi | +.14 | +.09 | |
| | sr. hi | +.28 | +.24 | +.15 |
| Parental affection | jr. hi | −.07 | −.16 | |
| | sr. hi | −.33 * | +.13 | −.10 |
| Multiple correlation | jr. hi | .55 * | .57 | |
| | sr. hi | .49 | .57 | .54 ** |
| (N) | jr. hi | (38) | (30) | |
| | sr. hi | (43) | (40) | (151) |

Note: Cell entries are partial correlation coefficients between the Combined Aggression Sum and each independent variable, controlling all other independent variables. The multiple correlation entries represent the total relationship with the entire set of independent variables. All independent variable measures are comparable to Maryland measures.

Table 33: Grand multiple regression analysis of combined self- and other-reports of aggressive behavior, by exposure and reactions to television violence: Wisconsin data

| Independent variable | Grade | Boys | Girls | Overall |
|---|---|---|---|---|
| Overall violence viewing (now) | jr. hi | +.01 | +.25 | |
| | sr. hi | +.23 | +.13 | +.16 |
| Violence viewing when younger | jr. hi | +.29 | −.01 | |
| | sr. hi | +.14 | +.02 | +.20 * |
| Perceived learning of aggression | jr. hi | +.21 | +.38 | |
| | sr. hi | +.04 | +.26 | +.36 ** |
| Multiple correlation | jr. hi | .36 | .51 | |
| | sr. hi | .30 | .32 | .50 ** |
| (N) | jr. hi | (38) | (30) | |
| | sr. hi | (43) | (40) | (151) |

Note: Cell entries are partial correlation coefficients between the Combined Aggression Sum and each independent variable, controlling all other independent variables. The multiple correlation entries represent the total relationship with the entire set of independent variables.

Table 34: Correlations between violence viewing and aggressive behavior, at high *vs* low parental emphasis on nonaggressive behavior: Wisconsin data

| Aggression index | Grade | Boys | | Girls | | Overall | |
|---|---|---|---|---|---|---|---|
| | | Low | High | Low | High | Low | High |
| SELF-REPORT | jr. hi | +.15 | +.03 | +.42 | +.31 | +.34 | +.23 |
| SUM | sr. hi | −.12 | +.56 | +.30 | +.10 | | |
| OTHER-REPORT | jr. hi | +.05 | −.12 | +.33 | −.27 | +.33 | −.08 |
| SUM | sr. hi | +.24 | +.20 | +.24 | −.20 | | |
| COMBINED SUM | jr. hi | +.16 | −.06 | +.55 | +.01 | +.39 | +.15 |
| | sr. hi | +.06 | +.45 | +.30 | +.02 | | |
| (N) | jr. hi | (22) | (15) | (15) | (14) | (82) | (65) |
| | sr. hi | (23) | (19) | (22) | (17) | | |

Note: Cell entries are zero-order correlation coefficients between the Violence Viewing Index and each aggression index. Respondents were sorted into high *vs* low groups on the Parental Emphasis on Nonaggression Index by cutting at the midpoint within each grade level. For the junior high group, Low = 0-3 and High = 4-8; for the senior high group, Low = 0-2 and High = 3-8. Higher scores indicate a greater parental stress on non-violent responses to social conflict situations.

Table 35: Multiple regression analysis of aggression approval, by violence viewing, perceived learning of aggression from television, and parental affection and punishment: Wisconsin data

| Independent variable | Grade | Boys | Girls | Overall |
|---|---|---|---|---|
| Overall violence viewing | jr. hi | +.11 | −.19 | +.02 |
| | sr. hi | +.04 | −.07 | |
| Perceived learning of aggression | jr. hi | +.20 | +.19 | +.31** |
| | sr. hi | +.22 | +.15 | |
| Parental punishment sum | jr. hi | −.19 | +.09 | +.05 |
| | sr. hi | +.04 | +.22 | |
| Parental affection | jr. hi | −.22 | +.06 | −.13 |
| | sr. hi | −.22 | −.11 | |
| Multiple correlation | jr. hi | .30 | .26 | .36** |
| | sr. hi | .34 | .36 | |
| (N) | jr. hi | (38) | (30) | (151) |
| | sr. hi | (43) | (40) | |

Note: Cell entries are partial correlation coefficients between the Approval of Aggression Index and each independent variable, controlling for all other independent variables. The multiple correlation entries represent the total relationship with the entire set of independent variables. All independent and dependent variable measures are comparable to Maryland measures.

Table 36: Multiple regression analysis of aggression approval, by violence viewing, perceived learning of aggression from television, and parental affection and punishment: Maryland data

| Independent variable | Grade | Boys | Girls | Overall |
|---|---|---|---|---|
| Overall violence viewing | jr. hi | −.02 | +.13 | |
| | sr. hi | +.17 | .00 | +.10* |
| Perceived learning of aggression | jr. hi | +.08 | +.35** | |
| | sr. hi | +.39** | +.13 | +.29** |
| Parental punishment sum | jr. hi | −.12 | −.11 | |
| | sr. hi | +.03 | +.15 | +.01 |
| Parental affection | jr. hi | −.20* | −.03 | |
| | sr. hi | +.05 | −.20* | −.10* |
| Multiple correlation | jr. hi | .25 | .41** | |
| | sr. hi | .44** | .35** | .36** |
| (N) | jr. hi | (122) | (108) | |
| | sr. hi | (107) | (136) | (473) |

Note: Cell entries are partial correlation coefficients between the Approval of Aggression Index and each independent variable, controlling for all other independent variables. The multiple correlation entries represent the total relationship with the entire set of independent variables.

Table 37: Grand multiple regression analysis of aggressive attitudes: Wisconsin data

| Independent variable | Grade | Boys | Girls | Overall |
|---|---|---|---|---|
| Overall violence viewing | jr. hi | −.07 | −.22 | |
| | sr. hi | +.23 | +.07 | +.09 |
| Perceived learning of aggression | jr. hi | +.52** | +.12 | |
| | sr. hi | +.04 | +.01 | +.32** |
| Parental punishment sum | jr. hi | −.06 | +.21 | |
| | sr. hi | +.13 | +.07 | +.09 |
| Parental affection | jr. hi | −.42* | −.36 | |
| | sr. hi | −.31 | −.26 | −.27** |
| Socio-oriented FCP | jr. hi | +.24 | +.15 | |
| | sr. hi | +.05 | +.02 | +.05 |
| Concept-oriented FCP | jr. hi | −.04 | −.13 | |
| | sr. hi | −.29 | −.09 | −.15 |
| Multiple correlation | jr. hi | .62** | .47 | |
| | sr. hi | .55* | .41 | .52** |
| (N) | jr. hi | (38) | (30) | |
| | sr. hi | (43) | (40) | (151) |

Note: Cell entries are partial correlation coefficients between the Aggressive Attitudes Index and each independent variable, controlling for all other independent variables. The multiple correlation entries represent the total relationship with the entire set of independent variables. The Aggressive Attitudes Index subsumes the Approval of Aggression Index. The first four independent variables are comparable to Maryland measures.

# Attitudes Toward Violence: The Interaction of Television Exposure, Family Attitudes, and Social Class

Joseph R. Dominick and Bradley S. Greenberg

*Michigan State University*

This project examines the interaction of exposure to television violence with children's attitudes toward violence, within the context of family attitudes toward violence and the child's social environment.[1] Several researchers have specified that television is likely to be most influential when the child is exposed to a set of ideas or behaviors which recur from program to program, when he or she is a heavy user of the medium, and when he or she is likely to have limited contact with or information from other socialization agencies and consequently to have less firm values against which to compare the media themes (Schramm, Lyle, and Parker, 1961; Himmelweit, Oppenheim, and Vince, 1958; Maccoby, 1964).

314

Our basic rationale posits that a child who is a heavy viewer of television violence and whose family has not actively pointed out that violence is noxious will have a more positive view of aggression as a mode of conduct. To test this rationale, we must first specify what ideas about violence television presents to the child, then identify the likely role of family and environment in shaping the ideas he or she brings to this area of socialization.

Content analyses indicate that the television world is a violent one. Although definitions of violent content vary greatly, several studies are consistent in this conclusion. A survey by the *Christian Science Monitor*, conducted six weeks after Robert Kennedy's assassination in 1968, found 84 killings in 85 1/2 hours of prime time and Saturday programming. The most violent evening hours, according to the newspaper's study, were 7:30-9 p.m., when approximately 27 million children aged two to 17 were watching. During that time period, one violent incident occurred every 16 minutes, a murder or killing every half-hour.

Gerbner (1969) substantiated these findings in a more sophisticated analysis. He found that acts of violence occurred in eight of every ten programs. Dramatic programs averaged seven violent episodes; cartoon shows had three times that number. During one week, 400 people were killed on prime time programs. Gerbner (1969b) also analyzed certain personality attributes of violent characters, who were judged to be more logical and efficient than nonviolent characters in most programs.

More germane to the present research are studies which examined the role of violence in problem solving. Stempel (1969) identified the means used to solve problems during one week's network television programs. Of 202 problems presented, nearly 60 percent were solved by violent tactics. One-third were solved nonviolently, and the remainder went unresolved.

Larsen, Gray, and Fortis (1968) identified "program goals" and the means by which these goals were achieved. Violent means were the most prevalent. These researchers also found that children's programs were even more likely than adult programs to use violence to achieve goals. These studies support certain generalizations:

1. A child who watches an average amount of television is likely to see a substantial amount of violent content;

2. Violence typically is presented as a highly successful means of goal achievement;

3. During the 1968-69 season, violence was the predominant means of conflict resolution found in television drama.

What the child brings to this television experience will be the result of his or her prior socialization experiences. Research indicates that the family is the key factor in the development of most children's attitudes toward violence. Most likely a family member becomes the child's first target for violence. As the child grows older, most of his or her conflicts are with siblings. It is primarily the parent who rewards or punishes this aggressive behavior (Sears, Maccoby, and Levin, 1957). The family not only administers positive and negative reinforcements for aggression, but also may provide alternative models for problem solving which are essentially nonviolent: decision-making, arbitration, compromise. Use of these methods varies from family to family. An early study (Sewell, Mussem, and Harris, 1955) isolated one major family pattern along a democracy-autocracy continuum and found parent-child conversations and formalized techniques for solving family conflicts used more frequently in the more democratic families.

McLeod, Chaffee, and Eswara (1966, 1967) have suggested that communication patterns within families can affect a child's socialization. Among four family types they identified, they labeled one "pluralistic." In such a family, they said, a child is likely to be exposed to both sides of an issue, and discussion of controversial matters is encouraged. This family style appears to expose the child more readily to nonviolent methods of problem solving.

Parents may also influence their children's ideas about violence in a more direct way. Adult comments about television content can serve as important learning cues for children (Hicks, 1965). If a parent says violence is inappropriate while watching a violent scene with his or her children, the children may develop more negative attitudes about violence. A child who repeatedly sees his parents watching violence while they calmly eat dinner may come to accept violence as more normative. Parents seem to have the opportunity to either counteract or legitimize television aggression while they watch it with their children (Sakuma, 1968). These studies support certain propositions:

1. The family is the first agency to deal with a child's aggressive behavior;

2. Families can influence a child's attitudes toward violence by giving positive or negative feedback when the child is aggressive, by using violent or nonviolent methods of problem solving within the family, and by commenting on scenes of violence.

3. Families vary in their uses of these techniques.

Socioeconomic background may also influence the pattern of effects that stem from exposure to television violence. A child from a low-income family is on the average a far heavier television viewer than is his middle-class counterpart (Schramm, Lyle, and Parker, 1961; Greenberg and Dominick, 1969-70) and is thereby exposed to more violent episodes automatically. Economic background also may effect what the child brings to the television viewing situation. Allinsmith (1960) found that children of low socioeconomic status were likely to respond to potentially frustrating situations with the most direct forms of aggression. Lower-income youngsters habitually expressed more aggression than did their middle-class peers. Further, the environment of the poor contains more frequent acts of physical violence than does the middle-class environment (U.S. National Commission on Civil Disorders, 1968). Fighting with peers, violent incidents among neighbors, and disputes with police characterize many lower-class environments.

The lower-class family may also do less to inhibit aggression. Among low-income families, parent-child interactions are often erratic and inconsistent. Parents and children may see one another on a less systematic, more disorganized basis (Minuchin, Braulio, Gurney, Risman, and Schumer, 1967). Because fewer fathers are present in families, mothers are forced to work, further fragmenting interaction with their children.

To this point, we have attempted to pinpoint the interactive roles of exposure to televised violence, the family, and social class in contributing to the child's attitudes about aggression and violence. In essence, the question becomes to what extent the norms of television violence (its frequency, effectiveness, and acceptability), the presence or absence of perceived family sanctions, and the child's social class environment affect the following attitudinal components:

1. *Approval of violence:* To what extent does the child perceive that violence is an acceptable mode of behavior?

2. *Willingness to use violence:* When presented with hypothetical "real-life" problems, to what extent will the child choose violent solutions?

3. *Effectiveness of violence:* How effective does the child perceive violence to be as a means of problem solving?

4. *Solutions to conflict situations:* Given an opportunity to propose a solution to a problem, does the child suggest a violent one?

The child's sex is another important factor in the way he or she expresses hostile and aggressive behavior. Not surprisingly, boys have been found to be more overtly aggressive in many studies (Walters, Pearce, and Dahms, 1957). Boys have been shown to be significantly more aggressive in play (Levin and Sears, 1956) and their play to be more violent and physically damaging than that of girls (Sears, 1951). Attitudes toward the use of aggression show similar differences. Sears (1961) found that girls displayed higher levels of anxiety about aggression than did boys and were significantly less tolerant of what Sears termed "antisocial" aggression.

In one study of the effects of mediated violence, girls exhibited less imitative behavior than boys after watching adults perform violent acts (Bandura, 1965). When offered an incentive, however, girls remembered as many aggressive acts as did the boys.

## Hypotheses

Three main antecendent variables (exposure, family attitudes, and social class) have been discussed; each should exert a separate influence on a child's attitudes toward violence. In addition, the child's sex may affect violence attitudes and behavior. The rationale of this study yields these hypotheses:

1. Youngsters with more exposure to television violence will indicate greater approval of violent acts, be more willing to use violence, perceive violence to be a more effective way of solving problems, and more readily suggest a violent means of resolving a problem.

2. Youngsters who perceive that their families are strongly opposed to the use of aggression will indicate less approval of violence, perceive violence to be a less effective means of solving problems, and less readily suggest a violent means of resolving a problem.

A discussion of the effects of social class differences yields parallel hypotheses, but the separate impact of this variable is of secondary interest here. Youngsters from more disadvantaged homes are expected to indicate greater approval of violence, to believe it to be more effective, and so on. Of more interest is the predicted interaction of social class with the other antecedent variables.

The impact of exposure to television violence should interact both with a child's social class and with his or her family's attitudes. Low-income children who watch more television are more likely to have preexisting favorable attitudes about violence than are middle-class youngsters. Therefore, in terms of first-order interactions, a third hypothesis is:

3. More exposure to television violence in conjunction with low socioeconomic status will result in greater approval of violence, more willingness to use violence, higher perceived effectiveness of violence, and greater readiness to suggest violent solutions to problems.

In addition, as Schramm, Lyle, and Parker (1961) emphasized, television's potential effects should be the reciprocal of the influence of more personal sources. Given families which provide the child little or ambiguous information about the appropriateness of violence, and in which he is heavily exposed to television violence, a fourth hypothesis directly parallels those made for the interaction of exposure and social class:

4. More exposure to televised violence among children whose families have not stipulated antiviolence attitudes willbe related to greater approval of violence, more willingness to use violence, higher perceived effectiveness of violence, and greater readiness to suggest it in problem solving.

Finally, the intersect of all these antecedent conditions is expected to maximize tolerance for aggression. The lower-class youngster who is a heavy viewer of violence and who receives little contrary information from his family should be most accepting of the norms of the world of television violence. Thus:

5. The interaction of more exposure to televised violence with low exposure to counterinformation and low socioeconomic status will manifest itself in more approval of violence, higher perceived effectiveness of violence, and higher salience for violent solutions to problems.

Data obtained from boys and girls were analyzed separately. The general expectation was that the same antecedent variables would be related to the shaping of aggression attitudes among both boys and girls. If anything, television exposure was expected to be an even more important factor in the shaping of such attitudes for girls than for boys, since girls generally have fewer experiences with physical violence and aggression in their daily lives.

## METHODS

Questionnaires were completed by 434 boys and 404 girls in the fourth, fifth, and sixth grades in six Michigan schools during class sessions in May 1970. The schools were chosen on the basis of social and economic variation. About nine percent of the sample were black. Data from boys and girls were obtained at the same time, although they were analyzed separately.

## Antecedent variables

For each sex, three antecedent variables were examined: the children's exposure to televised violence, their perceptions of their families' attitudes toward violence, and their families' socioeconomic status.

*Exposure to television violence.* Each youngster received a list of 28 locally available television programs. Twenty of these programs had been judged by a sample of newspaper and magazine critics to contain violence (Greenberg and Gordon, 1971). The number of programs of these 20 which the respondents reported watching each week were summed. Totals ranged from none to 20 among the boys and from none to 19 among the girls and were normally distributed with a standard deviation of 3.7 for boys and 4.4 for girls.

*Family attitudes toward violence.* The children were asked seven questions about how they thought their parents felt about various forms of violence—for example, "Suppose you and your parents were watching a TV show together and one of the people on TV shot another person. What do you think your parents would say?" or "Suppose one of your friends hit you. What do you think your parents would want you to do?" Each item had two, three, or four response categories. The answers to all seven items correlated significantly with one another. Correlations ranged from .38 to .70. The seven item scores were summed into an index ranging from 7 (low approval of violence) to 17 (high approval of violence).

*Social class.* Each child wrote down the job(s) of his parents. The principal job was coded on a 13-position scale of occupational prestige (Troldahl, 1967).

The three antecedent variables were found to be intercorrelated from −.09 to .10 for the boys and from −.17 to .12 for the girls.

# Dependent variables

Four dependent variables were used.

*Approval of violence.* Eight modified items from the Sears (1961) Antisocial Aggression Scale were used. These were declarative sentences (for example, "I see nothing wrong in a fight between two teenage boys" or "It's all right if a man slaps his wife") with three response categories (agree; not sure; disagree). Scores were summed for the eight items into an index ranging from 8 (low approval) to 24 (high approval).

*Willingness to use violence.* This index measured the child's willingness to use violence in "real life." Five scale items were adopted from the Buss-Durkee Hostility Inventory (Buss, 1957), with "agree" to "disagree" as the available responses. Declarative sentences dealt with whether or not the individual would use some sort of physical violence in certain situations ("Anybody who says bad things about me is looking for a punch in the nose"). Item scores were summed into an index with scores of 5 indicating low willingness to resort to violence and 10 indicating high willingness.

*Perceived effectiveness of violence.* Five constructed items measured the children's opinions of how effective violence was as a means of solving problems ("Sometimes a fight is the easiest way to get what you want" or "A fight is the best way to settle an argument once and for all"). Three agree-disagree response categories were used. Item scores were summed; 5 represented low perceived effectiveness, and 15 represented high perceived effectiveness.

*Suggested solutions to conflict situations.* In four open-ended questions, a potentially frustrating situation was described. The child wrote down the one thing he would most likely do on that situation ("Pretend somebody you know takes something from you and breaks it on purpose. What would you do?" or "Pretend somebody you know tells lies about you. What would you do?") Responses judged to be nonviolent were scored 1, those judged violent scored 2. Violence was defined as behavior which would produce physical pain in another. An index score of 4 indicated all nonviolent responses; a score of 8 represented all violent responses.

All items for each dependent variable were summed into the constructed indices. Interitem correlations for the modified Sears Antisocial Aggression items were low and inconsistent. Interpretation of results for this index should be restrained. Although some items in other indices had low interitem correlations, they were retained for these analyses because of the overall interitem reliability for those indices.

The four dependent variables intercorrelated from .13 to .37 among girls and from .22 to .43 among boys. Therefore, they are to be interpreted not as completely independent attitudinal assessments, but as partial replicates of general attitudes toward the use of aggression. Each was analyzed as a dependent variable.

## Analytic procedures

The respondents were divided into eight subgroups of boys and eight subgroups of girls. A median split was made according to the occupational prestige of the child's family. Those in the three lowest categories of the 13-step prestige scale (218 boys, 153 girls) were classified in the low-income category; those in the other prestige categories (216 boys, 251 girls) were classified in the middle-income group.

A second median split for each subgroup was made according to the number of violent programs each child watched each week. The median was eight programs per week for the boys and seven programs for the girls.

Finally, each subgroup was divided according to the index of the child's family's attitudes toward violence. The distribution was skewed toward the low-approval end of the scale. Scores of 7-10 (216 boys, 210 girls) were placed in the low-approval group. More than 90 percent of the remaining children's scores indicated that they were unsure or didn't know how their parents felt about violence. Scores of 11 or higher (218 boys, 194 girls) were categorized as "undefined." Fewer than ten percent of the boys reported that their families gave strong approval to violence.

Data for the girls' and boys' samples were analyzed separately. The results will be presented separately for Analysis 1 (boys' sample) and Analysis 2 (girls' sample).

## RESULTS—ANALYSIS 1

Results are presented for four dependent behaviors: the boys' approval of aggression; their willingness to use violence; the extent to which they perceive violence to be effective; and their readiness to suggest violent solutions to problems.

For each, hypotheses were made step-wise through main effects and interactions. The results will be discussed in that fashion, although the interactions, where found, qualify interpretations of the main effects.

Because of the lack of correlation among the antecedent variables, a three-way analysis of variance with unequal cells (Snedecor, 1956) was performed on each of the dependent measures.

# Approval of aggression

Table 1 presents the results of the three-way analysis for this measure as well as the individual cell means.

Table 1:  Approval of aggression (boys)

| Cell means | | | | |
|---|---|---|---|---|
| (The higher the score, the more approval of aggression) | | | | |
| Exposure to TV violence: | Middle class Family attitudes toward aggression | | Lower class Family attitudes toward aggression | |
| | Low approval | Undefined | Low approval | Undefined |
| Low | 14.13 (n=47) | 15.03 (n=60) | 15.29 (n=62) | 16.65 (n=40) |
| High | 14.14 (n=57) | 16.52 (n=52) | 14.68 (n=50) | 16.17 (n=66) |

| Analysis of variance table | | | | |
|---|---|---|---|---|
| Source of variation | MS | df | F | P |
| Exposure to violence | 4.0 | 1 | 0.59 | n.s. |
| Family attitudes | 223.0 | 1 | 33.14 | .0005 |
| Social class | 54.0 | 1 | 7.86 | .025 |
| TV Violence X Family attitudes | 28.0 | 1 | 4.15 | .05 |
| TV Violence X Social class | 24.0 | 1 | 3.56 | .10 |
| Social class X Family attitudes | 1.0 | 1 | 0.01 | n.s. |
| Violence X Family X Class | 30.0 | 1 | 4.46 | .05 |
| Error | 6.74 | 426 | | |
| Total | | 433 | | |

Significant differences were obtained in terms of perceived family attitudes toward aggression and the social class of the youngster, but there was no main effect difference between those more and less exposed to television violence.

Cell comparisons indicate that in the four possible comparisons between youngsters whose families gave low approval to violence and those whose attitudes were ill-defined, the mean differences were consistent and large. Three of four social class cell comparisons yielded similar results.

The two first-order interactions—of exposure to television violence with either family attitudes or social class—were also as predicted. High exposure to television violence coupled with less certainty about family attitudes maximized the approval of aggression. Low exposure to television violence in conjunction with a middle-class background minimized the approval of aggression. Thus, although television exposure by itself was insufficient to yield differences in aggression approval, its interaction with each of the other antecedent variables was not trivial.

Table 1 also indicates a significant three-way interaction which is difficult to interpret, particularly because the pattern of means within the lower class is inconsistent with the predictions.

To clarify this anomaly, one additional analysis was done. This was a two-way analysis of variance (ANOVA) within each of the social class groupings. It was repeated for all dependent measures. The pattern found here was consistent. Among the middle-class youngsters, exposure to television violence made some difference ($p<.10$), as did family attitudes ($p<.01$) and the interaction of the two ($p<.05$). Among the lower-class boys, only family attitudes were an important discriminant ($p<.01$).

# Willingness to use violence

Table 2 contains the results of the three-way analysis of variance for this attitudinal variable.

Table 2: Willingness to use violence (boys)

| | Cell means | | | |
|---|---|---|---|---|
| | (The higher the score, the more willingness to use violence) | | | |
| Exposure to TV violence: | Middle class Family attitudes toward aggression | | Lower class Family attitudes toward aggression | |
| | Low approval | Undefined | Low approval | Undefined |
| Low | 7.27 (n=47) | 7.70 (n=60) | 7.77 (n=62) | 8.42 (n=40) |
| High | 7.28 (n=57) | 8.60 (n=52) | 7.64 (n=50) | 8.53 (n=66) |

| An analysis of variance table | | | | |
|---|---|---|---|---|
| Source of variation | MS | df | F | P |
| Exposure to TV violence | 6.9 | 1 | 4.06 | .05 |
| Family attitudes | 68.5 | 1 | 40.34 | .0005 |
| Social class | 16.0 | 1 | 9.41 | .005 |
| TV violence X Family attitudes | 12.2 | 1 | 7.18 | .025 |
| TV violence X Social class | 1.2 | 1 | 0.70 | n.s. |
| Social class X Family attitudes | 0.1 | 1 | 0.10 | n.s. |
| Violence X Family X Class | 5.2 | 1 | 3.06 | .10 |
| Error | 1.71 | 426 | | |
| Total | | 433 | | |

Main effects predictions were supported for all three antecedent variables. Maximum willingness to resort to violence in conflict situations came from more exposure to violent television content, from families with less defined attitudes toward aggression, and from the lower income groupings. Here, as for all attitude segments, the family variable was the most discriminating.

Exposure to violence and family attitudes interacted in the same manner as in the Approval of Aggression index. High exposure and undefined attitudes in the home maximized the willingness to use violence. The predicted interaction between exposure and social class was not supported.

The three-way interaction was weaker in this analysis but more consistent with predictions. Willingness to use violence was increasingly present in the lower-class conditions, except in the cell comprised of boys with high exposure to television violence and undefined family attitudes, where there was no mean difference.

Again the two-way analysis aided interpretation. Only among the middle-class youngsters was a difference attributable to extent of exposure to television violence (p < .05). It washed out among the lower-class boys. For both groups, family attitudes were critical (p < .01). But only for the middle-class youngsters did family attitudes interact significantly (p < .05) with television exposure. These latter results exactly parallel those found for the approval of aggression index.

## Use of violence in conflict situations

This measure was a second approach to the one just described. The principal difference was that the youngsters were freely suggesting violent or nonviolent solutions rather than evaluating proposed ones. Results of the analysis are in Table 3.

Main effects were found for family attitudes and for social class. Television exposure made no difference in the free responses. Neither predicted first-order interaction was significant. The second-order interaction was significant, but the same inconsistencies are present in the data for the lower-class youngsters.

In the analyses done for each of the social class groupings, family attitudes toward violence were again crucial. For the middle-class youngsters, the predicted interaction between television violence and family attitudes was again significant (p < .01), but not for the lower-class boys. For neither group was television exposure alone critical.

## Perceived effectiveness of violence

Table 4 contains the results of the three-way analysis of variance for this dependent variable. Each of the main effects was significant and large. Violence was considered to be more effective in all four high television exposure conditions, the four undefined family attitude conditions, and the four lower-class cells.

Table 3: Use of violence in conflict situations (boys)

Cell means

(The higher the score, the more often the child uses violence to solve conflicts)

| Exposure to TV violence: | Middle class Family attitudes toward aggression | | Lower class Family attitudes toward aggression | |
|---|---|---|---|---|
| | Low approval | Undefined | Low approval | Undefined |
| Low | 4.57 (n=47) | 4.65 (n=60) | 4.85 (n=62) | 5.25 (n=40) |
| High | 4.49 (n=57) | 5.26 (n=51) | 4.78 (n=50) | 5.10 (n=66) |

An analysis of variance table

| Source of variation | MS | df | F | P |
|---|---|---|---|---|
| Exposure to TV violence | 2.0 | 1 | 2.08 | n.s |
| Family attitudes | 14.0 | 1 | 14.58 | .005 |
| Social class | 7.0 | 1 | 7.29 | .025 |
| TV violence X Family attitudes | 2.8 | 1 | 2.96 | n.s. |
| TV violence X Social class | 2.2 | 1 | 2.29 | n.s. |
| Social class X Family attitudes | 0.5 | 1 | 0.19 | n.s. |
| Violence X Family X Class | 4.5 | 1 | 4.68 | .05 |
| Error | 0.96 | 425 | | |
| Total | | 432 | | |

Table 4: Perceived effectiveness of violence (boys)

Cell means

(The higher the score, the more violence is seen as being effective)

| Exposure to TV violence: | Middle class Family attitudes toward aggression | | Lower class Family attitudes toward aggression | |
|---|---|---|---|---|
| | Low approval | Undefined | Low approval | Undefined |
| Low | 7.83 (n=47) | 9.22 (n=60) | 8.68 (n=62) | 10.90 (n=40) |
| High | 8.67 (n=57) | 11.08 (n=52) | 9.54 (n=50) | 11.50 (n=66) |

An analysis of variance table

| Source of variation | MS | df | F | P |
|---|---|---|---|---|
| Exposure to TV violence | 135.0 | 1 | 15.79 | .005 |
| Family attitudes | 416.0 | 1 | 49.81 | .0005 |
| Social class | 93.0 | 1 | 10.93 | .005 |
| TV violence X Family attitudes | 12.0 | 1 | 1.44 | n.s. |
| TV violence X Social class | 0.5 | 1 | 0.01 | n.s. |
| Social class X Family attitudes | 5.5 | 1 | 0.64 | n.s. |
| Violence X Family X Class | 12.0 | 1 | 1.44 | n.s. |
| Error | 8.55 | 426 | | |
| Total | | 433 | | |

None of the predicted two-or three-way interactions approached significance.

Parallel two-way analyses of variance were made for each of the social class groups. For both the middle-class and lower-class boys, television exposure and family attitudes were significant antecedent conditions. No interaction existed. Violence was judged to be maximally effective when television exposure was high or family attitudes were unclear.

## Summary of analyses

Given four dependent measures with moderate intercorrelations for three antecedent conditions, the degree of consistency across measures can be examined. Table 5 provides an overall summary of the analyses.

Table 5: Summary across dependent variables (boys)

| | Dependent variables | | | |
| --- | --- | --- | --- | --- |
| Antecedent variables | Approval of aggression | Willingness to use violence | Use of violence in conflict situations | Perceived effectiveness of violence |
| Exposure to TV violence | n.s. | .05 | n.s. | .01 |
| Family attitudes | .01 | .01 | .01 | .01 |
| Social class | .05 | .01 | .05 | .01 |
| TV Violence X Family | .05 | .05 | n.s. | n.s. |
| TV Violence X Class | .10 | n.s. | n.s. | n.s. |
| Family X Class | n.s. | n.s. | n.s. | n.s. |
| Violence X Family X Class | .05 | .10 | .05 | n.s. |
| Middle-class | | | | |
| Exposure | .10 | .05 | n.s. | .01 |
| Family attitudes | .01 | .01 | .01 | .01 |
| Exposure by Family attitudes | .05 | .05 | .01 | n.s. |
| Lower-class | | | | |
| Exposure | n.s. | n.s. | n.s. | .05 |
| Family attitudes | .01 | .01 | .05 | .01 |
| Exposure by Family attitudes | n.s. | n.s. | n.s. | n.s. |

For two of four measures—the individual's willingness to use violence and its perceived effectiveness when used—television exposure makes a direct contribution. With higher exposure comes more approval of violence.

For all four measures, both family attitudes toward aggression (as known to the child) and the social environment of the family have a persistent impact. Family attitudes account for the largest portion of variance, followed by social class differences.

Where television exposure does interact with either family attitudes or social class, the two variables serve to intensify the acceptance of violent norms, but exposure interacts irregularly, in three of eight possible instances.

The irregularities or inconsistencies are largely clarified in the analyses which partial out the social class differences. Among middle-class boys, the television exposure variable is more predictive, alone and in interaction with the attitudes of the youngsters' family. Among the lower-class boys, only family attitudes are a useful predictor of attitudes toward aggressive behavior.

## RESULTS—ANALYSIS 2

Results are presented for the four dependent variables.

# Willingness to use violence

Table 6 presents the three-way analysis of variance for this attitudinal variable. Two of the main effects were significant. The strongest predictor of willingness to use violence was the perceived attitude of the family. The main effect for exposure to television violence was also significant. Preteen girls who were more regularly exposed to television violence expressed more willingness to use violence than did those less exposed. Neither the main effect for social class nor any of the interactions was significant.

# Use of violence in conflict situations

The principal difference between this measure and the respondent's expressed willingness to use violence was that here a free response was given and coded. Results are in Table 7.

Again, main effects were found for the family attitude variable and for exposure to television violence. Social class did not further differentiate. Girls from families whose attitudes toward violence were ambiguous offered more violent solutions. Similarly, more violent suggestions were made by those youngsters who were heavier viewers of televised violence. No interactions existed.

# Perceived effectiveness of violence

As is evident in Table 8, family attitudes showed a strong relationship with this attitudinal measure. An equally strong relationship was found on the basis of exposure to television violence. In general, those girls who watched a great deal of television violence were more likely to perceive violence as effective. Social class differences did not emerge.

One interaction was significant. Maximum perceived effectiveness of violence existed among lower-class families whose attitudes toward violence were ambiguous; violence was minimally effective for the middle-class youngsters with clear antiviolence norms.

Table 6: Willingness to use violence (girls)

### Cell means

(The higher the score, the more willingness to use violence)

| Exposure to TV violence: | Middle class Family attitudes toward aggression | | Lower class Family attitudes toward aggression | |
|---|---|---|---|---|
| | Low approval | Undefined | Low approval | Undefined |
| Low | 6.60 (n=73) | 7.42 (n=64) | 6.71 (n=38) | 7.28 (n=29) |
| High | 7.02 (n=59) | 7.67 (n=55) | 6.90 (n=40) | 7.76 (n=46) |

### Analysis of variance table

| Source of variation | MS | df | F | P |
|---|---|---|---|---|
| Exposure to TV violence | 11.94 | 1 | 5.76 | .025 |
| Family attitudes | 57.16 | 1 | 27.49 | .0005 |
| Social class | 0.01 | 1 | * | n.s. |
| TV violence X Social class | 0.12 | 1 | 0.06 | n.s. |
| TV violence X Family attitudes | 0.72 | 1 | 0.34 | n.s. |
| Family X Class | 0.12 | 1 | 0.06 | n.s. |
| Violence X Family X Class | 0.01 | 1 | * | |
| Error | 2.07 | 396 | | |

*Less than 0.01

Table 7: Suggested use of violence in conflict situations (girls)

### Cell means

(The higher the score, the more frequently the child suggests violence to solve conflict)

| Exposure to TV violence: | Middle class Family attitudes toward aggression | | Lower class Family attitudes toward aggression | |
|---|---|---|---|---|
| | Low approval | Undefined | Low approval | Undefined |
| Low | 4.30 (n=73) | 4.72 (n=64) | 4.32 (n=38) | 4.41 (n=29) |
| High | 4.37 (n=59) | 4.89 (n=55) | 4.48 (n=40) | 4.93 (n=46) |

### Analysis of variance table

| Source of variation | MS | df | F | P |
|---|---|---|---|---|
| Exposure to TV violence | 4.00 | 1 | 5.88 | .025 |
| Family attitudes | 15.84 | 1 | 23.30 | .0005 |
| Social class | 0.01 | 1 | 0.02 | n.s. |
| TV violence X Social class | 1.28 | 1 | 1.88 | n.s. |
| TV violence X Family attitudes | 0.57 | 1 | 0.84 | n.s. |
| Family X Class | 1.16 | 1 | 1.78 | n.s. |
| Violence X Family X Class | 1.14 | 1 | 1.77 | n.s. |
| Error | 0.68 | 396 | | |

Table 8: Perceived effectiveness of violence (girls)

Cell means

(The higher the score, the more violence is seen as being effective)

| Exposure to TV violence: | Middle class Family attitudes toward aggression | | Lower class Family attitudes toward aggression | |
|---|---|---|---|---|
| | Low approval | Undefined | Low approval | Undefined |
| Low | 7.12 (n=73) | 8.80 (n=64) | 8.24 (n=38) | 9.03 (n=29) |
| High | 8.73 (n=59) | 9.91 (n=55) | 8.22 (n=40) | 10.77 (n=46) |

Analysis of variance table

| Source of variation | MS | df | F | P |
|---|---|---|---|---|
| Exposure to TV violence | 173.71 | 1 | 24.39 | .0005 |
| Family attitudes | 200.43 | 1 | 28.15 | .0005 |
| Social class | 15.16 | 1 | 2.13 | n.s. |
| TV violence X Social class | 0.01 | 1 | * | n.s. |
| TV violence X Family attitudes | 9.09 | 1 | 1.27 | n.s. |
| Family X Class | 65.61 | 1 | 9.21 | .025 |
| Violence X Family X Class | 11.99 | 1 | 1.68 | n.s. |
| Error | 7.12 | 396 | | |

# Approval of aggression

Only the main effect of the family attitudes variable was significant for this scale, the least reliable of the measures used. In Table 9, girls from families negatively inclined toward violence had lower scores than girls from families whose attitudes were more undefined. No other main effect nor any interaction was significant.

# Summary

The results show strong consistency for the four dependent measures. The measures themselves were moderately intercorrelated (.13 to .37). For all four measures, family attitudes toward aggression (as reported by the child) showed the most persistent relationship to the child's aggressive attitudes.

Exposure to television violence also made a consistent, independent contribution to the child's notions about violence. The greater the level of exposure to television violence, the more the child was willing to use violence, to suggest it as a solution to conflict, and to perceive it as effective.

Contrary to expectations, there were no social class differences in attitudes toward aggression. Perhaps both lower- and middle-class girls receive similar instructions about its undesirability, although the literature suggests otherwise.

Table 9:  Approval of aggression (girls)

Cell Means

(The higher the score, the more expressed approval of aggression)

| Exposure to TV violence: | Middle class Family attitudes toward aggression | | Lower class Family attitudes toward aggression | |
|---|---|---|---|---|
| | Low approval | Undefined | Low approval | Undefined |
| Low | 13.63 (n=73) | 15.09 (n=64) | 13.61 (n=38) | 14.34 (n=29) |
| High | 14.44 (n=59) | 14.93 (n=55) | 13.50 (n=40) | 15.61 (n=46) |

Analysis of variance table

| Source of variation | MS | df | F | P |
|---|---|---|---|---|
| Exposure to TV violence | 16.00 | 1 | 2.89 | n.s. |
| Family attitudes | 164.77 | 1 | 29.66 | .0005 |
| Social class | 3.84 | 1 | 0.69 | n.s. |
| TV violence X Social class | 2.56 | 1 | 0.48 | n.s. |
| TV violence X Family attitudes | 0.08 | 1 | 0.01 | n.s. |
| Family X Class | 10.94 | 1 | 1.98 | n.s. |
| Violence X Family X Class | 13.82 | 1 | 2.49 | n.s. |
| Error | 5.53 | 396 | | |

# DISCUSSION

The hypotheses and the rationale behind them were generally support-ed by the data. Among the middle-class boys, ill-defined family attitudes and above-average viewing of violence interacted to yield the highest level of approval of aggression, willingness to use violence, and suggest-ed use of violence to solve problems. Among the lower-class boys, the interaction was not evident; perceived family attitudes were the key predictors. Among the less advantaged, only perceived effectiveness of violence was directly related to television exposure.

Among the girls, the strongest indicator was undefined family atti-tudes toward aggression; this factor was associated with more approval of aggression, more willingness to use violence, more perceived effec-tiveness of violence, and more suggestions of violence to solve prob-lems. High exposure to television violence was related to more aggres-sive attitudes on all measures except the Approval of Aggression scale. Social class was not a significant predictor, nor did television violence interact with either family attitudes or social class to intensify any dif-ferences.

In this study, certain factors which were theorized to be critical in the kind of impact that large-scale exposure to televised violence would have on the impressionable minds of children were tested empirically. In par-ticular, we examined the notion that television would play a prominent role among youngsters who are less socialized by families and social environments and would influence their beliefs about the appropriate-ness and effects of using violence. By our approach to this problem, we found substantial support in the data. At the same time, it is incumbent on us to identify certain limits to this approach and to discuss certain of their implications in concert with the findings.

The model used implies causation, but the data-gathering process only permitted us to make associative statements. It cannot be stipulated from these data alone that among youngsters with minimum family influence, exposure to violence precedes and leads to the development of attitudes which are more accepting of violence. (That, however, seems to be as plausible a sequence as one which would argue that some socializing agent other than the family or the television set precedes. At the least, there is ample evidence that exposure to television violence accompanies the development of proviolence attitudes. There is no evidence that it countermands such development.)

Much variance in attitudes toward violence remains unexplained. Television exposure is a weak, but significant, predictor. Family attitudes and social class are stronger determinants. All together, however, only ten to 15 percent of the variance among the boys and eight to 15 percent among the girls has been explained by these factors. Studies exploring the contributions of peers, school, and other factors appear to be needed.

Television exposure is most extensively related, for these youngsters, to the perceived effectiveness of violence. Television violence works, for both the good and the bad guys; it gets things done. This may be a quite realistic assessment of the efficacy of that mode of conflict resolution. If the use of violence is also condoned or if alternate, effective means are not known or available to children for whom television is a principal socializing agency, the implications warrant consideration.

The study focuses solely on attitudes toward violence, not on actual uses of violent behavior. To what degree more favorable attitudes toward violence are manifested in greater use of violence remains equivocal. The focus of future studies might be directed toward ascertaining those conditions, if any, under which the more favorable attitudes are accompanied by reduced inhibitions or reduced anxiety about the uses of aggression. One could argue that the acceptance of violence as appropriate, effective, and useful is a behavior deserving of study in its own right. Does the greater acceptance of such beliefs, for example, interfere with or deter the development of other, more productive or socially accepted, behavior?

Some caution is necessary when we examine the present measure of exposure to television violence. A program is a gross unit of measure. Although a televised dramatic series may be consistently more violent than other programs, there is substantial variation among its episodes. What in the violent programs is having the observed effect is unknown. It may be the atmosphere of the entire program or series; it may be specific incidents. The segments called violent by researchers may not be the same items viewers would label violent. This lack of specificity is a crucial issue for subsequent research.

The children's perceptions of their parents' attitudes toward aggression was the predominant correlate of their own beliefs. The gap that remains here is that the data on parents' attitudes originated with the youngsters. More direct data from parents should be obtained. Does the youngster know, reflect, or guess at the parents' attitude? Is the youngster rationalizing his or her own beliefs by making those of key reference groups consistent with them? What of other viable reference groups like peers? And what of possible contradictory information from parents and peers about responding to frustrating or mutually aggressive situations? Current research by Chaffee and McLeod (1971) at the University of Wisconsin has obtained data from both parents and their children; this study may bear on the unanswered questions.

The central point of this discussion might well be the combination of findings which indicate the relatively greater impact of television exposure on girls and boys from middle-class homes. The literature abounds with arguments that if television has some kind of impact, it will be prevalent among the disturbed or "nonnormal." Although these arguments typically refer to the instigation of violent acts, rather than to the attitudes favorable to violent acts, the suggested locus of effect is the same. Yet the present findings, which allowed us to examine youngsters from more and less advantaged homes (the latter a common operationalization of "nonnormal") indicates more television impact on attitudes among the former. Among the middle-class boys and among most girls, persistent exposure to televised violence showed a clear relationship to attitudes about violence. For the middle-class boys, exposure interacted with family attitudes; for all the girls, exposure had its own independent impact on their attitudes. The girls' socialization experience in both low- and middle-income families seemed to have similar influences on their personal beliefs. The girls from different environments reported learning equally well the undesirability of being physically aggressive.

The fact that we do not observe this clear relationship between viewing and attitudes among the lower-class youngster may stem from other factors. Their consistently higher scores on all the dependent measures may have created a ceiling effect on the opportunity for exposure to interact with family attitudes. These youngsters' more likely direct experiences with violence could have superceded television influence or made it only reinforcing. Certainly the expectation that family attitudes would be less influential among the less advantaged was not borne out with respect to the one aspect of socialization studied here. But others have suggested that this lack of influence may be the case with respect to aggression (Maccoby and Gibbs, 1954; Sears, Maccoby, and Levin, 1957).

For relatively average children from average home environments, however, continued exposure to violence is positively related to acceptance of aggression as a mode of behavior. When the home environment also tends to ignore the child's development of aggression attitudes, this relationship is even more substantial and perhaps more critical.

Among the most disadvantaged boys, the pressures of their experience with real violence coupled with equivocal family attitudes may have effectively eliminated an added impact from television viewing. It is among the more advantaged boys, and among most of the girls, that programming seems to modify attitudes about aggression. If made available, alternatives to violence as problem solvers could alter acceptance of aggression as a mode of conduct among these children.

Females in our culture receive strong family training to inhibit display of physical aggression (Sears, Maccoby, and Levin, 1957; Sears, 1961). There is much variance in that training. Nevertheless, it would seem fruitful for future research to focus, not on whether television violence stimulates girls to initative acts of violence, but rather on whether the content of televised violence induces more proaggression attitudes—greater tolerance of violence and more reliance on its effectiveness. These attitudes could be in turn passed on to their own children by those women who become mothers.

## FOOTNOTES

1. The research upon which this report is based was performed pursuant to Contract No. HSM 42-70-32 with the National Institute of Mental Health, Health Services and Mental Health Administration, U.S. Department of Health, Education and Welfare. Professor Dominick is now at Queens College, New York City.

## REFERENCES

Allinsmith, B., cited in D. Miller and G. Swanson. *Inner conflict and defense.* New York: Holt, Rinehart, and Winston, 1960.

Bandura, A. Influence of models' reinforcement contingent on the acquisition of imitative responses. *Journal of Personality and Social Psychology*, 1965, **5**, 589-95.

Buss, A.B., and Durkee, A. Assessing different kinds of hostility. *Journal of Consulting Psychology*, 1957, **21**, 343-48.

Chaffee, S.H., and McLeod, J.M. Adolescent television use in the family context. In *Television and social behavior:* report to the Surgeon General's Scientific Advisory Committee (Vol. 3). Washington. D.C.: U.S. Government Printing Office, 1971.

Gerbner, G. The television world. In Baker, R.K., and Ball, S.J. (Eds.) *Mass media and violence:* staff report to the National Commission on the Causes and Prevention of Violence. Washington, D.C.: U.S. Government Printing Office, 1969.

Gerbner. G. The case for cultural indicators. Paper presented at the American Political Science Association, September 1969 (b).

Greenberg. B.. and Dominick, J. Race and social class differences in teenagers' use of television. *Journal of Broadcasting.* 1969, **13**, 331-44.

Greenberg. B.. and Dominick, J. Television behavior among disadvantaged children. In Greenberg. B.. and Dervin, B. *Use of the mass media by the urban poor.* New York: Praeger, 1967.

Greenberg. B.. and Gordon, T. Perceptions of violence in TV programs: critics and the public. In *Television and social behavior:* a report to the Surgeon General's Scientific Advisory Committee (Vol. 1). Washington, D.C.: U.S. Government Printing Office, 1971.

Hicks, D. Imitation and retention of film-mediated peer and adult models. *Journal of Personality and Social Psychology,* 1965, **2**, 97-100.

Himmelweit, H., Oppenheim, A.N., and Vince, P. *Television and the child.* New York: Oxford University Press, 1958.

Larsen, O.N., Gray, L., and Fortis, J. Goals and goal-achievement methods in television content: models for anomie? *Social Inquiry,* 1963, **33**, 180-96.

Levin, H., and Sears, R.R. Identification with parents as a determinant of doll play aggression. *Child Development,* 1956, **27**, 135-53.

Maccoby, E. Effects of the mass media. In Hoffman, M., and Hoffman, L. *Review of child development research.* New York: Russell Sage Foundation, 1964.

Maccoby, E., and Gibbs, P. Methods of child-rearing in two social classes. In Martin, W., and Stendler, C. *Readings in child development.* New York: Harcourt, Brace, and World, 1954.

McLeod, J., Chaffee, S., and Eswara, H. S. Family communication patterns and communication research. Paper presented to the Association for Education in Journalism, 1966.

McLeod, J., Chaffee, S., and Wackman, D. Family communication: an updated report. Paper presented to the Association for Education in Journalism, 1967.

Minuchin, S., Braulio, J., Gurney, J., Risman, B., and Schumer, F. *Families of the slums.* New York: Basic Books, 1967.

Sakuma, A. Values and the mass media. Unpublished paper, Syracuse University, 1968.

Schramm, W., Lyle, J., and Parker, E. *Television in the lives of our children.* Stanford: Stanford University Press, 1961.

Sears, R.R. A theoretical framework for personality and social behavior. *American Psychologist,* 1951, **6**, 476-83.

Sears, R.R., Maccoby, E., and Levin, H. *Patterns of child rearing.* New York: Row, Peterson, 1957.

Sears, R.R. Relation of early socialization experiences to aggression in middle childhood. *Journal of Abnormal and Social Psychology*, 1961, **63**, 466-92.

Sewell, W.H., Mussen, P.H., and Harris, C.W. Relationships among child training practices. *American Sociological Review*, 1955, **20** 136-48.

Snedecor, G.W. *Statistical methods*. Ames, Iowa: Iowa State University Press, 1956.

Stempel, G. Unpublished study cited in Baker and Ball (Eds.) *Mass media and violence*.

Troldahl, V. Occupational prestige scale. Department of Communication, Michigan State University, 1967 (mimeo).

U.S. National Commission on Civil Disorders. *Report of the National Commission on Civil Disorders*. New York: Bantam Books, 1968.

Walters, J.D., Pearce, D., and Dahms, L. Affectional and aggressive behavior of preschool children. *Child Development*, 1957, **28**, 15-26.

# Mass Media Use and Aggression: A Pilot Study

Herbert L. Friedman and Raymond L. Johnson

*American Institutes for Research*

The literature of research attempting to relate television programming to subsequent aggression on the part of its viewers presents a very confusing picture. The most clearcut evidence of the existence of such a relationship comes from laboratory studies whose subjects were not drawn from groups particularly noted for their aggression (Weiss, 1970). On the other hand, evidence from survey samples among adolescents and young adults—the groups responsible for most violent behavior in society—is contradictory (Eron, 1963; Schramm, Lyle, and Parker, 1961). No in-depth studies have been conducted which have attempted to identify specific ways in which television viewing might adversely affect youths who are predisposed to violent behavior.

The purpose of this pilot study was to advance understanding of the possible relationship between television viewing and social aggressiveness among adolescent boys. Attention was focused on developing adequate instruments for collecting and assessing data on the two topic areas.

## PROCEDURES

A junior high school in Baltimore was selected as the source of interviewees because of its racial (50 percent black and 50 percent white) and socioeconomic (predominantly blue and white collar families) mix of students. The director of research and development of the Baltimore public school system and the principal of the chosen school gave full cooperation to the researchers.

The vice principal in charge of discipline and the school counselors selected 19 white and 20 black eighth and ninth grade boys who had records of interpersonal aggressiveness in school. This group of 39 "aggressive" male students was matched with 41 other boys (equally drawn from both races) from the same classes who did not have notable records of aggressiveness. (Valuable consultation was provided throughout the project by a psychiatrist, Dr. Herbert S. Gross, of the University of Maryland School of Medicine.)

Robert L. Derbyshire, Ph.D., director of the Division of Human Relations and Urban Studies of the Psychiatric Institute of the University of Maryland School of Medicine, was retained as the supervisor of interviewing. Dr. Derbyshire provided and supervised the staff of interviewers, who were selected from participants in the Mental Hygiene Technicians Career program of the University of Maryland.

Since the investigators were interested in obtaining responses to numerous items in a number of different topic areas, they decided that the respondents would be asked to complete two separate questionnaires. This procedure would minimize the possibility of overtaxing the attention span of the subjects, would permit different kinds of answers to similar questions (i.e., enable the respondents to give both open- and closed-ended responses to some questions), and would compare the effectiveness of each of two ways of asking questions. In addition, the investigators felt some items lent themselves particularly well to one or the other of the two question methods used.

The first questionnaire was a paper and pencil form which was administered to subjects in a group setting. It required about 35 minutes to complete and, with a few exceptions, was made up of closed-ended, objective questions with appropriate response boxes to be checked off by the subjects. The ten-page questionnaire explored the subjects' television viewing parameters (time spent watching television; types and frequency of particular programs viewed; reasons for viewing; and complaints about television content) and their attitudes toward aggression (definitions of situations calling for aggressive actions; reactions to aggressive actions; personal propensities toward overt aggression, indirect aggression, and verbal aggression as taken from the Buss-Durkee scale and the Sears aggression scale).

The second questionnaire was an open-ended interview administered to each boy individually by a professional interviewer. The interview required about one hour and allowed each respondent to express in his own words the way he felt about many of the same aspects of television and social behavior covered in the first questionnaire.

The questions asked covered:

1) Favorite television programs: aspects of programs enjoyed, things learned from the programs, reality of the programs, characters enjoyed, least favorite programs, favorite advertisements;

2) Factors in a particular day's viewing. For each program watched on the preceding day, the subject was asked how much attention he paid to the program; his reason for choosing that program; how much he recalled of the program's plot; how he evaluated the program; who watched it with him and whether they influenced the program's selection; what parts of the program's content were upsetting; what parts were worth seeing again; what parts were missed because of other activity;

3) Television news programs: frequency of viewing; complaints about news; news material that was upsetting; reactions to coverage of the Vietnam war, civil disorders, and local news;

4) Use of other media: frequency of use and appealing content in newspapers, magazines, movies, and radio;

5) Personal sports activity and viewing of sports on television;

6) Background information: age, grades in school, parental occupations and education, place of birth, ages and sex of siblings, and number of close friends; and

7) Self-reported participation in antisocial activities.

Each of the 80 adolescent subjects completed one questionnaire administered in a group setting and one conducted by a professional interviewer during an individual interview session.

To encourage cooperation, the students were paid one dollar to complete each of the two questionnaires. Because of the many variances in students' individual schedules, school holidays, and the differences in the time required to get individual parents to consent to their child's participation, the interviews were scattered over several weeks. The majority of the group questionnaires were completed at school, though a few were administered in the interviewees' homes.

The group questionnaire was the least successful of the two in terms of completeness of responses and ease of administration. (The group questionnaire probably should be administered to groups no larger than ten or 15. In this study, a group of 30 behaved with greater cooperativeness and responsiveness than did the group of 57 students who were first treated.)

The setting of the individual interview is an important factor. When the interview was conducted in a quiet room at school, the subjects demonstrated considerable "openness" and seemed willing to respond with sincerity. When the interviews were conducted at home, particularly when siblings or parents were present, responses were more guarded and less expansive.

While individual interviews with the "aggressive" group of students were more difficult to arrange, members of this group tended to answer interview questions more honestly and thoughtfully than members of the "nonaggressive" group.

The use of two questionnaires with some question overlap between them gave rise to the suspicion among the interviewees that the repetition was an attempt to check on the honesty of their responses. The interviewers commented that when a question previously answered on the group questionnaire was repeated at the individual interview session, the subjects seemed to be less accurate and sincere in their responses.

# RESULTS

Three general research questions were explored in this study:

1. What types of mass media did teenage boys pay attention to in the early part of 1970?

2. Were there significant differences among boys labeled aggressive and nonaggressive in attention to and selection of this media content?

3. Could aggressive and nonaggressive boys be accurately distinguished by various self-administered questionnaire items?

*Media usage.* That these boys watch a good deal of television—between two and six hours on an average day—was obvious before the study began, but the exact amount of reported viewing depended on the question being asked. The respondents gave higher figures when asked how much TV they viewed "on an average day" than when asked about "yesterday," and both estimates were higher than when they were asked to check from a list all the specific programs they viewed on the preceding day. It is obvious that better measurement tools need to be employed to provide accurate estimates of actual viewing time.

In obtaining information about specific television content viewed by the subjects, the investigators found considerable agreement of responses to the interview and self-administered questionnaire approaches. Both methods showed that the boys' favorite programs were *Mod*

*Squad, It Takes a Thief, Hawaii Five-0, Mission Impossible, The Court-ship of Eddie's Father, Marcus Welby, M.D., The FBI, Laugh-In* and *The Bill Cosby Show.* Three programs—*The New People, Room 222* and *Music Scene*—were rated higher on the open-ended question form than on the checklist, and two programs—*Land of the Giants* and *Adam-12*—were rated higher on the checklist than in the open-ended questioning. More than half of these favorites are shows which emphasize a considerable amount of violent and aggressive behavior. Such programs were seldom mentioned spontaneously when the boys were asked to name three programs they would like to have taken off the air.

Television characters that these boys said they "would most like to be" tended to be drawn from these favorite programs. Alexander Mundy ( *It Takes a Thief* ), Linc Hayes ( *Mod Squad* ), Pete Dixon ( *Room 222* ), and Bill Cosby were among those most frequently named. However, three of the most popular characters—Tom Jones, Bronson, and Mannix—were drawn from less heavily viewed shows.

The boys were equally divided on the question of whether they had learned more about life in school or from television. However, when queried about what they had learned specifically from their favorite dramatic programs, less than half could give a concrete example. Those things they did list ranged from new words to the necessity of regular doctor visits; from (perhaps inaccurately) the way police and government agencies work to how life was in the Old West; from what it is like to take dope to how to get along without a parent; from methods of committing crime to the lesson that crime doesn't pay. The investigators were reminded of the Schramm, Lyle, and Parker (1961) conclusion that what children do to television is a better statement of the problem than what television does to children. A more complete listing of open-ended responses to questions about the ten most popular programs is presented in Appendix A.

The boys mentioned "enjoyment" and "time-killing" most often as general reasons for viewing. Nine in ten said they "usually" watched television to view a specific program they enjoyed very much; yet when asked about the programs they viewed on the preceeding day, the boys described 25 percent of them as "a waste of time." Twenty-nine percent of the total programs viewed on the day preceeding the interview "just came on" the particular channel the boys were watching. These reasons for watching are quite similar to those given by adults in Steiner's (1962) nationwide study, although the teenagers were more willing to admit they watch because "there is nothing better to do" or because they "get stuck for an evening" and less likely to say they view to "learn something." (Less than one in four said he usually watched television for this reason.) The boys in this study were considerably more likely than Steiner's adults to say they watched because they "might be missing something good."

Few of these teenagers felt there was too much sex (15 percent of the total group) or too much violence (20 percent on the television screen. Only 24 voiced any complaints at all, and only two boys spontaneously mentioned violence when asked for their complaints about television. More objectionable to these respondents were too many advertisements (80 percent) and too many news programs and news specials (65 percent). Blacks thought there should be more black actors in programs and advertisements; whites agreed with them about ads but not about regular programs.

The boys were critical of commercials and skeptical about their trustworthiness, social utility, entertainment value, or realism. Blacks were less negative about advertising than whites, however.

In response to questions about their specific television viewing on the day preceding the individual interviews, the boys indicated three-quarters of their viewing was done when they were alone in the viewing situation; even if others were present, the boys said they gave the program their complete attention. There seemed to be little conflict with others over choice of programs, and few respondents were unable to recall the main highlights of each program viewed. More than one boy in five reported being bothered or upset by something he had seen on television the previous day. While sports were the major source of dismay for these boys (if their favorite team lost the game), a variety of other concerns were also reported. These included: "A girl (in a movie) who was running around with other men even though she was married," "A man (in *Room 222*) tried to talk a student into going to a college who did not have good economic standing," "When the good guy always wins—that makes me mad," "A woman (in *The Survivors*) was about to stab the girl," and "The way the boys (in *The New People*) treated the colored boy."

More than half of the boys indicated their involvement with the programs by saying that there was something on television that day that they would like to see again. In addition, over one-quarter said that due to other obligations they missed something on television that they had wanted to watch. On the other hand, almost half said that there was some time during the day they wanted to watch television but didn't because there wasn't anything worthwhile on the air at that time.

One-third of these teenagers said they never watched either network or local news programs, but half said they watched at least two such programs each week. About 20 percent of the boys said they had seen things on television news that bothered or upset them; and in contrast with the entertainment programs, most of the disturbing news content dealt with violence (especially related to the fighting in Vietnam). Three respondents complained about local news coverage, one noting that this news should be broadcast throughout the day, another citing the lack of detailed local news, and the third wanting more pictures on the news.

One youngster was disturbed by "the way cameramen bug people who don't want to be bothered." There was little consensus about whether the media had given too much coverage to the fighting in Vietnam or to civil disorders.

Three-quarters of respondents said they read a newspaper at least a few times a week, and 43 percent said they read it every day. The comics appeared to be the most popular item in the newspaper[1]; sports ran a close second, the front page a distant third. Stories about "shootings and robberies" aroused more interest than those about Vietnam or civil disorders. Political stories were "skipped over" by 77 percent of these boys.

About 60 percent of the boys reported reading a magazine regularly. *Life, Look, Sports Illustrated,* and *Boy's Life* were read most often. Sixty-two percent of the boys said they read hot rod magazines, 35 percent read gun magazines, and 20 percent read crime and detective magazines.

Roughly three-quarters of the subjects had seen a movie during the previous six months, and 33 percent averaged at least one movie a month. Particularly favorite movies cited were rather high in violent content: *On Her Majesty's Secret Service* (the latest James Bond movie), *Butch Cassidy and the Sundance Kid, Goldfinger, Bullitt,* and *Bonnie and Clyde.* Less violent movies mentioned more than once included *The Reivers* and *Gone with the Wind.* Well over half the favorite movies listed seemed to have a high emphasis on violence, and practically all of the reasons that the teenagers gave for liking these movies had to do with the violence they contained. *(Cougan's Bluff:* "I like how the detectives crack down on people"; *Bonnie and Clyde* showed "cool robberies"; *Boston Strangler:* "I liked the fact he was killing women.")

Music is almost the sole reason that these boys listened to the radio two and one-half hours per day. Half of them listened to only one station. When asked to make a choice, 31 percent said they would most enjoy listening to their favorite music; 56 percent would rather watch their favorite television program, and 13 percent would rather read their favorite magazine.

Interest in playing and watching football was practically unanimous. Only about 10 percent had not played any football in the fall of 1969, and not one respondent had not seen at least one televised National Football League (NFL) game. The average respondent had seen three college games, ten NFL games, and four American Football League (AFL) games during the previous season. Twelve percent of the boys reported having watched more than ten college games. Sixteen percent reported having watched more than ten AFL games, and 49 percent reported having watched more than ten NFL games. There seemed little doubt that professional football had more appeal than the college game; many respondents mentioned that they preferred the pro game because of its more intense physical contact.

Presented with a list developed by the Michigan Survey Research Center's study of juvenile delinquency, respondents were asked to check off specific acts of antisocial behavior in which they had engaged. The results were much like those obtained from a nationwide study of tenth grade boys (except for school problems like expulsion). Sixty-two percent reported that they got into a serious fight with another student in school; 50 percent had taken part in a gang fight; 42 percent had gotten something by telling a person that something bad would happen to him if he did not cooperate; 25 percent had hurt someone badly enough to need bandages or a doctor; ten percent had hit a teacher, eight percent had used a knife or gun to get something from a person; five percent had hit their fathers; and five percent had hit their mothers.

*Differences between "aggressive" and "nonaggressive" boys.* The "aggressive" boys were considerably more likely than the nonaggressive boys to report getting into fights, participating in gang fights, hitting a teacher, or using a gun or knife to "get something" from another person. Overall, aggressive whites admitted to an average of seven aggressive acts; nonaggressive whites reported three. The distinction among blacks was consistent with this finding, but far less significant: 4.1 aggressive acts were admitted by aggressives and 3.5 by non-aggressives. Thus there was independent evidence to support the judgment of school counselors in assigning students to the aggressive and nonaggressive groups.[2]

Unfortunately for our research purposes, boys of both races who were tagged "aggressive" were significantly more likely to come from working class homes in which parents had less formal education.[3] This circumstance leads to some confusion about whether the differences were due to aggressiveness or to social status.

On all three questions about time spent viewing (average day estimate, previous day estimate, log of previous day), the "aggressive" boys reported roughly 20 percent more viewing than the "nonaggressives." However, when presented with a list of evening programs and asked to check those which they had seen at least five times during the previous fifteen weeks, the aggressive boys indicated far less viewing than the nonaggressive boys. Table 1 shows the breakdowns by race and by aggressiveness among the groups.

There were distinct differences among the groups in naming the top ten favorite dramatic series offered on the commercial networks (movies are not considered in Table 1). Aggressive whites listed eight violent programs among their top ten, while nonaggressive whites listed five. Among blacks the aggressives listed six, the nonaggressives three.[4]

In absolute viewing rates (as opposed to the Table 1 relative rates of viewing), however, no differences between aggressives and nonaggressives emerge, with one exception: the aggressive boys of both races viewed *Then Came Bronson* (a program not on the top ten listing of any of the four groups in Table 1) more than did nonaggressives.[5] The main reason for the overall lack of differences may be that nonaggressives listed more programs viewed than did aggressives.

Table 1: Television programs viewed most frequently by four types of boys (percent viewing program at least once between September and January in parentheses)

| Aggressive whites | | Nonaggressive whites | |
|---|---|---|---|
| 1. | *The FBI* (93) | 1. | *Mod Squad* (85) |
| 2. | *Mod Squad* (87) | 2. | *Bill Cosby* (80) |
| 3. | *Land of the Giants* (73) | 3. | *Land of the Giants* (75) |
| 4. | *Adam-12* (73) | 4. | *Courtship of Eddie's Father* (75) |
| 5. | *It Takes a Thief* (73) | 5. | *Mission Impossible* (74) |
| 6. | *Music Scene* (71) | 6. | *Hawaii Five-O* (74) |
| 7. | *Gunsmoke* (69) | 7. | *Laugh-In* (70) |
| 8. | *Hawaii Five-O* (69) | 8. | *Newlywed Game* (70) |
| 9. | *Mission Impossible* (76) | 9. | *Room 222* (68) |
| 10. | *Room 222* (67) | 10. | *Adam-12* (63) |

| Aggressive blacks | | Nonaggressive blacks | |
|---|---|---|---|
| 1. | *Mod Squad* (92) | 1. | *Bewitched* (94) |
| 2. | *It Takes a Thief* (85) | 2. | *Mod Squad* (94) |
| 3. | *Hawaii Five-O* (85) | 3. | *Room 222* (93) |
| 4. | *Room 222* (85) | 4. | *It Takes a Thief* (88) |
| 5. | *Mannix* (85) | 5. | *Mayberry RFD* (88) |
| 6. | *Mission Impossible* (79) | 6. | *Ed Sullivan* (88) |
| 7. | *Laugh-In* (79) | 7. | *Green Acres* (88) |
| 8. | *Julia* (77) | 8. | *Bill Cosby* (88) |
| 9. | *Walt Disney* (77) | 9. | *Petticoat Junction* (87) |
| 10. | *Land of the Giants* (77) | 10. | *Land of the Giants* (84) |

The conclusion that does emerge from both the relative and absolute viewing rates (derived from the check list) is that the aggressive boys view family comedy shows like *The Courtship of Eddie's Father, My Three Sons, Green Acres,* and *Family Affair* with considerable distaste. The same conclusion emerges from an analysis of the questionnaire item which asked respondents to list their four favorite programs. The number of times family comedies were listed was twice as high among nonaggressives as among aggressives.

The aggressive boys listed an average of 1.8 violent programs among the four programs they said were their favorites, while the non-aggressives listed an average of 1.6. On other questions, aggressives were only half as likely as nonaggressives to name a violent program as one they would like to take off the air. Not one aggressive boy spontaneously mentioned excess violence to the interviewer as a complaint about television.

Aggressive boys were also less likely to agree with the statement that there was "too much violence" on television. (Thirteen percent agreed versus 30 percent of the nonaggressives.) In line with their rejection of family comedy shows, the aggressives were more likely to endorse the statement (74 percent versus 52 percent of the nonaggressives) that there were "not enough comedy shows" on television. No further systematic differences of this magnitude between the two groups could be found among other complaints about television or television commercials.

The two groups differed little about other viewing parameters such as things learned, the amount of realism subjects felt the shows depicted, and preference for the stories over the characters in the stories. There was some evidence of more selective and intensive viewing among aggressives: aggressives were more likely to use television guides; they had greater ability to recall program themes; they were more likely to report being upset or bothered by some of what they saw on television; they appeared to regret missing their favorite programs more; and they reported a higher incidence of turning off the set because of poor program choice. However, many of these factors would have to be adjusted by more extensive analyses because the aggressives viewed more programs.

There were no systematic differences between the two groups in the amount of television news watched. However, while the aggressive boys voiced more complaints about news programs, they reported being less upset by specific news content than the nonaggressive boys.

Differences in the amount and type of newspaper and magazine reading between the two groups were not significant, although aggressives reported somewhat more interest in newspaper stories about shootings and robberies than about riots and civil disorders. Aggressives were more likely to name *Popeye, Dick Tracy,* and *Peanuts* as their favorite comic strips.

More noteworthy differences emerged in responses about movie attendance and radio listening. Aggressives attended movies less often than nonaggressives, but when they did attend, their favorite movies tended to be considerably more violent than the favorites of nonaggressive boys. Aggressive boys listened to the radio more, and they were more than twice as likely as nonaggressives to say they would prefer listening to their favorite music to watching television or reading a magazine.[6]

Aggressives were no more likely than nonaggressives to report active engagement in sports, nor did they watch more football on television. The aggressives felt that they had significantly more close friends than nonaggressives thought *they* had, and they were less likely to have been born in the Baltimore area. Their grades in school (60 percent had a C average or below) were considerably lower than those of nonaggressive boys.

*Discriminating power of aggression items.* The various psychological inventories used in this research effort failed to distinguish with satisfactory validity between the aggressive and the nonaggressive boys. The experimenters hoped that this pretest would provide a base for developing a short scale of optimal reliability and validity which could be used to relate personal aggressiveness to the viewing of violent television content. Of the 85 items drawn from various scales, less than ten elicited substantial response differences between aggressives and nonaggressives.[7] Items from the scales with widest use, those of Buss-Durkee (1957) and Sears (described in Schramm, Lyle, and Parker, 1961) fared less well than those from other sources. As can be seen in Table 2, only two Buss-Durkee items and one Sears item showed satisfactory validity. The lack of satisfactory discrimination held for entire scale scores for these instruments as well as the individual items.

Listed at the bottom of Table 2 are a few items, adapted from a hostility scale developed by Grace (1949), which did generate satisfactory discrimination between aggressives and nonaggressives. The items are in forced choice format and may be seen as verbal equivalents of the Rosenzweig Picture Frustration Test. Even here, however, some items which elicited a good deal of responses in a hostile direction (what would you do if your younger brother is beaten up by an older child, or if a child throws a glass on the floor) failed to discriminate between the two groups.

Table 2: Items showing clear distinctions between aggressives and nonaggressives

|  | Percent agreement | |
|---|---|---|
|  | Aggressives | Nonaggressives |
| Whoever insults me or my family is asking for a fight (Buss—Durkee) | 65 | 44 |
| Lately I have been kind of grouchy (Buss—Durkee) | 52 | 27 |
| Even if you don't like a person, you should still try to help him | 50 | 78 |
| It makes me uncomfortable to see two of my friends fighting (Sears) | 28 | 53 |
| You're waiting in a long line and someone tries to cut in ahead of you. You feel like: a) pushing him out of line | 63 | 52 |
| A friend of yours tells other people a secret about you that embarrasses you. You feel like: b) threatening to beat him up | 45 | 22 |
| A car splashes mud on your clothes. You feel like: c) throwing something at the car | 35 | 23 |

Two sets of items—one asking the respondent if he felt people could be trusted and one probing into his feelings of alienation—were included mainly as "dummy items" to detect possible differential answers due to response set. Aggressives gave slightly more alientated responses than nonaggressives, but much larger differences were obtained with the "trust-in-people" items. As would be expected, aggressive whites evidenced much lower trust in people than nonaggressive whites. These items did not discriminate within the black population, however. Moreover, in this study aggressive blacks were not likely to be much different in self-reported aggressive behaviors than nonaggressive blacks.

*Replicability of these results.* In the previous section we noted some uncomfortable implications of our designation of boys as either aggressive or nonaggressive. Boys noted as aggressive were more likely to come from lower status families. In addition, the aggressive boys were identified as such by school counselors; identification was made on the basis of the boys' misbehavior at school, not on the basis of their interpersonal aggressiveness or self-reported deviancy.

In order to extend the generalizability of our findings, the above analyses were replicated using the self-report aggressive behavior items as the criterion of aggressiveness rather than the designations of school counselors. This procedure did not offer direct control on social class differences, but it was employed as an attempt to provide independent verification of the aggressiveness dimension. A number of the findings did not survive the replication check.

The major casualty of the replication was the set of findings regarding the subject groups' viewing of certain types of television shows. Whereas Table 1 showed aggressives placing almost twice as many violent programs on their top ten list as nonaggressives (in terms of frequency of viewing), exactly the opposite occurred with comparable data from the new groupings based on self-reports. White boys who said that they had engaged in a good deal of aggressive behavior listed six violent programs among their top ten; those who reported themselves less aggressive listed seven. Among blacks, aggressives noted only three violent shows; less aggressives noted six. The earlier findings of aggressive boy's aversion to family comedy shows also failed to hold when this self-report criterion was used for aggression.

On the other hand, the item which asked the boys to list their favorite programs (rather than how often they viewed each program) showed the rate of choice of violent programs among aggressive boys to be even higher than it had been in the previous analyses. Among their four favorites, aggressive boys (according to the self-report criterion) mentioned 2.2 violent programs; less aggressives mentioned 1.5. Furthermore, the aggressives were still only half as likely (12 percent versus 26 percent of nonaggressives) to say that there was too much violence on television.

In the other question areas in which differences between aggressives and nonaggressives had been found in the previous analyses, the record is also mixed. As before, aggressives reported more overall television viewing, but the difference between the groups was less than ten percent; previously it had been 20 percent. Aggressives again appeared slightly more selective in their television viewing habits. In answer to questions about their use of the other mass media, aggressives again reported more attention to newspaper stories about robberies and civil disorders, and again preferred listening to their favorite music to watching their favorite television programs.

In a number of other question areas, the results obtained in the initial analyses failed to hold, but the new criterion resulted in new avenues of exploration. The small sample sizes and definitional problems are already apparent. But it might be constructive to note the personality items which consistently differentiated between aggressives and nonaggressives. Of the seven items in Table 2, the first three[8] and the final items survived replication; these four items deserve special consideration in future questionnaires where measures of aggression are desired.

## CONCLUSIONS

In this brief review of a pilot study of the television habits of 80 teenage boys from a lower middle class urban junior high school, we have found a number of interesting ways in which teenagers interact with the mass media. When attempting to establish a link between television viewing and aggressive behavior, it is necessary to take into account the fact that teenagers are exposed to violence in other media as well. We have seen that while almost half of the subjects' favorite television programs emphasized violence, these adolescents also pay a good deal of attention to newspaper stories emphasizing violence and are quite likely to attend movies in which violence (usually more blatant and prevalent than that shown on television) is a central element. Inquiry into the effects of exposure to popular music might be fruitful, since this study confirms earlier evidence that aggressive boys enjoy popular music more than nonaggressive boys (Halloran, 1969). Inquiring into the ways in which their peers influence boys' perceptions of when aggression and violence are justified would also be useful.

This research has relied on multiple indicators in various question areas: closed-ended and open-ended questions, personal interviews and questionnaires, check-lists and direct questions. As in most research using this multiple indicator approach, the varying research methods do not consistently point in the same direction. On balance, however, more evidence suggests that aggressive boys are more attracted to violent television content than nonaggressive boys than suggests the reverse. This tendency shows up most consistently in responses to questions about favorite television programs and to questions about whether there is "too much violence" on television.

Statistically, however, the results offer no direct evidence of television's "deleterious effects." Much larger and more representative samples and appropriate statistical controls on all the other variables would be needed before any claims of that nature could be advanced. Even with such evidence, researchers will eventually require data on how viewers interact with what they see on the screen on a continuing day-to-day basis before we can begin to understand the processes by which television affects its audience. The data on a single day's viewing habits in this present study reinforce the views of previous researchers (Schramm, Lyle, and Parker, 1961) that there is tremendous variation in how viewers react to television and that we should begin to develop measurement techniques that will reflect the subtle ways in which television "affects" its viewers.

## FOOTNOTES

1. *Blondie, Peanuts, Dick Tracy,* and *Beatle Bailey* were the most popular comic strips.
2. However, the antisocial item that shows greatest distinction was "been suspended or expelled from school," which indicates that the counselors used this as their major criterion of aggression.
3. The following percentage data were obtained for various parental characteristics:

|  | White | | Black | |
| --- | --- | --- | --- | --- |
|  | *Aggr.* | *Nonaggr.* | *Aggr.* | *Nonaggr.* |
| Father attended college | 10% | 40% | 25% | 38% |
| Father in white collar job | 20 | 55 | 15 | 60 |
| Mother attended college | 0 | 17 | 5 | 25 |
| Mother is housewife | 45 | 65 | 25 | 25 |
| Mother in white collar job (if employed) | 75 | 80 | 57 | 93 |

4. The designation of a program as violent conforms to ratings obtained from the critics and the public by Greenberg and Gordon in a separate report to the NIMH Television and Social Behavior program.
5. Bronson was named by aggressive whites as a television personality they would most like to be; and Linc Hayes performed this role for black teenagers. Aggressives and nonaggressives of both races identified with Alexander Mundy, the thief on *It Takes a Thief.*
6. This finding of interest in music jibes with results from a British study of delinquents by Halloran et al. (1969).
7. Almost as many items worked in the opposite direction of that predicted.

8. The Sears item, "It makes me uncomfortable to see two of my friends fighting," is especially interesting theoretically since it suggests that aggressive people value aggression above cognitive balance, the latter phenomenon considered an extremely strong drive by social psychologists.

# REFERENCES

Buss, A., and Durkee, A. An inventory for different kinds of hostility. *Journal of Consulting Psychology*, 1957, 21, 343-49.

Eron, L. Relationship of TV viewing habits and aggressive behavior in children. *Journal of Abnormal and Social Psychology*, 1963, 67, 193-96.

Grace, H. A study of the expression of hostility in everyday, professional, and international verbal situations. Unpublished doctoral dissertation, Columbia University, 1949.

Halloran, J., Brown, R., and Chaney, D. Mass media delinquency project. Appendix A in *Television Research Committee's second progress report and recommendations*. Leicester, England: Leicester University Press, 1969.

Schramm, W., Lyle, J., and Parker, E.B. *Television in the lives of our children*. Stanford, Calif.: Stanford University Press, 1961.

Steiner, G. *The people look at television*. New York: Alfred A. Knopf, 1963.

Weiss, W. Effects of mass media communication. In Lindzey, G., and ronsen, E. (Eds.) *Handbook of social psychology*, Vol. 5. Reading, Mass.: Addison-Wesley, 1970.

# Appendix A: Responses to
# open-end questions
# regarding favorite television programs

Mod Squad

Why watch?

1. like detective stories
2. about young people who become cops
3. lots of fighting and pretty girls
4. police show with kids in it
5. to see who they are going to help
6. exciting climaxes
7. about teenagers and things they do
8. for story and plot
9. like to see how the stars changed from hippies to police work
10. like policemen who fight crime
11. lots of action
12. it is exciting
13. likes detective stories
14. teaches a lesson
15. excitement, adventure
16. different problems of college people who take dope
17. the fights the squad gets into
18. something always active going on
19. exciting
20. likes stories and people
21. learn how today's police work

What is learned from watching this show?

1. learn about different countries
2. that "crime doesn't pay"
3. learn about self-defense
4. about how it is to be on dope
5. learn how to keep out of trouble
6. how police rule
7. learn how guys catch thieves
8. learn about crime
9. people should not steal
10. not to do anything bad around people you don't know
11. how real life is for police officers
12. learn about being addicted to drugs

How is this show realistic?

1. real life things happening to young people
2. shows how easy to get in trouble if not careful
3. stories seem real
4. how they catch robbers
5. students getting killed while participating in rallies
6. situations are not way out
7. how rich people do bad things
8. all the crime that is real
9. shows real crimes
10. shows everyday teens with adult problems
11. shows things like rioting
12. shows how young people get kids their own age out of trouble
13. shows how people are today

How is this show unrealistic?

1. TV hardly ever tells the real truth
2. just not like everyday life
3. I don't believe they have any young cops
4. because all that happens is exaggerated
5. things on show do not happen in real life

Why are people in show liked?

1. like Pete, Linc, and Julie because they are not like other police
2. the kids—they act kinda cool like kids today do
3. the kids—good actors
4. the kids—way they help people out
5. the kids—the experience they have
6. the kids—action they get into
7. shows that black people are just as important as whites
8. way they try to help others

| It Takes a Thief |

Why watch?

1. exciting
2. suspense in the story
3. likes Alexander Mundy
4. exciting—great deal of action
5. different from other shows
6. lots of action, suspense

7. likes fights Mundy is in and tricks he does
8. the way he operates looks real
9. likes private agent shows
10. likes the stories—the way Munday has different assignments
11. unusual—man steals for the U.S.

What is learned from watching this show?

1. educational because he travels to foreign lands
2. learn about government
3. learn what foreign countries are like

How is this show realistic?

1. way he steals looks professional
2. in real life there is a secret service and thieves
3. way they get their information

How is this show unrealistic?

1. not natural life
2. because no thief steals and gets away with it all the time
3. gets out of jams unrealistically
4. fictitious stories
5. too phony

Why are people in show liked?

1. Mundy—the way he's never afraid
2. Mundy—seems so smooth a person
3. Mundy—because he acts like he really knows what he's doing
4. Mundy—plays especially cool like nothing is happening
5. the way they do their thing

Hawaii Five-0

Why watch?

1. filmed in Hawaii
2. likes detectives
3. likes the 'chasing' action
4. good plot, interested in law and police action
5. mysterious happenings
6. people getting shot
7. likes the way the police arrest people

What is learned from watching this show?

1. that crime doesn't pay
2. how he captures criminals
3. how to be a detective
4. how criminals escape
5. how to find criminals

How is this show realistic?

1. criminals get chased
2. programs seem as if they could really happen
3. lots of realistic devious methods of criminals
4. the crimes are punished
5. because they base shows on real crime

Mission Impossible

Why watch?

1. to see how they make all kinds of escapes
2. lots of action and suspense
3. likes private agent shows
4. shows different problems government has
5. stories with weird gadgets
6. suspenseful, can't tell what's coming next

What is learned from watching this show?

1. learn that some people can be detectives; learn the problems involved in crime
2. how to handle people in an organization
3. way some people try to overrun governments
4. how to operate gadgets

How is this show both realistic and unrealistic?

1. stories could be real, but not ways missions are carried out

How is this show unrealistic?

1. people aren't as mean as some of the characters
2. might be done but isn't real

Courtship of Eddie's Father

Why watch?

1. like the little boy
2. shows how small boy and father get along
3. like the sense in boy
4. like Eddie
5. for the trouble boys get into
6. cute, educational, it's funny
7. likes how boy and father get along without mother

What is learned from watching this show?

1. how some people have to get along without one parent
2. how a small boy lives without a mother
3. when you're in trouble you should tell your parents so they can help you
4. learn about how little kids ask questions

How is this show realistic?

1. how kids without mothers do the best they can
2. how the father helps Eddie learn right from wrong
3. how Eddie confronts his dad with why not fight with girls
4. how some people can tell parents about their troubles without being punished
5. how some people live with only one parent

Why are people in show liked?

1. Eddie's father understands his son
2. Eddie and father play their parts well
3. Eddie is advanced for his age
4. Eddie and his dad get along so well

Marcus Welby, M.D.

Why watch?

1. adventures
2. the doctor is real and is like a father image
3. shows real people having medical problems
4. find out different diseases
5. shows different problems of a doctor

What is learned from watching this show?

1. more about medicine and human drama
2. how doctor gets involved with patients
3. how they go about operations
4. how to treat medical problems

How is this show realistic?

1. there are doctors like Marcus Welby
2. Dr. Welby's character is real
3. problems similar to those of my friends
4. good account of some things in real life
5. operations seem real

Why are people in show liked?

1. way they try to help people
2. Welby never panics
3. Welby, understanding father image

## The New People

Why watch?

1. entertaining
2. how young people can act mature and live on an island
3. comedy—like it
4. young people and adults are appealing
5. teaches a lesson
6. likes idea of starting new civilization
7. likes the teenagers in it
8. likes different ways they live on the island and how they try to get off
9. learn how people live on deserted islands
10. interesting stories
11. fun the way they started a new life

What is learned from watching this show?

1. truth of segregation
2. shows how to survive stranded on an island
3. teenagers could start their own civilization and have own laws
4. shouldn't join bad groups
5. why teens fight and have arguments

6. that not all young people take pot
7. about taking dope

How is this show realistic?

1. people take dope as in real life and also lots of realistic fights
2. plots are realistic
3. the people seem sorta real
4. trying to promote unity like the world today
5. people gamble in real life
6. yes, because it *could* happen

Why are people in show liked?

1. George—he's strong and smart
2. act like teenagers of today
3. leader—way he keeps control over everyone

### Room 222

Why watch?

1. related to show life
2. likes stories with kids in them
3. to get a laugh—funny show
4. learn about classroom life
5. not too funny nor too serious
6. because it is funny
7. likes the comedy
8. shows what real life is like
9. interesting facts about daily life
10. all about school—people are up to date
11. it's funny—not everyday thing

What is learned from watching this show?

1. shows clothes and things that really happen in school
2. how high school students behave, their manners, how they deal with teachers
3. how to choose a college
4. how problems can be worked out
5. you can get into trouble in school easily

How is this show realistic?

1. shows how people live and behave
2. shows all races work and live together

3. shows true high school life
4. believe people really act this way
5. can see some of the characters in my friends
6. most of the things really happen
7. same courses
8. same things happen in my school
9. things on show really happen in school
10. faculty and kids help each other in realistic way

How is this show unrealistic?

1. teachers don't act as in real life
2. teachers pick on individual students instead of letting students volunteer

Why are people in show liked?

1. Pete is a good teacher, doesn't just teach
2. Dixon, the way he teaches history
3. Jason, way he smiles
4. Karen because she's silly
5. Pete is smart and understanding
6. they act realistically
7. objectivity of people and liberalness
8. Dixon's understanding toward kids

### Gunsmoke

Why watch?

1. entertainment, comical action
2. likes to see show-downs
3. likes cowboy stories
4. likes cowboy shows
5. shooting guns
6. likes westerns
7. likes westerns, hard life and guns and horses

What is learned from watching this show?

1. ways different people act
2. how life was in the past
3. learn not to steal because you'll get caught anyway
4. learns about old west

How is this show realistic?

1. shows real life in long ago west
2. real life when Marshall Dillon grew up
3. Marshall had to clean out the fast shooters
4. duel and gun draws

How is this show unrealistic?

1. westerns aren't real for today
1. western days are over
3. aren't that many fights in real life

Why are people in show liked?

1. the characters' fighting is comical
2. characters are good actors
3. especially Festus and Marshall Dillon

## Then Came Bronson

Why watch?

1. interesting way Bronson is so free
2. way he drives motorcycle
3. lots of action, travels all over
4. because of his understanding of problems and way of helping others
5. always wanted a motorcycle
6. Bronson's cool and free and travels all over
7. Bronson's always free despite how people get involved with one another
8. because he sings and does different things

What is learned from watching this show?

1. how people react to freeness
2. likes where he travels—would like to do it
3. about dishonest situations and how young people must be careful
4. need an education to move up—can't live on motorcycle alone

How is this show realistic?

1. different patterns of living around the U.S.A.
2. many real life situations

  3. in life you see free guys riding around like Bronson
  4. men do roam country like Bronson
  5. lots of teens travel and like to be on their own
  6. shows how a person can work to help others

How is this show both realistic and unrealistic?

  1. situations sometimes real, sometimes not

Why are people in show liked?

  1. especially Bronson
  2. especially Bronson because he rides motorcycle and has long
     hair
  3. especially Bronson's sensibility, what he thinks
  4. Bronson—his understanding toward people

# Four Masculine Styles in Television Programming: A Study of the Viewing Preferences of Adolescent Males

Raymond L. Johnson, Herbert L. Friedman
*American Institutes for Research*
and
Herbert S. Gross
*University of Maryland School of Medicine*

The influence of television in changing a person's attitudes or behavior may be most evident when the person is already undergoing change. While experiencing the uncertainties of transition, a person becomes active and purposeful in seeking relevant information (Feather, 1967), and television can be a ready and profuse source. In this study, we attempted to interpret observed patterns of selective exposure to television programs as an instance of information seeking stimulated by one of the major transition phases in human development, the onset of adolescence.[1]

Erikson (1968) describes adolescence as one of the eight critical periods of change in the life cycle of an individual. The male, at about age 14, begins to consolidate a sense of identity around the biological nucleus of his maturing sexuality. He searches for a way of thinking about himself that provides a coherent account of his childhood successes and failures, enabling him to view his own life in continuous perspective. At the same time, he is concerned with the question of what kind of man he might become:

> Young people, beset with the physiological revolution of their genital maturation and the uncertainty of the adult roles ahead. . .are. . .preoccupied with what they appear to be in the eyes of others as compared with what they feel they are, and with the question of how to connect the roles and skills cultivated earlier with the ideal prototypes of the day (Erikson, 1968, p. 128).

To achieve a viable concept of the self, the boy chooses and conforms to a masculine style from among the options available in the society. The definition of manliness which the boy adopts as his own will enter into the formation of his sense of identity. Television programs portray a wide variety of masculine styles, and this aspect may become television's most salient feature for adolescent boys seeking information about ideal prototypes.

The purpose of this study was to identify and describe some of the styles of masculine behavior depicted on programs especially popular among teenage viewers. The end result was a provisional classification schema for television programs, based upon variants of the masculine "image."

# METHOD

*Subjects.* The eighty boys who participated in this study attended the eighth grade of a racially mixed junior high school in a lower-to-middle-income neighborhood of Baltimore, Maryland. School counselors selected 39 boys with histories of aberrant social aggressiveness and 41 who had not exhibited marked aggressive tendencies.

|  | White ($A_1$) | Black ($A_2$) |
|---|---|---|
| Aggressive ($B_1$) | n=20 <br> $A_1B_1$ | n=19 <br> $A_2B_1$ |
| Non-aggressive ($B_2$) | n=20 <br> $A_1B_2$ | n=21 <br> $A_2B_2$ |

Table 1: Types of adolescent male viewers. The two variables used to categorize the subjects (race and interpersonal behavior) are designated by the letters A and B, respectively.

*Procedure.* Subjects filled out a questionnaire which listed all prime time (7:30-11 p.m.) network television programs seen in the Baltimore area during the 1969-70 season. The instructions were to indicate which programs a subject had watched at least five times in the preceding four months (the period from September to December).

*Data Analysis.* The plan of this study was to empirically construct a classification schema for a set of selected television programs. Relationships among the programs were inferred from the degree of overlapping (i.e., substantially duplicated) audience. Our assumption was that programs attracting the same viewers portrayed similar versions of the masculine role. By ranking programs on the basis of shared audience, it was possible to identify programs similar in appeal and to form hypotheses about the nature of the shared attributes. Once abstracted, the attributes provided the conceptual framework needed to construct a classification schema.

As the initial step in constructing the schema, 12 programs were selected for detailed examination. Discarded were programs popular among all four groups of subjects: *Mod Squad, Room 222, It Takes a Thief, Bill Cosby, Hawaii Five-0, Land of the Giants.* Retained were programs more likely to have been frequently watched by the viewers belonging to one group than by those belonging to the other three. *The FBI,* for example, was watched (at least five times) by 80 percent of white aggressive viewers, while 63 percent of the others indicated they had seen the program that often. White aggressives were also more likely to have often watched *Then Came Bronson* (55 percent, compared with 30 percent for others) and were slightly more attracted to *Adam 12* (65 percent, others 60 percent). White nonaggressives showed a differentiating preference for *The Courtship of Eddie's Father* (75 percent, others 63 percent), *The Newlywed Game* (70 percent, others 50 percent), and *My Three Sons* (55 percent, others 30 percent). Popular programs among black aggressive boys were *Mannix* (84 percent, others 60 percent), *Mission Impossible* (84 percent, others 65 percent), and *Julia* (74 percent, others 45 percent). Black nonaggressives were more likely than others to have watched *Bewitched* (76 percent, others 60 percent), *Green Acres* (76 percent, others 55 percent), and *Mayberry R.F.D.* (67 percent, others 40 percent). The program preferences of each group of subjects were thus represented by three different programs.

To measure the audience overlap among these twelve programs, the identities of the viewers watching any two programs were determined, and tallies were made of the number who watched both programs, the number who watched one but not the other, and the number who reported watching neither program. These frequency tallies were cast in the form of two-by-two tables, and a phi-coefficient was computed as an index of correlation between each of the 66 pairs of programs.

The phi-coefficients were then used to rank-order the programs on the basis of audience overlap. But this step raised a procedural question: where should the list begin? There was no necessary starting point. Hence, the ranking had to be a circular one which would allow each program, in turn, to be ranked first. Our approach was to attempt to arrange the phi-coefficients to form a circumplex (Guttman, 1966).

In a correlation matrix exhibiting "circumplicial" structure, the correlations are largest next to the principal diagonal which runs from the upper left corner to the lower right corner. Moving away from the diagonal, the correlations first decrease and then begin to increase in a consistent way. This systematic descending-ascending pattern is observed in both the rows and the columns of the matrix. Guttman has shown that a correlation matrix that can be arranged to form a circumplex represents a circular rank ordering of variables. The arrangement is circular because it represents a sequence with neither a beginning nor an end.

A circumplex can be graphically displayed as a circle by spacing the variables around the circumference. Starting with any one variable and tracing around the circle (in either direction), correlations decrease in magnitude and then increase again as the departure point is neared. Variables which occupy adjacent positions are most highly correlated, and thus more similar, while variables on the opposite side have the smallest correlations and are least similar.

## RESULTS

It was possible to arrange intercorrelations among five of the programs to form a circumplex. The matrix of phi-coefficients is found in Table 2 , and a graphic version is displayed in Figure 1.

|  | Bronson | Eddie's Father | Bewitched | Mayberry R.F.D. | Mannix |
|---|---|---|---|---|---|
| Bronson | 1.00 | .11 | .02 | .05 | .11 |
| Eddie's Father | .11 | 1.00 | .23 | .13 | .02 |
| Bewitched | .02 | .23 | 1.00 | .27 | .05 |
| Mayberry R.F.D. | .05 | .13 | .27 | 1.00 | .19 |
| Mannix | .11 | .02 | .05 | .19 | 1.00 |

Table 2:  Circumplex matrix of intercorrelations among five television programs.

The differences in audience composition between any two programs were usually slight. The number of viewers watching one program but not another was statistically significant in only four of the 66 pair-wise comparisons. Nevertheless, the shifts in the makeup of audiences as one moves around the circle are systematic.

The action-adventure series popular among aggressive viewers (*Bronson* and *Mannix*) occupy adjacent positions around the circle, as do the situation comedies preferred by nonaggressive viewers (*Eddie's Father, Bewitched,* and *Mayberry, R.F.D.*). Likewise, programs especially popular among black viewers (*Mannix, Mayberry, R.F.D.,* and *Bewitched*) are contiguous, as are those programs which appealed especially to white viewers (*Bronson* and *Eddie's Father*). The turnover pattern from program to program around the circle is encoded as the changing sequence of letters and subscripts in Figure 1.

The circumplex includes at least one program especially popular among each type of viewer. Other programs could be substituted, but the result would be a less well-formed circumplex. However, the descending-ascending pattern of correlations is less seriously violated if

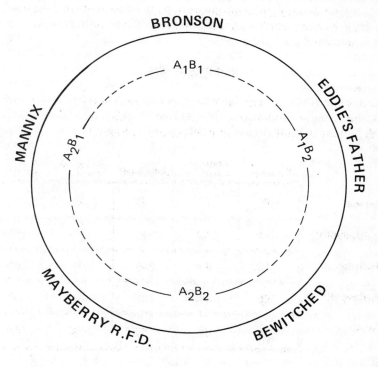

Figure 1: A graphic representation of the circumplex Matrix. Letters with subscripts correspond to the viewer categories in Table 1, and indicate program(s) preferred by each type of viewer.

the replacement is another program popular with the same type of viewer. For example, *The FBI* and *Adam-12* are partially interchangeable with *Bronson*. All three series were favorites of white aggressive viewers. But neither is a permissible substitute for other programs in the circumplex. These constraints on interchangeability indicated that the three programs preferred by each of the four types of viewers formed discrete, cohesive sets (an interpretation confirmed by a cluster analysis of the complete 12 x 12 matrix of correlations).

The construction of a circumplex was useful in helping us recognize the common features among seemingly dissimilar programs. Each program most resembled (in the make-up of its audience) the two on either side, and this relationship implied that adjacent programs possessed some attribute in common. Such a circumplex, linking a diversity of television programs, enabled us, in this study, to structure our thinking about the determinants of program preferences.

## DISCUSSION

A male's understanding of his sexual role develops during two periods, each lasting about six years (Kagan, 1969). Before puberty, a boy learns about the expectations and demands of the masculine role through his associations with other boys. During adolescence, his understanding is significantly altered as he learns to relate to girls. The fourteen-year-olds who participated in this study were at the juncture of these two periods. The information-seeking hypothesis proposes that under these conditions of transitional uncertainty, the adolescent male is highly motivated to search for prototypes of adult masculine behavior. Television is a readily accessible source of high-definition portraits of the masculine styles common in our mass culture.

Masculine style refers to those characteristic aspects of a man's relationships (with either women or other men) which are relatively invariant from person to person or across social contexts. The results of our data analysis of television program preferences led us to devise a classification schema of styles using two sets of paired, contrasting attributes. Within this format it was possible to elaborate a definition of masculine style which resembled semantic differential definitions of concepts. Indeed, the specific meanings we chose to assign to the abstract attribute system were derived from semantic differential studies intended to determine the meanings of diverse social roles (Friedman and Gladden, 1964) and of nonverbal communications (Mehrabian, 1970). These attributes reflect two different aspects of interpersonal behavior: status and reactivity. The status relationship between two people is determined when one person assumes the dominant role (i.e., high status) and the other assumes the subordinate role. Reactivity refers to a person's tendency either to actively initiate interpersonal contacts or to passively react to the social moves of others.

Permutations of these contrasting attributes yield four styles of masculine portrayal, presented in Table 3 together with our inferred trait characterization for each style. These are briefly discussed, in turn.

| | White (A$_1$) | Black (A$_2$) |
|---|---|---|
| **Aggressive (B$_1$)** | high status/active<br><br>'THE FORCEFUL MALE'<br><br>A$_1$B$_1$ | low status/active<br><br>'THE TACTICAL MALE'<br><br>A$_2$B$_1$ |
| **Non-aggressive (B$_2$)** | high status/passive<br><br>'THE PROTECTING MALE'<br><br>A$_1$B$_2$ | low status/passive<br><br>'THE VULNERABLE MALE'<br><br>A$_2$B$_2$ |

Table 3: Four Styles of Masculine Behavior Portrayed in Television Programs Popular among Adolescent Boys.

*The vulnerable male* (low status/passive) is portrayed in the three series preferred by nonaggressive black viewers: *Bewitched, Green Acres,* and *Mayberry, R.F.D.* In these programs, a common plot device is to entrap a man in a humiliating situation which exposes his impotence. Too weak and inept to rescue himself, he is dependent upon others for help. The help often comes from a masterful woman. Darrin, in the *Bewitched* series, depicts a fantasy version of this style. He is the lone mortal in a family of witches and warlocks, and his total subjugation through the malevolent magic of Endora, the hostile mother-in-law, is staved off only through the repeated interventions of his wife, Samantha. *Green Acres* portrays the harried life of a gentleman farmer outmaneuvered by his witless wife and the crafty folk of Hooterville. The comic incompetence of the male is the recurrent story idea of another program in this category, *Mayberry, R.F.D.* In one episode, fixit man Emmett Clark broke his arm and had to hire a high school boy to help in the shop. The townspeople soon discovered that the boy was much better at repair work than Clark. In another episode, one of the main characters, Sam Jones, unsuccessfully competed with a hired farm hand for the respect and admiration of his own son.

*The tactical male* (low status/active), a favorite of aggressive black viewers, is represented by *Mannix, Mission Impossible,* and by certain aspects of *Julia.* The lead characters are all adept problem solvers. A client is in trouble or in danger and must be rescued. One writer for the *Mannix* series considers Joe Mannix a "Christ figure," noting that "he really is everybody's ombudsman: he'll make it right" (quoted in *TV Guide*, October 31, 1970). As a consequence of his low status, however, the tactical male must work under severe handicaps. He is always in an exposed, vulnerable position: a private detective who must act aggressively without the legal authority of the police, an undercover team sent on dangerous missions behind enemy lines, a black nurse (the widowed mother of a small boy) who works for a domineering white doctor. In each case, their underdog positions require that they resort to cunning strategy and surprise rather than force and coercion.

The tactical male maintains close ties with others, and his band of associates often includes a woman. The continuing characters on *Mission Impossible* form a closely-knit group of collaborators with one woman in a supporting role. Mannix depends upon his black secretary. At least one black actor appears regularly in all three series.

*The protective male* (high status/passive) describes the key adult roles in *The Courtship of Eddie's Father*, *My Three Sons*, and *The Newlywed Game*, three programs especially popular among nonaggressive white viewers. The emphasis of these series is the man's capacity to fill a woman's place in the family.

*Eddie's Father* and *My Three Sons* both are concerned with fathers' determined attempts to rear their motherless sons. The affectionate relationship between father and son is clearly conveyed in *The Courtship of Eddie's Father*. As originally conceived, the "courtship" was to denote the boy trying to fix up dad with dates every week. But as the show evolved in concept, the courtship became that between father and son. In the 26 episodes of the 1969-70 season, only twice did eight-year-old Eddie try to find a wife for his father. James Komack, the producer, considers the single parent format necessary for delving into the parent-child relationship with any depth. He said, "A woman would interfere— would take away half the time, half the affection, half the moment" (*TV Guide*, July 4, 1970).

The vividness of the protective male style was demonstrated by Foster (1964), who found that even the most acceptable real-life fathers seemed less attractive to their sons than did the fathers portrayed on popular television series. In our study, the appeal of this style was relatively limited to white boys, however, since blacks avoided white family-type situation comedies. A similar racial pattern in program preferences was reported several years ago by Carey (1966).

The role of the protective male is seen in a somewhat different version in *The Newlywed Game*. Success in playing the game depends on the collaboration, not competition, of husband-and-wife teams. To score, a husband or wife must be able to correctly guess how the other partner answered a question. The winning team is the couple which can best take the place of each other.

*The forceful male* (high status/active) was a style attractive to white aggressive viewers. High status is accorded the male lead either because he is empowered to compel compliant behavior from others (Inspector Erskine of *The FBI*, officers Reed and Malloy of *Adam-12*), or because he is so unassailable in his independence that he alone determines his own actions ( *Bronson* ). The forceful male is dominating, self-sufficient, aggressively on the offensive. His response to threat is immediate and direct. There is seldom need for subterfuge or surprise.

Typically, these shows have few continuing characters and shift locales from one episode to another. The male leads are constantly on the move, and hence plot development does not depend upon complex interactions among characters. Moreover, the fictional world the forceful male inhabits is a man's world. No women appear regularly in any of the three series, and the roles which are assigned to women are usually incidental. The low involvement of women characters is reminiscent of Hemingway's short story collection, *Men Without Women*, in which the thrills of fishing, boxing, and bullfighting are preferred to the pleasures of women.[2]

The style of the forceful male further resembles a conventional Hemingway character in its associations with high adventure and violence and its hard-sell presentation as a life style worthy of imitation. The Soames (1969) have argued that "much of the effect of observational learning depends upon the success and prestige of the model who is imitated." Heavy propaganda infuses all three series which portray the forceful male. *The FBI* is an officially sanctioned account of Bureau heroics, while *Adam-12* often introduces law-and-order editorializing into its dialogue. *Bronson* promotes a quick getaway life style throughout each program, from the opening title vignette (which shows a man beset with the cares of middle age betraying his envy of Bronson's easyriding freedom) to the lyrics of the closing theme: "Goin' down that long, lonesome highway. . . gonna live like my way. . .I won't be hangin' 'round." Of the four masculine styles described, the forceful male is the most escapist since, as Lucy Komisar (1970) has noted, "this definition of manhood can no longer exist for most men, except through the shallow medium of television."

The programs we have considered both reflect and perpetuate mass culture stereotypes of masculine roles. The popularity of these particular programs among adolescent boys is probably due to the clarity with which the male leads embody stock styles of masculine behavior. When television influences a boy to adopt one of these styles as his own, his choice serves to maintain and reinforce its viability as a model for manhood.

## FOOTNOTES

1. This study was based upon data gathered for the Surgeon General's Scientific Advisory Committee on Television and Social Behavior, under contract with the National Institute of Mental Health. The authors acknowledge the assistance of Dr. Robert L. Derbyshire, University of Maryland School of Medicine, who supervised the survey phase of the research, and Mary G. Kalis, for the statistical analyses.

2. One consequence of a program winning popularity among white aggressive viewers may be a loss of women viewers. According to the Home Testing Institute, *Adam-12* was the only program in our selection to appear among its TvQ "top ten" list of nighttime network shows toward the end of the 1969-70 season. A TvQ score is the proportion of all viewers familiar with a program who single it out as one of their favorites. For each nighttime network show, the Home Testing Institute releases separate TvQ scores for men and women (18 years and older), children (6-11), and teenagers (12-17). The audience strength of *Adam-12* derived from the fact that it was the most popular show among teenage viewers, the second most popular among children (close behind *The Wonderful World of Disney*), and was one of two top-rated nightime shows more popular with men than women (*Bonanza* was the other). No other program on the "top ten" list, however, had a lower TvQ score among women viewers. (Source: *Advertising Age*, July 13, 1970.)

## REFERENCES

Carey, J. Variations in negro/white television preferences. *Journal of Broadcasting*, 1966, **10**, 199-212.

Erikson, E.H. *Identity: youth and crisis*. New York: W.W. Norton and Co., 1968.

Feather, N. T. An expectancy-value model of information-seeking behavior. *Psychological Review*, 1967, **74**, 342-60.

Foster, J. E. Father images: television and ideal. *Journal of Marriage and the family*, 1964, **26**, 353-55.

Friedman, C. J., and Gladden, J. W. Objective measurement of social role concepts via the semantic differential. *Psychological Reports*, 1964, **14**, 239-47.

Guttman, L. Order analysis of correlation matrices. In Cattell, R. B. (Ed.) *Handbook of multivariate experimental psychology*. Chicago: Rand McNally and Co., 1966.

Kagan, J. Sex-role identity. *Psychology Today*, 1969, **3**, 39-42.

Komisar, L. Violence and the masculine mystique. *The Washington Monthly*, 1970, **2**, 39-48.

Mehrabian, A. A semantic space for nonverbal behavior. *Journal of Consulting and Clinical Psychology*, 1970, **35**, 248-57.

Soames, L. M., and Soames, A. T. Social learning and social violence. *Proceedings, 77th Annual Convention*, American Psychological Association, 1969.

# Television Viewing Habits and Aggression

John P. Robinson and Jerald G. Bachman

*Survey Research Center, University of Michigan*

The Survey Research Center's Youth-in-Transition project has been studying a national probability sample of about 2,200 young men to determine their attitudes, plans, and behaviors, particularly those relating to educational and occupational aspirations. Data collections, using personal interviews and written questionnaires, have spanned a period of nearly four years. The first data (autumn 1966) were collected when the boys were in tenth grade at 87 public high schools scattered throughout the United States. The second collection (spring 1968) was made when the majority of boys were finishing eleventh grade. The third (spring 1969) took place before those boys still in high school had graduated.

The final data were collected during June and July of 1970 from 70 percent (or more than 1,500) of the boys in the original sample. Most of the boys had been out of high school for about a year; a large proportion had just finished their first year of college, although many others were in military service or in the work force. The Youth-in-Transition project added questions on television use to this final data collection, with the objective of examining the ways in which experiences with television might relate to the massive body of attitude and behavioral variables already available from the project. Of particular interest was the relation between television viewing and the self-reports of delinquent behavior (much of which was highly aggressive in nature) which had been regularly included in all four data collections.

Boys in the age range encompassed by this project are probably in a stage of life characterized by considerably more active, aggressive, and destructive behavior than any other stage of the life cycle; hence they comprise a most crucial sample in which to examine possible relationships between television violence and aggressive social behavior. From the level of delinquent behavior reported in each data collection, it would appear that these boys' aggressive behavior at age 19 was about the same as that when they were in eleventh or twelfth grade. The boys have reported dramatically higher levels of participation in aggressive delinquent behavior than one would surmise from the already shockingly high official public records of such behavior.

Further details on study design and sampling procedures of the Youth-in-Transition project can be found in Bachman (1970).

## Media questions

Three television use questions were asked in the final (June-July 1970) interview. Each boy was asked how many hours of television he watched on an average day, what his four favorite television programs were, and whether he felt he had learned more about life from television or in school. The last question—in answer to which some 15 percent of these boys chose television, while 80 percent named school—is examined in a separate report in this series (Robinson, 1971).

Respondents reported using television 1.7 hours on an average day—a low figure when compared with the three-hour figure given by national samples of adults (Roper, 1969; LoSciuto, 1971). Some 18 percent of the boys estimated no hours per day; 37 percent estimated an average of one hour, 22 percent two hours, and 23 percent three hours or more. (The last viewing figure is at or above the national average for adults.) Differences between college and noncollege youth were surprisingly trivial.

The 19-year-olds' aversion to television is further evidenced by the high proportion (44 percent) who would not or could not list at least three favorite television programs when asked to do so. For the 56 percent who did list at least three or four favorites, an index was developed to assess the preponderance of violent content in these programs. All television programs rated as notably violent by both the public and critical samples surveyed by Greenberg and Gordon (1971, elsewhere in this series) were given a score of 2. Those rated as moderately or occasionally violent were given a score of 1; those with little or no violence, a score of 0. Programs scored as 2 included *Mod Squad, Mannix,* and most of the other programs falling into the "adventure" category. Such programs as *Walt Disney, Get Smart, Bracken's World, Bronson,* and *Hogan's Heroes* were scored as 1. Programs like *Marcus Welby, M.D., Family Affair, Laugh-In,* and *Dean Martin* were scored as 0. Two types of programs not evaluated by Greenberg and Gordon's raters but still listed by several respondents were football (arbitrarily rated 2) and movies (rated 1).

Thus a respondent who listed *Mod Squad, NFL Football, Get Smart,* and *Dean Martin* as his four favorites would receive a score of 5 on this index (2 + 2 + 1 + 0). The favorite programs of those young men who listed three or four favorites skewed somewhat toward the nonviolent end of the index (with an average score of 3.0 on a scale running from 0 to 8), but more than 40 percent scored 4 (the theoretical midpoint) or more on the index. Only about 14 percent listed favorites that contained no rated violence.

## Relation between violent programs and aggressive behavior

For purposes of analysis, scores on this violence viewing index were divided into four categories: "almost none" (scores 0-1), "some" (scores 2-3), "much" (scores 4-5), and "a great deal" (scores 6-8). The group which failed to list at least three favorites was also considered; it served as a useful "control" group against which to compare the differential behavior of young men who mentioned favorite programs with varying amounts of violence.

The eight items dealing with interpersonal aggression in the delinquent behavior scale are listed in Table 1, along with the proportions who reported having engaged in such behaviors in the previous year for each of these violence viewing categories.[1] Thus, in the first row of Table 1, it can be seen that 37 percent of young men whose favorite programs contained "a great deal" of violence reported getting into a serious fight, compared with 33 percent of those listing programs containing "much" violence, 30 percent of those who listed programs containing "some" violence, and 25 percent of those listing programs containing "almost no" violence. Thus the percentage of those who got into serious fights is almost half again as high among those with heavy concentrations of violence in their favorite programs as among those who mentioned no violent favorites. A steady monotonic increase in aggressive behavior is reported by those with intermediate television violence preferences. The 37 percent rate of participation in aggressive behavior reported by

Table 1: Percent engaging in various aggressive behaviors by viewing of TV violence (June – July 1970)

| Item: | Amount of violence in four favorite programs | | | | |
| --- | --- | --- | --- | --- | --- |
| | Almost none | Some | Much | Great deal | Could not mention at least three favorites |
| Total sample (n=1559) | (n=244) | (n=283) | (n=239) | (n=120) | (n=673) |
| | Percent | Percent | Percent | Percent | Percent |
| 1. Gotten into a serious fight at school or work | 25 | 30 | 33 | 37 | 26 |
| 5. Gotten something by telling a person something bad would happen to him if he didn't | 15 | 19 | 20 | 18 | 13 |
| 9. Hurt someone bad enough to need bandages or a doctor | 17 | 23 | 21 | 28 | 18 |
| 12. Hit an instructor or supervisor | 6 | 7 | 7 | 11 | 6 |
| 14. Hit your father | 5 | 8 | 8 | 8 | 6 |
| 17. Taken part in a fight where a bunch of your friends are against another bunch | 19 | 23 | 24 | 28 | 21 |
| 18. Hit your mother | 3 | 3 | 4 | 4 | 2 |
| 21. Used a knife or gun or some other thing (like a club) to get something from a person | 2 | 4 | 3 | 8 | 3 |
| Interpersonal aggression index (based on the above eight items) | 119 | 125 | 126 | 132 | 119 |

boys who showed extreme preferences for violent programs was also considerably higher than the 26 percent participation rate reported by young men (presumably less serious television fans) who failed to list at least three favorite programs. The participation rate for these nonwatchers was comparable to that reported by preferrers of nonviolent programs.

Very much the same pattern emerges for each of the seven remaining items indicating interpersonally aggressive delinquent behavior. In several instances no differences or reversals can be observed, but, by and large, the higher the concentration of violence in a young man's favorite programs, the more likely he is to report having participated in aggressive behavior. Particularly dramatic differences appear in reports of hitting an instructor/supervisor and using a weapon to get something from another person.

At the same time, these progressive increases in aggressive behavior among more avid fans of violent television are not of sufficient magnitude to gain statistical significance for many items. In order to obtain a clear overall picture for such statistical testing purposes, these eight items have been merged into a single interpersonal aggression index of from 100 (no reported aggression in the previous year) to 400 (participation five or more times during the previous year for all eight items).[2] From the low participation rates in Table 1, we can infer that scores would skew highly toward the low end of this scale; this is borne out by the overall average score of 122 for the entire sample. Deviations around this average score for individuals with varying numbers of violent television favorites are presented at the bottom of Table 1.

It can be seen that there is a clearly monotonic, although not strong, relation between the two variables. As favorite television programs contain more violence, reported aggressive behavior inches upward. Moreover, the amount of aggressive behavior by those listing some, much, or a great deal of violent favorites does turn out to be significantly higher than that reported either by young men listing less than three favorites (t = 4.7, 1305 df.) or by those listing favorites with no violence (t = 3.9, 878 df.).

The question naturally arises whether such a result could be attributed to other factors like social class or personal characteristics. Controls on four such competing explanatory factors are examined in Table 2. These factors include mother's education (one key indicator of social class), race, amount of television viewed, and interpersonal aggression reported in the previous interview (spring 1969). Of these four variables, only hours of television viewing fails to predict higher reported aggressive behavior. Sons of mothers with less education, blacks, and those reporting more aggressive behavior as high school seniors all reported more aggressive behavior at age 19 than the sons of the better educated, whites, and those reporting less high school aggressive behavior.

Table 2: Scores on interpersonal aggression by viewing of television violence for certain demographic groups

| | Amount of violence in favorite TV shows | | | | Less than three favorite programs mentioned |
|---|---|---|---|---|---|
| | Almost none | Some | Much | Great deal | |
| Total sample | (n=244) | (n=283) | (n=239) | (n=120) | (n=673) |
| Interpersonal aggression index (n=1559) | 119 | 125 | 126 | 132 | 119 |
| Mother's education | | | | | |
| Did not finish high school (n=458) | 131 | 130 | 127 | 139 | 123 |
| High School graduate (n=722) | 115 | 123 | 125 | 125 | 120 |
| At least some college (n=292) | 110 | 127 | 117 | 121 | 113 |
| Race | | | | | |
| Whites (n=1351) | 115 | 121 | 125 | 125 | 118 |
| Blacks (n=167) | 139 | 149 | 133 | 160 | 137 |
| Amount of viewing | | | | | |
| 0 – 1 hours/day (n=845) | 117 | 128 | 127 | 132 | 119 |
| 2 – 3 hours/day (n=541) | 119 | 119 | 126 | 131 | 118 |
| 4 + hours/day (n=167) | 125 | 133 | 117 | 134 | 140 |
| Interpersonal aggression reported in previous year (i.e., Spring 1969) | | | | | |
| Average-below average (n=1243) | 113 | 115 | 115 | 115 | 112 |
| Somewhat above average (n=149) | 131 | 146 | 139 | 137 | 135 |
| Well above average (n=156) | 159 | 205 | 167 | 221 | 172 |

The smooth monotonicity found overall fails to hold up when controls for these subdivisions of the sample are applied. Monotonicity holds for sons of mothers who were high school graduates, but not among sons of mothers who did not finish high school or who attended college. It holds for whites, but not for blacks who fall into the moderate violent viewing category. The same nonmonotonic pattern holds true for young men who watch the most hours of television.

Perhaps the most dynamic test, however, is whether the television violence-interpersonal aggression relation continues to hold for respondents reporting varying amounts of identical aggression in the interview one year earlier. If it can be shown that viewers with a strong preference for violent programs were previously more prone to aggressive behavior and that this relation serves to essentially nullify any differentials noted in Table 1, a strong argument can be made that the Table 1 results are more attributable to previous levels of aggression than to any contributing factor from television violence.

The relation, examined at the bottom of Table 2, indeed indicates that no consistent difference in aggressive behavior accompanies increased preference for television violence among young men who reported average or somewhat above-average aggressive delinquent behavior in the previous year. The picture for the most aggressive individuals (self-reportedly) in the previous interview is more complex, however. Within this group, those mentioning favorites with almost no violence report the least aggressive behavior (159), while those listing favorites containing a good deal of violence report the most aggression (221). However, we are again faced with contradictory results for the middle groups. Respondents listing few violent favorites reported more aggressive behavior (205) than respondents listing a moderately high number of violent favorites (167). Overall, however, the contrast between those listing programs with "some," "much," or "a great deal" of violent favorites (mean = 196) and those listing "almost no" favorites (mean = 159) is statistically significant ( $t$ = 2.8, 93 df.), as is the contrast between the some-much-great deal groups and respondents listing less than three favorite programs (mean = 175; $t$ = 2.3, 142 df.).

In essence, then, once previous aggression is controlled, we are able to corroborate a link between aggressive behavior and preference for violent television programs only among those subjects who reported themselves most aggressive to begin with. Even here the link is neither monotonic nor dramatic enough to implicate preference for violent television as a primary determinant of aggressive interpersonal behavior.

Before concluding this examination of the relation between television preferences and behavior, it might be worthwhile to consider one further set of data that could offer a further competing explanation for the Table 1 results. That explanation centers around the greater activity levels, tendencies toward any delinquent behavior (interpersonally aggressive or not), or adventure-seeking of those who expressed greater preference for violent television. Such relations are examined in Table 3 for 13 delinquent (but not interpersonally aggressive) types of behavior.

It can be seen in Table 3 that the more avid fans of television violence are not more likely to report engaging in seven of these 13 actions: petty theft, trespassing, arguing with parents, running away from home, school vandalism, shoplifting, and drinking. These more avid viewers of television violence are slightly more likely to report arson, getting into trouble with the police, and minor car theft; they are *considerably* more likely to report major theft, especially of cars and car parts. Overall, these results tend to suggest that boys who are more likely to prefer violence on television are distinguished from those whose tastes run to less violent fare (or who have few favorite television programs) by their greater participation in more serious delinquent behavior. Only insignificant differences by varying television taste patterns exist for less serious delinquency.

# Summary and conclusions

We have found a significant and monotonic relation between participation in aggressive delinquent behaviors (fighting, armed robbery) and preference for violent television programs among a national probability sample of over 1,500 boys who are one year out of high school. The relation tends to become nullified or qualified as controls for mother's education, race, amount of viewing, and previous aggressive behavior are imposed. There is limited support for the view that preference for violent television content is associated with higher aggressive behavior among boys previously most active in such behavior.

The latter finding is our most ambitious attempt to add any causal flavor to the interpretation of these results. Nevertheless, even this limited evidence must be advanced with utmost caution. The predictor variable used here—the mention of violent programs among one's favorites—is a most subjective measure, which obviously says more about the tastes of the respondent than about the effects of what he has seen on television. In essence, then, preference for violent television content is primarily a personality variable, much in the way that Rorschach or thematic apperception test cards are intended to elicit those features of one's environment that are most salient to the individual.[3] While it probably does correlate significantly with pure exposure to such violent fare, it remains a contaminated measure of this variable.

At best, then, the strongest possible conclusion boils down to the well-worn maxim that media content only serves to reinforce the pre-existing tendencies of its viewers. While this is a relatively commonplace finding for effects of the media in other areas (e.g., in changing attitudes, increasing passivity or knowledge), seldom has appropriate rec-

Table 3: Percent participating in various delinquent behaviors (not interpersonally aggressive) by viewing of TV violence (June – July 1970)

| Item | Amount of violence in favorite television program | | | | |
| --- | --- | --- | --- | --- | --- |
| | Almost none | Some | Much | Great deal | Less than three favorite programs mentioned |
| | Percent | Percent | Percent | Percent | Percent |
| 2. Taken something not belonging to you worth under $50 | 46 | 49 | 47 | 44 | 43 |
| 3. Went onto someone's land or into some house or building when you weren't supposed to be there | 56 | 52 | 54 | 52 | 53 |
| 4. Set fire to someone else's property on purpose | 4 | 3 | 6 | 5 | 4 |
| 6. Argued or had a fight with either of your parents | 64 | 75 | 70 | 68 | 70 |
| 7. Run away from home | 13 | 12 | 11 | 15 | 9 |
| 8. Gotten into trouble with police because of something you did | 31 | 30 | 42 | 37 | 30 |
| 10. Damaged school property on purpose | 16 | 20 | 22 | 16 | 15 |
| 11. Taken something from a store without paying for it | 40 | 44 | 47 | 43 | 39 |
| 13. Drunk beer or liquor without parents' permission | 74 | 75 | 74 | 65 | 69 |
| 15. Taken a car that didn't belong to someone in your family without permission of the owner | 4 | 8 | 6 | 10 | 6 |
| 16. Taken an expensive part of a car without owner's permission | 6 | 7 | 9 | 12 | 7 |
| 19. Took something not belonging to you worth over $50 | 10 | 12 | 13 | 16 | 10 |
| 20. Taken an inexpensive part of a car without owner's permission | 8 | 12 | 13 | 13 | 12 |

ognition been given to the dysfunctional consequences of such a reinforcement effect in the case of violent media content. Put another way—
that violent content only serves to support or activate the violent tendencies of people who are already violent—this research finding takes on
entirely different implications.

The present analysis, however, is not sufficient to argue decisively for
such a reinforcement effect, since numerous other variables must be
considered at length before the Table 1 linkages can be advanced without undue skepticism. Many of these variables are available in the enormous file of background variables that the Youth-in-Transition project
has assembled: sources of frustrations and disappointments at school or
at home, relations with parents, self-esteem, life satisfaction, irritability, impulse to aggression, and so on. The present analysis represents
only a superficial mining of this rich body of data. It does indicate, however, that preference for violent television content is a variable that deserves further exploration as a facilitating factor in the expression of
aggressive interpersonal behavior.

# FOOTNOTES

1. These questions on delinquent behavior, unlike most of the information obtained from these boys, were answered individually in a special booklet marked "Confidential Information." This procedure was
   followed because we felt that anyone would find it extremely embar-
   rassing to truthfully reveal this type of information verbally to an interviewer. Scrupulous care was taken to ensure the confidentiality of
   this information. The boys were asked their frequency of participation in each activity, although Tables 1 and 3 differentiate only between those who took part in the activities and those who did not.
2. There is a compelling rationale for examining results with the index
   rather than as individual behaviors. Because of the highly confidential and self-incriminating nature of these questions, responses to all
   individual items were destroyed soon after they were coded. Frequency counts and the runs on Tables 1 and 3 were the only analyses
   performed with these variables before they were destroyed.
3. In this sense it is interesting to find a strong correlation between preference for violent television content and support for the Vietnam war
   in these data. Thirty-one percent of the young men who became more
   supportive of the war between 1969 and 1970 listed "much" or "a
   great deal" of violent content; only 21 percent of those who became
   more opposed to the war during that period listed violent content.
   Among those who were opposed to the war in both years, only 13
   percent list favorite programs with much or a great deal of violence.

# REFERENCES

Bachman, J.G. *Youth in transition, Vol. 2.* Ann Arbor, Mich.: Survey Research Center, Institute for Social Research, 1970.

Greenberg, B.S., and Gordon, T. Perceptions of violence in television programs: critics and the public. In *Television and social behavior,* Vol. 1 (this series). Washington, D.C.: U.S. Government Printing Office, 1971.

LoSciuto, L.A. A national inventory of television viewing behavior. In *Television and social behavior,* Vol. 4 (this series). Washington, D.C.: U.S. Government Printing Office, 1971.

Robinson, J.P. On defining the functions of television. In *Television and social behavior,* Vol. 4 (this series). Washington, D.C.: U.S. Government Printing Office, 1971.

Roper, B. *A ten-year view of public attitudes toward television and other mass media, 1959-1968.* New York: Television Information Office, 1969.

# Television Violence and Deviant Behavior

Jennie J. McIntyre and James J. Teevan, Jr., with the
assistance of Timothy Hartnagel

*University of Maryland*

The role of the church in moral education has withered to a pallid weekly session at Sunday school. As we have seen, the family, primarily because of changes in the larger social order beyond its control, is no longer in a position to exercise its responsibilities. As for the school—in which the child spends most of his time—it is debarred by tradition, lack of experience, and preoccupation with subject matter from concerning itself in any major way with the child's development as a person. . . .The vacuum, moral and emotional, created by this state of affairs is then filled—by default—on the one hand by the television screen with its daily message of commercialism and violence, and on the other by the socially isolated, age-graded peer group, with its impulsive search for thrills and its limited capacity as a humanizing agent (Bronfenbrenner, 1970, pp. 115-16).

Although more emphatic than many, the above statement by a social scientist concerned with the socialization of youngsters in the United States is illustrative of the widespread concern with television's influence, particularly on the character development of children.

In part this question of the influence of television stems from its ubiquity. Although the most recent, it is the most popular of the mass media. The 1969 report of the staff of the National Commission on the Causes and Prevention of Violence notes that by 1968, 94 percent of American homes had sets, that average daily operating hours per set varied from 4.8 in midsummer to 6.8 hours in January, and that of the 66 percent of adults who do watch some television on a given day, the average daily viewing time was just over three and one-half hours (Baker and Ball, 1969).

Another reason for the widespread concern about the possible influence of television is the belief, exemplified by the above quotation, that it may be a major factor in the socialization of the young. At an age when their character development may be most susceptible to influence, children not only spend much time in front of the television set, but do not limit their viewing to those programs intended for them. The Commission data show that more children are watching in the early evening than during the late afternoon "children's hours" and that their viewing continues into the late evening. On one Monday during the period covered, over five million children under the age of 12 and nearly 6.4 million 12- to 17-year-olds were still watching between 10:30 and 11 p.m. (Baker and Ball, 1969, p. 207).

Given the amount of public (and especially of children's) exposure to television, it is not surprising that recent years have seen much attention focused on the content of television programming. The purpose of this scrutiny has been to examine the possible relationship between the increasing use of television and the concomitant increase in many social problems—for example, crime. It seemed to many people that the simultaneous occurrence of these two developments was not coincidental (see references 46-49 cited in Baker and Ball, 1969, p. 452).

Violence in television programming thus became the focus of much public attention. Many observers felt that there was a possibility that the viewer of television violence would be more likely to engage in criminal or violent behavior. Others suggested that the violence on television might influence the viewer's perception of the amount of crime and violence in the country, thereby affecting his level of fear and anxiety (President's Commission on Law Enforcement and Administration of Justice, 1967, p. 52).

While there may not be consensus regarding the effects of television violence, there is more agreement on the presence of violence in program content. Baker and Ball, for example, reported the following conclusions:

1. . . . There is a great deal of violent content available, at all times of the day, for all manner of intended audience.
2. The presentation of violence is typically as a means of achieving virtually any type of goal.
3. Violence is the predominant means of conflict resolution suggested in television drama, as of 1968.
4. The use of violence, whether sanctioned or not, is likely to be a successful means of obtaining such goals.
5. Character depictions are stereotyped, emphasize the unusual behavior, and promote (through both emphasis and absence) certain behavioral values, a majority of which are socially disapproved or undesirable. (Baker and Ball, 1969, pp. 441-42).

Furthermore, on the basis of a content analysis of commercial television entertainment programming done for the Commission's Media Task Force, it was concluded that violence is pervasive, occurring in 81 percent of all 1967 programs analyzed and 82 percent in 1968. The content analysis also revealed that though the extent of violence varies by type of program, a majority of all types of programs contains violence and that no network had less than 77 percent of all its programming (prime time, Oct. 1-7, 1968) containing violence (Baker and Ball, 1969, p. 333).

The question which follows from a consideration of the content of television programming, the extensive exposure to such programming, and its possible effects on behavior, attitudes, and beliefs has been stated as follows:

> If models for violent behavior are repeatedly presented with few competing notions, and people, particularly children, repeatedly expose themselves to such materials, what could be a more favorable arrangement for learning about violence, if not learning to do violence? (Baker and Ball, 1969, p. 237).

Professor Otto Larsen, who poses this question, also points out, however, that the abundance of violent media content and the frequency of exposure to it do not suffice to prove that the mass media can modify attitudes or induce violent behavior. He goes on to argue that the question cannot be simply whether the media have an effect. It must be discovered under what conditions, for whom, how much, and what kind of effect the media are likely to have. Furthermore, whatever may be the effects of the mass media upon their audience, these must be assessed in relation to the way other aspects of the larger social system affect these same persons (Baker and Ball, 1969, pp. 238-40).

In the pages that follow the present investigators take seriously the recommendations of Professor Larsen and the other authors of the staff report.[1] They first present a brief review of the relevant literature concerning the effects of television. They then proceed to the specification of a conceptual model for analyzing the effects of television violence and the development of hypotheses from this model. These hypotheses are followed by a discussion of the methodology of the present study and the presentation of the findings. Throughout the report the central concern will be questions raised but not answered in the National Commission's Media Task Force report: 1) does exposure to television violence increase the probability of violent and/or deviant behavior; 2) do norms and values projected by the television world of violence affect the viewers' norms for violence; and 3) does the world view presented by television foster belief in a society characterized by a high level of violence?

## Previous findings

A comprehensive review of the literature is unnecessary since this task has been done quite recently (Weiss, 1968; Baker and Ball, 1969. Rather, this section looks selectively at three different aspects of the literature pertinent to this research: 1) the effects of television on deviant behavior; 2) the social psychology of mass communications; and 3) adolescent deviant behavior.

There has been much discussion of the possible effects of television on deviant behavior. Much of the research has been confined to laboratory studies of aggression. The results of these experiments, however, are not uniform. Some researchers have concluded that television has little if any effect in causing aggression or deviant behavior in adolescents. According to this position, when presented with the same television stimuli, aggressive children will be aggressive, adjusted children will not. Banay argues before a congressional subcommittee on juvenile delinquency: ''. . . The young people who are influenced by television toward crime seem to be different from others who are not so influenced, even before they are influenced by television'' (Schramm, 1961, p. 164). Schramm concurs: ''Television then interacts with the needs and emotions the child brings to it. . . .The most that television can do is to feed the malignant impulses that already exist'' (p. 166). According to these views, television plays but a minor part in causing deviant behavior. It elicits that behavior which is already in the child's repertoire. Schramm (1961, p. 165) concludes, ''Therefore, our belief is that the kind of child we send to television, rather than television itself, is the chief element in delinquency.''

Agreement comes from Bailyn (1959) in one study and Haines (1955) in another, who concur that it is ''misfits'' who select violent shows and that television has an effect only on ''susceptible teenagers.'' Riley and Riley (1951) discovered that children who do not wish to be isolates, yet who cannot gain peer group acceptance, use television for compensatory fantasy purposes. Those children who are well integrated with their peers have less preference for action and violence on television. Gerson (1963) reports that a family/school context in which an adolescent is not integrated is more likely to generate the use of the mass media as a socializing agency than is a social context in which the adolescent is well integrated.

In their review of the findings regarding the effects of observer characteristics, Bandura and Walters (1963, p. 85) report that a person's previous experiences are among the major determinants of the influence of a model. Persons with low self-esteem, who are incompentent, who have been previously rewarded for the same behavior, who are highly dependent persons, or who believe themselves to be similar to a model, are especially likely to imitate or to match the responses of a model and hence, by inference, to be influenced by the behavior of television characters.

The demographic comparisons made in Baker and Ball (1969) are consistent with these views that previous experiences affect the way in which an individual uses television. Baker and Ball report that adults and teenagers who approve of violence or who have experienced violence (as victim, observer, or assailant) have the same age, sex, race, and residence characteristics as those respondents who: 1) most frequently choose television for relaxation; 2) approve of television's portrayals of violence; 3) prefer programs including violence.

Other researchers have found, however, that even the *normal* child can learn violence from television. Eron (1963) found a positive relationship between violence ratings of favorite programs and aggressive behavior among third-grade boys (but not girls). Zajonc (1954) and Brodbeck (1955) found that children will imitate heroes who are successful, whatever their means. Schramm (1961) summarizes the implications of Brodbeck's studies: ". . . Children may remember (and presumably be able to use) violence, even though it is in conflict with their ethics and values" (p. 163). Thus violence on television may lead to actual violence and deviant behavior. Bandura, for example, finds that imitative responses may be acquired from observation, although performance of that response may be dependent on expectations of reward for that behavior. The response pattern has been learned and is available if there later is an incentive for the behavior. Goranson (1969), in his recent review of the psychological effects of media portrayals of violence, summarizes the literature as follows:

> Novel aggressive behavior sequences are learned by children through exposure to realistic portrayals of aggression on television or in films. A large proportion of these behaviors are retained over long periods of time if they are practiced at least once. . . .The actual performance of aggressive behaviors learned from the media is largely contingent on the child's belief in the effectiveness of aggression in attaining his goals while avoiding punishment. The mass media typically present aggression as a highly effective form of behavior (Baker and Ball, 1969, pp. 409-10).

Learning from television includes the learning of attitudes as well as of behavior patterns. Walters's investigation of responses to a violent film sequence, for example, found that the outcome for observers was not using a weapon as such but taking the expressed motivations of the model as their own (Walters and Llewellyn-Thomas, 1963).

In a similar vein, Himmelweit, Oppenheim, and Vince (1958) found that although television does not make kids more aggressive, children pick up values and information from television if they are needed and not available elsewhere. Thus adolescents watching television may pick up the information and attitudes needed for the commission of deviant acts.

Some additional issues cut across these two major positions in the literature. First, does television lead to aggression or does it lead to the draining off of aggression? Bandura's studies (1963) as well as those of Berkowitz (1964) cast doubt on these catharsis or drive reduction theories. The catharsis controversy has been summarized in papers by Goranson and Feshbach in Baker and Ball (1969).

If television violence does not lead to aggression and deviance directly, a second issue is whether it might not lead to an acceptance of violence in others and a belief that violence is both common and socially acceptable. The Lovibond (1967) and the Thompson (1959) studies raise this issue. Wertham makes the similar suggestion that television makes viewers callous to the ugly aspects of violence: "The trouble is not that they get frightened (by television), but that they *do not* get frightened" (quoted in Larsen, 1968, p.38; emphasis added).

Other writers have suggested directions in which future research on the effects of mass media violence should move. Maccoby (1968), for example, argues that the central question should be reformulated to read: how much effect on what kind of children, and under what circumstances will the effects be exhibited? She points out further that the occurrence of television-stimulated violence depends to some degree on the probability of the occurrence of appropriately corresponding real-life situations. Halloran (1968) suggests the hypothesis that where a television program can be associated with an individual's personal conflicts, the individual is more likely to carry the stimulation over into real life and to increase the amount of directly expressed aggression. In his review of the effects of the mass media, Weiss (1968) states the view that whether symbolically acquired information is ever used depends on a number of factors, such as the motivation to exhibit the learning in actual behavior, the ability to do so, the proper opportunity to do so, the strength of internal and external restraints against doing so, and the similarity between the individual's actual environment and the media setting (p.126).

Bandura (1968) has argued for a distinction between learning and performance. He found that subsequent rewards to a child may elicit the performance of earlier learned forms of aggression. In another context, Maccoby (1954) notes that tendencies toward performing aggressive behavior will enter as one element in the set of behavior tendencies aroused later in some relevant situation. Whether it actually occurs is a function of the strength of competing responses and the restraints acting upon the media-acquired behavior. Thus the media can be seen as a source of norms, but, as Larsen points out, it is necessary to investigate its relative rank *vis-a-vis* other sources of norms. Thus he states that we must establish how children perceive, identify with, and use mass media content and sort this impact from the continuing impact of other agencies of socialization which influence audience members before, during, and after exposure to mass communication. In another context, Larsen not only poses the question of the promotion of violence as a norm by the media but also asks whether there may be the further effect of opportunity lost. The media, by focusing so strongly on violence, does not present to the audience the use of alternative means of goal attainment (Baker and Ball, 1969, pp. 237-46). DeFleur (1966) has noted that persuasive messages presented via the mass media may provide the appearance of consensus with respect to a given object or goal, shortcutting the process of consensual validation. This shortcutting occurs particularly with respect to objects or practices about which groups do not yet have institutionalized cultural interpretations. DeFleur further notes that such messages can imply that adoption of the communicator's goal is normative in the group and hence the individual's adoption of it will result in social approval (p. 136). Such functioning of the media may be particularly applicable to children and adolescents who are in the process of being socialized and may not as yet have acquired the existing normative standards about appropriate means for achieving goals.

In a review of the literature on mass communications, Larsen (1964) has pointed out that while early work conceived of the media as having direct effects upon the individual, this view has given way to the position that social linkages between individuals play an important part in mediating the influence of mass communications. Selectivity in exposure and reaction arise out of organized social processes. Wright (1959) makes the similar point that although the individual is anonymous to the communicator, he is rarely anonymous in his social environment. Rather, he is ordinarily a member of a network of primary and secondary groups which influence his opinions and attitudes. Inevitably these groups affect the way in which he is exposed to mass communication, how he interprets or reacts to any specific communication, and the extent to which he will or can modify his behavior in compliance with the message.

Since the mass media of communication are only one of a number of socializing agents, one important question to be raised concerns the interrelationships among these several agents. It would appear necessary to incorporate into the model a set of variables which at least potentially can be conceived of as either increasing or decreasing the effects of media stimuli.

First, with respect to individual recipients of communications, Hovland et al. (1953) demonstrated that persons with low self-esteem are more easily persuaded by a communication than are persons with higher self-esteem. Voting behavior studies (Lazarsfeld et al., 1948) indicate that audience self-selection occurs such that individuals listen to that which they want to hear and which supports what they want to believe. However, although perception is selective, it is also related to the groups to which the individual belongs. Kelley and Volkart (1952) demonstrated that boys who were most strongly motivated to retain their membership in the Boy Scouts were the most resistant to a communication that ran counter to their group standards. But groups weakened by external or internal stresses may accept new attitudes which under other conditions would have been resisted (Riley et al., 1951).

Kelley and Woodruff (1956) have shown that perceived support for a contrary opinion leads to a change in attitudes and norms. Experiments by Schramm and Danielson (1958) and by Zimmerman and Bauer (1956) have shown that when positive reference groups are tied in with the receipt of a communication, these groups influence the individual to interpret the message as being consonant with the attitudes of the group. However, others (Festinger, 1950; Kelley, 1955; Charters and Newcomb, 1958) have shown that a reference group must be salient before it is able to affect the attitudes of individuals. Variables such as these must be utilized in the model.

Since one of the dependent variables of interest is deviant behavior on the part of adolescents, the model being developed must, of necessity, also incorporate variables that have been shown to affect such behavior.

A major school of thought is the anomie tradition. It has been oriented primarily to explaining lower-class delinquency and has focused much of its attention on occupational aspirations and class-based differences in the opportunity structure (Merton, 1938; Cohen, 1955; Cloward and Ohlin, 1960). On the other hand, Miller (1958) has argued that delinquency is largely the natural result of conformity to lower-class cultural expectations which conflict with the legal norms established by the middle class. Cohen (1966) has recently pointed out that much of deviant behavior, rather than being a means to some end, may perhaps represent an expression of an individual's self-concept formed in his social relationships with others. This notion is in turn related to labeling theory, which emphasizes that the way in which others define and behave toward the individual may have the effect of confirming him in a deviant career (Lemert, 1967; Becker, 1963; Scheff, 1966).

Whether children and adolescents who are motivated to deviate actually do so depends in part on the degree to which they experience constraints against such behavior (Briar and Piliavin, 1965). These constraints or commitments to conformity include not only fear of material loss and punishment resulting from discovery, but also concern about the consequences of such a discovery on one's attempts to maintain a consistent self-image, to sustain valued relationships, and to preserve current and future statuses and activities.

The point to be emphasized in the present context, however, is that if one wishes to examine the impact of television stimuli on deviant behavior among adolescents, it is necessary to include in the model those variables which have been prominent in the literature on delinquency. The broader implication of this view is that there is no simple direct relationship between television stimuli and adolescent deviance. On the contrary, the present researchers expect to observe some rather complex interactions among the sets of variables drawn from both the mass media and delinquency literature—variables which they conceive of as mediating the effect of television stimuli.

## MODEL AND HYPOTHESES

The preceding review of the literature suggests, then, that certain distinctions should be made with respect both to the independent and the dependent variables and to the relationship between them. With respect to the independent variable—television violence—at least two elements are crucial: the objective character of television programming and the respondent's subjective perception of the character of these programs. Thus, given a set of television shows, it is necessary first to inquire into the objective amount of violence (defined in some standardized manner) present in these shows. The subject's viewing habits must also be ascertained: how much time he spends watching television, which programs he watches, and which are his favorites. The favorite programs take on a special significance because these are likely to be the programs he watches attentively.

Given some objective measure of the violent content of programs actually watched, it must be determined, for the same set of programs, how the subjects perceive that violence. For example, do they think that it is a true reflection of the way people behave in the real world or that it is make-believe? Perhaps equally impoitant, do the programs seem to the adolescent to present a picture of the way people ought to behave? Is violence seen as the means used to achieve goals; is it effective in achieving these goals, or is the user of violence punished for his behavior?

The literature on mass communications indicates that additional sets of variables have an impact upon the way in which an individual uses the media. For present purposes these variables can be broken down into two classes: (1) demographic—broad social categories such as race, age, and social class, which indicate an individual's position in the social structure; (2) primary group relationships—social relationships with parents and peers in particular.

Turning to the dependent variable, violence and/or deviance, an essential distinction must be made between *attitudes and beliefs* about violence and deviance, and deviant and violent *behavior*. In making this distinction, the investigators are explicitly raising and testing the notion, expressed by several authors, that the effect of television violence may vary from the attitudinal to the behavioral realms. More specifically, they will inquire into the subject's commission of delinquent acts, using self-report techniques. In addition, data about the subjects' personal acceptance of various levels of violent behavior faced with varying levels of provocation will be examined, as well as data about their beliefs about the level of violence in their schools and neighborhoods.

Since the data do not permit a clear identification of the temporal sequence, it is difficult to answer the question of whether it is television or the kind of child sent to television which causes any observed relationship between television violence and the child's behavior and attitudes. One question which *can* be answered, of course, is whether watching violent television programs is associated with increased deviance or with attitudes such as approval of violence. Additionally, however, by controlling for gender, race, socioeconomic status, age, and various ties to the social structure—loosely labeled insulating factors, it becomes possible to see whether television violence is related to certain behavior and attitudes, whether it has an effect for some but not all categories of children, or whether its effect varies according to these characteristics of the child.

The major hypotheses of the present study are:

1. There is a relationship between television violence watched and both deviant behavior and attitudes and beliefs about aggression. These attitudes and beliefs include personal and perceived social acceptability of violence and perception of the level of violence present in American society.

2. This relationship will be strengthened for those respondents who subjectively perceive the violence in their favorite shows as an effective means to an end, who find it realistic, and in general who perceive violence to be an accepted mode of behavior in such shows. Those who do not perceive these factors should be less affected by objective violence.

3. The relationship between television violence and deviant behavior will be stronger for these categories of respondents who are more vulnerable to deviance, specifically: younger respondents, males, blacks, lower-class respondents, and those individuals who have fewer ties to the social structure.

## THE SAMPLE

The data for this and several related studies were collected during April 1970 in public junior and senior high schools in Prince Georges County, Maryland, bordering the District of Columbia.[2] This county was selected because it includes areas which are quite rural, middle-class and blue collar suburbs, and some areas which approximate conditions in an inner city.

The schools, five high and eight junior high schools, were selected in such a way as to provide a probability sample of students, with two restrictions: roughly equal numbers were selected from each grade, seventh through twelfth, although lower grades were somewhat larger; and a predominantly black school was oversampled to provide sufficient black respondents to facilitate comparisons.

The diversity of the sample schools can be noted from the proportion of respondents who were black and from varying socioeconomic levels (Table 1). Although the median percentage of black respondents was 4.4, in three of the schools more than 45 percent of the respondents were black. Three schools could be considered relatively affluent, with more than 40 percent of the respondents for whom this information was available reporting father's occupation classified as high.[3] In another three schools, 30 percent of the respondents were classified as low socioeconomic status, using father's occupation. Two of these schools are located near the District of Columbia; many of their students had recently moved the short distance from the city. The third, in a rural area, has a student population with farm backgrounds as well as parents who work in the District of Columbia or at service jobs in the area.

Table 1: The sample

| | |
|---|---|
| Senior high school students | 1242 |
| Junior high school students | 1057 |
| Total | 2299 |
| White male | 964 |
| Black male | 146 |
| White female | 1011 |
| Black female | 168 |

## ADOLESCENTS' VIEWING HABITS

One can estimate the potential influence of television by examining the amount of television viewing. Respondents were asked: "On an average day, about how many hours do you personally spend watching television?" In spite of the attempt to ask the question in a manner calculated to focus attention on actual viewing time, there may have been a tendency to overstate. The impression gained, nonetheless, is one of many youngsters spending hours in front of a television set (Table 2). Nearly 50 percent say they watch more than three hours a day. Some of these hours may represent time spent in the same room with a set which is turned on, rather than time spent paying close attention to what is on the screen. If the tendency to overstate the case is constant from one race, age, or gender category to another, it is possible at least to estimate the relative amount of viewing for these subsamples. The younger

Table 2: Hours television viewing by age, race, and gender

| Hours TV | White | | | | Black | | | | Total |
|---|---|---|---|---|---|---|---|---|---|
| | Male | | Female | | Male | | Female | | |
| | (11 – 14) | (15 – 19) | (11 – 14) | (15 – 19) | (11 – 14) | (15 – 19) | (11 – 14) | (15 – 19) | |
| 0 – 1 | 7% | 16% | 5% | 14% | 4% | 2% | – | 3% | 10% (221) |
| 2 – 3 | 43% | 49% | 37% | 48% | 13% | 21% | 14% | 24% | 41% (890) |
| More than 3 | 51% | 35% | 58% | 39% | 83% | 77% | 87% | 74% | 48% (1038) |
| | (320) | (578) | (367) | (596) | (46) | (87) | (74) | (81) | (2149) |

adolescents spend more time viewing than the older adolescents, females more than males, and black youngsters more than white. Adolescents from lower socioeconomic status homes watch television more hours per day than do those from higher status homes (Table 3).

News programs, while not the focus of the present study, are an important aspect of an individual's television habits. At least one writer has suggested that newscasts may have greater influence on violence potential than comparable dramatic programs (Greenwald, 1971). The young viewer may, in fact, be acquiring beliefs and attitudes about a variety of subjects in this fashion. Adolescents in the present study generally watch news programs quite frequently (Table 4). More than 50 percent say they watch news at least two or three times a week; 20 percent say every night. There is no clearcut pattern of subsample differences, although males and blacks tend to watch news more frequently than females and whites. Within the white subsample, older adolescents watched somewhat more frequently, but the converse was true for the black respondents. There was little difference between news watching of poor and of the more affluent youngsters (Table 5). Thus, the pattern of news watching is quite different from the pattern for overall viewing. This finding suggests the importance of measuring *what* is watched on television, not how much.

Table 3: Hours of television viewed daily by social class

| Hours | Social class | | |
| | Lower | Middle | Upper |
| --- | --- | --- | --- |
| 0 – 1 | 7% | 10% | 17% |
| 2 – 3 | 33% | 42% | 47% |
| More than 3 | 60% | 48% | 37% |
| Total | 100% (270) | 100% (812) | 100% (559) |

A major question in the present study is the level of violence in the programs being watched. Respondents were asked to list their four favorite programs, "the ones you try to watch every time they are on the air." They were then asked to select from that list their one most favorite show. Attention is focussed on the favorite programs because it seems liekly that they may be the most influential. As suggested above, it is possible that some viewing time is simply time spent in the same room with a television set. A person might watch the screen rather casually or might be more likely to watch a favorite show attentively from the beginning until it is finished.

A violence rating was assigned to each favorite program, and a summary average was computed for the four favorite programs. The ratings are taken from a survey of television critics and a sample of adults in a large city (Greenberg and Gordon, 1970). The definition of violence used

Table 4: Frequency of watching news by age, race, and gender

| Watch news | White | | | | Black | | | | Total |
|---|---|---|---|---|---|---|---|---|---|
| | Male | | Female | | Male | | Female | | |
| | (11 – 14) | (15 – 19) | (11 – 14) | (15 – 19) | (11 – 14) | (15 – 19) | (11 – 14) | (15 – 19) | |
| Every night | 22% | 25% | 14% | 18% | 31% | 18% | 26% | 19% | 20% |
| 2 – 3 times weekly | 35% | 35% | 30% | 33% | 25% | 37% | 25% | 27% | 33% |
| Once a week | 21% | 15% | 20% | 21% | 15% | 17% | 16% | 22% | 19% |
| Less than once a week | 14% | 16% | 22% | 20% | 19% | 20% | 25% | 27% | 19% |
| Never | 7% | 9% | 14% | 9% | 10% | 8% | 8% | 6% | 9% |
| | (326) | (606) | (375) | (629) | (48) | (93) | (80) | (83) | (2240) |

was as follows: "By violence I mean how much fighting, shooting, yelling, or killing there usually is in the show." The correlation between ratings by critics and by adult public was .86.

A problem arises in the case of shows which cannot be coded—for example, *Saturday Night at the Movies*. The violence level may vary from one episode to another, and there was no rationale for including these shows in either the low, moderate, or high violence categories.

Table 5:  Frequency of watching television news by social class

|  | Social class | | |
| --- | --- | --- | --- |
| Frequency | Lower | Middle | Upper |
| Every night | 18% | 18% | 20% |
| 2 — 3 times weekly | 33% | 35% | 34% |
| Once weekly | 21% | 18% | 21% |
| Less than once weekly | 20% | 20% | 18% |
| Never | 8% | 10% | 7% |
| Total | 100% (277) | 100% (839) | 100% (582) |

About one-third of the respondents listed a program rated as "low violence" as their favorite; 12 percent named moderate violence programs; a quarter selected high violence shows, and another quarter picked shows which could not be rated (Table 6). There were no great differences in the selections of subsamples, although females, younger adolescents, and upper-class respondents named low violence shows somewhat more frequently. Distribution of average violence ratings (of four favorite shows) is very similar.

It might seem reasonable to assume that the more time a child spends watching television, the greater is the likelihood that he will be exposed to violent program content. The present study does not include a measure of a child's total exposure to violent programs for any period of

Table 6:  Violence ratings, favorite program, by race, gender, age, and social class

|  | Violence rating | | | | |
| --- | --- | --- | --- | --- | --- |
|  | Low | Moderate | High | Not codeable | Number |
| White male | 27% | 12% | 28% | 33% | (953) |
| White female | 42% | 14% | 22% | 22% | (997) |
| Black male | 30% | 7% | 31% | 32% | (142) |
| Black female | 40% | 3% | 36% | 21% | (164) |
| 11 — 14 years | 39% | 13% | 22% | 26% | (824) |
| 15 — 19 years | 33% | 11% | 28% | 28% | (1415) |
| Lower-class | 33% | 11% | 22% | 34% | (273) |
| Middle-class | 36% | 12% | 27% | 25% | (823) |
| Upper-class | 39% | 12% | 25% | 23% | (566) |
| Total | 35% | 12% | 26% | 27% | (2266) |

time. It can be noted, however, that the respondents who spend much of their time viewing television are neither more nor less likely to choose violent programs as their favorites (Table 7).

Table 7: Hours of television viewed daily and violence, favorite program

| Violence, favorite program | Hours | | |
| --- | --- | --- | --- |
| | 0 – 1 | 2 – 3 | 4 or more |
| Low | 49% (69) | 46% (301) | 50% (398) |
| Moderate | 19% (27) | 18% (120) | 14% (110) |
| High | 33% (46) | 36% (233) | 37% (295) |
| Total | 100% (142) | 100% (654) | 100% (803) |

# TELEVISION VIOLENCE AND DEVIANT BEHAVIOR

## Deviance measures

In order to measure deviance, a self-report checklist of deviant behavior was compiled from the usual measures of delinquency found in the literature. In order to comply with the requirements of the school systems, items concerning sexual behavior, drugs, and the more serious types of delinquency, such as stealing, were not included.

For this study, five measures representing different types of deviance were used. The first type is aggressive or violent acts. It was measured by responses to the questions about how often the respondents: (1) got into a serious fight with a student at school; (2) got something by telling a person something bad would happen to him if they did not get what they wanted; (3) hurt someone badly enough for him to need bandages; (4) had taken part in a fight where a bunch of their friends were against another bunch. The second type of deviance is composed of petty delinquent acts. Respondents were asked how often they: (1) went onto someone's land or into a house or building when they weren't supposed to; (2) damaged school property on purpose. The third type of deviance is defiance of parents and was measured by how often the respondents said they: (1) stayed out later than parents said; (2) ran away from home; (3) argued or had a fight with either of their parents; (4) drank beer or liquor without parent's permission.

Political action by the young can be and often is defined as a form of deviance. Merton calls this deviant behavior nonconformity, as opposed to aberrant behavior; the individual knows but does not accept the norms and violates them openly in an effort to bring about change (Merton, 1966). It was measured through responses to questions on how often the students: (1) participated in a sit-in or demonstration at school; (2) participated in a sit-in or demonstration at places other than school;

(3) asked a school official to change any regulations or courses.

The last measure of deviance—involvement with legal officials—is presumably the most serious and may be used as a substitute for some of the serious delinquencies not listed. The students were asked about their contacts with the police and how often they had: (1) been stopped by the police; (2) been picked up and taken down to the police station; (3) been arrested; (4) been brought to the juvenile court; and (5) spent time in a juvenile detention facility. Such involvements may be used as an indirect measure of serious delinquency.

Table 8: Aggressive deviance by race, gender, and social class

| Aggressiveness | White males | White females | Black males | Black females |
|---|---|---|---|---|
| | | Lower class | | |
| Low | 32.4 | 52.0 | 25.0 | 58.8 |
| Moderate | 33.3 | 31.6 | 46.9 | 23.5 |
| High | 34.3 | 16.4 | 28.1 | 17.7 |
| Total | 100% (108) | 100% (95) | 100% (32) | 100% (34) |
| | | Middle class | | |
| Low | 39.3 | 59.2 | 21.6 | 47.4 |
| Moderate | 32.2 | 31.1 | 43.2 | 34.2 |
| High | 28.5 | 9.7 | 35.2 | 18.4 |
| Total | 100% (351) | 100% (402) | 100% (37) | 100% (38) |
| | | Upper class | | |
| Low | 45.9 | 67.2 | a | 45.0 |
| Moderate | 33.7 | 25.5 | a | 30.0 |
| High | 20.4 | 7.3 | a | 25.0 |
| Total | 100% (270) | 100% (271) | a | 100% (20) |

[a] Number too small for stable percentages (less than 20)

Items were included in the various indices on the basis of an *a priori* relationship between the behavior reported and the type of deviance being measured. Summary scores, based simply on cumulative incidence, were derived for the five types of deviance (scored one for "did it once" and two for "twice or more"). Based on the marginals, each type is divided into three logical subdivisions of low, moderate, and high deviance for tabular presentation; original scores are used to compute correlations. In this section each type of deviance is examined in turn in order to discover the relationship between deviance and television violence.

## Distribution of deviant behavior

In order to determine if the present data are comparable with those of previous studies, the distribution of the five deviant behavior measures are presented, controlling for race, gender, and social class as measured by father's occupation. Since race and social class are often related, the effects of race are presented controlling for social class. The results are presented in Tables 8 through 12.

Inspection of Table 8 reveals that among lower-class respondents, gender and not race is the important variable in explaining aggression. Boys are more aggressive than girls, and this holds true for both races. Among middle-class respondents, however, race and gender are both important. Again, boys are more aggressive than girls, but in this social class blacks are also more aggressive than whites. This same pattern holds again for the upper-class respondents. Being middle- or upper-class insulates whites from aggression but does not insulate blacks. The general conclusion is that as social class increases, aggression decreases, but only for whites. The opposite is true for blacks. Upper- and middle-class blacks tend to be more aggressive than do lower-class blacks. In every social class, boys are much more aggressive than girls.

A different pattern emerges with respect to petty delinquency (Table 9). There is a positive relationship between social class and this type of deviance. Upper-class respondents admit to more of these petty delinquencies than do lower-class respondents. This type of deviance is the kind that erases social class differences in self-reported delinquency studies and shows the middle and upper classes to be more deviant than they appear to be in official statistics (Gibbons, 1970, pp. 20-31). As before, there is more male than female deviance in all social classes. Race, however, presents a different and inconsistent picture. White males are more deviant than blacks except in the upper class, where the N is too small to make a comparison. Among females, however, it is the upper- and middle-class white girls who commit more petty delinquent acts than do their racial counterparts. In the lower social class, whites and blacks do not differ. A possible explanation for this mixed pattern is that petty delinquency is the domain of the privileged, their normal deviance, and thus is found among the advantaged—that is, whites and upper-class respondents. In addition, compared with aggressive deviance, girls commit much more of this more minor type of deviance.

The differences in rates between boys and girls and among the social classes narrow considerably for fighting with parents (Table 10). This deviance is the most prevalent of the five and appears to be neither gender- nor class-specific. There are racial variations, however, in all social classes and for both genders. Black respondents appear to fight much less with their parents than do whites.

Table 11 presents the results for the distribution of political deviance. The gender differences reported for aggression again disappear; boys and girls are almost equally involved in political action. One might predict that the more advantaged social classes would be more politically sophisticated and thus engage in more political activity. This appears to

Table 9: Petty delinquency by race, gender, and social class

| Amount of petty crime | White males | White females | Black males | Black females |
|---|---|---|---|---|
| | | Lower class | | |
| Low | 43.4 | 62.6 | 37.5 | 57.1 |
| Moderate | 15.1 | 22.2 | 40.6 | 25.7 |
| High | 41.5 | 15.1 | 21.8 | 17.1 |
| Total | 100% (106) | 100% (99) | 100% (32) | 100% (35) |
| | | Middle class | | |
| Low | 39.0 | 60.8 | 50.0 | 65.8 |
| Moderate | 14.7 | 17.2 | 10.5 | 21.1 |
| High | 46.3 | 22.0 | 39.5 | 13.1 |
| Total | 100% (354) | 100% (401) | 100% (38) | 100% (38) |
| | | Upper class | | |
| Low | 37.6 | 50.7 | a | 50.0 |
| Moderate | 18.1 | 20.8 | a | 40.0 |
| High | 44.2 | 28.4 | a | 10.0 |
| Total | 100% (271) | 100% (274) | a | 100% (20) |

a Number too small for stable percentages

Table 10: Fighting with parents by race, gender, and social class

| Amount of fighting | White males | White females | Black males | Black females |
|---|---|---|---|---|
| Low | 25.0 | 27.5 | 48.4 | 71.4 |
| Moderate | 31.5 | 30.6 | 25.8 | 14.3 |
| High | 43.5 | 41.9 | 25.8 | 14.3 |
| Total | 100% (100) | 100% (98) | 100% (31) | 100% (35) |
| | | Middle class | | |
| Low | 21.4 | 24.5 | 35.1 | 44.8 |
| Moderate | 26.9 | 30.1 | 37.8 | 39.5 |
| High | 51.7 | 45.3 | 27.0 | 15.8 |
| Total | 100% (350) | 100% (399) | 100% (37) | 100% (38) |
| Low | 24.7 | 27.0 | a | 21.1 |
| Moderate | 28.8 | 34.3 | a | 63.2 |
| High | 46.4 | 38.7 | a | 15.8 |
| Total | 100% (271) | 100% (274) | a | 100% (19) |

a Number too small for stable percentages

Table 11: Political deviance by race, gender, and social class

| Amount of political deviance | White males | White females | Black males | Black females |
|---|---|---|---|---|
| Lower class | | | | |
| Low | 52.3 | 49.5 | 40.6 | 42.9 |
| Moderate | 15.9 | 24.2 | 9.4 | 17.1 |
| High | 31.8 | 26.3 | 49.8 | 40.1 |
| Total | 100% (107) | 100% (99) | 100% (32) | 100% (35) |
| Middle class | | | | |
| Low | 50.4 | 47.9 | 36.1 | 37.8 |
| Moderate | 21.4 | 24.8 | 25.0 | 27.0 |
| High | 28.3 | 27.4 | 38.9 | 35.1 |
| Total | 100% (351) | 100% (399) | 100% (36) | 100% (37) |
| Upper class | | | | |
| Low | 42.8 | 44.9 | a | 50.0 |
| Moderate | 23.6 | 23.5 | a | 10.0 |
| High | 33.6 | 31.6 | a | 40.0 |
| Total | 100% (271) | 100% (272) | a | 100% (20) |

a Number too small for stable percentages

be the case; the amount of "low" political activity decreases as social class increases. Blacks, perhaps because of the momentum of the Black Movement, have attempted political action more often than whites. This is not unexpected, and again it is the upper-status blacks who are the most active; they were also the most aggressive.

For males there is an inverse relationship between social class and involvement with legal officials or serious deviance (Table 12). Thus, these data agree with most other studies of involvement with legal authorities. Boys greatly outnumber girls for this type of deviance, again in line with other research. What is not expected is that there are no racial variations. Social class is more important than race, and when social class is held constant, the differences between the races disappear. Most other studies, including those which use self-report data, however, show an overrepresentation of blacks among those youngsters involved with the police. A possible explanation for this study's discrepant finding is the sample. All of the respondents were students. It is possible that among school dropouts there is a higher rate of official involvement and that blacks may be overrepresented in the dropout population. Had a truly representative sample of all adolescents been taken, the racial differences would perhaps appear.

Table 12: Serious deviance by race, gender, and social class

| Amount of serious deviance | White males | White females | Black males | Black females |
|---|---|---|---|---|
| Lower class | | | | |
| Low | 28.3 | 64.6 | 30.3 | 65.7 |
| Moderate | 54.7 | 30.3 | 51.5 | 34.3 |
| High | 17.0 | 5.0 | 18.2 | 0 |
| Total | 100% (106) | 100% (99) | 100% (33) | 100% (35) |
| Middle class | | | | |
| Low | 34.6 | 64.7 | 30.6 | 73.7 |
| Moderate | 47.6 | 30.0 | 52.8 | 23.7 |
| High | 17.8 | 5.1 | 16.7 | 2.6 |
| Total | 100% (353) | 100% (400) | 100% (36) | 100% (38) |
| Upper class | | | | |
| Low | 44.9 | 68.2 | a | 70.7 |
| Moderate | 41.9 | 26.6 | a | 25.0 |
| High | 13.1 | 5.2 | a | 5.0 |
| Total | 100% (267) | 100% (274) | a | 100% (20) |

a Number too small for stable percentages

To summarize the distribution of the five dependent variables, one notes that in general boys are more deviant than girls, especially on the more extreme types of deviance such as aggression and serious deviance. Similarly, blacks and lower-class respondents are overrepresented for these same two types of deviance. Thus, generally speaking, with the one exception of official involvement (which is apparently due to the lack of inclusion of school dropouts in the present sample), the deviance scores are distributed by gender, race, and class in a manner consistent with the literature on deviance. These findings give some measure of confidence in the reliability of the self-report measures of deviance used in this research.

# The effects of television

The general hypothesis is that there will be a weak but positive relationship between the amount of violence viewed on television and deviant behavior. However, this hypothesis is qualified in three respects. First, it is predicted that the relationship will be stronger for certain types of deviance. For example, it is predicted that the relationship between television violence and aggressive deviance will be stronger than the relationship between television violence and nonaggressive or less violent types of deviance.

The second qualification concerns the effects of the respondent's perception of the content of television programming. It is argued that such perception is an important variable to be considered in examining the effects of television violence on behavior. The literature suggests that the perception of the content of the media presentation interposes itself between the objective content and any behavioral response. For present purposes, then, it is relevant to examine not only the relationship between the objective amount of violence viewed and deviance, but also the relationship between the subject's perception of the media content and that same deviance. It is hypothesized that the relationship between television violence and deviant behavior will be increased for those respondents who perceive that violence is an effective means to an end and that the characters portray acceptable behavior.

The third qualification refers to the effects of other variables known to have a relationship with deviant behavior. For example, there are gender differences in both the rate and the type of deviant behavior; males have higher rates in general and also are more likely to engage in the more aggressive types of deviance. It is predicted that the relationship between television violence and deviant behavior will be stronger for those respondents who are more vulnerable to deviance: males, blacks, lower-class or young respondents, and those respondents with fewer ties to the social structure. Thus the main interest is the examination of the possible joint effects of television violence and other variables on deviant behavior.

Tables 13 through 17 present data on the objective violence rating of the respondent's favorite television program and his score on each type of deviant behavior. These tables indicate that there is a very small positive relationship between the objective violence rating of the respondent's favorite program and deviant behavior; correlation coefficients are not significant except for serious deviance. They do, however, consistently show more deviance in the high violence condition than in the low violence condition. Thus the general hypothesis receives slight support. The first qualification to the general hypothesis is in part rejected since the relationship between television violence and deviance is not stronger for aggressive deviance but is stronger for serious deviance.

When the average violence rating of the adolescent's four favorite shows is considered, however, the relationships with deviance are somewhat stronger (Tables 18 and 25). The general hypothesis is confirmed then, using this latter measure of television violence viewed. The first qualification is also confirmed, as the relationships are stronger for average violence and for aggressive and serious deviance than for the other deviance measures.

It will be remembered that respondents were asked to list as their favorite shows those which they "tried to watch every time they are on the air," and then to select their most favorite from that list. It is, of

Table 13: Aggressive deviance by violence, favorite program

| | Violence, favorite program | | |
|---|---|---|---|
| Aggressiveness | Low | Moderate | High |
| Low | 49.9 | 48.6 | 48.2 |
| Moderate | 31.6 | 34.7 | 30.9 |
| High | 18.5 | 16.7 | 21.0 |
| Total | 100% (776) | 100% (259) | 100% (573) |

r = .038 (n.s.)

Table 14: Petty delinquency by violence, favorite program

| | Violence, favorite program | | |
|---|---|---|---|
| Amount of petty delinquency | Low | Moderate | High |
| Low | 49.1 | 51.3 | 46.3 |
| Moderate | 19.7 | 18.0 | 17.6 |
| High | 31.2 | 30.7 | 36.1 |
| Total | 100% (782) | 100% (261) | 100% (579) |

r = .043 (n.s.)

Table 15: Fighting with parents by violence, favorite program

| | Violence, favorite program | | |
|---|---|---|---|
| Amount of fighting | Low | Moderate | High |
| Low | 28.4 | 27.7 | 28.4 |
| Moderate | 30.6 | 25.8 | 30.2 |
| High | 41.1 | 46.5 | 41.4 |
| Total | 100% (772) | 100% (256) | 100% (570) |

r = .017 (s)

Table 16: Political deviance by violence, favorite program

| | Violence, favorite program | | |
|---|---|---|---|
| Amount of political deviance | Low | Moderate | High |
| Low | 48.4 | 46.9 | 46.1 |
| Moderate | 22.9 | 23.3 | 22.8 |
| High | 28.7 | 29.8 | 31.1 |
| Total | 100% (783) | 100% (258) | 100% (571) |

r = .029 (n.s.)

Table 17:  Serious deviance by violence, favorite program

|  | Violence, favorite program | | |
| Amount of serious deviance | Low | Moderate | High |
|---|---|---|---|
| Low | 56.9 | 50.8 | 46.5 |
| Moderate | 34.5 | 38.0 | 43.9 |
| High | 8.5 | 11.3 | 9.6 |
| Total | 100% (780) | 100% (258) | 100% (574) |

$r = .058$ *

* $p < .01$

course, not feasible to obtain a violence rating of all programs watched by the subjects of this study. Their four favorite programs, however, will represent a substantial proportion of their total viewing in addition to being an indicator of preference *per se*. In comparing results using the two measures, it should also be remembered that no violence rating was available for a quarter of the respondents' most favorite shows. The average violence rating, on the other hand, could be computed for nearly all respondents. (If one of the four could not be coded, average was computed for the remaining three.)

Table 18:  Aggressive and serious deviance by average violence rating of four favorite shows

| Amount of aggressive deviance | Violence rating | | |
|  | Low | Moderate | High |
|---|---|---|---|
| Low | 53.8 | 48.0 | 40.4 |
| Moderate | 31.7 | 31.5 | 34.2 |
| High | 14.4 | 20.4 | 25.5 |
| Total | 100% (637) | 100% (1104) | 100% (339) |

$r = .109$ **

| Amount of serious deviance | | | |
|---|---|---|---|
| Low | 63.1 | 49.1 | 42.4 |
| Moderate | 30.9 | 40.9 | 41.5 |
| High | 5.9 | 10.0 | 16.1 |
| Total | 100% (640) | 100% (1109) | 100% (335) |

$r = .158$ **

** $p < .001$

Since the objective violence rating of the respondent's most favorite television show does not bear any strong relationship to the amount of deviant behavior, it is important to examine the possibility that a stronger relationship may exist between the subject's perception of the violence content of his favorite show and his deviant behavior. The following were included in a list of statements and the respondent asked to select those which describe his favorite show: (1) the main character pushes the others around; (2) the guy who gets rough gets his way. Selection of the first statement is taken as evidence that the respondent perceives violence to be used; selection of the second, that it is rewarded. Table 19 presents the data for these relationships between subjective perception of television violence and deviant behavior. Only the more violent and serious deviances are presented. (It should be noted that these tables use the entire sample of respondents who rated their favorite shows and are not limited to those respondents for whose favorite shows there was an

Table 19: Perception of television violence

Aggressive deviance by perception of television violence

| Aggressiveness | Violence used as means | Violence not used as means | Violence rewarded | Violence not rewarded |
|---|---|---|---|---|
| Low | 31.5 | 49.6 | 28.3 | 50.3 |
| Moderate | 27.0 | 32.1 | 27.0 | 32.1 |
| High | 41.4 | 18.2 | 44.7 | 17.6 |
| Total | 100% (111) | 100% (2081) | 100% (159) | 100% (2034) |

Petty delinquency by perception of television violence

| Amount of petty crime | Violence used as means | Violence not used as means | Violence rewarded | Violence not rewarded |
|---|---|---|---|---|
| Low | 36.8 | 49.9 | 35.0 | 50.4 |
| Moderate | 17.5 | 17.9 | 20.0 | 17.7 |
| High | 45.6 | 32.2 | 45.0 | 32.0 |
| Total | 100% (114) | 100% (2096) | 100% (160) | 100% (2051) |

Serious deviance by perception of television violence

| Amount of serious deviance | Violence used as means | Violence not used as means | Violence rewarded | Violence not rewarded |
|---|---|---|---|---|
| Low | 43.2 | 52.1 | 37.2 | 52.9 |
| Moderate | 36.0 | 38.1 | 44.9 | 37.4 |
| High | 20.7 | 9.8 | 17.9 | 9.7 |
| Total | 100% (111) | 100% (2085) | 100% (156) | 100% (2041) |

objective rating.) Those subjects who perceive violent means as being used on their favorite show are somewhat more likely to engage in deviant behavior; those who perceive the use of violence as being rewarded are similarly somewhat more likely to engage in deviance.

In addition to the violence used and rewarded, other subjective perceptions expected to increase the likelihood of deviance included perceived realism and normative content. Perceived realism was indicated by the item "it shows life as it really is" and normative content by "it shows the way people ought to act." A combined index was constructed, scoring one for each of these items indicating perceived violence, realism, and normative content. The relationship between this index (labeled "perceived violence and realism") and deviant behavior is generally greater than that between the objective violence rating of the favorite program and deviance (Table 27). It should be remembered that only a very small minority perceive their favorite show as violent, however. It is not known how often violence is subjectively perceived on the four favorite shows, so the comparison between objective and subjective violence can be made for this one show only.

Summarizing the findings to this point, then, the data indicate a small but generally consistent relationship between the objective violence rating of television shows and deviant behavior. As expected, a stronger relationship does exist between the subject's perception of the violence content of his favorite television show and the amount of deviant behavior, and this relationship is strongest with respect to aggressive deviance. It appears, then, that the subject's perception of violence is more closely related to deviant behavior than is the objective rating of the violence content of television shows. This comparison is made for violence rating and perception of the respondent's one favorite show only, as it is for this program that both kinds of information are available.

The next point to be considered concerns the possible joint effect of objective television violence and the subject's perception of that violence on deviant behavior. It would be expected that the amount of deviance, particularly the more aggressive type, would be increased with the joint occurrence of a high objective violence rating and the subject's perception of the presence of such violence.

Examination of Table 20 reveals that this is not the case. There is no consistent pattern of relationship between the objective violence rating of favorite program and deviant behavior, even among those respondents who perceive violence used and rewarded on their favorite shows. With respect to petty delinquency, it does appear that if the respondent perceives violence as not rewarded, and if his show is objectively violent, then there is a tendency toward higher deviance. It can be noted in Table 25, however, that controlling for perceived violence and realism does not change the relationships between favorite program violence and deviance.

Table 20: Objective and subjective measures of television violence

Aggressive deviance by violence, favorite program, and perception of favorite program

| Aggressive deviance | Violence used as means | | | Violence not used as means | | |
|---|---|---|---|---|---|---|
| | Low | Moderate | High | Low | Moderate | High |
| Low | 38.2 | a | 24.2 | 50.4 | 49.2 | 49.4 |
| Moderate | 17.6 | a | 45.5 | 32.3 | 35.3 | 30.0 |
| High | 44.2 | a | 30.3 | 17.3 | 15.5 | 20.5 |
| Total | 100% (34) | a | 100% (33) | 100% (742) | 100% (252) | 100% (536) |

| | Violence rewarded | | | Violence not rewarded | | |
|---|---|---|---|---|---|---|
| Low | 36.8 | 17.6 | 27.8 | 50.6 | 51.0 | 50.1 |
| Moderate | 18.4 | 29.4 | 29.6 | 32.2 | 34.9 | 31.1 |
| High | 44.8 | 52.9 | 42.6 | 17.1 | 14.2 | 18.8 |
| Total | 100% (30) | 100% (17) | 100% (54) | 100% (735) | 100% (241) | 100% (515) |

Petty delinquency by violence, favorite program, and perception of favorite program

| Petty delinquency | Violence used as means | | | Violence not used as means | | |
|---|---|---|---|---|---|---|
| | Low | Moderate | High | Low | Moderate | High |
| Low | 40.0 | a | 29.4 | 49.5 | 52.0 | 47.1 |
| Moderate | 11.4 | a | 17.6 | 20.1 | 17.7 | 17.6 |
| High | 48.5 | a | 52.9 | 30.3 | 30.3 | 31.2 |
| Total | 100% (35) | a | 100% (34) | 100% (745) | 100% (254) | 100% (541) |

| | Violence rewarded | | | Violence not rewarded | | |
|---|---|---|---|---|---|---|
| Low | 37.8 | 41.2 | 33.9 | 49.7 | 51.9 | 47.4 |
| Moderate | 21.6 | 11.8 | 17.9 | 19.5 | 18.5 | 17.5 |
| High | 40.5 | 47.0 | 48.3 | 30.8 | 29.6 | 35.1 |
| Total | 100% (37) | 100% (17) | 100% (56) | 100% (742) | 100% (243) | 100% (519) |

Serious deviance by violence, favorite program, and perception of favorite program

| Amount of serious deviance | Violence used as means | | | Violence not used as means | | |
|---|---|---|---|---|---|---|
| | Low | Moderate | High | Low | Moderate | High |
| Low | 35.3 | a | 44.1 | 57.9 | 50.8 | 46.8 |
| Moderate | 47.1 | a | 32.4 | 33.9 | 38.1 | 44.4 |
| High | 17.6 | a | 23.4 | 8.2 | 11.1 | 8.7 |
| Total | 100% (34) | a | 100% (34) | 100% (744) | 100% (252) | 100% (536) |

Table 20 (Cont.)

| | Violence rewarded | | | Violence not rewarded | | |
|---|---|---|---|---|---|---|
| Low | 27.8 | a | 29;6 | 58.4 | 51.9 | 48.4 |
| Moderate | 50.0 | a | 55.6 | 33.6 | 37.8 | 42.4 |
| High | 22.2 | a | 14.9 | 7.9 | 10.3 | 9.2 |
| Total | 100% | a | 100% | 100% . | 100% | 100% |
| | (36) | | (54) | (741) | (241) | (516) |

The issue was previously raised that the joint occurrence of violent television and other variables related to deviant behavior could increase deviance rates. An examination of the relationship between the objective violence rating and aggressive deviance, while controlling for these other variables, reveals that this is not correct (Tables 21 to 23). Neither gender, race, social class, nor age strengthens the original relationship between favorite program violence and deviance. The differences between the deviance rates of those who watch the low and those who watch the high violence shows are still quite small; in some tables there are reversals and in general no consistent pattern emerges. One tentative generalization is that the relationship is strongest for lower-class respondents.

Table 21:  Aggressive deviance by violence, favorite program, gender, race, social class, and age

| | White males Violence, favorite program | | | Black males Violence, favorite program | | |
|---|---|---|---|---|---|---|
| Aggressiveness | Low | Moderate | High | Low | Moderate | High |
| Low | 43.3 | 34.2 | 38.0 | 23.8 | a | 30.0 |
| Moderate | 29.9 | 36.0 | 31.8 | 35.7 | a | 32.5 |
| High | 26.8 | 29.7 | 30.2 | 40.5 | a | 37.5 |
| Total | 100% | 100% | 100% | 100% | a | 100% |
| | (254) | (111) | (255) | (42) | a | (40) |

| | White females Violence, favorite program | | | Black females Violence, favorite program | | |
|---|---|---|---|---|---|---|
| Aggressiveness | Low | Moderate | High | Low | Moderate | High |
| Low | 56.9 | 62.9 | 63.0 | 46.0 | a | 50.8 |
| Moderate | 31.3 | 32.6 | 29.6 | 38.1 | a | 28.8 |
| High | 11.8 | 4.5 | 7.5 | 15.9 | a | 20.4 |
| Total | 100% | 100% | 100% | 100% | a | 100% |
| | (415) | (132) | (216) | (63) | | (59) |

Table 21 (Cont.)

| Aggressiveness | Young (11-14) Violence, favorite program | | | Older (15 +) Violence, favorite program | | |
|---|---|---|---|---|---|---|
| | Low | Moderate | High | Low | Moderate | High |
| Low | 44.9 | 44.6 | 40.6 | 53.4 | 51.3 | 52.3 |
| Moderate | 34.3 | 45.5 | 34.9 | 29.6 | 27.9 | 28.8 |
| High | 20.0 | 9.9 | 24.5 | 17.0 | 20.7 | 18.9 |
| Total | 100% | 100% | 100% | 100% | 100% | 100% |
| | (312) | (101) | (175) | (459) | (154) | (392) |

| Aggressiveness | Lower class Violence, favorite program | | | Middle class Violence, favorite program | | |
|---|---|---|---|---|---|---|
| | Low | Moderate | High | Low | Moderate | High |
| Low | 40.4 | 43.7 | 47.5 | 50.3 | 44.6 | 48.0 |
| Moderate | 34.8 | 40.6 | 25.4 · | 30.8 | 36.6 | 31.2 |
| High | 24.7 | 15.5 | 27.2 | 18.8 | 18.9 | 20.8 |
| Total | 100% | 100% | 100% | 100% | 100% | 100% |
| | (89) | (32) | (59) | (292) | (101) | (221) |

| Aggressiveness | Upper class Violence, favorite program | | |
|---|---|---|---|
| | Low | Moderate | High |
| Low | 56.6 | 61.4 | 55.6 |
| Moderate | 29.4 | 31.4 | 28.5 |
| High | 14.0 | 7.2 | 16.0 |
| Total | 100% | 100% | 100% |
| | (221) | (70) | (144) |

[a] Number too small for stable percentages

It may be, however, that race, gender, and age are not the crucial characteristics of the child for understanding the effects of television. There is some reason to expect that the strength of the child's ties to the social structure may influence the manner in which he uses television. Family troubles, insecurity, and unsatisfactory social relationships, for example, have been found characteristic of "heavy viewers" (Himmelweit et al., 1958; Schramm et al., 1961). Empey has suggested that the absence of strong personal relationships would make the child more dependent on the images portrayed by television and movies (1967, p. 40). Maccoby's investigation supports that hypothesis (1954).

Another argument, concerning deviant behavior rather than television, is that strong ties to the social structure will inhibit deviant behavior (Briar and Piliavin, 1965). This argument includes personal relationships but also other kinds of ties to the social structure. High occupa-

Table 22: Petty delinquency by violence, favorite program, gender, race, social class, and age

| Amt. of petty delinquency | White males Violence, favorite program | | | Black males Violence, favorite program | | |
|---|---|---|---|---|---|---|
| | Low | Moderate | High | Low | Moderate | High |
| Low | 40.8 | 45.9 | 31.4 | 35.7 | a | 53.7 |
| Moderate | 18.0 | 9.0 | 18.6 | 31.0 | a | 14.6 |
| High | 41.2 | 45.0 | 50.1 | 33.3 | a | 31.7 |
| Total | 100% (255) | 100% (111) | 100% (258) | 100% (42) | a | 100% (41) |

| Amt. of petty delinquency | White females Violence, favorite program | | | Black females Violence, favorite program | | |
|---|---|---|---|---|---|---|
| | Low | Moderate | High | Low | Moderate | High |
| Low | 53.7 | 54.5 | 59.2 | 58.7 | a | 57.6 |
| Moderate | 19.3 | 24.6 | 16.5 | 22.2 | a | 20.3 |
| High | 27.0 | 20.8 | 24.3 | 19.1 | a | 22.0 |
| Total | 100% (419) | 100% (134) | 100% (218) | 100% (63) | a | 100% (59) |

| Amt. of petty delinquency | Young (11–14) Violence, favorite program | | | Older (15 +) Violence favorite program | | |
|---|---|---|---|---|---|---|
| | Low | Moderate | High | Low | Moderate | High |
| Low | 47.6 | 50.5 | 46.3 | 49.8 | 50.6 | 46.2 |
| Moderate | 20.2 | 24.3 | 20.3 | 19.6 | 14.3 | 16.7 |
| High | 32.2 | 25.3 | 33.3 | 30.7 | 35.0 | 37.1 |
| Total | 100% (317) | 100% (103) | 100% (177) | 100% (460) | 100% (154) | 100% (396) |

| Amt. of petty delinquency | Lower class Violence, favorite program | | | Middle class Violence, favorite program | | |
|---|---|---|---|---|---|---|
| | Low | Moderate | High | Low | Moderate | High |
| Low | 52.2 | 51.6 | 48.3 | 50.9 | 52.5 | 49.8 |
| Moderate | 25.6 | 19.4 | 19.0 | 18.8 | 12.9 | 16.1 |
| High | 22.0 | 29.1 | 32.8 | 30.4 | 34.6 | 34.1 |
| Total | 100% (90) | 100% (31) | 100% (58) | 100% (293) | 100% (101) | 100% (223) |

Table 22 (Cont.)

| | Upper class Violence, favorite program | | |
|---|---|---|---|
| Amount of petty delinquency | Low | Moderate | High |
| Low | 46.6 | 40.3 | 39.3 |
| Moderate | 18.1 | 27.8 | 22.8 |
| High | 35.3 | 32.0 | 37.9 |
| Total | 100% (221) | 100% (72) | 100% (145) |

a Number too small for stable percentages
* p < .01

tional aspirations and expectation of apprehension and punishment for wrongdoing are two such inhibiting factors. The individual with high occupational aspirations would have more to lose by getting into trouble than would the child who has no such aspirations. The child who be-

Table 23: Serious deviance by violence, favorite program, race, gender, social class, and age

| | White males Violence, favorite program | | | Black males Violence, favorite program | | |
|---|---|---|---|---|---|---|
| Amount of serious deviance | Low | Moderate | High | Low | Moderate | High |
| Low | 45.8 | 25.7 | 30.7 | 35.7 | a | 36.6 |
| Moderate | 41.9 | 53.2 | 52.9 | 50.0 | a | 56.1 |
| High | 12.3 | 21.1 | 16.4 | 14.3 | a | 7.3 |
| Total | 100% (253) | 100% (109) | 100% (257) | 100% (42) | a | 100% (41) |
| | r = .078 (n.s.) | | | r = .055 (n.s.) | | |

| | White females Violence, favorite program | | | Black females Violence, favorite program | | |
|---|---|---|---|---|---|---|
| Amount of serious deviance | Low | Moderate | High | Low | Moderate | High |
| Low | 65.6 | 72.9 | 62.3 | 59.7 | a | 64.4 |
| Moderate | 28.2 | 24.8 | 34.4 | 33.9 | a | 32.2 |
| High | 6.2 | 2.3 | 3.2 | 6.5 | a | 3.4 |
| Total | 100% (419) | 100% (133) | 100% (215) | 100% (62) | a | 100% (39) |
| | r = .032 (n.s.) | | | r = .022 (n.s.) | | |

Table 23 (Cont.)

| Amount of serious deviance | Young (11–14) Violence, favorite program | | | Older (15 +) Violence, favorite program | | |
|---|---|---|---|---|---|---|
| | Low | Moderate | High | Low | Moderate | High |
| Low | 66.6 | 70.6 | 54.6 | 50.8 | 38.2 | 43.4 |
| Moderate | 29.0 | 22.5 | 37.4 | 38.1 | 47.4 | 46.7 |
| High | 4.4 | 6.9 | 8.0 | 11.2 | 14.5 | 9.9 |
| Total | 100% | 100% | 100% | 100% | 100% | 100% |
| | (317) | (102) | (174) | (457) | (152) | (394) |
| | $r = .110$ ** | | | $r = .013$ (n.s.) | | |

| Amount of serious deviance | Lower class Violence, favorite program | | | Middle class Violence, favorite program | | |
|---|---|---|---|---|---|---|
| | Low | Moderate | High | Low | Moderate | High |
| Low | 53.3 | 41.9 | 40.0 | 53.4 | 49.5 | 47.1 |
| Moderate | 40.0 | 38.7 | 46.7 | 37.3 | 35.6 | 43.9 |
| High | 6.6 | 19.3 | 13.4 | 9.3 | 14.8 | 9.1 |
| Total | 100% | 100% | 100% | 100% | 100% | 100% |
| | (90) | (31) | (60) | (292) | (101) | (221) |
| | $r = .112$ (n.s.) | | | $r = .022$ (n.s.) | | |

| Amount of serious deviance | Upper class Violence, favorite program | | |
|---|---|---|---|
| | Low | Moderate | High |
| Low | 62.6 | 62.9 | 49.7 |
| Moderate | 29.3 | 32.9 | 41.3 |
| High | 8.1 | 4.3 | 9.1 |
| Total | 100% | 100% | 100% |
| | (222) | (70) | (143) |
| | $r = .063$ (n.s.) | | |

a Number too small for stable percentages
** $p < .001$

lieves that wrongdoers are likely to be punished has more reason to abstain from misbehavior than the child who thinks such punishment is unlikely.

The general question being asked here is whether such ties to the social structure mediate between television violence and aggressive deviance. It is predicted that weaker and fewer insulating ties to the social structure will strengthen the relationship between television violence and deviance.

The insulating factors are as follows: 1. Educational expectations (Do you expect to finish high school, go to college, finish college?) 2. Occupational aspirations (What kind of job would you *like to have* when you completely finish school?) 3. Occupational expectations (What kind of job do you think you *actually will get* when you completely finish school?) 4. Participation in school activities. 5. Relationship with peers (How often in the past have you found yourself with someplace to go but no friends to go with?) 6. Fear of punishment (Suppose that a person your age beats up another kind at school and hurts him badly enough so a doctor is called. Do you think he would a) be arrested; b) be picked up by police and taken home; c) be lectured by the police; d) get a talking to by a principal or teacher; e) get beaten up by the other kid's friends; f) get in trouble with his parents; g) get suspended from school; h) nothing would happen. If a person your age gets into trouble with the police, what effect would this have on his life when he is older? i) no effect at all; j) no difference in the long run; k) might affect the kind of job he could get; l) might make his whole life harder. A summary score, expectation of punishment, was assigned based on the number of positive responses to a - g, k, and l. The combined index, insulating factors, is described in Table 1, Appendix A.

As can be noted in Table 24, respondents with few or weak insulating ties to the social structure do have higher aggressive deviance scores (see percentages in "total" column). There is not a consistent pattern of stronger relationships between favorite program violence and aggression, however. As can be noted in Table 25, the relationships between either measure of television violence and each of the deviance measures is not changed appreciably when insulating factors are controlled. It is not possible to conclude, based on the present evidence, that weakness of these ties to the social structure leaves the child more vulnerable to the effects of television violence.

To summarize this section, it can be pointed out that the objective violence rating of the most favorite program is not consistently related to deviance. The percentage differences tend to go in the predicted direction, but they are very small. This relationship is not strengthened when characteristics of the child, insulating ties to the social structure, or perception of violence on favorite program are controlled. There is, however, a small but consistent relationship between the average violence rating of four favorite programs and the deviance scores. The relationship remains significant when age, social class, and insulating ties to the social structure are contolled; the relationship is strongest for aggressive and serious deviance.

Table 24: Aggressive deviance by violence, favorite program, and insulating factors

(Percent with high aggressive scores)

| | Low | Moderate | Violence High | Total | |
|---|---|---|---|---|---|
| **Educational expectations** | | | | | |
| Low | 25% | 21% | 23% | 25% | (623) |
| Moderate | 27% | 29% | 30% | 26% | (196) |
| High | 14% | 12% | 19% | 16% | (1369) |
| **Occupational expectations** | | | | | |
| Low | 29% | a | 36% | 38% | (94) |
| Moderate | 18% | 12% | 20% | 19% | (736) |
| High | 15% | 8% | 14% | 14% | (560) |
| **Occupational aspirations** | | | | | |
| Low | 32% | a | 36% | 37% | (96) |
| Moderate | 19% | 13% | 22% | 20% | (650) |
| High | 17% | 11% | 19% | 16% | (766) |
| **School activities** | | | | | |
| Low | 20% | 20% | 23% | 21% | (820) |
| Moderate | 18% | 16% | 20% | 20% | (1120) |
| High | 8% | 14% | 12% | 10% | (164) |
| **Fear of punishment** | | | | | |
| Low | 22% | 27% | 20% | 21% | (391) |
| Moderate | 18% | 15% | 21% | 20% | (1172) |
| High | 17% | 14% | 21% | 18% | (617) |
| **Integrated with peers** | | | | | |
| Poor relationship | 20% | 12% | 20% | 20% | (1403) |
| Good relationship | 17% | 24% | 22% | 19% | (804) |
| **Combined index** | | | | | |
| 1 (low) | 37% | a | 14% | 28% | (87) |
| 2 | 23% | 21% | 24% | 24% | (1060) |
| 3 | 14% | 13% | 19% | 15% | (954) |
| 4 (high) | 51% | a | 23% | 8% | (88) |

a Number too small for stable percentage

# TELEVISION VIOLENCE AND APPROVAL OF VIOLENCE

The finding that those adolescents who watch violent programs exhibit only slightly more aggressive behavior does not mean that they are not learning about aggression and violence. They may learn about patterns of behavior which then are available for use when an appropriate occasion arises. What could have more important long-term consequences, both for the individual and for the society, then, may be the attitudes formed about violence. If the adolescent views violent program content, begins to believe that violence is a usual rather than an extraordinary means of achieving goals and that many people apparently approve of such means, then he too may be more likely to approve of such behavior. If he has not yet acted out this behavior, he may more readily do so at some later date. Moreover, he may be more tolerant of violence on

Table 25: Summary of relationships between television violence and deviance

| | x = Violence, favorite program | | x = Average violence, four favorites | | x = Perceived violence and realism |
|---|---|---|---|---|---|
| | r x y | r x y.a | r x y | r x y.a | r x y |
| y = aggressive deviance | .038 (n.s.) | | .109 ** | | .152 ** |
| a = age | | n.s. | | .106 ** | |
| a = ses | | n.s. | | .108 ** | |
| a = insulating factors | | n.s. | | .096 ** | |
| a = perceived violence and realism | | n.s. | | | |
| y = petty delinquency | .043 (n.s.) | | .083 ** | | .053 ** |
| a = age | | n.s. | | .045 * | |
| a = SES | | n.s. | | .063 * | |
| a = insulating factors | | n.s. | | .079 ** | |
| a = perceived violence and realism | | n.s. | | | |
| y = fighting with parents | .017 (n.s.) | | .089 ** | | -.041 (n.s.) |
| a = age | | n.s. | | .060 * | |
| a = SES | | n.s. | | .089 ** | |
| a = insulating factors | | n.s. | | .079 ** | |
| a = perceived violence and realism | | n.s. | | | |
| y = political deviance | .029 (n.s.) | | .063 ** | | .064 ** |
| a = age | | n.s. | | .045 * | |
| a = SES | | n.s. | | .063 * | |
| a = insulating factors | | n.s. | | .060 * | |
| a = perceived violence and realism | | n.s. | | | |
| y = serious deviance | .058 * | | .158 ** | | .049 * |
| a = age | | n.s. | | .144 ** | |
| a = SES | | n.s. | | .157 ** | |
| a = insulating factors | | n.s. | | .142 ** | |
| a = perceived violence and realism | | n.s. | | | |

* p < .01
** p < .001

the part of others and less ready to interfere, come to the rescue of a victim, or be concerned about the fate of others. On a societal level, an entire population may become indifferent to large-scale violence or may approve the use of indiscriminate mass violence. Whatever might be the consequences of ever larger numbers of persons approving of violent behavior, if such an increase were to occur, or if it is occurring, the formation of such attitudes as a possible consequence of media program content is in itself worthy of consideration. In this section the hypothesis that viewing violent programs leads to the approval of violent behavior is tested.

The measures of television violence again are the objective violence rating of the adolescent's favorite program and the average violence rating of his four favorite programs. To reiterate, although there are other potential indicators of the independent variable, the violence score of the youngster's favorite program may be of special significance. The youngster is more likely to watch his favorite shows attentively from beginning to end than to let his attention shift to other things from time to time. If this is so, he will be more aware of the characters' actions and their consequences as well as the general context in which violence occurs.

Assuming that approval of violence depends at least in part on (1) the characteristics of the assailant and the victim, (2) the level of provocation, or the context in which the behavior occurs, and (3) the level of violence under consideration, these dimensions are included in the measures of approval. The assailant-victim pairs include man and adult male stranger, teenage boy and teenage boy, and policeman and adult male citizen. For each pair the respondent was asked first whether he would approve a lesser degree of violence under various circumstances and then a more serious violent act under similar sets of circumstances.

## Approval of adult violence

Approval of adult male-adult male violence was measured by the following items (scored 1 for each "yes" response): Would you approve of a man punching an adult male stranger if the stranger: (a) was in a protest march showing opposition to the other man's views; (b) was drunk and bumped into the man and his wife on the street; (c) was beating up a woman and the man saw it; (d) had broken into the man's house; (e) had knocked the man down and was trying to rob him? Would you approve of a man shooting a stranger if the stranger: (a) was in a protest march showing opposition to the other man's views; (b) was drunk and bumped into the man and his wife on the street; (c) was beating up a woman and the other man saw it; (d) had broken into the man's house; (e) had knocked the man down and was trying to rob him?

There is a small but positive relationship between the violence rating of the respondent's favorite program and approval of violence (Table 26). The respondent's subjective perceptions of his favorite program are expected to influence the likelihood of violence approval, just as it has influenced the likelihood of aggressive behavior. It will be recalled that a number of phrases were listed and the respondent asked to check those which described his favorite program. The results can be summarized as follows: When violence is viewed as having been a means to a goal (main character "pushes the others around"), and when it is rewarded (the "guy who gets rough gets his way"), approval is more frequent than if these features are not checked as descriptive of the program (Table 27). Whether the characters were viewed as behaving the way people ought to act has no effect on the frequency of approval.

Table 26: Approval, adult violence by violence, favorite program

| Approval, adult violence | Violence, favorite program | | |
|---|---|---|---|
| | Low | Moderate | High |
| Low | 13.2 | 12.1 | 10.4 |
| Moderate | 38.9 | 44.5 | 37.6 |
| High | 47.9 | 43.5 | 52.1 |
| Total | 100% (786) | 100% (265) | 100% (588) |

$r = .071$ **

** $p < .001$

The relationship between the perceived violence and realism index and approval of violence is statistically significant for two of the three indices of approval (Table 36). The relationship between favorite program violence and approval of violence is not appreciably changed when perceived violence is controlled.

## Approval of teen violence

The second measure of approval of violence included items concerning teenage male victim and assailant. The items are as follows: "Would you approve of Andy, a teenage boy, punching Bill, another teenage boy, if: Andy didn't like Bill; Bill had made fun of Andy and picked on him; Bill had challenged Andy to a fist fight, Bill had hit Andy; Bill had attacked Andy with a knife?" "Would you approve of Andy, a teenage boy, knifing Bill, another boy, if: Andy didn't like Bill; Bill had made fun of Andy and picked on him; Bill had challenged Andy to a fist fight; Bill had hit Andy, Bill had attacked Andy with a knife?"

There is a relationship between the objective level of favorite program violence and approval of teen-teen violence (Table 28), but again the relationship is stronger when the average violence rating is used (Table

Table 27: Approval, adult violence, by violence, favorite program, and perception of favorite program

| Violence, favorite program | Violence used as means (% with high approval) | | Violence not used as means (% with high approval) | |
|---|---|---|---|---|
| Low | .54% | (35)b | 47% | (749) |
| Moderate | a | a | 44% | (259) |
| High | 72% | (34) | 52% | (550) |
| Total c | 54% | (116) | 48% | (2123) |

| | Violence rewarded (% with high approval) | | Violence not rewarded (% with high approval) | |
|---|---|---|---|---|
| Low | 53% | (38) | 47% | (745) |
| Moderate | 65% | (17) | 42% | (247) |
| High | 67% | (57) | 50% | (527) |
| Total c | 63% | (165) | 47% | (2075) |

| | The way people ought to behave (% with high approval) | | Not the way people ought to behave (% with high approval) | |
|---|---|---|---|---|
| Low | 51% | (217) | 47% | (569) |
| Moderate | 39% | (66) | 45% | (198) |
| High | 51% | (80) | 52% | (503) |
| Total c | 48% | (475) | 48% | (1767) |

a Number too small for stable percentage
b Number in parentheses is number on which percentage is based
c Total sample, including respondents for whom there is no violence rating for favorite program

36). This relationship between average violence and approval of adult violence remains when age, socioeconomic status, and ties to the social structure are controlled. Those adolescents whose favorite programs are more violent more frequently approve of a teenage boy punching or knifing another teenage boy. If the favorite program is described as depicting violence as a means to an end or violence rewarded, teen vio-

Table 28: Approval, teen violence by violence, favorite program

| Approval, teen violence | Violence, favorite program | | |
|---|---|---|---|
| | Low | Moderate | High |
| Low | 18.0 | 23.0 | 17.5 |
| Moderate | 47.5 | 42.6 | 44.3 |
| High | 34.5 | 34.4 | 38.2 |
| Total | 100% (787) | 100% (265) | 100% (589) |

r = .021 (n.s.)

lence is approved more often than if the program is not so described (Table 29). Whether or not the program "shows the way people ought to act" does not influence frequency of approval. When perceived violence and realism are used as controls, the effect of objective violence is not appreciably changed (Table 36).

Table 29: Approval, teen violence, by violence, favorite program, and perception of favorite program

| Violence, favorite program | Violence used as means (% with high approval) | | Violence not used as means (% with high approval) | |
|---|---|---|---|---|
| Low | 44% | (34)[b] | 34% | (751) |
| Moderate | a | a | 34% | (259) |
| High | 56% | (34) | 37% | (551) |
| Total | 49% | (114) | 35% | (2122) |

| | Violence rewarded (% with high approval) | | Violence not rewarded (% with high approval) | |
|---|---|---|---|---|
| Low | 38% | (37) | 34% | (747) |
| Moderate | a | a | 33% | (247) |
| High | 53% | (57) | 37% | (528) |
| Total [c] | 51% | (162) | 35% | (2075) |

| | The way people ought to behave (% with high approval) | | Not the way people ought to behave (% with high approval) | |
|---|---|---|---|---|
| Low | 38% | (219) | 33% | (568) |
| Moderate | 35% | (66) | 34% | (198) |
| High | 35% | (81) | 39% | (503) |
| Total [c] | 35% | (476) | 36% | (1763) |

[a] Number too small for stable percentages
[b] Number in parentheses is number on which percentage is based
[c] Total sample, including respondents for whom there is no violence rating for favorite program

## Approval of police violence

The approval of violent behavior, or the use of force, by a policeman has a somewhat different significance than approval of the behavior of a private citizen. The policeman is a representative of a law enforcement agency and therefore of society itself, and there is a general understanding that he may on occasion be required to use force either to defend himself or to carry out his responsibilities. It is to be expected that adolescents, as well as adult citizens, will approve the use of force on the part of a policeman at least as often as they would approve similar behavior on the part of a private citizen. It is not possible to make clear comparisons between the approval of violence on the part of policemen, adult males, or teenage males, because the number and content of the items which make up the indices are not identical. There does not, however, appear to be a great disparity between the number of approval responses for roughly comparable items in the three indices. (Tables of responses to individual items omitted.)

Table 30: Approval, police violence, by violence, favorite program

| Approval police violence | Violence, favorite program | | |
|---|---|---|---|
| | Low | Moderate | High |
| Low | 56.5 | 58.8 | 58.0 |
| Moderate | 35.7 | 34.1 | 31.1 |
| High | 7.8 | 7.1 | 10.9 |
| Total | 100% (791) | 100% (267) | 100% (588) |

$r = .013$ (n.s.)

The items included in the approval of police violence index are as follows: "Would you approve of a policeman striking an adult male citizen if the citizen: had said vulgar and dirty things to the policeman; was demonstrating against the war in Vietnam; was being questioned as a suspect in a murder case; was attempting to escape from custody; was attacking the policeman with his fists; was threatening the policeman with a weapon?" "Would you approve of a policeman shooting an adult male citizen if the citizen: had said vulgar and dirty things to the policeman; was demonstrating against the war in Vietnam; was being questioned as a suspect in a murder case; was attempting to escape from custody; was attacking the policeman with his fists; was threatening the policeman with a gun?"

There is not a significant relationship between violence rating of favorite program and approval of police violence (Table 30). Again, however, the relationship between the average violence rating of *four* favorite programs and approval is positive although small (Table 36). The respondents who have indicated that in their favorite programs violence has been used as a means to an end are more likely to be high approvers of police violence (18 percent compared to nine percent high approvers) (Table 31). The perception of violence having been rewarded is also related to approval, but normative content is not. The index of perceived violence and realism of favorite program was not significantly related to approval, however, nor did it strengthen the relationship between the objective rating of the favorite program and approval (Table 36).

Considering race and gender, the positive relationship appears consistently only for white males (Tables 32, 33, and 34). This finding does not indicate that race and gender, *per se*, are the important determinants

Table 31: Approval, police violence, by violence, favorite program, and perception of favorite program

| Violence, favorite program | Violence used as means (% with high approval) | | Violence not used as means (% with high approval) | |
|---|---|---|---|---|
| Low | 14.3 | (35)[b] | 7.4 | (754) |
| Moderate | a | a | 7.3 | (260) |
| High | 23.5 | (34) | 10.2 | (550) |
| Total [c] | 17.7% | (119) | 8.8% | (2131) |
| | Violence rewarded (% with high approval) | | Violence not rewarded (% with high approval) | |
| Low | 10.5 | (38) | 7,6 | (750) |
| Moderate | 11.1 | (18) | 6.9 | (248) |
| High | 19.6 | (56) | 10.1 | (528) |
| Total [c] | 16.3% | (166) | 8.8% | (2085) |
| | The way people ought to behave (% with high approval) | | Not the way people ought to behave (% with high approval) | |
| Low | 9.6 | (220) | 7.2 | (571) |
| Moderate | 12.1 | (66) | 5.5 | (200) |
| High | 9.8 | (82) | 11.2 | (501) |
| Total | 10.1% | (483) | 9.2% | (1770) |

[a] Number too small for stable percentages
[b] Number in parenthesis is number on which percentage is based
[c] Total sample, including respondents for whom there is no violence rating for favorite programs

of the level of approval of violence, however. There is no consistent relationship between approval and race/gender across the three measures of approval. White males consistently approve more violence than white females, but no other pattern emerges. White males approve more adult violence but less teenage violence than do black males, for example (Table 2, Appendix A). It seems more reasonable to conclude at this point that race and gender are not major determinants of approval of violence nor of the manner in which television influences approval.

Age, however, is negatively related to approval of teen violence ($r = -.094$, $p < .001$). The relationship between average violence and approval remains but is not greatly strengthened when age is controlled (Table 36).

Social class is negatively associated with approval of teen violence ($r = -.114$, $p < .001$), and with approval of adult violence ($r = -.082$, $p < .001$), with lower-class respondents approving more violence than upper-class respondents; when the assailant-victim pair is policeman-adult male, there is no such relationship. The relationships between violence ratings of favorite programs and approval do not change appreciably when social class is controlled (Table 36).

Table 32: Approval, adult violence, by violence, favorite program, race, and gender

| Approval, adult violence | White males | | | White females | | |
|---|---|---|---|---|---|---|
| | Low | Moderate | High | Low | Moderate | High |
| Low | 10.8 | 8.0 | 4.9 | 14.9 | 15.2 | 15.1 |
| Moderate | 34.0 | 38.1 | 27.5 | 43.4 | 48.6 | 50.5 |
| High | 55.2 | 54.0 | 67.5 | 41.7 | 36.2 | 34.4 |
| Total | 100% (259) | 100% (113) | 100% (265) | 100% (417) | 100% (138) | 100% (218) |

| | Black males | | | Black females | | |
|---|---|---|---|---|---|---|
| | Low | Moderate | High | Low | Moderate | High |
| Low | 16.3 | a | 13.6 | 11.1 | a | 13.8 |
| Moderate | 30.2 | a | 40.9 | 33.3 | a | 32.8 |
| High | 53.5 | a | 45.5 | 55.5 | a | 53.4 |
| Total | 100% (43) | a a | 100% (44) | 100% (63) | a | 100% (58) |

a Number too small for stable percentages

Table 33: Approval, teen violence, by violence, favorite program, race, and gender

| Approval, teen violence | Violence, favorite program White males | | | Violence, favorite program White females | | |
|---|---|---|---|---|---|---|
| | Low | Moderate | High | Low | Moderate | High |
| Low | 12.7 | 17.7 | 10.9 | 22.1 | 27.5 | 26.6 |
| Moderate | 42.9 | 34.5 | 41.1 | 52.4 | 50.0 | 50.0 |
| High | 44.4 | 47.8 | 47.9 | 25.5 | 22.4 | 23.4 |
| Total | 100% (259) | 100% (113) | 100% (265) | 100% (416) | 100% (138) | 100% (218) |

| | Violence favorite program black males | | | Violence, favorite program black females | | |
|---|---|---|---|---|---|---|
| | Low | Moderate | High | Low | Moderate | High |
| Low | 7.0 | a | 9.1 | 20.0 | a | 20.3 |
| Moderate | 34.9 | a | 36.4 | 43.1 | a | 45.8 |
| High | 58.1 | a | 54.5 | 36.9 | a | 33.9 |
| Total | 100% (43) | a | 100% (44) | 100% (65) | a | 100% (59) |

a Number too small for stable percentages

Some of the variables which have been termed insulating ties to the social structure may be of greater consequence than the demographic variables just considered. Occupational aspirations and expectations of the adolescent are both such ties to the social structure. The child who aspires to, or expects to achieve, a high rather than a low status occupation has stronger ties to the society. It was expected that television violence would have more influence on the respondents with lower aspirations and expectations. For similar reasons, educational expectations, grades in school, integration into school activities, and relationships with parents and peers are expected to serve as insulating factors.

Table 34: Approval, police violence, by violence, favorite program, race and gender

| Approval, police violence | White male Violence, favorite program | | | Black male Violence, favorite program | | |
|---|---|---|---|---|---|---|
| | Low | Moderate | High | Low | Moderate | High |
| Low | 41.1 | 49.1 | 45.4 | 62.8 | a | 68.2 |
| Moderate | 44.2 | 38.6 | 36.0 | 34.9 | a | 25.0 |
| High | 14.7 | 12.3 | 18.6 | 2.3 | a | 6.8 |
| Total | 100% (260) | 100% (114) | 100% (264) | 100% (43) | a | 100% (44) |

| | White female Violence, favorite program | | | Black female Violence, favorite program | | |
|---|---|---|---|---|---|---|
| | Low | Moderate | High | Low | Moderate | High |
| Low | 62.3 | 65.2 | 66.5 | 73.9 | a | 74.6 |
| Moderate | 32.7 | 31.2 | 29.8 | 23.1 | a | 18.6 |
| High | 5.0 | 3.6 | 3.7 | 3.1 | a | 6.8 |
| Total | 100% (419) | 100% (138) | 100% (218) | 100% (65) | a | 100% (59) |

a Number too small for stable percentages

Another measure of the strength of the child's ties to the society is his expectation that an offender will be apprehended and punished. These ties to the social structure were combined to form the index of "insulating factors" described earlier. The relationship between these insulating factors and approval of violence varies according to the assailant-victim category. Strength of ties to the social structure have no appreciable affect on approval of violence by the police ($r = .021$, n.s.). When adult males or teenage males comprise the assailant-victim pairs, however, the relationship between approval of violence and insulating factors is negative ($r = -.052$, $p < .01$; $r = -153$, $p < .001$). It might be suggested that strong ties to the social structure do not lessen approval of violent behavior by policemen because these youngsters expect that policemen are using force only when necessary and legitimate. The same legitimacy would not be accorded other assailants. These distinctions notwithstanding, the strength or weakness of these insulating factors does not alter relationships between either measure of television violence and approval of violence.

Table 35: Insulating factors

Approval, teen violence, by violence, favorite program, and insulating factors

| Violence, favorite program | Insulating factors (% with high approval) | | | | | | | |
|---|---|---|---|---|---|---|---|---|
| | 1 (low) | | 2 | | 3 | | 4 (high) | |
| Low | 46% | (35)b | 42% | (198) | 35% | (345) | 24% | (208) |
| Moderate | 50% | (22) | 43% | (84) | 31% | (109) | 20% | (49) |
| High | 58% | (40) | 46% | (166) | 36% | (255) | 26% | (128) |
| Total | 52% | (97) | 44% | (448) | 35% | (709) | 24% | (385) |

Approval, adult violence, by violence, favorite program, and insulating factors

| Violence, favorite program | Insulating factors (% with high approval) | | | | | | | |
|---|---|---|---|---|---|---|---|---|
| | 1 (low) | | 2 | | 3 | | 4 (high) | |
| Low | 46% | (33) | 54% | (197) | 48% | (347) | 42% | (208) |
| Moderate | 59% | (22) | 51% | (84) | 38% | (109) | 37% | (49) |
| High | 58% | (40) | 56% | (165) | 51% | (255) | 48% | (128) |
| Total | 54% | (95) | 54% | (446) | 47% | (711) | 44% | (385) |

Approval, police violence, by violence, favorite program, and insulating factors

| Violence, favorite program | Insulating factors (% with high approval) | | | | | | | |
|---|---|---|---|---|---|---|---|---|
| | 1 (low) | | 2 | | 3 | | 4 (high) | |
| Low | 6% | (35) | 6% | (199) | 10% | (348) | 6% | (208) |
| Moderate | 9% | (23) | 7% | (85) | 9% | (109) | 2% | (49) |
| High | 23% | (40) | 12% | (166) | 10% | (254) | 9% | (128) |
| Total | 13% | (98) | 9% | (450) | 10% | (711) | 7% | (385) |

b Number in parentheses is number on which percentage is based

In summary, it can be noted that there is a small relationship between the objective rating of the child's favorite television program and his approval of violent behavior on the part of adult males but not other categories of assailants. It should be noted that this relationship is found for the average rating of the four favorite programs and all three measures of approval, however. Furthermore, it is the objective rating rather than the subjective perception of violence which is more strongly related to approval.

Demographic characteristics of the respondents—race, gender, age, and social class—are not useful in explaining the relationship between television violence and approval of violence, although the lower-class

Table 36: Summary of relationships between television violence and approval of violence

| | s = Violence, favorite program | | x = Average violence, four favorites | | x = Perceived violence and realism |
|---|---|---|---|---|---|
| | r x y | r x y.a | r x y | r x y.a | r x y |
| y = approval, adult violence | .071 ** | | .096 ** | | .041 ** |
| a = age | | .074 ** | | .093 ** | |
| a = social class | | .071 ** | | .095 ** | |
| a = insulating factors | | .068 ** | | .092 ** | |
| a = perceived violence and realism | | .068 ** | | | |
| y = approval, teen violence | .021 (n.s.) | | .084 ** | | .110 ** |
| a = age | | n.s. | | .094 ** | |
| a = social class | | n.s. | | .086 ** | |
| a = insulating factors | | n.s. | | .072 ** | |
| a = perceived violence and realism | | n.s. | | | |
| y = approval, police violence | .013 (n.s.) | | .076 ** | | .026 (n.s.) |
| a = age | | n.s. | | .078 ** | |
| a = social class | | n.s. | | .075 ** | |
| a = insulating factors | | n.s. | | -.069 ** | |
| a = perceived violence and realism | | n.s. | | | |

\* p < .01
\*\* p < .001

respondents and the younger adolescents are more likely to approve. Nor was another set of variables, representing the strength or weakness of the child's ties to the social structure, more helpful in explaining the influence of television violence. Generally speaking, the children with more and stronger insulating ties are more likely to approve police violence, less likely to approve teenage violence, but equally likely to be influenced by television violence.

Although it is necessary to remember that the differences between children who watched low and high violence programs were in most cases small, the relationship was consistent for the four favorite programs and in no case was greatly reduced with the introduction of other variables.

## BELIEFS ABOUT LEVEL OF VIOLENCE IN SOCIETY

It has been demonstrated thus far that the child's viewing of television violence is associated with aggressive and deviant behavior and also with approval of violence on the part of others. A related question is whether the child believes that he is learning about the real world as he watches dramatic programs. If so, and if he often selects the high violent shows, he might well decide that he lives in a society with a high level of violence.

Table 37: Realism and violence, favorite program

| Realism | Violence, favorite program | | | | |
|---------|-----|----------|------|--------------|-------|
| | Low | Moderate | High | Not codeable | Total |
| 0 | 7% (57) | 10% (27) | 9% (54) | 13% (78) | 10% (216) |
| 1 | 28% (223) | 28% (75) | 28% (164) | 34% (206) | 30% (668) |
| 2 | 28% (218) | 26% (69) | 28% (165) | 28% (168) | 28% (620) |
| 3 | 37% (290) | 36% (95) | 34% (199) | 26% (158) | 33% (742) |
| Total | 100% (788) | 100% (266) | 100% (582) | 100% (610) | 100% (2246) |

Using a measure of how realistic the child believes his favorite program to be (shows life as it really is, people just like people in real life, and not much like the real world [reverse scoring]), fewer than half the respondents, about 40 percent, think that their favorite shows are not very true-to-life, while one-third think that both the situations and the characters are realistic (Table 37). It is conceivable that the children who think these shows are realistic are referring to educational programs, documentaries, or news programs. This is not the case, however, for more of the high violence shows than those in the "non-codeable" category were termed realistic, although the latter included news, documentaries, and similar shows. Furthermore, the high violence shows are just as likely to be considered realistic as the low or moderate shows (Table 37).

Table 38: Belief in frequency of crime by violence, favorite program

| Frequency of crime | Violence, favorite program | | |
|--------------------|-----|----------|------|
| | Low | Moderate | High |
| 1 (low) | c | c | c |
| 2 | 4% | 3% | 4% |
| 3 | 44% | 45% | 43% |
| 4 | 47% | 47% | 47% |
| 5 (high) | 5% | 5% | 6% |
| Total | 100% (775) | 100% (258) | 100% (584) |

c Less than one percent

Many of the programs which had been rated as violent include portrayals of crime and criminals. It might be expected, then, that many youngsters who selected these high violent shows would have a picture of their society as one in which serious crimes are frequent. To test this hypothesis, respondents were asked: How often do serious crimes like these (robbery, assault, car theft, burglary, etc.) occur "in your neighborhood," "in downtown Washington," and "in this part of the country?" Respondents were assigned summary scores based on their responses of "never," "rarely," "fairly often," or "very often" for crime in each location. As is apparent in Table 38, the children whose favorite is rated high in violence are neither more nor less likely to believe in a high level of crime in the society. As was the case with deviance and approval of violence, however, the average violence rating of respondents' four favorite programs is clearly related to belief in level of crime in the society. The relationship is not great, however, and is no longer significant when age is controlled (Table 39). Socioeconomic status and insulating ties to the social structure do not change the relationship greatly.

Table 39: Summary of relationships between television violence and belief in crime level

|  | r x y | r x y.a |
|---|---|---|
| x = violence, favorite program |  |  |
| y = belief in crime level | .012 (n.s.) |  |
| a = age |  | n.s. |
| a = socioeconomic status |  | n.s. |
| a = insulating factors |  | n.s. |
| a = perceived violence and |  |  |
| realism |  | n.s. |
| x = average violence |  |  |
| y = belief in crime level | .048* |  |
| a = age |  | .039 (n.s.) |
| a = socioeconomic status |  | .048* |
| a = insulating factors |  | .045* |

* $p < .01$

To summarize, two-thirds of the respondents, including those whose favorites are high in violence, believe that their favorite shows are true to life. The small but significant relationship between average violence of four favorite programs and belief in crime level in society gives additional support to the hypothesis that youngsters use these programs in forming their views of society.

## SUMMARY AND CONCLUSIONS

It had been anticipated that the violence ratings of the adolescents' favorite television programs would be associated with deviant behavior, especially with aggressive and serious deviance. This has been found to be true when the violence ratings of four favorite programs are considered, but (except for serious deviance) not for the violence rating of the one most favorite show. The four favorite programs, the ones "you try to watch every time they are on the air," constitute a greater proportion of all television programs viewed, and it seems likely that this may account for their greater relationship with behavior. It had been expected also that the adolescents' subjective perceptions of violence would be more strongly related to deviant behavior than would the objective violence ratings. This comparison is possible for the one favorite show only, and here it proves to be true. Nonetheless, four favorite shows are for the most part more strongly related to deviant behavior than the subjective perception of violence on the one most favorite show. If subjective perception of violence alone were associated with deviant behavior and approval of violence, it might be concluded that the relationship between television violence and deviant behavior existed only for certain youngsters—those already prone to deviance and aggression. It is not, however, only those youngsters who subjectively perceive violence for whom there is a relationship between the violent content of their four favorite shows and deviance. Nor is the latter relationship generally diminished by including in the analysis characteristics of the youngster which would be expected to increase the likelihood of his being deviant or aggressive.

When the adolescent's attitudes about violence (that is, approval of violence on the part of others) and his beliefs about violence in the society are considered, the ratings of the four favorite programs are again consistently associated with greater approval of violence and belief in higher level of violence in the society. The high proportion of youngsters who take their favorite programs to be a fairly accurate picture of the real world, including those youngsters whose favorite is a program with high violence content, may be related to this finding.

Many children choose to watch those shows which are more violent and take them to be a reflection of the real world; the selection of these shows is related to the belief that violence and crime are frequent occurrences in the society and to the approval of violent behavior. This finding is as important as the finding of an association between television violence and aggressive behavior itself. These youngsters may become inured to violence and later as citizens be indifferent to its occurrence. Second, it is also possible that the approval of violence may increase the likelihood of future violent behavior. Even if the consequences are limited to the first—that people become more willing to tolerate violence in others—the implications are not trivial.

There is one last issue: the discussion of causality. In the present investigation, which used survey research techniques, information is limited to the *associations* between television programs preferred (and viewed) and behavior and attitudes. The magnitude of correlations is not great, and certainly television can be no more than one among many factors influencing behavior and attitudes. However, there is consistently a significant relationship between the violence rating of four favorite programs and the five measures of deviance, three of approval of violence and one of beliefs about crime in the society. Furthermore, these relationships remain when variables expected to decrease the likelihood of deviance are introduced. The regularity with which these relationships appear suggests that they should not be overlooked.

# FOOTNOTES

1. The research upon which this report is based was performed pursuant to Contract No. HSM 42-70-52 with the National Institute of Mental Health, Health Services and Mental Health Administration, U.S. Department of Health, Education, and Welfare.

   The research staff for the project included Mary T. Batt, Douglas Schocke, and Stephen Wolfe. We are grateful to the public schools of Prince Georges County, the principals, the teachers, and the students whose cooperation made the project possible.

   Dr. Teevan is now at the University of Western Ontario.
2. Data were collected in one school in September 1970. The additional questionnnaires were administered to include a larger proportion of black students.
3. Father's occupation was coded using the Duncan Socio-Economic Index (Reiss, Duncan, Hatt, and North, 1961). Those occupations coded 24 or below (at fifth decile, included "bus driver") were arbitrarily considered "low" SES. Those from 25 to 64 were considered "middle" SES, and those 65 and over (included ninth and part of eighth deciles—professionals, technical and kindred workers, etc.) were considered "upper" SES.

# SELECTED BIBLIOGRAPHY

Bailyn, L. Mass media and children; A study of exposure habits and cognitive effects. *Psychological Monographs*, 1959, **73**, 1-48.

Baker, R.K., and Ball, S. J. (Eds.) *Mass media and violence: a staff report to the National Commission on the Causes and Prevention of Violence*. Washington, D.C.: Government Printing Office, 1969.

Banay, R. S. Testimony before the Subcommittee to Investigate Juvenile Delinquency. Committee on the Judiciary, S. Res., Apr. 1955, 62, Washington, D.C.: Government Printing Office.

Bandura, A. What television violence can do to your child. In Larsen, O. N. (Ed.) *Violence and the mass media*. New York: Harper and Row, 1968.

Bandura, A., and Walters, R. H. *Social learning and personality development*. New York: Holt, Rinehart and Winston, 1963.

Becker, H.S. *The outsiders*, New York: Free Press, 1963.

Berkowitz, L., Corwin, R., and Heiromimous, M. Film violence and subsequent aggressive tendencies. *Public Opinion Quarterly*, 1963, **27**, 217-29.

Block, H. A., and Niederhoffer, A. *The gang*. New York: Philosophical Library, 1958

Briar, S., and Piliavin, I. Delinquency, situational inducements, and commitment to conformity, *Social Problems*, 1965, **13**, 35-45.

Brodbeck, A. J. *The mass media as a socializing agency.* Paper presented at the meeting of the American Psychological Association, San Francisco, 1955.

Bronfenbrenner, U. *Two worlds of childhood: U.S. and U.S.S.R.* New York: Russell Sage Foundation, 1970.

Charters, W. W., and Newcomb, T. M. Some attitudinal effects of experimentally increased salience of a membership group. In Maccoby, E. E. *et al.* (Eds.) *Readings in social psychology* (3rd ed.). New York: Holt, Rinehart and Winston, 1958.

Cloward, R., and Ohlin, L. *Delinquency and opportunity.* New York: Free Press, 1960.

Cohen, A. K. *Delinquent boys.* Glencoe: Free Press, 1955.

Cohen, A. K. *Deviance and control.* Englewood Cliffs: Prentice Hall, 1966.

Cohen, A. K. Middle class delinquency and the social structure. Paper presented at the meeting of the American Sociological Association, Chicago, 1957.

Cohen, A. K., and Short, J. F. Research in delinquent subcultures. *Journal of Social Issues,* 1958, **14**, 20-37.

Commission on Law Enforcement and Administration of Justice, *The challenge of crime in a free society.* Washington, D. C.: Government Printing Office, 1967.

DeFleur, M. L. *Theories of mass communication.* New York: David McKay, 1966.

England, R. W. A theory of middle class juvenile delinquency. *Journal of Criminal Law, Criminology, and Police Science,* 1960, **50**, 535-40.

Eron, L. D. Relation of TV viewing habits and aggressive behavior in children. *Journal of Abnormal and Social Psychology,* 1963, **67**, 193-96.

Feshbach, S. The catharsis effect: research and another view. In Baker Ball (Eds.) *Mass media and Violence.*

Festinger, L. Laboratory experiments: the role of group belongingness. In Miller, J. G. (Ed.) *Experiments in social process: a symposium on social psychology.* New York: McGraw Hill, 1950.

Gerson, W. M. *Social structure and mass media socialization.* Unpublished doctoral dissertation, University of Washington, 1963.

Gibbons, D. C. *Delinquent behavior.* Englewood Cliffs: Prentice-Hall, 1970.

Goranson, R. E. A review of recent literature on psychological effects of media portrayals of violence. Baker and Ball (Eds.) *Mass media and violence.*

Greenberg, B. S., and Gordon, T. Perceptions of television violence: critics and the public. In *Television and social behavior,* Vol. 1. Washington, D.C.: U. S. Government Printing Office, 1971.

Greenwald, A. G. Do crime and violence in the mass news media modify behavior? Columbus: Ohio State University, 1971 (mimeo).

Haines, W. H. Juvenile delinquency and television. *Journal of Social Therapy*, 1955, 1, 192-98.

Halloran, J. D. Television and violence. In Larsen, O. N. (Ed.) *Violence and the mass media*. New York: Harper & Row, 1968.

Himmelweit, H. T., Oppenheim, A. N., and Vince, P. *Television and the child*. London: Oxford University Press, 1958.

Hovland, C. I., Janis, I. L., and Kelley, H. H. *Communication and persuasion*. New Haven: Yale University Press, 1953.

Kelley, H. H. Salience of membership and resistance to change of group-anchored attitudes. *Human Relations*, 1955, 8, 275-90.

Kelley, H. H., and Volkart, E. H. The resistance to change of group-anchored attitudes. *American Sociological Review*, 1952, 17, 453-65.

Kelley, H. H., and Woodruff, C. L. Members reactions to apparent group approval of a counter-norm communication. *Journal of Abnormal Social Psychology*, 1956, 52, 67-74.

Larsen, O.N. Social effects of mass communication. In Faris, R. E. (Ed.) *Handbook of modern sociology*. Chicago: Rand-McNally, 1964.

Larsen, O. N. *Violence and the mass media*. New York: Harper & Row, 1968.

Larsen, O. N. Posing the problem of effects. In Baker and Ball (Eds.) *Mass media and violence*.

Lazarsfeld, P. F., Berelson, B., and Gaudet, H. *The people's choice*. New York: Columbia University Press, 1948.

Lemert, E. M. *Human deviance, social problems, and social control*. Englewood Cliffs: Prentice Hall, 1967.

Lovibond, S. H. The effect of media stressing crime and violence upon children's attitudes. *Social Problems*, 1967, 15, 91-99.

Maccoby, E. E. Effects of the mass media. In Hoffman, M. L., and Hoffman, L. W. (Eds.) *Review of child development research*, Vol. 1. New York: Russell Sage Foundation, 1964.

Maccoby, E. E. Effects of the mass media. Larsen (Ed.) *Violence and the mass media*.

Marwell, G. Adolescent powerlessness and delinquency. *Social Problems*, 1966, 14, 35-47.

Matza, D., and Sykes, G. M. *Juvenile delinquency and subterranean values*. *American Sociological Review*, 1961, 26, 712-19.

Merton, R.K. Social structure and anomie. *American Sociological Review*, 1938, 3, 672-82.

Miller, W.B. Lower class culture as a generating milieu of gang delinquency. *Journal of Social Issues*, 1958, 14, 2-19.

National Commission on the Causes and Prevention of Violence. *Commission statement on violence in television entertainment programs.* Washington, D.C.: U.S. Government Printing Office, 1969.

Nye, F.I., and Short, J.F. Scaling delinquent behavior. *American Sociological Review*, 1956, **22**, 326-31.

Reiss, A., Duncan, O., Hatt, P., and North, C. *Occupations and social status.* New York: The Free Press, 1961.

Riley, M.W., and Riley, J.W. A sociological approach to communication research. *Public Opinion Quarterly*, 1951, **15**, 445-60.

Rilay, J.W., Schramm, W., and Williams, F.W. Flight from communism: a report on Korean refugees. *Public Opinion Quarterly*, 1951, **15**, 274-86.

Scheff, T.J. *Being mentally ill.* Chicago: Aldine, 1966.

Schramm, W., Lyle, J., and Parker, E.B. *Television in the lives of our children.* Stanford, Calif.: Stanford University Press, 1961.

Sellin, T. and Wolfgang, M. *The measurement of delinquency.* New York: John Wiley, 1964.

Thompson, R.J. *Television crime-drama: its impact on children and adolescents.* Melbourne: F.W. Cheshire, 1959.

Turk, A. T. Toward construction of a theory of delinquency. *Journal of Criminal Law, Criminology, and Police Science*, 1964, **55**, 215-29.

Walters, R. H., and Llewellyn-Thomas, E. Enhancement of punitiveness by visual and audio-visual displays. *Canadian Journal of Psychology*, 1963, **17**, 244-55.

Weiss, W. Effects of the mass media of communication. In Lindzey, G. and Aronson, E. (Eds.) *The handbook of social psychology.* Reading, Mass.: Addison-Wesley, 1968.

Wertham, F. We are teaching our children that violence is fun. In Larsen (Ed.) *Violence and the mass media.*

Wilensky, H. L., and Lebeaux, C. N. *Industrial society and social welfare.* New York: Russell Sage Foundation, 1958.

Wright, C. R. *Mass communication.* New York: Random House, 1959.

Zajonc, R. Some effects of the space serials. *Public Opinion Quarterly*, 1954, **18**, 367-74.

Zimmerman, C., and Bauer, R. A. The influence of an audience on what is remembered. *Public Opinion Quarterly*, 1956, **20**, 238-48.

# Appendix A

Table 1: Index of insulating tries to the social structure

One point was added to the summary score for each of the following factors for which the respondent scored high:

1. Peer relationships: How often have you found yourself with someplace to go but no friends to go with? (Hardly ever, Never)

2. Parental relationships: When you want to ask your parents for or about something are they around or willing to talk to you? (Always, Usually)

3. Grades in school: What are your average grades in school? (A's, A's and B's, or B's)

4. Fear of punishment. Range = 0 – 9; high = 6 or above.

5. School activities: What school activities do you participate in? (2 or more activities)

6. Educational expectations: Expects to go to college or finish college.

7. Occupational aspirations: What kind of job would you like to have when you completely finished school? (High = Duncan Socio=Economic Index score of 25 or above)

8. Occupational expectations: What kind of job do you think you actually will get when you completely finish school? (High = Duncan Socio-Economic Index score of 25 or above)

Table 2: Distribution of approval of violence scores by race, gender, age, and social class

(% with high approval)

|  | Approval adult violence | Approval teen violence | Approval police violence |
|---|---|---|---|
| White male | 59% | 45% | 06% |
| White female | 37% | 24% | 05% |
| Black male | 47% | 50% | 10% |
| Black female | 52% | 39% | 09% |
| Lower class | 56% | 44% | 11% |
| Middle class | 50% | 36% | 11% |
| Upper class | 44% | 29% | 07% |
| 11 – 14 years | 51% | 40% | 11% |
| 15 – 19 years | 46% | 34% | 09% |

**This book may be kept**
**FOURTEEN DAYS**
A fine will be charged for each
day the book is kept overtime.

| | | | |
|---|---|---|---|
| APR 3 0 '78 | | | |
| JAN 27 '78 | | | |
| DEC 1 4 '79 | | | |
| MAY 2 '80 | | | |
| MAY 2 '80 | | | |
| APR 9 '82 | | | |
| APR 26 '82 | | | |
| DEC 12 1988 | | | |
| MAY 0 4 1980 | | | |
| | | | |
| | | | |
| | | | |
| | | | |
| | | | |
| | | | |

HIGHSMITH  45—226

41862